SPIRIT, STYLE, STORY

Essays Honoring John W. Padberg, S.J.

SPIRIT
STYLE
STORY

Essays Honoring John W. Padberg, S.J.

Edited by Thomas M. Lucas, S.J.

an imprint of
LOYOLAPRESS.
CHICAGO

JESUIT WAY *an imprint of*
LOYOLAPRESS
3441 N. ASHLAND AVENUE
CHICAGO, ILLINOIS 60657
(800) 621-1008
WWW.LOYOLABOOKS.ORG

© 2002 Thomas M. Lucas, S.J.
All rights reserved

Scripture quotations in the essays by Michael J. Buckley, William A. Barry, Martin D. O'Keefe, and David L. Fleming are from the Revised Standard Version of the Bible, copyright ©1946, 1952, and 1971 by the Division of Christian Education of the National Council of the Churches of Christ in the United States of America. Used by permission. All rights reserved.

An earlier version of William A. Barry's essay appeared in *Presence: The Journal of Spiritual Directors International* vol. 7, no. 3, October 2001.

Thomas M. Lucas's essay first appeared as "Petrus Canisius: Jesuit Urban Strategist," in *Petrus Canisius, Humanist und Europäer,* edited by Rainer Berndt, Berlin: Akademie Verlag, 2000. Reprinted with permission.

Cover photography: Westrich Photography.
The photo of S. Giovannino, Florence, exterior is courtesy of Gauvin A. Bailey.
The photo of S. Giovannino, Florence, Apostles Chapel and tomb of Bartolomeo Ammannati is courtesy of Gauvin A. Bailey.
The photo of S. Giovannino, Florence, interior is courtesy of Gauvin A. Bailey.
The photo of S. Giovannino, Florence, plan is courtesy of Gauvin A. Bailey.
The photo of *Jacob's Ladder* is courtesy of Gauvin A. Bailey.
The photo of the Church of the Gesù is courtesy of Fordham University Press.
The photo of St. Martin's, Bamberg is courtesy of the Getty Institute.
The photo of the view of Bamberg is courtesy of *Deutschland: Baukunst und Landschaft* (Berlin: Atlantis, 1924).
The photo of the Industrial School for Native American boys is courtesy of the Jesuit Oregon Province Archives, St. Ignatius Mission Collection.
The photo of the Holy Family Mission, Montana is courtesy of the Jesuit Oregon Province Archives, Northwest Albums Collection.
The photo of Native American girls of Montana and their Ursuline teachers is courtesy of Jesuit Oregon Province Archives.

Cover and interior design by Megan Duffy Rostan

Library of Congress Cataloging-in-Publication Data
Spirit, style, story : essays honoring John W. Padberg / edited by
Thomas Lucas.
   p. cm.
Includes bibliographical references and index.
 ISBN 0-8294-1620-X
 1. Jesuits—Spiritual life. 2. Priesthood—Catholic Church. 3. Pastoral theology—Catholic Church. I. Padberg, John W. II. Lucas, Thomas M.
 BX3703 .S64 2003
 271'.53—dc21

2002151711

Printed in the United States
03 04 05 06 07 Bang 10 9 8 7 6 5 4 3 2 1

JOHANNI GUGLIELMO PADBERG, S.J.
FILIO MISSOURIAE
CIVI TOTIUS MUNDI

MAGISTRO SAPIENTISSIMO
NARRATORI FACETISSIMO
ADMINSTRATORI PROBISSIMO
JESUITAE MAGNANIMO
AMICO OPTIMO

GRATISSIMI AMICI
DIEI NATALIS EIUS SEPTUAGESIMI QUINTI
CELEBRANDI CAUSA
HOC OPUS
DDD

For John William Padberg, S.J.
Son of Missouri
Citizen of the world

Wise teacher
Raconteur extraordinaire
Trusted administrator
Magnanimous Jesuit
Best of friends:

To celebrate his seventy-fifth birthday,
his most grateful friends
give, devote, dedicate
this work.

CONTENTS

GREETING
from Very Reverend Peter-Hans Kolvenbach, S.J.
Superior General of the Society of Jesus ... ix

INTRODUCTION ... xi

PART I: SPIRIT

"Likewise You Are Priests . . . ": Some Reflections on
Jesuit Priesthood ... 3
   Michael J. Buckley, S.J.

Discernment of Spirits as an Act of Faith ... 33
   William A. Barry, S.J.

Jerome Nadal, S.J., on the Virtue of Obedience ... 45
   Martin D. O'Keefe, S.J. (Translator)

Keys to Spiritual Growth: Remembering and Imagining
in Ignatian Spirituality ... 71
   David L. Fleming, S.J.

Intellectual Conversion: Jesuit Spirituality and
the American University ... 93
   Joseph A. Tetlow, S.J.

Soul Education: An Ignatian Priority ... 117
   Howard J. Gray, S.J.

PART II: STYLE

The Florentine Reformers and the Original Painting Cycle
of the Church of S. Giovannino ... 135
   Gauvin A. Bailey

The International Jesuit Style: Evil Twin of National Styles ... 181
   Evonne Levy

PART III: STORY

The Council of Trent: Myths, Misunderstandings,
and Misinformation　　　　　　　　　　　　　　　　　　　205
　　John W. O'Malley, S.J.

Novices in the Early Society of Jesus: Antonio Valentino, S.J.,
and the Novitiate at Novellara, Italy　　　　　　　　　　　227
　　Peter J. Togni, S.J.

The Jesuits and the Santa Casa di Loreto:
Orazio Torsellini's *Lauretanae historiae libri quinque*　　269
　　Paul V. Murphy

Peter Canisius: Jesuit Urban Strategist　　　　　　　　　283
　　Thomas M. Lucas, S.J.

Jesuit Book Production in the Netherlands 1601–1650　　303
　　Paul Begheyn, S.J.

Sparrows on the Rooftop: "How We Live Where We Live"
in Elizabethan England　　　　　　　　　　　　　　　　327
　　Thomas M. McCoog, S.J.

"Habits of Industry": Jesuits and Nineteenth-Century
Native American Education　　　　　　　　　　　　　　365
　　Gerald L. McKevitt, S.J.

The Just Development of Mind and Heart: Jesuit Education
at the Turn of the Century in Milwaukee, Wisconsin　　403
　　Michael W. Maher, S.J.

CONTRIBUTORS　　　　　　　　　　　　　　　　　　431

INDEX　　　　　　　　　　　　　　　　　　　　　　433

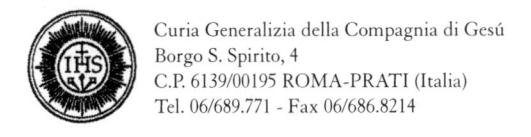

Curia Generalizia della Compagnia di Gesú
Borgo S. Spirito, 4
C.P. 6139/00195 ROMA-PRATI (Italia)
Tel. 06/689.771 - Fax 06/686.8214

14 February 2002

Rev. John W. Padberg, S.J.
Jesuit Hall
3601 Lindell Boulevard
St. Louis, MO 63108-3393
U.S.A.

Dear Father Padberg, P.C.

On the occasion of this slightly belated celebration of your 75th year of pilgrimage and exploration in the marvelous world of human life, it is a pleasure to greet you with a word of gratitude and appreciation from the General Curia. As the introduction to this volume puts it, you have loved this world since you love the God who made it.

Your love of God, as Saint Ignatius urges us, has manifested itself in deeds, and not just in words — although quite often your "deeds" have issued in the publication of many "words." Our Jesuit brotherhood has been richly blessed because of your great passion for our history and our life. You have not only explored that history in your research and work as editor, you have almost literally lived it, bringing insights from the past to bear on our contemporary world and the Society's role in it. And you have done this with great verve and an evident love for whatever topic you are treating.

I thank you, Father Padberg, for your many years of creative contributions to our life and work, and wish you many more years of happy service of the Lord's mission. Be assured of my prayers and best birthday wishes.

Sincerely in Our Lord,

Peter-Hans Kolvenbach, S.J.
Superior General

INTRODUCTION

*S*PIRIT, STYLE, STORY IS A COLLECTION OF ESSAYS HONORING a great and good American Jesuit, John W. Padberg, S.J. Its title is an attempt to capture the essence of the man: a Jesuit whose deep spirituality, humane style, and passion for history have inspired a generation of Jesuits and lay colleagues.

John William Padberg was born in St. Louis, Missouri, and entered the Society of Jesus at Florissant on the day before his eighteenth birthday in 1944. He holds a baccalaureate degree in classics, a master's degree in modern European history, licentiates in both philosophy and theology from St. Louis University, and a doctorate in the history of ideas from Harvard University. He also did postgraduate studies at the Institut Catholique in Paris.

Father Padberg taught history and theology at St. Louis University for two years before being named assistant to the dean of the graduate school, vice president for academic affairs, and then acting executive vice president. After serving for two years as one of the founding members of the U.S. Jesuit Conference staff in Washington, D.C., he was named president of the Weston School of Theology in Cambridge, Massachusetts, a position he filled with great distinction for a decade. In 1986 he returned to his native St. Louis where he was named director of the Institute of Jesuit Sources and chairman of the Seminar on Jesuit Spirituality. He also served as founding chair of the National Seminar on Jesuit Higher Education. He attended the Thirty-second and Thirty-fourth General Congregations of the Society of Jesus as an elected delegate from the Missouri Province. Throughout his career he has continued to teach and lecture.

Teaching and administrating, however, never detracted from his scholarly output. His magisterial *Colleges in Conflict: The Jesuit Schools in France from Revival to Suppression, 1815–1890* (Harvard University, 1969) remains the standard work on that subject. As director of the Institute of Jesuit Sources, he has made immense contributions to Jesuit historiography, including his detailed and colorful histories of the Society of Jesus' thirty-four General Congregations, his many monographic contributions to the Studies in Spirituality of Jesuits series, and countless articles in other important publications. During his tenure at the institute, he has edited and overseen the publication of more than forty books and eighty issues of the *Studies* periodical.

Father Padberg's generosity is renowned. He rarely turns down an invitation to lecture on Jesuit history and spirituality. At the age of seventy-two he reluctantly yet cheerfully accepted the position of rector of the St. Louis University Jesuit Community. For many years he has served as the U.S. coordinator for the triennial International Colloquium on Jesuit Spirituality and has frequently been invited to Rome as a consultant to the General Curia of the Society of Jesus. He has been a member of the board of trustees of a dozen universities, contributing historical, theological, and practical wisdom. It is rumored that his travel alone kept St. Louis–based TWA afloat during the last decade of its existence.

Underpinning his scholarly work is a spirituality of service and availability. A compassionate priest, Padberg has mentored innumerable young scholars, both lay and Jesuit. He has cared for the sick and dying in his own Jesuit community and has ministered to his beloved family and friends. Like the great Jesuit saint and scholar Peter Canisius, whom Padberg resembles in everything save disposition, he continues to preach, teach, and administer (recall that the root meaning of the word *administer* is "minister to") at an age when many of his contemporaries have retired from the fray.

While spirituality and history—spirit and story—have dominated his life, one needs to add a word about John Padberg's style. Anyone who has ever dined with him knows that during his years in France he studied not only great ideas but also *les grands crus*. His conversations sparkle with anecdotes on St. Margaret Mary

Alacoque and Madame de Sévigné, Ignatius and I. M. Pei. Simply put, he is the most urbane of men, yet one who carries his great learning lightly and with touching humility; he loves the world because he loves the God who made it.

The essays that follow touch on the passions of his life: spirit and spirituality, style and beauty, and most of all history. Each in its own way is an attempt to combine reverence for and knowledge of history, the fruits of modern scholarship, and a spirituality of mind and heart developed by Ignatius Loyola and lived out by men like John Padberg for the past 463 years. It is the writers' hope that in preparing these essays to honor a true scholar and good friend they will contribute to the work to which John has dedicated his life, the reasoned and humane exposition of history and the workings of history's Lord.

It was the compiler's intention that this *festschrift* see the light in 2001 in honor of John Padberg's seventy-fifth birthday. Such intentions are well-known paving materials, and I regret the delay. Things happen—and don't—in their own historical time.

This project gave me the opportunity to be in contact with many old friends and collaborators. The authors responded with great enthusiasm to the invitation to honor John with an essay, and they have endured many harangues and many months, even years, of waiting to see this project in print. I am most grateful to them: Michael Buckley, S.J.; William Barry, S.J.; Martin O'Keefe, S.J.; David Fleming, S.J.; Joseph Tetlow, S.J.; Howard Gray, S.J., whose essays focus on primarily Jesuit spirituality; Evonne Levy and Gauvin Bailey, who discuss art and architecture in the Jesuit context; and historians John O'Malley, S.J.; Peter Togni, S.J.; Paul Murphy; Thomas McCoog, S.J.; Paul Begheyn, S.J.; Gerald McKevitt, S.J.; and Michael Maher, S.J.

My old friend and trusted copy editor Ruth McGugan helped immensely in the preparation of the manuscript. Her diligence enhanced our prose and clarified our endless endnotes. Since its inception, Father George Lane, S.J., director of Loyola Press, Chicago, has supported this project with great interest and generosity. Rebecca Johnson, Matthew Diener, Daniel Connor, and the very capable staff at Loyola Press saw the project through to press with courteous and attentive professionalism. I am also grateful for generous grants from St. Louis University president Father Lawrence Biondi, S.J., the U.S. Jesuit Conference, and the Jesuit Community at USF that enabled this project to move forward. Darnise Martin and Siobhan Muenk at USF were also most helpful in all stages of manuscript preparation.

Most of all, though, I'm grateful for the example, mentoring, and friendship of John W. Padberg, S.J., to whom this work is affectionately dedicated.

Thomas M. Lucas, S.J.
University of San Francisco
Feast of St. Thomas Aquinas, 2002

PART I: SPIRIT

"Likewise You Are Priests...": Some Reflections on Jesuit Priesthood

Michael J. Buckley, S.J.

O N 8 SEPTEMBER 1973, THE GENERAL OF THE SOCIETY OF Jesus, Pedro Arrupe, formally summoned the Thirty-second General Congregation. The following week, Pope Paul VI sent a strong letter to the Jesuits, "In Paschae solemnitate," expressing his concerns about the Society and his hopes for the forthcoming Congregation.[1] The letter clustered four notes to sketch the Society's character as "an order that is religious, apostolic, priestly, and united with the Roman Pontiff by a special bond of love and service."[2] This description would repeat over and over again in the discussions preparatory to the Congregation, in the debates of its members once assembled, and in the decrees it legislated. The papal address to the Congregation as it opened on 3 December 1974 cited it explicitly and employed it as the algorithm to spell out the identity of the Society. The Congregation accepted this designation, and two of its more definitional documents advanced it crucially to delineate the nature of the Society.[3]

Of these four notes, none was more problematical than "priestly." There was some discussion about its appropriateness for Jesuits within the church following Vatican II, and in one province, a number of scholastics had petitioned to remain within the Society and to forgo ordination to the priesthood. But these were minor voices amid the consensus that the papal formula was authentic. Debates did ensue, but they centered on the nature and exercise of priesthood within the Society of Jesus, not its existence; upon the meaning of priesthood in the Society, not upon its fitting location among the essential notes of the Order. Paradoxically, neither this Thirty-second nor the Thirty-third Congregation explored the question of the character of Jesuit priesthood. It was the Thirty-fourth Congregation, ten years later, that recognized the need to formulate a decree, addressing explicitly "the priestly dimensions of Jesuit life more complete[ly] than the last three congregations were able to offer." It was a task urgent in its necessity and immensely complicated in its execution, and so the Congregation determined not to elaborate a "theology of priesthood, but only a way of considering the priestly dimension of Jesuit identity and mission in the light of our founding inspiration."[4]

The resultant decree six thus offered to the Society an orientation that was accepted as sound and promising, but necessarily containing within its pages the traces of a number of different theologies of the ministerial priesthood. This was obviously quite appropriate. It did not belong to a Congregation to elaborate a systematic theology of the priesthood, but to decree its constituents and requirements in the Society. This document would and should open the nature of ministerial priesthood in the Society of Jesus to further reflections that were *ex professo* theological. The question to be treated would be not so much how the Jesuits of the sixteenth century found themselves priests and took that priesthood for granted from the earliest redactions of the *Formula of the Institute*—though this history itself contains critically important theological determinations and clues. The theological question today is rather what is the character of the ministerial priesthood as a defining mark of the Society, i.e., what is the contemporary specification of the priesthood in the normative tradition of the church and in the commitments of the Society. The following pages hope to take up something of that question, and to do so as a tribute to a Jesuit, Fr. John Padberg, to whom the Society stands in so much debt both for the sound scholarship he has given to its understanding and for the abiding and generous leadership he has repeatedly lent to its deliberations and ministries.

When one attempts a "theology of" something, one is seeking to apprehend the subject in terms of the self-communication and self-revelation of God as they reach a normative intensity in Jesus of Nazareth and the transformation worked by his Spirit, and as they are further embodied and realized in the sacramental and evangelical life of the church and in all authentic religious experience. One does a "theology of" when one attempts to understand anything explicitly in terms of God. Obviously so vast a subject as that of the ministerial priesthood allows for only a fragmentary and truncated treatment in a single study. To attempt more would be to accomplish less; hence the emphatic "some" in the title of this essay. These remarks focus upon a single question: What is the theological meaning or appropriateness of the ministerial priesthood as it exists within and marks the ministries of the Society of Jesus?

The present article considers this question through two successive stages: how does the church understand the ministerial priesthood in general, and how is this understanding shaped and realized in the Society in such a way that recent Congregations and recent popes could repeatedly insist that "the exercise of the ministerial priesthood has been regarded as central to the Society's identity and apostolic mission"?[5]

This problematic intersection of a theology of the Catholic priesthood with the spirituality that is the Society of Jesus—conceived in the *Formula of the Institute* as a pathway to God *(via est quaedam ad Illum)*[6]—allows for a point of departure that is somewhat different from that found in the usual manual treatment of ordained priesthood; this point of departure finds its roots in two critically important convictions as they both emerge from and specify the tradition that gives definition to the Society of Jesus: the desire of human beings for God and the desire of God for human beings.

Section One.
The Ministerial Priesthood

Part One. Union with God

The first of these primordial convictions within the tradition of the spirituality of the Society can be found as effectively as in any other place in the opening statement of a seventeenth-century masterpiece of spiritual direction, *Doctrine spirituelle,* the teaching of a Jesuit tertian master, Louis Lallemant (1587–1635). So important, so critical did the redactors of his reflections judge this statement, that they used it to introduce what became Lallemant's spare, laconic, but massively perceptive and influential work. They transpose into a world of affectivity and experience the opening sentences of the "Principle and Foundation":

> Nous avons dans notre coeur un vide
> que toutes les créatures ne sauraient remplir.
> Il ne peut être rempli que de Dieu,
> qui est notre principe et notre fin.[7]

Lallemant begins with the human experience of an emptiness—of a void—of what is classically called "religious hunger" and whose very privation points to the destiny of the human person or of the human community. For this emptiness constitutes a longing for union with God—however God comes confusedly into human lives disguised as unrealized happiness or as the decisive offer of love or of complete meaning and fulfillment or as an absolute and permeating claim upon what human beings are and choose. There is this obscure, unthematic, yet continual personal experience that one is called to something more and that consequently one must continually change. Why? Because "this is not enough." Augustine's assertion has been repeated a thousand times because its truth is so established by experience: "You have made us for yourself, O Lord, and our heart is restless until it rests in You."[8] That phrase, "for yourself," will obtain its own transposition in the "Principle and Foundation": "The human being was created to praise, reverence, and serve God our Lord, and in this way, to save his or her soul."[9]

It is this first conviction—and the experience it names—that Karl Rahner cites as foundational for his theology, a conviction now transposed into the language of speculative or practical theology: the recognition that a human being is an emptiness for God, a question for which God is the only answer; and to attempt to fill that emptiness with anything finite, anything categorical or created, only increases the emptiness and the sense of fraud or frustration or even despair. Much of this marks the experience that has created the world in which we live, feeding a skepticism in postmodernity—the experience of alienation, of being religiously marginalized, of despair (even when this is not recognized as such). In Rahner's fundamental principle: "Wir sind auf God verwiesen. Diese ursprüngliche Erfahrung is immer gegeben."[10]

So many of our contemporaries have the experience—vague or definite—that *"this"* (whatever *this* is and however many things it encompasses) is not enough. Take but one example from someone who may well be the most popular spiritual author of our time. In his journal for 24 November 1941, a few weeks before he entered Gethsemani Abbey, the young Thomas Merton wrote: "I am not physically tired, merely filled with a deep, undefined vague sense of spiritual distress, as if I had a deep wound running inside of me, and it had to be stanched. . . . The wound is only another aspect of the fact that we are exiles on this earth. The sense of exile is inside me like a hemorrhage."[11] Unless it is suppressed or overwhelmed with distractions or lost in unacknowledged despair, there is within the human being that sense of privation and an aspiration for a coherence in which things make final sense and human longing is affirmed in the experience of love.

This conviction is also basic to all pastoral ministry. Any understanding of Catholic ministerial priesthood issues in part from this recognition that human beings, however covertly, inescapably long for union with God. This conviction figures often in effective preaching, spiritual direction, or conversations that stir in others this subtle, pervasive self-awareness and awakens in them the possibilities of its fulfillment. That is why Friedrich Wulf can say that the first stage of spiritual direction is to aid the directee to self-knowledge.[12]

This first conviction is true—but it is not true enough. It is secondary to and derivative of something far more primordial and fundamental. For God is not finally derived from human longings, however human needs point to God. Far more important is it, and especially for a spirituality marked by the contemplation of the "Call of the Temporal King," to recognize that the primacy even here belongs to God. Hence the primordial conviction: that God longs for union with us, with human beings. Behind human longing and desire is the desire of God to unite human beings with himself. Indeed this is the reason why human beings exist and are constituted as they are, i.e., as a question before God, however one understands the mystery of divine desire and longing. The human aspiration for God is a result of the divine causality, and it has as its fundamental cause God's desire for union with human beings. The desire of God is first and is sovereign.

In the Scriptures, this is an abiding theme—from God's coming to the Garden to speak with Adam and Eve, to the formation of a people through whom God would enter into all human history, to the Incarnation and the paschal mystery and the mission of the promised indwelling Spirit. This longing search of God reaches a particularly poignant expression in the fifteenth chapter of Luke, legitimately called "the gospel within the gospel."[13] For the sheep is not searching for the shepherd but the shepherd for the sheep. The coin is not frantically looking for the woman, but the woman for the coin. It is the Father who catches sight of his son a far way off, runs up to him, and embraces him; it is the Father who goes out to plead with the elder son to come into the house. The Father loves his two sons and wants them to be with him in an intensity and purity of love that neither of them had for him.

This theme runs through Christian theology. Augustine has given it classic expression in the question placed in the first paragraphs of the *Confessions:* "What am I to you, O Lord, that you have commanded me to love you?"[14] At the beginning of the great digression in his commentary on the third stanza of "The Living Flame," John of the Cross reminds the reader as a matter of primary importance that "if the soul is seeking for God, her Beloved is much more *(mucho más)* seeking for the soul."[15] In *The Spiritual Exercises,* the "Call of the Temporal King" introduces the contemplations upon the life of Christ, not with the religious hunger of humankind for the kingdom of God, but with the desires and determinations of Christ, "chosen by God" as his instrument: "It is my wish to conquer the entire world and all enemies and so to enter into the glory of my Father."[16] What is at issue is the glory of God. The foundational importance of this desire of God, a desire that is aboriginal and creative of the religious longing that constitutes human beings, is not so much recognized today, and yet it is crucial to the dynamism of the *Exercises* and to a religious order that speaks of serving the glory of God. The religious longings of human beings are the desires of God in shadow. All of creation and redemption point to this primordial understanding of God: that it means an enormous amount to God that he be known and loved by those whom he has created and loved. Thus, in the *Exercises,* the initiative toward union is not human longing, but God's. "It is my will to conquer the whole world."[17]

Hence, one can propose as the theological foundation for any understanding of Catholic priesthood—as indeed for any ministry in the church—this longing for unity between God and human beings: the longing of God for union with human beings, and its effect, the longing of human beings for union with God.

Part Two. Reconciliation with God

When Catholic theology talks about union with God within a prior history of sin and alienation (i.e., in a personal or collective history where the absence of the influence of God has been chosen or accepted and transmitted to subsequent generations as part of the cultural air one breathes or is being lived with unrecognized religious despair), and as one consciously and soberly appropriates with Christian realism something of the depths and pervasive presence of this situation, theology specifies or names the divine unity for which human beings long not so much as "union" but as "reconciliation." "Reconciliation" always denotes a restoration of union between persons. Whether that union be friendship or marriage or political concord, it is a union forged or achieved within an antecedent history of the destruction of that union through indifference or explicit repudiation or gradual alienation. When that choice rejects a personal influence or destroys a union with God, it is called "sin." To do evil is to effect the destructively antihuman; but to commit sin is to excise the influence of God that would deter one from doing evil. The distinction is important, though again one distinguishes in order to unite, and one can see it at work in any serious personal relationship.

A young couple comes to Berkeley, the University of California, where the husband is to study physics. His wife urges him to avoid at all cost the drug scene at the university. "In some places, it is very heavy—almost overwhelming—and you have had serious trouble with it before. For my sake and for the sake of our marriage, keep away from anything that has to do with drugs." The man promises, life takes off with his graduate studies, but in a year or so the wife finds that he is heavy into drugs. Her pain and sorrow are enormous as she recognizes two things: her husband is destroying himself and their marriage, and her love was not a strong enough presence in his life to deter him from doing this destruction. Something homologous can occur in the human relationship with God. The human destruction, the corrupting of so much that was promising and good within human beings, is evil; but the repudiation of the personal, divine influences that would have inhibited this evil is sin. Evil is any corruption of good; sin is the chosen absence of the influence of God. The first calls for amendment and healing; the second, for forgiveness and reconciliation.

"To reconcile" is to restore union, to bond once more into a deep personal union those who have been estranged. Reconciliation concludes in a renewed union that supplants the chosen absence of God. Reconciliation, then, is that reuniting of human beings with God that is the forgiveness of sins, and it issues from the longing of God and of human beings.

Reconciliation is how Paul understood what God was about in Christ. Consider how often and crucially the concept appears in 2 Corinthians:

> Therefore, if anyone is in Christ, he is a new creation;
> the old has passed away, behold, the new has come.
> All this is from God, who through Christ, *reconciled*
> *[katallaxantos]* us to himself and gave us the *ministry of*
> *reconciliation [diakonian tes katallages];* ...
> in Christ God was *reconciling the world to himself,*
> not counting their trespasses against them,
> and entrusting to us the *message [logon] of reconciliation.*
> So we are ambassadors for Christ *[presbeuomen],*
> God making his appeal through us.
> We beseech you on behalf of Christ,
> *be reconciled to God.*[18]

What 2 Corinthians calls the "ministry of reconciliation" begins with the desire of God for reconciliation. As God chose to effect creation, so does God work to bring about that reconciliation that is the new creation. But God makes his appeal through human beings. Christ thus becomes the agent of that reconciliation. The mission is first of all Christ's and then those who act on "behalf of Christ," those in whom and through whom Christ acts. In this human mediation, reconciliation continues to reach out to all aspects of human life. But it is crucial to see that this all begins with the desire of God for reconciliation and that this desire frames the mission of Jesus and of the church. When the New Testament deals with reconciliation, it is not dealing immediately with the subjectivity of religious hunger, but with that objective alienation or enmity with God that has found expression in later centuries as an aching inner hunger.[19] There are other ways of expressing this, such as entrenched social inequality, the degradation of the human, exploitation, and racism—all of which can be recognized as "objective" expressions of the human alienation from God.

And when this reconciliation—and the new union it embodies between God and human beings—was transposed into the terms of the letter to the Hebrews, one speaks explicitly of the priesthood that was Christ's. It was through this priesthood that reconciliation or forgiveness was effected and sin eliminated: "Therefore, he had to be made like his brothers in every respect, so that he might become a merciful and faithful high priest in service of God to make expiation for the sins of the people."[20] The agent of this union is *hiereus,* Christ. And all of the faithful, in being joined to Christ, share in his universal priestly ministry.

Part Three. The Priesthood of Christ

Classically, the ministry of reconciliation between God and human beings (the forgiveness of sins) was the function and the meaning of the priesthood in Hebrews.[21] Over and over again it is stated that Christ is priest—the *hiereus*—and thus the "source of eternal salvation for all who obey him, being designated by God as a high priest after the order of Melchizedeck" (5:9–10). His priesthood, as Avery Dulles has summarized, in some way includes his divine call (5:4–6), his earthly prayers of petition (5:7), his obedience by which his passion was made holy (5:8), his sacrificial death (9:18), and his existence now as the one who "always lives to make intercession for [us]" (7:25). Thus Dulles can maintain that this priesthood unites teaching (1:2), sanctifying (passim), and guiding/leading (5:2; 9–10).[22]

In this sense it is true to say that Jesus is the only priest, the only *hiereus,* who offered his own life for us and now lives perpetually "to make intercession for us," the One who is to bring about our union, our reconciliation, with God.[23] Hebrews stresses that this priestly reconciliation—calling Jesus the "mediator of the new covenant"[24]—occurs not only through his intercession but by his direction and word, which elicit our obedience. He is priest by his teaching and leadership; as high priest he is the "source of eternal salvation for all who obey him."[25] Christ exercises his priesthood for us—reconciles us—by teaching, sanctifying, and guiding us. All of these actions bear upon and are embodied definitionally in his priesthood.

Part Four. Priesthood of the Church

Concretely, how does Christ continue in the historical order to extend himself into human lives? This is the meaning and mission of the church, this community of those whose lives are consecrated to his discipleship through baptism. The church is to objectify and so to continue the priesthood of Christ in history, i.e., into this time and place and into every time and every place. The first Petrine epistle maintains that these people are a holy priesthood, a priesthood defined by the offering of "spiritual sacrifices acceptable to God through Jesus Christ" and by "announcing the praises of him who called you out of darkness into his wonderful light."[26] For the purpose of the church, of this community, is precisely to reconcile the world to God by making concretely present to the world Christ's priesthood of teaching, sanctifying, and guiding. This is what such theologians as Friedrich Wulf have recognized and retrieved for contemporary theology, the universal priesthood as "the priesthood of the Church."[27] This is what makes it possible for the priesthood of Christ to continue within human history. The "missing link" in so many attempts to understand the ministerial priesthood is the failure to see the priesthood of the church itself, the priesthood of the people of God.

The church is a priestly people insofar as the everlasting priesthood of Christ is realized in this community. The church is what it is only to the degree that it unites human beings with God; it fulfills this task by making available to all human life the teaching and sacrifice of Jesus, the Word that is Christ that guides human lives into union with him, the sacramental communication of his Spirit as that by which we live and by which we walk. Christ reconciles human beings to God through his Spirit, through the ongoing word and sacrament of his church, through the life and mission to the world of his church. Whenever the Christian people, severally or collectively, act to reconcile the world to God and thus to one another, the church precisely as a priesthood finds a place in this historical moment.

Part Five. The Ministerial Priesthood in the Church

Ministerial priests, presbyters, are those human beings who are called by Christ through his church and anointed by the Spirit explicitly to minister to the church in the name of the church in such a way that the priesthood of the faithful becomes actualized.

They are the servants of the church, consecrated to this task "in the name of the church," i.e., as commissioned and sent by the church that the priesthood of the people would become a reality in this time and this place. They exist as ministerial priests through the call and mandate of the church—freely given and freely accepted.

These ordained priests are to minister to the objectification of Christ in the world, i.e., to the church, so that (despite our sins) the church's word, guidance, and sanctification are authentic. The *presbyteroi*—to be sharply distinguished from the *hiereus* that is Christ—are those chosen by Christ to minister in the name of the church to his church, to sustain and foster the priesthood of the baptized. They represent and embody in this "official" or public way Christ's care for his church—both in its internal life and in its mission to the world—that the church would be priest to the world. What is of preeminent importance is the priesthood of the faithful, the priesthood of the entire church united with Christ. This ordained priesthood is instrumental to that great reality; it is to minister to and to serve the church. The ministerial priesthood allows the church to continue Christ's great work of reconciliation. This is what it means to say that ministerial priests are the servants of the people of God who are the church.

That is why decree six from the Thirty-fourth General Congregation so rightly insisted that through their baptism, all Christians participate in Christ's priestly work of reconciling the world to God; they form the whole Christ, who as St. Thomas says, "is the only true priest; all of the others are only his ministers" (Heb. 7:4).[28] One must be very clear on this: Christ alone is priest in the sense of the Greek term *hiereus*. The church is a priestly people as it is a "place/people" where Christ's mission of reconciliation is embodied and continued, where God is truly worshiped, where God's self-revelation and self-communication to the entire world are continued, and by which human lives in conformity with that teaching and that spirit are fostered. In this sense, the church is not simply the people *for* whom God is worshipped, confessed, and invoked; it is also the people *by* whom God is worshiped, confessed, and invoked. In this way, God's influence over human praxis is furthered, and the church realizes the priesthood that is uniquely Christ as *hiereus*.

Christ through his Spirit calls, forms, educates, examines, and finally officially ordains ministers who by mandate of the church are to serve the church; in this way the church becomes what it is—this kind of priestly people. These ministers are ordained to bring it about that the Word of God is continued and heard and understood, that the Eucharist and the other sacraments are present in this culture and this time, that this priestly people embody in their various commitments the love and care for human suffering that bespeak the reconciliation that is the purpose of Jesus. The priesthood of the church, the universal priesthood, is realized whenever and however human beings are so reconciled to God. The ministerial priests are not alone to foster and support that mind of Christ in the church, but they do so by special mandate, ministries (evangelical as well as sacramental), and responsibilities. In this sense, their ordained service to the church is to retrieve the Christ of Ephesians, who "loved the church and gave himself up for her, that he might sanctify her."[29]

These ministers we call "priests," not in the sense of *hiereis,* but in the sense of *presbyteroi*. They are those whom Christ calls and through whom he works so that the church may be the sacrament of our reconcilation. The ministerial priest serves the church in two ways: in a complexus of services to the church directly, that it be what it is, and in a complexus of services from the church to the world, that the church can care for the world redeemed by Christ. In both cases the key is reconciliation with God, reconciliation worked within the church and within the world. Perhaps it is warranted to spell out this twofold ministry of the ordained priests to the church in a little more detail.

Ministerial priests are to serve the people of God first of all by their teaching and preaching. This ministry of the Word is placed first among the defining responsibilities of the bishop by *Lumen Gentium:* "Among the principal tasks of the bishops the preaching of the gospel is preeminent."[30] This grounds the assertion of *Presbyterorum ordinis* and determines its discussion of the ministerial priesthood: "Priests, as the fellow workers of the bishops, have as their first charge *[primum habent officium]* to announce the gospel to all."[31] This is to understand the defining focus of the ministerial priesthood as Karl Rahner does: "The priest is he who, related to an at least potential community, preaches the Word of God by mandate of the church as a whole and therefore officially, and in such a way that he is entrusted with the highest levels of sacramental intensity of this Word. Expressed very simply, he has the mission to preach the gospel in the name of the church." And this immediately engages the Eucharist. Rahner continues: "He does this at the highest level at which this Word can operate in the anamnesis of Christ's death and resurrection through the celebration of the Eucharist."[32] All of the other sacraments either lead to the Eucharist or issue from it. Thus the ministerial priests serve the church both in its prophetic or evangelical life and in its sacramental life. They foster that Christian community which is constituted as the living priesthood of Christ and which is to continue in the social and political order the reconciliation that issues from the gospel.[33]

Ministerial priests represent the people of God in a unique way, so that they can speak in the name of the church in, for example, calling the world to hear the gospel, to hope in God, to have compassion for the suffering, to be reconciled from human enmities. All Christians can and should do this. In the name of the church, the ministerial priest does this himself, representing the church by the public commission of the church; he also (and very importantly) calls upon other Christians to commit themselves to this work of teaching, preaching, and sanctification.[34] The ministerial priest then is called by Christ to have a twofold relationship to the church: *ad intra* and *ad extra*. He is called to act for the sake of the church in its own priestly existence; to act on behalf of the church that the church might be the church, he is called to act in the name of the church in its presence within the world, so that the church can act through him.

There is a more lapidary way of phrasing this: Through the ministerial priesthood, Christ acts to make real and salvifically effective the priesthood of the faithful. The ordained priest is subordinate to the universal priesthood of the church; he is its servant.

The purpose of the ministerial priesthood is the actualization of the priesthood of the faithful at this time and this place. The ministerial priesthood is an instrumentality through which Christ ministers to his church and through his church to this world. This is how Christ continues to do what the book of Revelation with so much gratitude insists that he is doing: "To him who loves us and has freed us from our sins by his blood, and made us a kingdom, priests to his God and Father, to him be glory and dominion forever and ever. Amen."[35]

There are obviously many different charisms and ministries in the Church—as different as those of Dorothy Day, Mother Teresa, Gabriel Marcel, and Karl Rahner.[36] Each of these charisms emerges out of the presence of the Spirit given in baptism and confirmation; each of them realizes and re-presents the priesthood of Christ *(hiereus)*. Commitments and vocations such as religious life and Christian marriage bring baptism and confirmation to their completion, to their inherent fullness. But there is also a ministry of serving the church by fostering the actualization of the universal priesthood of the church—of acting in the name of the church to foster its reconciling missions of teaching, sanctifying, and leading. There is the ministry of being officially of service to the church and for the church in its life and in its mission. When Christ calls a person to care for the church and the world in this way and when the church confirms this call through the sacrament of orders, one speaks about the ministerial priest *(presbyteros)*, the servant of the church.

This ministerial priesthood that exists for the priesthood of the faithful can be realized in vastly divergent ways as even a glance at the history of the church will show. The second section of this essay will attempt to indicate the manner in which it has taken a particular shape in the Society of Jesus.

Section Two.
Ministerial Priesthood and the Society of Jesus[37]

Part One. The Reason for Founding the Society of Jesus

I. A Curious Clue

It is very hard to get at the special character of priesthood in the Society of Jesus, but perhaps one can take a clue from what seems a Jesuit anomaly—a unique protocol which the Society has always defended, even against massive opposition and figures as formidable as Pius V. The Society of Jesus is the first and only religious order in the church for whose members ordination to the priesthood precedes final vows. For all, except the obvious case of temporal coadjutors, one enters the Society as a priest. The scholastic fulfills his promise "to enter the Society" only after ordination to the priesthood.[38] The professed must be priests before their profession, as must the spiritual coadjutors before their final vows.[39] In all other religious orders at the time of Ignatius, the members made their solemn profession upon the completion of the novitiate, with ordination to the priesthood many years away.[40] The Society reversed that order and modeled a new structure of further probations and final incorporation that echoes much of the processes of the election and the confirmation of the election in the Spiritual Exercises.

But why? This procedure recapitulates the origins of the Society as a religious order and the incorporation of its first members; even more important, it indicates the unique relationship between this order and the ministerial priesthood. If one explores the history and the foundation of the Society, it is obvious that the Society was neither founded nor is it now conceived as a religious order some of whose members are priests and some are lay brothers. That distinction, indeed the title "lay brother," bespeaks a monastic origin and character, as in the monastery the differences between choir monks and lay brothers for centuries distinguished the priests from the brothers. This was not the distinction among grades in the Society. Indeed, in the mind of Ignatius, all Jesuits are brothers—and so Ignatius can write to Francis Borgia: "I accept and receive you as our brother."[41] Historically speaking, the Society of Jesus did not begin as a religious order that later determined that some of its members should be priests. On the contrary, the Society issued out of a group of priests—men already ordained and deeply engaged in priestly ministries, listed by them at its very beginning as "confessions, teaching, and other spiritual works." In *Regimini militantis ecclesiae* they identified themselves by the dioceses to which they belonged.[42]

Such distinctions as came to emerge in the early formation of the Society were fourfold, each stage of which gave the term "Society of Jesus" greater and greater comprehension: the first included the professed of the four vows, all of whom were priests (the "professed Society"); the second included with them the formed coadjutors of the professed society, either spiritual or temporal, priests or nonpriests; the third extended this to those still in formation or probation; and the fourth further comprised all of those who live under obedience to the General.[43] In all cases where ordination obtained, it preceded final vows. In this way, if one was a priest, he was a priest before finally entering the Society of Jesus. The Society itself had emerged as a consensus among priest-companions.

II. Available to Be Sent by the Pope

When these secular priests—already vowed to poverty and committed to the Roman pontiff for the determination of their apostolic missions—met to decide whether there would be a religious order, a community that would one day be named "the Society of Jesus," they posed the first of two questions for their *Deliberations:*

> Granted that we had offered and dedicated ourselves and our lives to Christ our Lord and to his true and legitimate vicar on earth, so that he might dispose of us and send us wherever he judged it to be more fruitful, whether to the Turks or to the Indies or to heretics or to others of the faithful or pagans—given that, would it or would it not be more advantageous for our

purpose to be so joined and bound together in one body that no physical distance, no matter how great, would separate us?[44]

The "Question" was asked by this group of secular priests. And it bore upon the strengthening of the mission they were already doing as priests and upon their prior availability to be sent by the pope—whether they were missioned to strengthen the church in word or sacrament or to confront the vast world of disbelief. Two were already being sent to Siena, and their mission occasioned this deliberation that was to form the Society of Jesus.

The "Answer" they gave was that "we ought day by day to stabilize our union . . . in order to effect the greater spiritual good of our fellow men. For united spiritual strength is more robust and braver in any arduous enterprise than it would be if segmented."[45] The union that they formed among themselves, which became the Society of Jesus, was conceived and chosen precisely as a way of strengthening a particular form of priestly ministry that was at the disposition of the pope for the service of the life and mission of the church throughout the world. In time, this service to the church and this availability to the determinations of the Roman pontiff were explicitly linked. The first *Formula of the Institute* (1539) framed this dedication as follows: "to serve the Lord alone and the Roman Pontiff." The final redaction of this *Formula* (1550) formulated it with far more theological accuracy and in a manner that was open to the later understandings of the ministerial priesthood at the service of the priesthood of the faithful: "to serve the Lord alone and the Church his spouse under the Roman Pontiff."[46]

There was nothing curious about this choice. The orientation of the Jesuit is to serve the worldwide church, as this final redaction of the *Formula Instituti* makes explicit. The bishop whose leadership is engaged by that responsibility is the bishop of Rome. Thus to be of service to the universal church in its mission to the entire world is to be of aid to the one who holds this charge, precisely in his task of a universal care. This conviction had been with the early companions before the foundation of the Society of Jesus. As early as 23 November 1538, "Peter Faber and the rest of his comrades and brothers" wrote to their old principal of the College de Sainte-Barbe to explain their decision:

> All of us who have bound ourselves together in this Society have pledged ourselves to the supreme pontiff, since he is the master of Christ's whole harvest. When we made this offering of ourselves to him, we indicated that we were prepared for anything that he might decide in Christ for us. Accordingly, if he will send us there where you are calling us, we shall gladly go. The reason why we subjected ourselves to his will and judgment in this manner was that we knew that he has a greater knowledge of what is expedient for Christianity as a whole.[47]

This orientation eventually concretized itself in terms of the fourth solemn vow of the members of the professed Society, which is not a vow of "loyalty," or of doctrinal submission, but of total availability to be sent on assignment. Thus, the *Declaration* on this section of the *Constitutions* could state explicitly: "The entire meaning of this fourth vow of obedience to the pope was and is in regard to missions."[48] The bishop whom the Jesuits were peculiarly bound to assist was the Roman pontiff; the manner in which they would serve the church would determine the nature of their priesthood.

Part Two. What Kind of Priestly Ministry?

Ignatius never enters into a discussion of the nature or status of the priesthood. The *Formula of the Institute* simply takes for granted and then states explicitly that all of the members are priests.[49] But the *Formula* does more than this: it defines the character of Jesuit priesthood by its ministries and enumerates these constituent ministries in the very first sentence of the *Formula of the Institute*. For the Jesuit is a member of "a Society founded chiefly for this purpose: to strive especially for the defense and propagation of the faith and for the progress of souls in Christian life and doctrine," and the means by which he pursues these objectives are the ministries that characterize his priesthood:

- Public preaching, lectures, and any other ministration whatsoever of the Word of God
- The Spiritual Exercises, the education of children and unlettered persons in Christianity, and the spiritual consolation of Christ's faithful through hearing confessions and administering the other sacraments
- Reconciling the estranged, assisting and serving those in prison or hospitals, and other works of charity[50]

The combination is a curious one, and it takes its focus from the ministry of the Word—the public imparting of this Word by preaching and teaching; the personal and social assimilation of the Word through the Spiritual Exercises, catechetics, and the sacraments, especially penance; and the social embodiment of the Word through the *obras de caridad*.

It is not hard to see that it is this conjunction that the Thirty-second General Congregation transposed into its now famous formulations of the promotion of faith and the service of justice. Nor is it difficult to understand how the Congregation subsumed its first articulation of this formulation under the rubric of "reconciliation": "The mission of the Society of Jesus today is the service of faith, of which the promotion of justice is an absolute requirement. For reconciliation with God demands the reconciliation of people with one another."[51] The "reconciliation" that was the focus of the priestly mission of Christ was advanced by the Congregation as the comprehensive principle by which both faith and justice were to be understood.

Part Three. The Character of Ministerial Priesthood in the Society of Jesus

One must see that ministerial priesthood in the Society of Jesus is not primarily a cultic priesthood. The distinction is important. Obviously the Jesuit priesthood is profoundly cultic because any Christian priest is a minister of praise, reverence, and service. Ignatius was "ordained for Mass," and his intense devotion to the Mass is well documented.[52] The daily Eucharist held a radical centrality in his own life and in that of his companions. When they traveled, provision was made for Mass no matter how difficult the surroundings. Ignatius's *Spiritual Diary* indicates the depth to which his own life depended on the daily Eucharist as he offered God the decisions or choices that eventually profoundly affected the composition of the *Constitutions* and, through that, the entire Society. He offered these decisions together with the everlasting offering of Christ. It is interesting to note that when Ignatius is portrayed in the vestments of Mass, it is not the missal that he is holding; it is the *Constitutions*. Much of Ignatius's understanding of the Mass was, of course, consistent with the church of his time and liturgically limited in this way. But what is of lasting significance is the unity between the habitual offering of his daily decisions and the eucharistic sacrifice that gave to this moment a fundamental and irreplaceable focus in the daily responsibilities of his life. He legislated daily Mass for the scholastics in addition to the hour that they were to spend in prayer in the course of their day.

But the *Constitutions* do not conceive the Jesuit's priestly ministry as that of the cathedral canon or of the parish pastor, someone whose principal function is either to preside over the Eucharist, or to administer the complexus of sacraments from baptism through marriage, or to devote sections of his day to the liturgical praise of God through the divine office in choir. Ignatius wanted the daily Eucharist to be a part of the life of every Jesuit, but nowhere does he insist that every Jesuit is to "say his own Mass." In fact, according to Gonçalves da Câmara, "Ignatius was accustomed to say the Hail Marys, which substituted for his breviary, after he arose. He then celebrated or attended Mass; after this he meditated for two hours."[53]

This alternative finds its way into the *Constitutions*. In the ceremony of solemn vows, for example, the *vovent* does not say Mass on that day according to the *Constitutions*. He attends Mass and receives Communion from the one who receives his vows.[54] On the day of election of the general "someone should celebrate the Mass of the Holy Spirit. All will attend it and receive communion during it."[55] For the average Jesuit, his "celebration of Mass should not be postponed beyond eight days without reasons legitimate in the opinion of the superior."[56] Here one should add to this Ignatius's mandate: "Our members will not regularly hold choir for the canonical hours or sing Masses and offices."[57] Most interestingly, the only exception that he would allow to this liturgical ban was the public recitation of vespers if it was done "for the purpose of attracting the people to more frequent attendance at the confessions, sermons, and lectures, and to the extent that it is judged useful for this."[58] Ignatius did not understand the priestly consecration of Jesuits as primarily cultic.

Secondly, even less was ministerial priesthood conceived as what one might call a kingly or administrative priesthood, the way that one understands a parish priest, in which the function of his priestly service of leadership is to gather believers into a community to receive the church's Word and its sacraments, and to stay there with them, ministering to their needs. Ignatius did not want his priests so committed to any one place. He expected them to be on the move, available for any mission to any place. Cardinal Newman grasped the austerity of this availability when he said, rather starkly: "The Jesuits do not know the word *home*." [59] Newman was contrasting the Jesuit with the Oratorian, who goes to a place, locates in that town, and becomes more and more stable so that he thinks of himself and his life in terms of one place. Ignatius was almost the opposite. His thoughts were primarily of being on the road, on mission.[60]

The original, primitive understanding of the Society was of a group of preachers in poverty making their way from town to town.[61] Gradually this understanding became more sophisticated, more elaborate, but the essence of the Society is its availability for mission: "Because the occupations which are undertaken for the aid of souls are of great importance, proper to our Institute, and very frequent, and because, on the other hand, our residence in one place or another is so highly uncertain."[62] Or even more sharply: "Because the members of this Society ought to be ready at any hour to go to some or other parts of the world where they may be sent by the sovereign pontiff or their own superiors, they ought not to take a curacy of souls and still less ought they to take charge of religious women."[63]

So what did Ignatius envisage as the Jesuit priesthood? A prophetic priesthood, one that was concerned to speak out the Word of God in any way that it could be heard, assimilated, and incarnated within the social life of human beings; a priesthood that spoke out of and to the religious experience of human beings and—as did the prophets of the Old Testament—coupled this care for authentic belief and life with a concern for those in social misery: the ministry of the Word, the ministries of interiority, the ministry to social misery.[64]

This is not an arbitrary collection of concerns. The preaching and teaching of the Word very naturally tends to the ministries of interiority by which the Word can be heard and assimilated, and this tends very naturally to the ministries of justice through which it can be lived and shared with others in the historical living out of human life. What the last few Congregations have done with their emphasis upon faith and the justice it includes was to restore focus once more to the priestly identity of the Society in the idiom characteristic of our times.

What is more, the contemporary church, through its reform in lectionary and in language and through its biblical and patristic scholarship, has restored to the celebration of the Eucharist its prophetic, proclamatory function. To allow Ignatius's definition of the Jesuit priesthood its own evolution within the contemporary church is to acknowledge that the Word is present in its most profound depths in the eucharistic anamnesis and in the words of forgiveness spoken in the sacrament of reconciliation. As the Eucharist proclaims far more effectively today than in the sixteenth century the death of the Lord Jesus until he comes, the ministry of the Word within the church has itself developed to subsume into a more profound unity certain other aspects of ministerial priesthood while conserving its primordial orientation toward the speaking, hearing, and embodiment of the Word of God.

So it is that in recent decrees from general congregations the vocabulary of "reconciliation" appropriately frames both the mission of the church and the ministry of Jesuits in service "to Christ our Lord and to the church, his spouse, under the Roman pontiff."[65] The normative decisions of the Society have so stated the character of the ministerial priesthood and the common task of the Society "of continuing Christ's saving work in the world, which is to reconcile men to God and men among themselves, so that by the gift of his love and grace they may build a peace based on justice."[66]

Out of this fundamental orientation of Jesuit priestly mission come the massively varied enterprises that have characterized the commitments of the Society of Jesus: the academic, the missionary, the educational, the pastoral, the intellectual, the social, the scholarly, and the artistic. All of them are concerned that the Word, the message, and self-communication of God be articulated and heard within a particular form of human culture and experience. But for this, it is imperative that priests be able to speak its word within every varied form of culture. They must be of the culture so that they can speak an intelligible word to the culture. They must be incarnate in a particular form of human culture to encourage the church as a whole to be incarnate in a particular culture. Otherwise the church and its ministerial priests become a sect. These engagements bespeak not the "hyphenated priest" but the incarnate priest, who identifies with a culture in order to speak with a culture.

At root, these are all forms of radical reconciliation between the human and the divine. They objectify the Ignatian conviction that nothing is foreign to the glory of God, that God "desires to be glorified both through the natural means, which He gives as Creator, and through the supernatural means, which He gives as the Author of grace."[67] There is, then, an organic relationship between this prophetic priesthood and every aspect of human life and aspiration, both in theory and in the history of the Society. But to trace out that relationship would be the work of another essay.

Endnotes

1. The title of this monograph, "Likewise you are priests . . ." comes from the "Address of Pope Paul VI to the Members of the 32nd General Congregation (December 3, 1974)," *Documents of the 31st and 32nd General Congregations of the Society of Jesus,* ed. John W. Padberg, S.J. (St. Louis, Mo.: The Institute of Jesuit Sources, 1977), 525. This edition will be cited for references to these congregations. In general, decrees from general congregations will be referenced by congregation, decree, and paragraph number, e.g., GC 34, d. 6, #1. For the Latin, English, French, and Spanish versions of "In Paschae solemnitate," see *Acta Romana Societatis Iesu,* XVI.1 (Anno 1973), 11–25.

2. Paul VI, "In Paschae solemnitate," 18.

3. GC 32, d. 2, #24; d. 4, #15.

4. GC 34, d. 6, #1. *Documents of the Thirty-fourth General Congregation of the Society of Jesus,* ed. John L. McCarthy, S.J. (St. Louis, Mo.: The Institute of Jesuit Sources, 1995). This edition will be cited for references to this Congregation. The reflections of the above essay are obviously coordinate with this sixth decree, as anyone who inspects both documents will see. I have decided, therefore, not to cite the decree at each point of agreement or confirmation.

5. GC 34, d. 6, #8.

6. *Formula Instituti* 3 [1]. *The Constitutions of the Society of Jesus,* trans. and introd. George E. Ganss, S.J. (St. Louis, Mo.: The Institute of Jesuit Sources, 1970). Hereafter, *Constitutions.*

7. Louis Lallemant, S.J., "Doctrine spirituelle," in *Collection Christus,* No. 3, ed. François Courel, S.J. (Paris: Desclée de Brouwer, 1979), Premier principe, 1:77.

> We have in our heart an emptiness
> which all creatures, taken together, cannot fill.
> It is not able to be filled except by God,
> who is our source and our purpose
> (our beginning and our end).

8. "Tu excitas ut laudare te delectet, quia fecisti nos ad te et inquietum est cor nostrum donec requiescat in te." Augustine, *Confessions,* vol. 1, ed. James J. O'Donnell (Oxford: Clarendon Press, 1992), I. 1:3.

9. Ignatius of Loyola, *The Spiritual Exercises,* "Principle and Foundation," 23. All references to the writings of Ignatius are taken from the critical

editions published as part of the *Monumenta historica Societatis Iesu*. The abbreviations for the volume cited are modeled upon those in Ganss, *Constitutions*, 359–62. Hereafter, *SpExx*.

10. Karl Rahner, *Grundkurs des Glaubens: Einführung in den Begriff des Christentums*, vol. 2 (Freiburg: Herder, 1976), 2:62. "We are oriented to God. This original experience is always given." *Foundations of Christian Faith: An Introduction to the Idea of Christianity*, trans. William V. Dych (New York: Crossroad, 1982), 53.

11. Thomas Merton, *Run to the Mountain: The Journals of Thomas Merton*, vol. 1, ed. Patrick Hart, O.C.S.O. (San Francisco: Harper, 1995), 452.

12. Friedrich Wulf, "Spiritual Direction," *Sacramentum Mundi* (New York: Herder and Herder, 1968–70), III:165.

13. See John R. Donahue, *The Gospel in Parable* (Philadelphia: Fortress Press, 1988), 146–62.

14. "Quid tibi sum ipse, ut amari te iubeas a me?" Augustine, *Confessions*, 1, 5:4.

15. San Juan de la Cruz, "Llama de amor viva," in *Vida y Obras de San Juan de la Cruz*, ed. Crisognono de Jesus, Matias del Niño Jesus, and Lucinio frl DD. Sacramento (Madrid: Biblioteca de Autores Christianos, 1964), 885.

16. "Mi voluntad es de conquistar todo el mundo y todos los enemigos, y así entrar en la gloria de mi Padre." St. Ignatius of Loyola, *Ejercicios Espirituales*, no. 95, in *Obras Completas de San Ignacio de Loyola* (Madrid: Biblioteca de Autores Christianos, 1963), 219.

17. *SpExx*, "The Call of the Temporal King," #92.

18. 2 Cor 5:17–20. Line breaks and italics are the author's. All scriptural citations taken from the *New Oxford Annotated Bible with the Apocrypha: Revised Standard Version*, (Oxford University Press: New York, 1977). Decree six of the Thirty-fourth Congregation cites this text as thematic.

19. See Joseph A. Fitzmeyer, S.J., "Pauline Theology," in *The New Jerome Biblical Commentary*, ed. Raymond E. Brown, S.S., Joseph A. Fitzmeyer, S.J., and Roland E. Murphy, O.Carm. (Englewood Cliffs, N.J.: Prentice Hall, 1990), 1398–99.

20. Heb. 2:17.

21. Heb. 2:14–18. See GC 34, d. 6, #6: "Through their baptism, Christians participate in Christ's priestly work of reconciling the world to God and all are called to mediate this reconciliation in their lives."

22. Avery Dulles, S.J., *The Priestly Office: A Theological Reflection* (New York: Paulist Press, 1997), 6–7.

23. Heb. 7:25.

24. Heb. 12:24. See also 8:6, 8.

25. Heb. 5:9.

26. 1 Pet. 2:5, 9.

27. Friedrich Wulf, "Commentary on the Decree, *Presbyterorum ordinis,*" in *Commentary on the Documents of Vatican II,* ed. Herbert Vorgrimler, trans. Hilda Graef, W. J. O'Hara, and Ronald Walls (New York: Herder and Herder, 1969), 4:221. This set of commentaries is henceforth cited as Vorgrimler.

28. GC 34, d. 6, #7.

29. Eph. 5:25–26.

30. *Lumen Gentium,* #25. This *predicatio evangelii* includes both teaching and preaching. Karl Rahner comments: "It is noteworthy (and important for an ecumenical theology) that the more doctrinal concept of teaching attributed to the bishops as *doctores* is subordinated to the biblical and more comprehensive or existential concept of preaching." Vorgrimler, 1:208.

31. *Presbyterorum ordinis,* #4. Friedrich Wulf comments: "Thus in actuality preaching is the start of all priestly activity as it is its centre also; for in the kerygma of the Church as a society of believers the Lord himself, crucified, and risen, the one who unites all in faith and creates unity, is effectively present." Vorgrimler, 4:228.

32. Karl Rahner, "What is the Theological Starting Point for a Definition of Priestly Ministry?" in *The Identity of the Priest,* vol. 43, ed. Karl Rahner. (Concilium, vol. 43) (New York: Paulist, 1969), 85.

33. GC 34, d. 6, #7.

34. GC 34, d. 6, #7.

35. Rev. 1:5–6. See also 5:10.

36. cf. GC 34, d. 6, #3.

37. An earlier draft of much in this section appeared twenty-five years ago in the author's "Jesuit Priesthood: Its Meaning and Commitments," in *Studies in the Spirituality of Jesuits* 8, no. 5 (December 1976): 148–50.

38. *Constitutions,* V. 1. A. [#511c/d].

39. GC 1, #12.

40. See Antonio M. de Aldama, S.J., *An Introductory Commentary on the Constitutions,* trans. Aloysius J. Owen, S.J. (St. Louis, Mo.: The Institute of Jesuit Sources, 1989), 192.

41. Ignatius to Francis Borgia (9 October 1546), EppIgn 1:442–44, in *Letters of St. Ignatius of Loyola,* ed. and trans. William J. Young, S.J. (Chicago: Loyola University Press, 1959), 109.

42. For the text of the *Deliberatio primorum patrum* in English translation, reference is made to "The Deliberation That Started the Jesuits: A Commentario on the 'Deliberatio primorum patrum,'" in *Studies in the Spirituality of Jesuits,* trans. Jules J. Toner, S.J. (June 1974), 6:4. (Hereafter cited as *Del* with paragraph references, e.g., *Del,* 6k.) For the identification of the first companions in the papal bull, *Regimini militantis ecclesiae,* see *Impelling Spirit: Revisiting a Founding Experience: 1539. Ignatius and His Companions,* Joseph F. Conwell, S.J. (Chicago: Loyola Press, 1997), 33–64.

43. See *Constitutions,* V. 1. A. [#511].

44. *Del,* 3e.

45. *Del,* 3f.

46. For the texts of the three redactions of the *Formula Instituti,* see *Constitutiones et Regulae Societatis Iesu,* 4 vols. (Rome: Monumenta Historica Societatis Iesu [MHSI], 1934–48), 1:14–21, 24–32, 373–83. For a commentary upon the *Formula Instituti,* see Antonio M. de Aldama, S.J., *The Formula of the Institute: Notes for a Commentary,* trans. Ignacio Echániz, S.J. (St. Louis, Mo.: The Institute of Jesuit Sources, 1990).

47. *Sancti Ignatii de Loyola epistolae et instructiones,* 12 vols., (Madrid: MHSI, 1903–11), 2:581, I:132–133.

48. *Constitutions,* V. 3. C. [#529].

49. See *Formula Instituti* of 1550, chap. 5: "Socii autem omnes, cum Presbyteri esse debeant" in *Cons,* MHSI, I:380.

50. *Formula Instituti* of 1550 in Ganss, *Constitutions,* 66–67.

51. GC 32, d. 4, #2.

52. Ignatius of Loyola, *Autobiography,* #93, in *Obras completas de S. Ignacio de Loyola,* ed. Candido de Dalmases, S.J. (Madrid: Biblioteca de autores Cristianos, 1963), 150.

53. See Georg Schurhammer, S.J., *Francis Xavier: His Life, His Times,* trans. M. Joseph Costelloe, S.J. (Rome: The Jesuit Historical Institute, 1973), 1:483, n. 112, 485.

54. *Constitutions,* V. 3. 2. [#525].

55. *Constitutions,* VIII. 6. 3. [#697].

56. *Constitutions,* VI. 3. 2. [#584].

57. *Constitutions,* VI. 3. 3. [#586].

58. *Constitutions,* VI. 3. B. [#587].

59. "Newman's Oratorian Papers No. 6," in *Newman: The Oratorian, His Unpublished Oratory Papers,* ed. Placid Murray, O.S.B. (Dublin: Hill and Macmillan, 1969), 215: "Here again the Jesuits do not know the word *home;* they are emphatically strangers and pilgrims upon earth."

60. For a brilliant and insightful treatment of ministry in the early formative years of the Society of Jesus, see John O'Malley, S.J., *The First Jesuits* (Cambridge, Mass.: Harvard University Press, 1993).

61. GC 34, d. 6, #16.

62. *Constitutions,* VI. 3. 4. [#586].

63. *Constitutions,* VI. 3. 5. [#588]

64. GC 34, d. 6, #14.

65. See, for example, GC 32, d. 4, #2, #18, #27, #33; d. 2, #21; or GC 34, d. 6, #6, #10, #14, #15.

66. "Jesuits Today," GC 32, d. 2, #21.

67. *Constitutions,* X. 3. [#814].

Discernment of Spirits as an Act of Faith

William A. Barry, S.J.

RECENTLY, WHILE DIRECTING A RETREAT, I REALIZED that discerning the spirits requires an act of faith. One of the retreatants had stated early and quite openly that she hated retreats. I asked her why she continued to make them if this was the case. She said, "Because religious have to." She could pray in short periods, she said, but the idea of spending an hour at a time in prayer sent her into a tizzy. At the same time, she desired to experience the presence of God. The desire was strong enough to bring tears to her eyes as she spoke of it. Nevertheless, she did not have much hope that her desire would be fulfilled.

When I asked her what she liked to do, she told me that she enjoyed listening to music, doing puzzles, and going for walks in the woods. I suggested that she spend the day doing those things with the desire that God make his presence felt. She was afraid that she would feel guilty if she spent her retreat time in this way; it did not seem like prayer. Over the next day or so I prevailed on her to give enjoyment a try. She later recounted that on the evening of the third day she said to herself with a laugh, "I'm actually enjoying this retreat." She also had the sense that God might be enjoying it too. But the guilt feelings did not disappear; she still felt that this could not be the way a good retreat should go. During the session after this day we looked at the two different experiences: the enjoyment of the retreat and the feelings of guilt. I then asked her,

"Which of these experiences are you going to believe in?" At that moment I had the insight that the discernment of the spirits is not complete until it ends up in an act of faith. I thanked her for helping me to arrive at this clarity. By exploring this insight I hope to help spiritual directors and others.

In *Jesus and the Victory of God,* the second of a projected three or four volumes on the New Testament and the question of God, N. T. Wright develops a historical hypothesis about the nature of Jesus' vocation and his self-consciousness. It is a Christology from below, as it were, but it arrives at a very high Christology. One of his statements concerns our topic. He notes that to speak of Jesus' vocation is not the same as to speak of Jesus' knowledge of his divinity. "Jesus did not . . . 'know that he was God' in the same way that one knows one is male or female, hungry or thirsty, or that one ate an orange an hour ago. His 'knowledge' was of a more risky, but perhaps more significant, sort: like knowing one is loved. One cannot 'prove' it except by living it."[1] In other words, Jesus had to take the risk of faith that any human being takes when he discerns a vocation from God. But Jesus' vocation, as he saw it, included within it actions that Israel's God had reserved to himself. Jesus, by entering Jerusalem on a donkey, symbolically enacted the return of Yahweh to Zion; Jesus took upon himself the role of Messianic shepherd, God's role. Jesus' discernment of his vocation, in other words, required an act of faith in a unique relationship with God. He "proved" it by living it. I am going to argue that every discernment of spirits is like this; it is not complete until we prove its truth by acting on it.

As many know, Ignatius of Loyola included rules for the discernment of spirits in the little book, *The Spiritual Exercises.* We know from his memoirs, which he dictated to Luis Gonçalves da Câmara, that he developed these rules on the basis of his own experiences during his recovery at Loyola and his months of prayer at Manresa. At Loyola he engaged in two sets of daydreams. In one set he was a knight doing great deeds to win the favor of a great lady. In the other he was a follower of Christ after the manner of saints like Francis of Assisi or Dominic. Both sets of daydreams gave him great pleasure while he was engaged in them, but after the first set he found himself "dry and dissatisfied," while after the second set he remained "satisfied and joyful." He continues:

> He did not notice this, however; nor did he stop to ponder the distinction until the time when his eyes were open a little, and he began to marvel at the difference and to reflect upon it, realizing from experience that some thoughts left him sad and others joyful. Little by little he came to recognize the difference between the spirits that were stirring, one from the devil, the other from God.[2]

Here, for the first time, Ignatius discerned the movements of his heart. Notice that his discernment meant an act of faith that God was acting to inspire him to follow Jesus. Insight must be followed by action for the discernment to be complete, and the action is an act of faith in God's direction of him. Like Jesus, Ignatius proves that he is being called by acting on his insights.

The next instance makes the act of faith even clearer. After some time of great consolation at Manresa, Ignatius of Loyola began to be deeply troubled by scruples. He wrote:

> But here he began to have much trouble from scruples, for even though the general confession he had made at Montserrat had been quite carefully done and all in writing . . . still at times it seemed to him that he had not confessed certain things. This caused him much distress, because although he had confessed that, he was not satisfied. . . . Finally, a doctor of the cathedral, a very spiritual man who preached there, told him one day in confession to write down everything he could remember. He did so, but after confession the scruples still returned, becoming increasingly minute so that he was in great distress.
>
> Although he was practically convinced that those scruples did him much harm and that it would be good to be rid of them, he could not break himself off.
>
> Once when he was very distressed by them, he began to pray, and roused to fervor he shouted out loud to God, saying,

> "Help me, Lord, for I find no remedy in men nor in any creature; yet if I thought I could find it, no labor would be too hard for me. Yourself, Lord, show me where I may find it; even though I should have to chase after a puppy that it may give me the remedy, I will do it."[3]

Things got so bad that he was tempted to commit suicide. He decided to embark on a total fast to beg God for relief, and he did so for a week. When he went to confession the next Sunday, his confessor ordered him to break his fast. With some reluctance he did so and was without scruples for a couple of days. But on Tuesday the scruples returned with a vengeance. He then goes on:

> But after these thoughts [of all his sins], disgust for the life he led came over him with impulses to give it up.
>
> In this way the Lord deigned that he awake from his sleep. As he now had some experience of the diversity of the spirits from the lessons God had given him, he began to examine the means by which that spirit had come. He thus decided with great lucidity not to confess anything from the past any more; and so from that day forward he remained free of these scruples and held it certain that Our Lord had mercifully deigned to deliver him.[4]

Earlier, Ignatius says, he knew that these scruples were doing him great harm, but he did not, perhaps could not, act on this knowledge. He still believed in a God who was an exacting taskmaster, almost a celestial accountant who was waiting to catch him out. This was the faith he showed in practice. In effect, he could not believe in a God who wanted his peace. After the last bout of scruples, however, Ignatius came to the conclusion that he faced a choice. He may not have formulated the choice in terms of faith, but that is what it amounted to. Ultimately Ignatius had to decide what God he believed in. When he chose not to confess his past sins again, he had no guarantee that he was right. He had to act in faith, hope, and love that God was not an ogre ready to pounce on mistakes and forgotten sins.

This incident in the life of Ignatius reminds us of the first two "Rules for the Discernment of Spirits" more suitable for the First Week of the Exercises.

> *The First Rule.* In the case of the persons who are going from one mortal sin to another, the enemy ordinarily proposes to them apparent pleasures. He makes them imagine delights and pleasures of the senses, in order to hold them fast and plunge them deeper into their sins and vices.
>
> But with persons of this type the good spirit uses a contrary procedure. Through their good judgement on problems of morality he stings their consciences with remorse.
>
> *The Second.* In case of persons who are earnestly purging away their sins, and who are progressing from good to better in the service of God our Lord, the procedure used is the opposite of that described in the First Rule. For in this case it is characteristic of the evil spirit to cause gnawing anxiety, to sadden, and to set up obstacles. In this way he unsettles these persons by false reasons aimed at preventing their progress.
>
> But with persons of this type it is characteristic of the good spirit to stir up courage and strength, consolations, tears, inspirations, and tranquility. He makes things easier and eliminates all obstacles, so that the persons may move forward in doing good.[5]

From his experience (and perhaps from the experience he had in directing others who were very scrupulous, such as one of his first companions in Paris, Blessed Pierre Favre) Ignatius came to believe that God acts differently with people depending on their orientation in life. For those who are trying to lead a good life (those of the second rule), troubling, anxious thoughts about sin are not from God; rather they emanate from the enemy of human nature, the evil one. Most people who want to make the Spiritual Exercises or who seek spiritual direction would surely be in this category, as Ignatius was after his conversion and during all his time at Manresa. Hence, they are asked to make an act of faith that God is not the author of their worried and anxious movements, that God wants their peace and deep contentment. (A sign that these anxieties are not from God, by the way, is that they put the focus on the self, not on God and God's activity.)

It was clear to us both that by the end of her retreat, the retreatant who occasioned these reflections was faced with this faith choice. Once again, we note that there is no guarantee that God will act in any given way with those who are trying to live a good life; one plants one's feet firmly in midair and marches on in faith, hope, and trust. The only verification we get is the continued peace and joy we experience on the journey. The "fruit of the Spirit is love, joy, peace, patience, kindness, goodness, faithfulness, gentleness, self-control." [6]

Of course, events can distort our discernment of how we are being led. Ignatius provides a good example of this. During his stay at Manresa, Ignatius determined that his vocation was to go to Jerusalem and live and "help souls" there. Some commentators believe that this decision was, for Ignatius, an election made according to the pattern for "The First Time" described in *The Spiritual Exercises*. In the section entitled "Three Times . . . suitable for making a sound and good election," Ignatius writes: *"The First Time* is an occasion when God our Lord moves and attracts the will in such a way that a devout person, without doubting or being able to doubt, carries out what was proposed. This is what St. Paul and St. Matthew did when they followed Christ our Lord."[7]

In his memoirs Ignatius makes it quite clear that he determined "to remain in Jerusalem, continually visiting those holy places; and in addition to this devotion, he also planned to help souls," although he kept this latter idea to himself. When he spoke to the provincial of the Franciscans who had charge of the Holy Places about his desire to stay, he was told that he could not remain because other pilgrims who had remained had been captured and enslaved and had to be redeemed at great cost. Ignatius replied to this that he was very firm in his purpose and was resolved that on no account would he fail to carry it out. He frankly insisted that even though the provincial thought otherwise, if there was nothing binding him under sin, he would not abandon his intention out of any fear. To this the provincial replied that they had authority from the Apostolic See to have anyone leave the place, or remain there, as they judged, and to excommunicate anyone who was unwilling to obey them, and that in this case they thought that he should not remain.[8]

We can see how strongly Ignatius believed that he was being led by God in his determination to remain in Jerusalem. But when he was threatened with excommunication, he concluded that "it was not Our Lord's will that he remain in those holy places."[9] Ignatius acted in faith that God was leading him to live and die in Jerusalem. Only by such an act of faith could he discover that he was in error with regard to his discernment. Note, however, that it took another act of faith to change his direction. Ignatius believed that God was speaking through the provincial who had the authority from the Holy See to excommunicate anyone who disobeyed him. In our own day many a person has discerned a vocation and has been convinced that God inspired the decision only to have events disconfirm it. For example, a young man discerns that he has a vocation to be a Jesuit priest but finds that the Society of Jesus will not accept him. He had to act in faith on his best lights and move forward with his application, trusting that he would discover in the process that he was correct in his discernment. How he now goes forward with his life will be a sign of how openly he is seeking what God desires.

Later Ignatius had other occasions to discern "spirits" and to note how the evil spirit cloaks himself as an angel of light for those who have advanced a bit in their journey into a deeper intimacy with God. For example, upon his return from Jerusalem he decided that he needed to study in order to be able to help souls.

> So, returning to Barcelona, he began to study with great diligence. But one thing was very much in his way: when he began to memorize, as one must in the beginnings of grammar, there came to him new insights into spiritual matters and fresh relish, to such an extent that he could not memorize, nor could he drive them away no matter how much he resisted.
>
> So, thinking often about this, he said to himself, "Not even when I engage in prayer and am at Mass do such vivid insights come to me." Thus, little by little, he came to realize that it was

a temptation. After praying he went to Our Lady of the Sea, near the master's house. So when they were all seated, he told them exactly all that went on in his soul and what little progress he had made until then for that reason; but he promised this same master, saying, "I promise you never to fail to listen to you these two years, so long as I can find bread and water in Barcelona with which I might support myself." As he made this promise with great determination, he never again had those temptations.[10]

In this instance Ignatius had to decide in faith that these "spiritual favors" were not from God. Such experiences lie behind his fourth rule for discernment appropriate for the Second Week of the Exercises.

It is characteristic of the evil angel, who takes on the appearance of an angel of light, to enter by going along the same way as the devout soul and then to exit by his own way with success for himself. That is, he brings good and holy thoughts attractive to such an upright soul and then strives little by little to get his own way, by enticing the soul over to his own hidden deceits and evil intentions.[11]

Ignatius had to act in faith on his discovery that God is not the only source of pious thoughts.

The discernment of the spirits rests on the belief that the human heart is a battleground where God and the evil one struggle for mastery. Jesus of Nazareth himself believed this. In the desert he had been tempted by the evil one masquerading as an angel of light. If these were real temptations, then he, like us, had to discern the movements inspired by God from those inspired by the evil one. He, too, had to make an act of faith in who God really is, based on his experiences and his knowledge of the Scriptures of his people. Jesus came to recognize who the real enemy of God's rule is. He cast out demons and equated his power over the demons as a sign of God's coming to rule: "But if it is by the finger of God that I cast out demons, then the kingdom of God has come upon you."[12] The majority party of the Pharisees and most

Jews of the time saw the real enemy of Israel, and therefore of God, as the pagans, and especially the Roman occupiers. Over and over again Jesus warned his hearers that the real enemy was Satan. Jesus faced this enemy and refused to use the strategies and means of the evil one to carry out his vocation.[13] God's rule cannot come about through the means proposed by Satan. Jesus, like any faithful Jew, believed that God was acting in history to bring about his rule (this notion may be called "God's project" or "God's intention"). He also believed that whoever is not God's enemy "is for us."[14] John Meier puts the matter this way:

> It is important to realize that, in the view of Jesus, . . . human beings were not basically neutral territories that might be influenced by divine or demonic forces now and then. . . . Human existence was seen as a battlefield dominated by one or the other supernatural force, God or Satan (alias Belial or the devil). A human being might have a part in choosing which "field of force" would dominate his or her life, i.e., which force he or she would choose to side with. But no human being was free to choose simply to be free of these supernatural forces. One was dominated by either one or the other, and to pass *from* one was necessarily to pass *into* the control of the other. At least over the long term, one could not maintain a neutral stance vis-à-vis God and Satan.[15]

Jesus' own discernment of spirits rested on his Jewish belief that God was acting in history and that the evil one was acting to thwart God. Once again, we see that the discernment of spirits is a matter of faith put into practice.

Indeed, faith is not just an intellectual affirmation of truths; faith is a verb. Faith is a graced response to our self-revealing God. This goes for the faith of the church as well as for the faith of the individual who is trying to discern a path through life. Perhaps we can get a better grasp on how discernment requires an act of faith from the philosophy of the person of John Macmurray. In the first volume of his Gifford Lectures, Macmurray argues that the world is ruled by intention. He ends that volume with the following statement:

> If we act as if the world, in its unity, is intentional; that is, if we believe in practice that the world is one action . . . we shall act differently from anyone who does not believe this. We shall act as though our own actions were our contributions to the one inclusive action which is the history of the world. If, on the other hand, we believe that the world is a mere process of events which happen as they happen, we shall act differently. Our conception of the unity of the world determines a way of life; and the satisfaction or dissatisfaction of that way of life is its verification.[16]

In other words, if we believe that the world is one action ruled by one intention, we are committed to a way of life in conformity with this belief. If we do not act on our belief, we act in bad faith. At the end of the second volume Macmurray fleshes out this insight in more theistic terms:

> There is, then, only one way in which we can think our relation to the world, and that is to think it as a personal relation, through the form of the personal. We must think that the world is one action . . . contained in it, subordinated within it, and necessary to its constitution. To conceive the world thus is to conceive it as the act of God, the Creator of the World, and ourselves as created agents, with a limited and dependent freedom to determine the future which can be realized only on the condition that our intentions are in harmony with His intention, and which must frustrate itself if they are not. . . .
>
> It would be a mistake to suppose that this vindication of the validity of religious belief in general constitutes an argument for the truth of any system of religious belief in particular. Religious doctrines are as problematic as scientific theories and require like them a constant revision and a continual verification in action. Their verification differs in this, that it cannot be experimental, since they are not merely pragmatic; they can be

verified only by persons who are prepared to commit themselves intentionally to the way of life which they prescribe.[17]

In other words, all religious beliefs are only verified in action. Indeed "religious beliefs" that do not issue in complementary action are not religious beliefs at all; they are thoughts about the world, not beliefs. Someone may object: "But I am a sinner and often do not act according to my beliefs." That is true, but the very fact that you know that you are a sinner who does not act according to your beliefs shows that you have beliefs that must be verified in action. If I say that I believe God acts with purpose in this world, that belief must lead to attempts, however feeble, to discern how my own actions might be attuned to God's one action. Moreover, these attempts to discern must lead to action; otherwise I will be acting with "bad faith" and will experience malaise, the pricking of conscience that Ignatius mentions in the first rule cited earlier.

Jesus did not leave us a list of truths to affirm, but a task to carry out. We must try to discern in our time and place how God wants us to live our lives in this world in tune with God's Spirit, the one divine action at work in this universe. This is what the discernment of spirits is all about. Followers of Jesus have been given a task to carry out and the means to do it. Impelled by God's Spirit they must try to live in this world with the conviction that with the life, death, and resurrection of Jesus all the needful has been done, that God has won the victory he intends. Our task, therefore, is to follow the prompting of the Spirit, who has been poured out in our hearts, to follow the way of Jesus, the way of peace, of love, of the cross. We discern the spirits in order to act as followers of Jesus, as believers. Every act of discernment is an act of faith in what God has done in Jesus of Nazareth and continues to do through the indwelling of God.

Endnotes

1. N. T. Wright, *Jesus and the Victory of God* (Minneapolis: Fortress, 1966), 653.

2. Ignatius of Loyola, *A Pilgrim's Testament,* trans. Parmananda R. Divarkar (St. Louis, Mo.: The Institute of Jesuit Sources, 1995), 9–10.

3. Ibid., 34–36.

4. Ibid., 37–38

5. Ignatius of Loyola, *The Spiritual Exercises,* trans. George E. Ganss (St. Louis, Mo.: The Institute of Jesuit Sources, 1992), 121, nn. 314–315.

6. Gal. 5:22–23. All scriptural citations taken from the *New Oxford Annotated Bible with the Apocrypha: Revised Standard Version,* (Oxford University Press: New York, 1977).

7. Ibid., 76, n. 175.

8. *Pilgrim's Testament,* 60–62.

9. Ibid., 63.

10. Ibid., 79–80.

11. *Exercises,* 126–27, n. 332.

12. Luke 11:20.

13. See Luke 4:1–13.

14. Mark 9:40.

15. John Meier, *Mentor, Message, and Miracles,* vol. 2 of *A Marginal Jew: Rethinking the Historical Jesus* (New York: Doubleday, 1994), 414–15.

16. John Macmurray, *The Self as Agent* (Atlantic Highlands, N.J.: Humanities Press, 1978), 221.

17. John Macmurray, *Persons in Relation* (Atlantic Highlands, N.J.: Humanities Press, 1979), 222–23.

Jerome Nadal, S.J., on the Virtue of Obedience

Martin D. O'Keefe, S.J. (Translator)

TRANSLATOR'S INTRODUCTION

JEROME NADAL, S.J. (1507–80), WAS NOT ONE OF THE ORIGINAL group of six men who came together with St. Ignatius of Loyola in 1534 to form what would eventually be the Society of Jesus. Nadal joined the Society in 1545. Nonetheless, he turned out to be one of the most influential forces in the formation and development of that nascent Society. For it was to Nadal that St. Ignatius entrusted oral promulgation of the Society's *Constitutions* to Jesuits throughout Italy, Spain, Portugal, France, Germany, Austria, and the Low Countries. Thus the early understanding that Jesuits had of the spirit and teachings of Ignatius and of the *Constitutions* of their order was by and large the understanding that Jerome Nadal possessed. This is not to assert that Nadal's understanding of the *Constitutions* differed from Ignatius's; there is little evidence to support such a claim. However, it does point up the crucial importance of this peripatetic vicar of Ignatius in the formation and self-understanding of the early Society of Jesus.

The selection of Nadal's thoughts on obedience that is translated below is taken from Jerome Nadal, *Commentarii de Instituto Societatis Iesu*, ed. Michael Nicolau, S.J., in *Monumenta Historica Societatis Iesu*, vol. 90 (Rome, 1962). The particular *monumentum* that constitutes the selection carries the Latin title "Monumentum 7: De Virtute Obedientiae." The selection contains four parts:

(1) On the Perfection of Obedience within the Society of Jesus, (2) Canons on Obedience, (3) On Blind Obedience, and (4) Twenty Ways in Which the Virtue of Obedience Is Commonly Hindered, Weakened, or Lessened. Ends of original manuscript folios are marked in square brackets in this translation.

One might or might not wish to adopt Nadal's thoughts on obedience when developing a personal twenty-first-century spirituality of this particular virtue within the Society of Jesus. But it seems imprudent to attempt to develop such a spirituality without knowing what obedience in the Society was in the order's earliest years. Knowledge of history, and the history of the Society in particular, continues to be critical to those who wish to live in or understand the Jesuit order. Therefore, may the translation of the following selection be a fitting part of this tribute to historian *par excellence* John Padberg, S.J., whose knowledge of the beginnings of the Society and most if not all of its subsequent history has been both astonishing and inspiring to all of us who have been privileged to know him.

I. On the Perfection of Obedience within the Society [of Jesus]

[1] The Role Perfection Plays in Religious Obedience

The nature of obedience, as it is grounded by vow in religious orders, is greatly different from that found in any other circumstances. For religious obedience is not even envisaged unless there is question of a striving for perfection. Consequently, this sort of obedience seeks after items which are matters of counsel and supererogation, by whatever means it can bring itself into possession of perfection.[1] In any other sort of obedience, it is sufficient, at most, if there be no question of becoming entangled in venial sin or if, as is minimal and entirely necessary, there is care to stay outside the boundaries of mortal sin.

[2] Threefold Obedience: In the External Action, in the Will, in the Intellect

Obedience should be offered in the external action, in the will, and at the same time in the intellect, and that not merely in the sense that the intellect of the one who offers it is blind in regard to whatever is commanded so that it sees none of those matters that could hinder or lessen the perfection of obedience, but also in this sense, that once this blindness has been attained, the one offering obedience also, in the fullness of the Spirit, examines the matter and thinks well of it so that he tries to obey not what has in fact been commanded, but also whatever has been merely hinted at or can, by any sort of prudent reasoning, be seen as coming forth from superiors as manifested by whatever sign. For the will does not render perfect obedience, unless by its action and influence it leads the intellect fully to its own obedience, etc.[2]

[3] Analogies with Faith, with the Intellect by Itself, with Original Justice, and with Revelation

Obedience has a distinctive character of quiet, but of determination as well, which is quite similar to that possessed by faith.[3] Obedient persons so preserve their stance, and are persuaded so to act, as if they wished neither to understand nor to will by means of any intellect or will other than that of the superior.[4]

Obedience is not unlike the state of original justice, which, led on by simplicity and purity of heart in the fullness of innocence, subordinates to God its higher part; from this as source, subordination of the soul's other powers and actions follows.[5]

The practice of obedience is like the public revelation of God.[6] For whenever I hear a superior speaking, I should feel that it is exactly what it would be were I to hear God himself present to me.[7]

Obedience is rendered to a human being as if to God himself, not only because I obey a human out of love for God, but also because that vow is made to God himself and also to a human being, and that with the selfsame obligation.[8]

[4] What If Something Should Be Commanded That Is Impossible or Sinful

Even should a superior order something that cannot be done, nonetheless obedience impels us to obey, taking no account of difficulty or impossibility.[9] If the obedience in question is perfect, as that of certain of the saints has been [f. 266v], it would overcome any natural impossibility and conquer any difficulty in the power of Christ.[10] On the other hand, if the obedience under discussion is not perfect, but is nonetheless true obedience, it will encounter the impossibility with simplicity of heart, and then only in sorrow will it by the nature of the case leave off its efforts and transfer its earnestness of spirit to the superior, [telling him] in humble simplicity of heart that he, the subject, was not able to carry out what had been commanded. And this he will do shamefacedly, as if he were manifesting a fault that is his.[11] An obedient person never thinks, nor, at least as long as the force and the reality of obedience is at work and is activating his powers, can he think (unless there be some other reason therefor) that a superior would command or wish either what is impossible or what is sinful, unless the superior be engaged in what would have to be pure and simple speculation, in which matter he could scarcely be aware or serious. Should, however, such a thought ever occur in practice, that is to say, in such wise that it would influence anyone's judgment, let all be aware that this is a temptation that seeks in subtle fashion to tear down the purity and simplicity of obedience.[12]

All this being the case, should the thought, or the temptation, ever occur to anyone that a superior is ordering something which is impossible or sinful, let him not deliberate about or decide the matter by his own private judgment, but rather by that of the superior, and should the superior be (a state from which may God preserve us) openly and clearly in the wrong, let the obedient person himself consider him so as a theoretical matter, but let him leave the determination itself to the judgment of worthy professed fathers or of his own confessor.[13]

[5] Obedience Should Be Partly Blind, and Partly Sighted; the Perfection of Obedience

Obedience ought to be partially blind, but partially sighted: blind to all considerations that could deflect or hinder it, as well as to those that could diminish the superior's authority in our minds. Thus obedience does not see faults in the superior; to that extent it is blind.[14] If there is question of having sight in matters such as these, it will be that sight that, understanding all reasons in the light of obedience, flees the darkness of all reasoning and of everything else that could render it weaker. For obedience is indeed clear-sighted and considers as good everything that comes forth from the superior in whatever way, ever beholding clearly in it both the presence and the authority of Christ himself. The light that obedience possesses is not unlike the light of true Christian contemplation, whereby the truth stands forth brightly and whereby whatever is false and idle simply cannot be understood.[15]

True obedience involves three faculties [executive, will, and intellect] and the perfections of their actions. In the executive faculty are found promptness, courage, ease, and, in brief, all those characteristics that are sought as external accompaniments for the perfection of the powers and acts of the will [f. 267r] and the intellect. In the [faculty of the] will is found an application that is pleasant, sweet, and filled with the aid of perseverance and of all the virtues. In the [faculty of the] intellect we find a splendid light whereby the intellect easily gives its assent and seems unable to think or perceive anything other than what obedience proposes; moreover, it discovers abundant further reasons whereby obedience is confirmed.[16]

Obedience is blind, since it is governed by the will of another; in it, since it is blind (for the power that is the will is not a cognitive one either) both the carrying out of the command and the desires of my will, as well as the judgment of the intellect, should find themselves transformed.

II. Canons on Obedience

[6]

- One who examines the reasons why a superior issues a command is not an obedient person.[17]
- One who entertains the idea of debating whether a superior has commanded properly is not an obedient person.
- One who seeks the reason why a superior commands in a certain way is not an obedient person.
- One who obeys because of a given reason, and not solely because of the will of the superior in Christ, is not an obedient person.[18]
- One who obeys because what is commanded is somehow or other pleasing to him is not an obedient person.
- One who obeys only the expressed will of the superior, and not the slightest sign of his will,[19] is not an obedient person.
- One whose obedience lacks internal unity and, whatever superior he obeys,[20] does not refer his obedience to God is not an obedient person.
- One who does not perceive God himself in superiors[21] is not an obedient person.
- One who obeys a superior more because that superior is good or wise, etc.,[22] is not an obedient person.

[7]

- One who more readily obeys one of his superiors, even though he be the highest superior, to a degree greater than he obeys another, even the lowest in rank, is not an obedient person.
- One who considers in his heart whether superiors are in disagreement or at loggerheads is not an obedient person.
- One who acts inquisitively, questioning whether a superior is a good man or a learned one or something of the sort[23] is not an obedient person [f. 267v].

- One who wants a superior to favor him or to agree with what he himself wishes is not an obedient person.[24]
- One who is not indifferent as to whatever the superior may command is not an obedient person.
- One who is not blind to all imperfections superiors may have or to whatever difficulties may stand in the way of obeying is not an obedient person.

[8]

- One who believes that in the Society he can commit something confidential to someone else while at the same time being unwilling that a superior should be at all aware of the matter[25]—that is to say, by means of entrusting the matter under secrecy or under the sacrament of confession (as is commonly said, even though confession itself does not take place)—is not an obedient person.
- One who in the context of sacramental confession either makes known or hears secret matters of this sort, if in fact they do not pertain to the confession itself, is not an obedient person.
- One who does not take in good spirit what is commanded, and even examines it and weighs it, is not an obedient person.[26]
- One who perceives a difference in whether a superior simply speaks and makes his will known,[27] or if he merely gives a command, or if he actually gives a command in virtue of holy obedience is not an obedient person.
- One who says that he wishes to obey and to understand what is commanded, but nevertheless says that he experiences hardship in carrying it out, alleging as excuse the fact that nature itself opposes it,[28] is not an obedient person.

[9]

- One who appeals to theologians, particularly scholastic theologians, and to those who construct theological summaries when there is question of obedience, is not an obedient person. For this is not to delineate one's obligation by the opinions of learned men, but rather to do so by what one has convinced himself are the opinions of learned men. Now, if one appeals to the opinions of the learned, then the matter is to be transacted by means of the judgment of outsiders, and once again the individual will not be perfect in obedience, since for him a legitimate superior ought to stand in the place of learned men, unless that superior were to command something openly sinful or impossible; however, of the obligation involved in this case we have already spoken.[29]

- One who says that, for his part, he desires and thinks according to the word of the superior, but that it would not be impossible for some other opinion to be presented to him is not an obedient person [f. 268r].[30]

- One to whom, when he is under obedience to a superior, there first presents itself reasoning that is contrary to obedience or presents difficulties to it, even though afterwards there immediately ensues the greatest degree of abnegation and perfection in obedience, is not an obedient person.[31]

- One who entertains the idea that the Constitutions and Rules are interpreted according to his own reading of them and does not on the contrary submit to the interpretation of superiors is not an obedient person.

[10]

- One who only imperfectly obeys immediate superiors, excusing himself and making appeal on the grounds that some other mediate superior has spoken otherwise, or else that the Constitutions and Rules speak otherwise, is not an obedient person. In such a case, nonetheless, let it suffice for such a one to represent to the immediate superior what the other superior has said or commanded, in peaceful perfection of obedience. But if the immediate superior nonetheless indicates that it is his will that the subject should do as he commands, then the subject should obey him and should believe that the immediate superior knows the mediate superior's will. Still, it will be possible for the subject, after prayer, to relate the entire matter to one of the consultors,[32] whereby he can bring the matter to the attention of the provincial or the General; however, let each one always remain in the wholeness, simplicity, and purity of holy obedience.

- One who feels that indulgence should be granted him, since he has labored long in the Society, or that he should be allowed to use his own judgment, or that he ought to be promoted to some other grade[33] is not an obedient person.

[11]

- One who says that he is, indeed, obligated to obey according to the manner of the Society, but only in those matters that pertain to the rule and not to others is not an obedient person. For he is obligated to obey in all things that are not sinful.[34] Additionally, it is stated in the rule and in the Constitutions that nothing can be excluded from the scope of the rule.[35]

- One who, although he is not a superior, nevertheless acts in the authoritative manner toward his brothers that superiors are wont to use with inferiors is not an obedient person [f. 268v].

- One who, having been given a command by a superior or having come to know the superior's will, asks whether he would sin if he does not obey, or what kind of sin he would commit,[36] is not an obedient person.

- One who states that he thinks as does the superior because of obedience, but indicates that otherwise he would not have come to the same judgment, or that the matter commanded is not otherwise good and righteous, is not an obedient person.

[12]

- One who, when a superior is about to depart, requests from him that something be allowed to him during that superior's absence and is not entirely subject to his ordinary superior in simplicity and humility is not an obedient person.

- One who in prying fashion inserts himself into the office of another[37] is not an obedient person.

- One who deals in familiar fashion with a superior in such wise that he seems to forget, because of the superior's gentleness and friendship, the reverence he owes that superior is not an obedient person.

- One who, as a consultor, has been asked by a superior for his opinion [and] is saddened because the superior does not do what he suggests is not an obedient person.

- One who, upon seeing what command comes forth from the superior, does not consider it good from every point of view, but rather says that the superior's secretary or someone on the superior's staff is responsible for it is not an obedient person.

- One who is led by his own judgment and opinion more than by obedience, even though he should seem to be a spiritual person, is not an obedient person.

- One who, having been given a penance to lead him to repentance, nonetheless does not repent as the superior seems to understand and will is not an obedient person, for true obedience brings it about that one repents joyfully.

[13]

- One who has a number of superiors in hierarchical rank and betakes himself to the highest of these in receiving commands and does not rather go to immediate and mediate superiors and is not satisfied with being obedient to them is not an obedient person.

- One who, when requested to perform an external office of serious moment, undertakes to do so without permission,[38] however much he may add to this the promise that he will refer it to his superior, is not an obedient person.

- One who so governs matters that are within his legitimate scope in such wise that he looks more to his own vision and knowledge than to that which is proper to the Society, which he can determine whether by his superior or by the Constitutions or by the rules or by our customs, is not an obedient person.

[14]
- One who, having heard the command of a superior, obeys, to be sure, but does so in such wise as to be led by an inclination that stems from himself alone, rather than also from the principle that is the vow of obedience, is not an obedient person.
- One who by himself is unable to obtain or has no hope of obtaining from his superior what he desires (whether this has to do with persons or with colleges or undertakings of the Society, even those which seem to have great usefulness attached to them) [and] takes measures that what he desires should be sought from superiors by some other person acting as intermediary is not an obedient person.
- One who convinces himself that the superior does not esteem him, or else esteems some other person more than he esteems him, or indeed esteems any of the brethren more than any other one is not an obedient person.

Let similar canons be formulated from the words of St. Ignatius,[39] from the Constitutions, and from the rules [f. 269v; f. 270r].

III. On Blind Obedience

[15] Obedience Should Be Examined by Spiritual Understanding, by Arguments from Authority, and by Arguments from Reason

Let our treatment of obedience be first based on spiritual knowledge; then let the same thing be considered on the basis of authorities and of reason so that those who rely on spiritual knowledge may be further reassured and so that those who do not understand in this way may by authority and reason be assisted toward the spirit of obedience and thus be led forward.

[16] Examples Favoring Blind Obedience

Obedience ought to be blind. The opposite of this [blindness] rendered Lucifer disobedient, either when he viewed his own perfection without the eyes of self-denial,[40] or when he did not take it well that God should become a human rather than an angel.[41] Again, Lucifer in the same manner tempted Eve so that she might resist the sacred blindness of the command she had been given,[42] and, indeed, then for the first time did she fall into sin when, having lost this blindness, she saw that the fruit of the branch was good, etc. In the case of Christ, on the other hand, while we should not use the term *blindness*,[43] nonetheless do we notice that he, practically speaking, took account of nothing that could have weakened the obedience that he owed to the Father, even though there could have been some other means of redeeming the human race than through the death of God himself, etc. For he truly possessed that degree of self-denial in obedience from which shone radiantly outward the most perfect and splendid reasons for redemption's taking place in that fashion. The Virgin Mary, too, obeyed in the most perfect fashion in the conception of the eternal Word, making no judgment in that most mysterious of all events, which surpassed entirely every type of human knowledge [f. 270v].

Abraham, likewise, obeyed most perfectly in the announcement of the conception of Isaac.[44] "In hope he believed," said St. Paul, "against hope."[45] Again, in the sacrifice of Isaac, he reasoned that God can raise one even from the dead.[46] He also obeyed when he went forth into a place that he himself did not know: "Go from your country . . . to a land which I will show you",[47] as if God had said to him, as Chrysostom remarks, "Come to where you know not."[48]

[17] Why Blindness Is Part of the Nature of Obedience

Learned men see obedience as pertaining to the will both of the one who commands and of the one who obeys. Now since the will itself is blind or unseeing, only the will of the superior ought to be considered and nothing else; the intellect of the one who obeys ought to represent to his will only what the superior wills. When the will of the one who obeys comes into play, once again blindness recurs, since my will, which ought to be moved by obedience alone, is blind, etc. There is therefore nothing in this strict sense of obedience that would not be consonant with the quality of blindness.

[18] An Argument from the Similarity between Obedience and Faith

When there is question of faith, a pious disposition stemming from divine grace and from the action of the Holy Spirit brings it about that the intellect becomes blind toward those things that are to be believed. So also, in the obedience found in the Society, God grants much the same, even though faith is a much more perfect virtue than obedience.[49]

[19] An Argument from Indifference, As Found in the Exercises

From the Principle and Foundation of the Exercises[50] and from a spiritual understanding of it, we can easily imagine the Society's indifference in spirit and its resignation, not only of the will but of the intellect as well. For from the fact that mankind was created to praise and reverence God and from the fact that every creature was likewise created for this purpose, that it assist us in doing this, it follows that we ought not choose one creature in preference to another for this purpose [f. 271r] except to the extent that we are moved to do so, not by our own preferences, but rather by the will of God and his grace,[51] given the fact that we are already, in virtue of this Principle and Foundation, denying ourselves the influence of our own preferences. It is therefore no surprising thing if in the Society we are obligated to follow that sort of obedience that finds its base in the full abnegation and surrender of the intellect and will.

[20] If Someone Is Burdened beyond His Due, That Is His Glory

Should the idea stealthily come upon you that the superior is treating you unjustly, never take this in any other way but that he is doing this as your lack of merits warrants. And if he should do so even beyond what you in fact deserve, that truly would be for you a wonderful thing, for he, acting in the person of God himself, is testing you. Receive, therefore, with full awareness of spirit from him everything he does as coming from the hand of God and Christ Jesus, with joy of spirit under the light of holy obedience.

[21] The Will Is Prompt to Obey If the Intellect Does Not Consider Whatever Stands in the Way

Learned men associate obedience with the will, for they say that it renders the will prompt to fulfill the will of the one who commands.[52] And so, if obedience is perfect, it will render the entire will prompt to obey. The intellect, on the other hand, will not extend itself to considering or commanding something that is contrary to obedience or hampers it, or else it will not, as a matter of practice, consider something that is thus contrary to obedience and an impediment to it. And should something of the sort occur to an uncautious person unexpectedly, he would direct the intellect away from that.[53] All these matters can, even apart from interior knowledge, be persuasively argued by theological reasoning on obedience or by moral reasoning on it.

[22] Obedience As Joined with Simplicity of Judgment

Obedience has joined to it a certain simplicity and humility of spirit and judgment from which it derives strength, as in the case of the obedience of the Abbot John, who watered a dry stick[54] and who with full knowledge attempted to move a huge stone.[55]

Obedience is said to be greater than other virtues because it spurns goods of the mind so as to cleave to God;[56] it therefore will be even more perfect [f. 271v] if it subordinates both will and intellect rather than simply the will alone [f. 272r].

IV. Twenty Ways in Which the Virtue of Obedience Is Commonly Hindered, Weakened, or Lessened

1. The first is that of those who, although they obey in certain matters, nevertheless in others are less obedient; Paul reproaches this in his second letter to the Corinthians: "For this is why I wrote, that I might test you and know whether you are obedient in everything."[57]

2. The second is that of those who, while they do perform the item commanded, do not do so fully; Paul reproves this in his letter to Philemon: "Confident of your obedience, I write to you, knowing that you will do even more than I say."[58]

3. The third is that of those who, although they do what is commanded, nonetheless [they] do so in a different way from that commanded (and sometimes in a perverse manner). "The disciples went and did as Jesus had directed them."[59]

4. The fourth is that of those who make themselves so difficult to deal with as far as obedience is concerned that only with great effort and trouble can they be moved from what they themselves desire to doing anything else, much in the same way as a person is put upon who tries to move large stones to a high place. Against such people Paul says to the Hebrews, "Obey your leaders and submit to them; for they are keeping watch over your souls, as men who will have to give

account. Let them do this joyfully, and not sadly, for that would be of no advantage to you."[60] It is as if he were saying obey in this way, namely, that you do not cause them to grieve about the difficulty of commanding obedience but rather so that they may rejoice in the ease of its exercise, since to the obedient person nothing is difficult. For Bernard [?][61] says, "Nothing is impossible for those who believe; nothing is difficult for those who love; nothing is harsh to the meek; nothing is found to be difficult for the humble, for whom grace provides assistance, and to the obedient, devotion softens the roughness of command."[62]

5. The fifth is that of those who are unwilling to obey at the simple expression of the superior's will, but rather insist that the matter be enjoined upon them; against this is what Paul says to Titus, "Bid slaves to be submissive to their masters and to give satisfaction in every respect."[63] And if earthly servants ought to act in this way, how much more so the servants of God? As St. Bernard says, "In acting under obedience it is very helpful if [f. 272v] humility, with no one enforcing it, be the guardian of whatever the sternness of discipline imposes."[64]

6. The sixth is that of those who occasionally obey, not because of love, but rather because of fear of punishment; against this, Gregory states, "Obedience ought to be rendered, not out of fear of punishment, but out of love for justice."[65]

7. The seventh is that of those who always do obey but are accustomed to engage in long discussions about what is commanded. Against this position St. Jerome states, "You should fear the head of the monastery as a lord, love him as a parent, and believe that whatever he commands is for your good. Nor should you pass judgment on the view of a superior, for it is your office to obey and carry out what has been commanded."[66]

8. The eighth is that of those who, while they do carry out what is commanded, nonetheless [they] are sad and sorrowful in undertaking it. The psalmist, on the other hand, says, "As soon as they heard of me they obeyed me."[67]

9. The ninth is that of those who are always found unprepared to obey, saying that at that particular time they are unable to do what is commanded; against this the psalmist says, "I hasten and do not delay to keep thy commandments."[68]

10. The tenth is that of those who never prepare themselves, by previous prayer or thought, for obeying well; Bernard says in that regard, "He who is perfectly obedient offers his ears so as to hear, his hands so as to work, his tongue so as to speak, etc."[69]

11. The eleventh is that of those who do obey, to be sure, but they carry out what is enjoined with murmuring, not unlike the obedience of the demons who at the command of the Lord were forced to go forth from bodies, but [were] crying out as they did so.[70] In their regard, Benedict says, "Then will obedience be pleasing to God and pleasant for humankind, if what is commanded is not carried out with murmuring."[71]

12. The twelfth is that of those who, while not actually murmuring, nonetheless perform what is commanded with sadness. Benedict says, "The obedience which is rendered to superiors, is rendered to God: 'He who hears you hears me.'"[72] And that obedience ought to be given by subjects in good heart [f. 273r], for the Lord loves a cheerful giver.[73]

13. The thirteenth is that of those who obey in greater matters, but spurn lesser ones. Bernard: "O you, the most obedient of all monks, who do not pass over even one word of whatever superiors utter."[74]

14. The fourteenth is that of those who have no concern for fulfilling the intention of a superior who gives an

order, provided that they do accomplish the general thrust of the order. Whereas, quite the opposite, among faithful and loyal minds more concern should be had for the intention of the superior than for his actual words. In Ephesians 6, we read, "Slaves, be obedient to those who are your earthly masters, . . . not in the way of eye-service."[75]

15. The fifteenth is that of those who, when something displeasing to them is commanded, calumniate the intention of the superior, judging that he has commanded this for some unworthy reason. Bernard says, "It is not enough to obey our superiors externally only, unless we also, from the depths of our hearts, think in most upright fashion about them."[76]

16. The sixteenth is that of those who, in order to excuse themselves from having to obey, allege their inability. St. Benedict says, "If a superior should enjoin something that is impossible, nevertheless the subject should attempt to carry it out;[77] towards this end the words of the Apostle are consoling when he says, 'I can do all things in him who strengthens me.'"[78]

17. The seventeenth is that of persons who show themselves to be of such a temperament that superiors do not dare enjoin anything upon them, just as in the case of a wild horse, which bites and kicks: people do not dare to place a burden on it. Against this is the advice of the holy man who said to an individual who desired to enter the religious life and who asked how he should conduct himself, "You and a donkey must be as one. Just as a donkey indifferently and peacefully accepts whatever burden is placed upon it, so ought a religious to conduct himself in religious life."[79] In the Epistle of James [f. 273v]: "Receive with meekness the implanted word."[80] The word of obedience may be said to have taken root in you because it draws one who receives it to its own nature, in the fashion of a young shoot inserted into the trunk of a tree.

18. The eighteenth is that of those who, relying on a presumptuous confidence in their own wisdom, find it unworthy to be ruled by another. And thus they are less obedient. St. Jerome says, "It is good to obey people who are better than oneself and, following the instruction of the Scriptures, to learn from others the way of one's life, and not to rely on that worst of all instructors, one's own confident assurances."[81]

19. The nineteenth is that of those who prefer to be obeyed by superiors rather than to obey them, since they draw superiors into doing what such people themselves wish. Bernard: "The ill will of many demands today that it be said to them, 'What shall I do for you?'[82] and not that they themselves should say, 'Lord, what would you have me to do?'[83] O brief saying, but wonderfully full, efficacious and worthy of acceptance by all! For thus it is entirely worthy, Lord, that not my will should be sought and done by you, but rather yours by me."[84]

20. The twentieth is that of those who, though they do perform what is commanded, nevertheless knowingly do so badly, deceitfully, so that no other commands be imposed on them. They are like a deceiving horse that, led from its stable, walks badly so that he will not be led from his stable on any other occasion. Against this we read in Jeremiah, "Cursed is he who does the work of the LORD with slackness."[85]

A religious person, acting under obedience, ought to be very careful to avoid all these [twenty] things, lest by falling into any of them he or she be bereft of obedience and lose its reward in whole or in part. St. Bernard says, "Remember, my brothers: so that Christ might not violate obedience, he sacrificed his life."[86] But if Christ so behaved, how much the more ought we to take care not to lose the good of obedience?[87]

Endnotes

1. Cf. Jerome Nadal, "Exhortation #16 at Coimbra," in *Commentarii de Instituto S.I.* (Rome: Monumenta Historica Societatis Iesu [MHSI], 1962), 64–165, 167, nn. 2–3, 9.

2. Cf. Ignatius of Loyola, "Letter on Obedience to the Brethren at Portugal," in *Monumenta Ignatiana, Letters,* 4:672–77, nn. 5–19; Jerome Nadal, "Exhortation #16 at Coimbra," 167–69, nn. 10–13; "Exhortation #11 at Alcalá," in Jerome Nadal, *Commentarii de Instituto S.I.* (Rome: MHSI, 1962), 424–39; "Dialogue II," in Jerome Nadal, *Commentarii de Instituto S.I.* (Rome: MHSI, 1962), 709–11. Among Nadal's works published in Italian (in *Monumenta Ignatiana, Letters,* [Rome: MHSI, 1903–11], 12:663–65, hereafter *MI, Letters*) is an item "On the Threefold Grade of Obedience," in which he propounds his teaching on the threefold way of perfection in the matter of obedience. The same selection is translated into Spanish by José Manuel Aicardo, *Comentario a las constituciones de la Compañía de Jesús,* 6 vols. (Madrid: Blass, 1919–32), 1:816–17.

3. Cf. "Letter on Obedience," in *MI, Letters,* 4:679, n. 23; "Exhortation #16 at Coimbra," 169–70, n. 15; "Exhortation #11 at Alcalá," 433–35; "Dialogue II," 712–14.

4. Cf. "Exhortation #17 at Coimbra," 171–72, nn. 2–3; "Exhortation #11 at Alcalá," 433–35.

5. Cf. "Exhortation #10 at Coimbra," 169, n. 14.

6. Cf. "Exhortation #16 at Coimbra," 169, n. 13; "Exhortation #11 at Alcalá," 433–35.

7. Cf. "Exhortation #16 at Coimbra," 169, n. 13; "Exhortation #11 at Alcalá," 427–28.

8. Cf. "Exhortation #16 at Coimbra," 169, n. 13.

9. Cf. "Exhortation #17 at Coimbra," 174–75, nn. 11–12; "Exhortation #11 at Alcalá," 436–38; "Dialogue II," 711–12.

10. Cf. "Letter on Obedience," in *MI, Letters,* 4:679.

11. Cf. "Exhortation #17 at Coimbra," 174–75, nn. 11–12; "Exhortation #11 at Alcalá," 436–38; "Dialogue II," 711–12.

12. Cf. "Exhortation #17 at Coimbra," 174–75, nn. 11, 13; "Exhortation #11 at Alcalá," 438.

13. Cf. Ibid.

14. Cf. "Exhortation #16 at Coimbra," 170, n. 16; "Exhortation #11 at Alcalá," 430–31.

15. Cf. "Exhortation #16 at Coimbra," 170, nn. 16–17; "Exhortation #17 at Coimbra," 178, n. 25; "Exhortation #11 at Alcalá," 430–31.

16. Cf. "Exhortation #16 at Coimbra," 167–70, nn. 10–13, 16; "Exhortation #11 at Alcalá," 430–31; "Dialogue II," 712–14.

17. Cf. "Exhortation #11 at Alcalá," 431.

18. Cf. Ibid..

19. Cf. *Constitutions*, [547]; "Exhortation #17 at Coimbra," n. 24.

20. Cf. *Examen*, [84]; *Constitutions*, [286]; "Exhortation #17 at Coimbra," n. 20. (Translator's note: the footnote reference in the *Monumenta Historica Societatis Iesu* from which the text is taken is incorrect here and elsewhere in its references to *Constitutions* 1:3, n. 24; it should be 3:3, n. 24.)

21. Cf. *Constitutions*, [284]; "Exhortation #16 at Coimbra," n. 8; "Exhortation #11 at Alcalá," 427—28.

22. Cf. "Letter on Obedience," in *MI, Letters*, 4:671, n. 3.

23. Cf. Ibid.

24. Cf. "Letter on Obedience," in *MI, Letters*, 4:674, n. 6.

25. Cf. *Constitutions*, [424].

26. Cf. *Constitutions*, [284].

27. Cf. *Constitutions*, [547]; Nadal, "Exhortation #17 at Coimbra," n. 24.

28. Cf. *Constitutions*, [284].

29. In section 1, n. 4, above.

30. Cf. "Letter on Obedience," nn. 5ff.m, in *MI, Letters*, 4:672ff.

31. Cf. "Exhortation #17 at Coimbra," nn. 9, 11.

32. Cf. "Exhortation #17 at Coimbra," n. 13.

33. Cf. *Constitutions*, [542]; *Examen*, [116–17].

34. Cf. "Exhortation #16 at Coimbra," nn. 3–4, 10; "Exhortation #11 at Alcalá," 435–36.

35. *Constitutions*, [284].

36. Cf. "Exhortation #17 at Coimbra," nn. 11, 13; "Exhortation #11 at Alcalá," 436–38.

37. Cf. *Constitutions*, [428].

38. Cf. *Constitutions*, [591].

39. Writings of St. Ignatius concerning obedience can be found in *MI, Letters*, 2:54–65 (letter to Fr. Andrew de Oviedo, written by Fr. Polanco at St. Ignatius's behest, 27 March 1548); *Letters*, 3:156–57 (on blind and prompt obedience, written to the brethren living in the Roman houses, 24 August 1550); *Letters*, 4:559–63 (to Fr. James Miró, on the obedience required of a subject, 17 December 1552); *Letters*, 4:669–81 (the renowned letter to the brethren in Portugal, 26 March 1553); *Letters*, 12:659–65 (various writings concerning obedience).

40. The allusion here is to the theological opinion, fairly common at Nadal's time, of those who placed the sin of the angels in a disordered evaluation of their own excellence.

41. In these words is expressed the view of those who, assuming that the future incarnation of the Word had been revealed to the angels, thought that he (Lucifer) had sinned in desiring the hypostatic union for the angelic nature (rather than the human one). Cf. St. Augustine, *Ench.*, chap. 28, n. 9, Migne, *Patrologia Latina*, 40, 246; Suárez, *De angelis,* book 7, chap. 13, n. 13; Vives, *Opera*, 2: 885.

42. Cf. Gen. 3:1–6. All scripture citations taken from the *New Oxford Annotated Bible with the Apocrypha: Revised Standard Version*, (Oxford University Press: New York, 1977); Nadal, "Dialogue II," 712–14.

43. For it is known that the beatific vision was proper to the human nature of Christ from the very moment of his incarnation and that his human nature did in fact possess it.

44. Gen. 17:15–19; cf. Gen. 15:6.

45. Rom. 4:18.

46. Cf. Gen. 22:1–18; Rom. 4:21.

47. Cf. Gen. 12:1; Nadal, "Exhortation #11 at Alcalá," 428–29.

48. Cf. Council of Orange II (A.D. 529), canon 5, in Migne, *Patrologia Graeca*, 53, 286; Denzinger, *Enchiridion Symbolorum,* n. 178.

49. Cf. section 1, n. 3.

50. Ignatius of Loyola, *Spiritual Exercises and Selected Works,* ed. and trans. George Ganss (St. Louis, Mo.: Institute of Jesuit Sources, 1991), n. 23.

51. Nadal provides an explanation of the Principle and Foundation in his *Apologia Exercitorum;* cf. *Letters of Nadal,* 4:826ff.

52. St. Thomas Aquinas, *Summa Theologiae,* II–II, q. 104, art. 2, ad. 3.

53. Cf. Ignatius of Loyola, "Letter on Obedience," in *MI, Letters,* 4:677, n. 19.

54. John Cassian, *De institutis coenobiorum,* book 4, chap. 24; *CSEL* 17, 63–64; Migne, *Patrologia Latina,* 49, 183.

55. De institutis, chap. 26; *CSEL,* 17, 65; Migne, *Patrologia Latina,* 49, 185–86. Cf. Ignatius's "Letter on Obedience," in *MI, Letters,* 4:679, n. 23; Nadal, "Exhortation #17 at Coimbra," 175, n. 12.

56. St. Thomas Aquinas, *Summa Theologiae,* II-II, q. 104, art. 3, c.

57. Cf. 2 Cor. 2:9.

58. Cf. Philem., v. 21, where the text actually is addressed, not to a group of people, but rather to a single person. (The manuscript mistakenly has "to the Philippians.") Nadal changes the original text *"confidens de obedientia tua scripsi tibi, sciens quod super id quod dico facies"* to the following: *"confidens in obedientia* vestra *scripsi* vobis, *sciens quod super id quod dico* facietis".

59. Cf. Mt. 21:6.

60. Cf. Heb. 13:17.

61. Translator's note: the [?] appears in the *Commentarii de Instituto* text.

62. St. Leo the Great expresses similar sentiments in his *Sermo 35 (de Epiphania),* chap. 3, in Migne, *Patrologia Latina,* 54, 252A: "Therefore, my most beloved brothers and sisters, nothing is harsh for the humble, nothing difficult for the meek; and all commands come easily into execution when grace extends its help and obedience softens the harshness of command."

63. Titus 2:9.

64. In a similar vein speaks St. Bernard in his *Sermones super Cantica: iuxta Thomam Hibernium, Flores Doctorum* (Venice, 1550), under title of *Disciplina,* fol. 160v, letter c.

65. Cf. St. Gregory the Great, *Moralia,* book 35, chap. 14, n. 32, Migne, *Patrologia Latina,* 76, 768A. Cf. Thomas of Ireland, *Flores Doctorum,* under the title *Obedientia,* fol. 353r, letter c.

66. Letter 125 ("To the Monk Rusticus"), n. 15; *CSEL,* 556, 134; Migne, *Patrologia Latina,* 22, 1081.

67. Ps. 18:44.

68. Ps. 118 (119):60.

69. Cf. *Sermo 41 de diversis* (On the Virtue of Obedience and Its Seven Degrees), n. 7 (4th degree), Migne, *Patrologia Latina*, 183, 657B. In the *Flores Doctorum* see under the title "Obedience," fol. 353v, letter h.

70. Cf. Luke 4:41.

71. Cf. *Rule of St. Benedict,* chap. 5 (on obedience), n. 14; *CSEL,* 75, 37; Migne, *Patrologia Latina,* 66, 750B.

72. Luke 10:16. Cf. *Rule of St. Benedict,* chap. 5, n. 15; *CSEL* 75, 37; Migne, *Patrologia Latina,* 66, 750B.

73. 2 Cor 9:7. Cf. *Rule of St. Benedict,* chap. 5, n. 16; *CSEL* 75, 35; Migne, *Patrologia Latina,* 66, 750B.

74. Along the same lines, see *Liber de praecepto et dispensatione,* chap. 7, nn. 14–16; Migne, *Patrologia Latina,* 182, 869–870.

75. Eph. 6:5–6.

76. *Sermon 2 on the Coming of the Lord,* n. 4; Migne, *Patrologia Latina,* 183, 45c.

77. Cf. *Rule of Saint Benedict,* chap. 68 ("If Impossible Commands Should Be Given"); *CSEL* 75, 158–59; Migne, *Patrologia Latina,* 66, 917–18. See also note 40 in "Exhortation #11 at Alcalá."

78. Phil. 4:13.

79. Thus the Abbot Nesteron is said to have regarded entrance into religious life. See *De vitis Patrum,* book 5 ("Sayings of the elders" and "On Humility"), n. 30; Migne, *Patrologia Latina,* 960B. Cf. A. Rodriguez, *Practice of Perfection and Christian Virtues,* pt. 3, trat. 5, chap. 8, wherein the same example is cited.

80. James 1:21.

81. Cf. *Epist.* 130 (to Demetrias), n. 17; *CSEL* 565, 198; Migne, *Patrologia Latina,* 22, 1121.

82. 2 Kings 4:2.

83. Acts 9:6.

84. Cf. St. Bernard, *Sermon #1 on the Conversion of St. Paul,* n. 6; Migne, *Patrologia Latina,* 183, 363CD.

85. Jer. 48:10.

86. Cf. *On the Customs and Office of Bishops,* chap. 9, n. 33: Migne, *Patrologia Latina* 182, 831A. There we read: "He indeed *gave* his life, so that he might not sacrifice obedience." But elsewhere we find: "He who

had obedience to such a degree, that he preferred to *sacrifice* life rather than save it, being obedient to the Father all the way unto death." *Ad milites templi,* chap. 3: Migne, *Patrologia Latina,* 182, 939.

87. In the manuscript text that follows, fol. 274r–79v, we find the *Letter on Obedience to the Brethren in Portugal,* edited by Nadal's own hand; these editorial emendations can be found in *Epistulae Natalis,* 4:9.

Keys to Spiritual Growth: Remembering and Imagining in Ignatian Spirituality

David L. Fleming, S.J.

WHAT DOES A WRITER OF HISTORY DO? A HISTORIAN, perhaps through his or her own experience, and certainly through reading and research, takes in or gathers the data of past events. I call this the remembering function of the historian. But this is only the first activity. In the second function of communicating the data that the historian has gathered or *re-membered,* he or she creatively puts events into a pattern of meaning, intelligibility, or interpretation. This second activity I identify as the imaginative function of the writer of history. Historians are praised or vilified on how well they can balance both functions.

Although Ignatius of Loyola is not identified as a historian, Ignatian spirituality finds its dynamic power in the interplay of the two activities of remembering and imagining—they are the key elements of Ignatian spirituality and essential to its dynamism. Both elements in balance are necessary for living an integral Ignatian spirituality. Over the last thirty years, the renewed study of Ignatian spirituality has ordinarily placed a greater stress on the remembering function than on the imagining one. Perhaps this stress comes from the Jesuit tradition—the bearers of the Ignatian heritage—to be associated more with the methodical approach to prayer and spiritual practice than with the creative, romantic, and mystical approach. Despite the past prevalent rational or philosophical explanations of the Principle and Foundation introduction to the Ignatian Exercises and even thereby the rest of the structural pieces of the retreat, the affective or feeling emphasis embedded in the text of Ignatius has never been completely ignored. The affections that ground the discernment practice of Ignatius are integrally connected with his imaginative way of praying the Gospels. It is this imaginative element that is the source of Ignatian spirituality's dynamism and the reason for its popular contribution to living a rich spiritual life in the midst of a worldly busyness. Although the imaginative element of Ignatian spirituality was never entirely lost, I believe that we need to examine it closely so that we better understand and appreciate the holistic balance of this particular spirituality.

For example, our ability to discern—so central to Ignatian decision making—demands the interworking of memory and imagination. In a similar way, our ability to have a *live* spirituality—one that adapts to changing circumstances of time and culture—calls for the active use of memory and imagination. Our efforts to be evangelizers today—those who can respond to Pope John Paul II's call to a new evangelization—look to people who work with their powers of remembering and imagining. Because of the centrality of the relationship of these two elements in the overall dynamic movement in Ignatian spirituality, I want to give a quick overview of remembering and imagining and then trace more carefully their relationship in the lived experience of Ignatius and in his book *The Spiritual Exercises*.

Remembering

We associate the word *remembering* with Ignatius's use of the word *memory* as a necessary part of our way of praying. In the meditation form of prayer found especially in the First Week of the Exercises, Ignatius refers to the use of memory, understanding, and will—traditional ways of describing the use of our human faculties in the process of this way of praying. In Ignatius's directions for praying the Gospel contemplations found in the Second, Third, and Fourth Weeks of the Exercises, we again note his insistence on recalling or remembering the Gospel passages given for this particular prayer time. Since people did not often have Bibles for their personal use in the first one hundred years or more of Jesuit retreat giving, memory played an important part in the Ignatian director's recalling of the Gospel mystery. Gospel stories took their place along with the director's other stories—to be told and to be remembered for the progress of the retreat.

Remembering so permeates Ignatian spirituality that it can be characterized as a *reflective* spirituality. People who are either not naturally reflective or, even with training, little so inclined do not find a home in Ignatian spirituality. Ever since the now classic article "The Examen of Consciousness" by Fr. George Aschenbrenner was published in *Review for Religious* in 1972, much attention has been given to this element of Ignatian spirituality.

The Examen

One indication of the central importance of remembering is Ignatius's stress on examination. He often describes this exercise by his favored shortened expression, transliterated into English as *examen*. We note that Ignatius does not begin the text of the First Week with a content matter of meditation, but rather by explaining the use of various kinds of examens. In this way he gives a hint right at the beginning for the one making the Exercises that this spirituality approach demands that one be reflective. A person should be able to look back, to recall thoughts and interior movements, to remember insights and stirring desires.

Ignatius suggests that it is important that the examen be made every day; in fact, he suggests that about midday and again at the end of the day one should spend some time (identified as a quarter of an hour) reflecting on where God has been present or absent in one's day. There is also the possibility of the particular examen within the daily examen: an examination aimed at a focused area of one's life—a virtue to be practiced so as to make it one's own by God's grace or a fault to be overcome, again by God's grace inspiring and strengthening one's effort. Neither of these examens is restricted to a retreat time, but rather both are meant to be a part of daily life with God. Then there is the examination preparing oneself for the sacrament of reconciliation, whether in its regular rhythm of church life or in its special use when one makes a general confession of one's life, especially in the context of the thirty-day retreat experience.

As we move into the prayer periods of the retreat according to the Spiritual Exercises, we find Ignatius again stressing the importance of a time for examen upon completing the prayer period. Rather than letting us get distracted and self-focused within our prayer, Ignatius suggests that we devote some time—marked by a different bodily position like sitting or walking if we have been praying kneeling or standing—to reflect on where God has met us in prayer, our own response or lack of response, and any other movements we discover as we look back at our prayer time. As a general overview, these are some of the favored ways that remembering is effected in the Ignatian Exercises. There is no doubt that Ignatian spirituality finds its home in a reflective person.

Imagining

If a retrospective action is easily associated with Ignatian spirituality, the use of imagination may not come so readily to mind. We may often easily overlook evidence of the important role imagination played in Ignatius's life. In the first chapter of his *Autobiography*, he gives full play to the romantic way he imaged his life as a courtier. Even his desire to while away the hours of his convalescence from the cannonball incident at Pamplona took shape in the request for romance novels, stories about knights and their ladies. He acknowledges that he was much given to reading such "worldly books of fiction," especially those dealing with chivalry. (Ignatius once alluded to a love poem that he had written to a young woman; too bad that it has been lost since it would be another indication of his imaginative abilities.) When he is presented with the only books in the Loyola family castle—a life of Christ and lives of saints—he so enters into this reading that he imaginatively sees himself doing great things for God after the manner of a St. Francis of Assisi or a St. Dominic. A romantic or imaginative vision gives focus to his pilgrimage to the Holy Land; his dream of spending his life there, however, is cut short by the local Franciscan provincial's threat of excommunication. It seems to me that much of Ignatius's appeal to the people he had dealings with, and especially to the first companions who gathered around him in Paris, was due to his visionary or imaginative character.

We expect, then, to find imaginative qualities present in the text of *The Spiritual Exercises*. We are not disapppointed, but we do not find these imaginative gifts immediately in evidence the way that we may have expected. In a cursory reading, the text may seem dry, almost telegraphic in expression, with little colorful or emotive language. But Ignatius indicates, though subtly, at the very beginning of the text of the *Exercises* that he wants a director who uses imagination. That *The Spiritual Exercises* begins with a section called "Annotations" is significant. By beginning the text with these directions for the retreat director, Ignatius makes clear that the Exercises in practice must always be adapted to those making the retreat. He is underlining the necessity of the director's own imaginative adaptation for the good movement of the retreat. Yet the most evident call upon imagination is found in the consistent way that Ignatius approaches the mysteries of Jesus' life as it is presented in the Gospels.

Ignatian Contemplation

Although Ignatius is not usually identified with original spiritual practices, his way of entering into prayer on the Gospel mysteries of Jesus' life has credited him with a prayer method known as Ignatian contemplation. We find an explanation of this way of praying as we enter into the Second Week of the Exercises.

Ignatius presents us with two approaches to this way of praying that draw upon our imagination. In the first contemplation of the first day of the Second Week, Ignatius indicates that, looking with the same gaze as the triune God, we see first the world with its mix of peoples and their relationships, and then the angel Gabriel and Mary and their conversation about God's plan to become a human being. With God we are deeply moved by the plight of those who people our earthly globe, and with God we experience the expectant wait for Mary's response so that we may acknowledge with great wonder the decisive moment of God's Word made flesh. In the second contemplation Ignatius suggests the same kind of intimate involvement in the mystery under consideration, but our involvement is *from within* rather than the previously described *from above*. When we consider the Gospel nativity scene, we are encouraged to take our places as participants in the events described. Ignatius suggests that we might imagine ourselves being servants ready to help Joseph and Mary in any way that they might call upon us. With these two relatively brief indications of how to enter into this kind of Gospel contemplation, Ignatius presumes that he has given the retreatant enough help, along with the director's continuing guidance, to enter into this form of contemplation in the Second Week.

In broad strokes, then, we have pictured the element of remembering, especially in the consistency of a reflective examen permeating the retreat exercises, and the element of imagining, especially engaged in the pervasive way of praying Ignatian contemplations. To appreciate the dynamism provided for this spiritual approach by these two elements, it is important for us to trace the interplay of remembering and imagining throughout the text of the *Exercises* and the experience it engenders.

Four-Week Movement

The progress of the retreat in the full thirty-day experience of the Spiritual Exercises is in the movement relating one Week to another—what we might call "grace building upon grace." We need to remember how God has worked with us in the past Week in order that we can be more readily available for his continuing guidance in our lives. In terms of our Judeo-Christian heritage, each of us enters into the Israelite experience of needing to look back at, to remember, God's ways of acting so that they might shed light on our present and future directions. The Bible is a memory document, and through its God-given light, memory, or *re-membering,* has its importance in allowing us to gather and put together our experiences in relation to God. As Ignatius framed each day and each Week of his Exercises, remembering is meant to give us a God perspective: we are not locked into having our personal response be a reaction only to the anonymous "What happens?"

The First Week

Movement from consideration of the Principle and Foundation to the First Week exercises takes place as a natural flow because of human memory. As we reflect on our Judeo-Christian vision of God, ourselves, and our world, and as we consider our responsibility to make choices among the goods meant to help lead us to God, we find ourselves remembering not only our delight in these gifts but also our misuse of them. This natural movement of memory leads us, with a director's guidance, into the first meditation exercise on sin as the rejection of God made visible in the choice of angels and human beings, the first free creatures of God's creation. From recalling and pondering these objective biblical stories, we progress to the second meditation, which is subjective consideration of our own lives. In order to recall in what ways we have sinned and rejected God, Ignatius asks us to remember and consider (1) the places we have lived, (2) the people we have dealt with, and (3) the occupations or responsibilities we have held.

In the first prelude of each prayer time of the First Week, Ignatius calls us to a composition of place. We enter into this composition through the seeing of the imagination—seeing a physical setting derived from reality or a metaphorical setting from an abstract context. This imaginative way of composing our very being—that is, positioning ourselves in a felt way consistent with our prayer content—serves as a centering element of Ignatian prayer.

In the colloquy of the first exercise, Ignatius uses a few carefully chosen words to paint a picture of Christ on the cross, the Christ who is the Word through whom "all things were made through him, and without him was not anything made that was made."[1] Christ described as Creator, even while he hangs on a cross, is in keeping with the focus of the Principle and Foundation and the Bible stories of angels and first parents. To the mystery of evil, this Creator God responds, in continuing love, with the mystery of the cross. In the Ignatian meditations of the First Week, we do not pray for the grace of understanding evil or sin—these remain a mystery. Instead we pray for the grace of shame or confusion— because we do not understand others, such as Adam and Eve and the angels, and their behavior in the face of God's loving goodness, or even ourselves and our own inability to act with consistency in doing the good. In the second prayer period we look to our own lives, praying for the grace of sorrow, even to the point of tears, in our sinful response to God. The shame and confusion, the sorrow and tears, with which God's grace gifts us, are embedded in the foundational response of gratitude to God. Gratitude is the permeating response of the First Week prayer—a gratitude to a God who never stops loving and providing the gifts of love.

The imaginative placing of ourselves before Christ on his cross is the setting that opens up our personal conversation with God about evil and sin, the part we play in it, and God's response. In the prelude requesting grace and the colloquy we realize that Ignatius finds an engine for movement within the retreat day and Week: the grace prelude and the colloquy subtly become our expressions of an Ignatian imagination where we make ourselves available to God.

The content of the next two prayer exercises in the Ignatian text flows from the prayer examens following the previous prayer exercises. In each examen after the prayer period, we have noted where we felt moved either by greater consolation or desolation, or generally by greater spiritual appreciation. These movements and the thoughts that elicited them, remembered and noted, provide the content matter of the third prayer exercise. Ignatius identifies this prayer period as a "repetition," and he makes frequent use of this manner of praying throughout the weeks of the Exercises. The fourth prayer exercise of this First Week is a "summary" or "resumé" of the previous period. Ignatius once again makes the content of this prayer period our recollection of significant movements of the previous repetition. It is truly another form of repetition—perhaps the choice by Ignatius of a new identity word reinforcing his direction that the prayer matter is not just a return to or a rethinking of the same material. Rather the Ignatian repetition always starts from thoughts or feelings that have been significant in the preceding prayer experience—and then we see where God will continue to lead and interact with us from *this* starting point. So there is both a remembering (a going back to a previous response) and an imagining (an openness to the new, a future not within our control) in the Ignatian repetition.

In the final or fifth prayer exercise of the First Week, Ignatius enters us into an imaginative experience of hell. Interpretations about the makeup of this imagining have always differed, since Ignatius in the other weeks refers to this final prayer period as an application of the senses. Some say that Ignatius is much more centered on imagining with the true physical senses, granted some metaphorical use of tasting the bitterness of tears and sorrow. Others point out that Ignatius is alluding rather to the spiritual senses, after the manner of the descriptions given in the spiritual writings of the Franciscan St. Bonaventure. If we consider what we might describe as the *distilling process* of prayer that is evident in the Ignatian use of repetition, it would be jarring to introduce at the end of the day a new kind of prayer that demands a lot of activity. More in keeping with Ignatian movement is an explanation that sees this fifth or last prayer period of the day (for the first time in this week's meditation prayer pattern calling upon a prayer of imagination) as a more passive way of praying by allowing the total experience of all our prayer times of this day to sweep over us just as our senses drink in the total environment without our personal effort. The prayer matter—thoughts and feelings—is not new and requires no new effort on our part. We let ourselves be immersed in what has involved us during this retreat day, and it becomes for us our imaginative experience of hell.

However we understand this imagination prayer, I want to turn our attention to Ignatius's directions for the colloquy—the interchange with God or what we might call the "actual praying" time. He suggests that we bring to mind people before Jesus' coming who chose hell by what they did or failed to do, people during Jesus' life who similarly chose hell, and finally people since Jesus' resurrection who continue to choose hell by their sins of commission or omission. Recalling such people, we can only give thanks for God's mercy in our lives. With this exercise of imagination and memory, the material content of the First Week closes.

Although there are times of imagining, as in the prayer period on hell, the First Week stresses exercises that more evidently use memory. Remembering is urged because there is no moving forward unless we are aware of and accept our past. Remembering for Ignatius is never nostalgic. It is rather a time to look for God's footprints, a time to see the devil's tail, a time to note our own past blindness or insensitivity to God's gifts or to God's action in our lives. Noting that God's response to sin and evil is Jesus on the cross and thereby a continuity with Love's outpouring of gifts upon us, we experience the grace of being loved and forgiven sinners. We have come to know the justice of God in his loving mercy. Only by taking time to remember God's response can we choose to act differently—with gratitude. Remembering always remains essential in shaping the Ignatian imaginative choice of a future.

The Second Week

Just as we consider the Principle and Foundation as part of the First Week movement, so we may see the "Call of the King" as introductory to, but a part of, the Second Week movement. There is a long tradition among Ignatian commentators of identifying the "Call of the King" as a second Principle and Foundation. It is true that it fits more the consideration model of the Principle and Foundation since Ignatius himself suggests no colloquy or proper prayer time in either exercise. Just as the Principle and Foundation leads naturally into the exercises of the First Week, so too the "Call of the King" flows into consideration of the mysteries of Christ's life. If we pray for the grace not to be deaf to Christ's call in our own lives, we find the stirrings of desire to know him better so that we may be able to follow him more surely.

The comparison Ignatius draws between the temporal king and Christ our Lord is based upon a summary picture of Jesus taken from the Gospels. Ignatius wants us to remember the calls of Jesus and his desire to have followers whose lives, like his, are concerned with God and the coming of God's kingdom. Although Ignatius could have chosen a particular Gospel passage that sums up Jesus' call and identity of mission,[2] he instead imaginatively paints his own synoptic picture of Jesus making his call to every man, woman, and child. He has the risen Jesus (the *now* Jesus) issue a biblical battle cry for war against evil in all its death-dealing forms. Ignatius is tapping into the imaginative stirrings of the human heart to evoke a vision and mission that is worth the gift of one's life.

This structural exercise is imaginative in a number of ways. First, in looking back to the First Week, it fulfills the idea of a meditation on mercy. Our saving God does not let us be passive recipients of his merciful justice. Christian salvation is not limited to a "saving from" sin. Rather the salvation offered by God in Christ is the very empowering of God's own life in us so that we may live as the sons and daughters God has created us to be. In the Ignatian exercise, through our Savior's invitation we are welcomed as participants in the salvation mission.

In imagination, we observe people responding in two different ways—some logically or rationally and others generously or magnanimously. Ignatius very carefully does not ask us as retreatants to make our own response at this time. We need to know more about Jesus and what his call to us entails. And so our desires are naturally led to contemplations of Jesus' life. The "Call of the King" acts both as a conclusion to the First Week of experiencing

God's merciful justice and as a foundation for the Second Week and beyond for all of the contemplations on Jesus' life. This exercise acts dramatically as a concrete instance of a grace building upon a grace between the Second Week and the First.

The second way this exercise is imaginative is in its Ignatian presentation. When we do not appreciate the Ignatian emphasis on imagination, we easily lose the magic that his structural piece had for his contemporaries and for many throughout history. It takes imagination to adapt to and use this second foundation to launch us into the exercises of the Second Week. For example, we can imaginatively say that Ignatius is asking us to enter into Jesus' dreams for God's kingdom and our part in it. This exercise in itself is an engine of movement, once again combining the elements of remembering and imagining, attracting us to Christ and so to his mission.

Finally, the "Call of the King" is imaginative in its reality as a foundation piece or a refining of the Principle and Foundation. The newness of this foundation is the person of Christ and identification of his mission of proclaiming the kingdom of heaven, or reign of God. From our first foundation we are still in the context of God's continuing love, God's showering of gifts, and our effort to make the choices of response to God's love. Ignatius is careful in presenting his vision pieces—the Principle and Foundation, the "Call of the King," and the "Contemplation on the Love of God"—to emphasize always the same vision and yet each time with a further refinement or completeness. It is the imaginative element in the presentation that triggers the movement for the next stage of living our response to God more fully.

We enter into the contemplations proper to the Second Week with the Gospel Annunciation mystery, but placed in a context of the triune God looking upon the world and choosing to enter into creation and heal it from within by being born a human being. We touched upon this scene when we were describing Ignatian contemplation earlier. The second prayer period of the day is the biblical mystery of the Nativity, which provides Ignatius with the opportunity to give a second explanation of how to enter into this form of contemplation.

Ignatius suggests a three-day period for entering into this contemplative way of praying, coming to appreciate the beginnings of Jesus' life and settling into a restful and quiet pace after the demands of the First Week. Imaginative adaptation to the retreatants either lengthens or shortens these first days of the Second Week.

The Ignatian-designated fourth day is a total change of pace, with a return to the prayer of meditation for the whole day. We pray for the grace of understanding: understanding of the deceitful methods used by the evil spirit to ensnare us, and understanding of the values that Jesus chooses for himself and for us that enable us to live freely as the adult children God has called us to be. Between the meditative way of praying and the grace of understanding that we are asking for, this seems to be a very rational, thinking kind of day. And yet Ignatius is particularly imaginative in presenting the meditative material of the day. He draws the picture of two opposing forces, each flying its own flag of allegiance over earthly cities: Jerusalem, a place-name signifying the peace of God, where Christ is the commander in chief of the good, and Babylon, a biblical place-name identified with noise and confusion and division among people, where Lucifer is the chief of the enemy. To whom is Lucifer enemy? Lucifer, whose name means "a bearer of light," is identified as the mortal enemy of human nature. Ignatius's choice of verbs piques the imagination: contrast Lucifer, who "issues a summons," "scatters," and "casts out nets and chains," with Jesus, who "chooses," "sends," and "recommend[s] . . . them to want to help." Lucifer is seated on a great chair, obscured with fire and smoke; Jesus stands with his followers, on the level plain.

Lucifer tries to entrap through riches, honors, and finally pride. From these three allurements people are led to all other vices. Jesus holds up the seemingly obscure values of poverty, powerlessness, and humility. But from these three values people are led to all other virtues. Ignatius has imaginatively chosen to emphasize these three not-very-apparent values from Jesus' life in the Gospels in the face of three evident worldly values that are common across cultures and centuries. It is from this prayer exercise that Ignatius expects God's grace to enlighten the mind of the retreatant so that it may guard against Lucifer's wiles. Our meditation will help us to understand Christ's choice of values so that we may imitate and follow him.

Although the final prayer period of this fourth day is uncharacteristically a meditation on new matter, Ignatius brings a lightness to it by employing imagination. He makes use of a case study model to bridge the gap between understanding and action. Objectively considering different groupings of people and how they face decisive action is the method for eliciting our own subjective readiness to follow Christ in his chosen way of living.

With the fifth day of the Second Week we return to our contemplative way of praying. But Ignatius provides two more exercises that draw us further into the use of imagination. The first exercise has usually been given the title "Three Manners [Kinds, Degrees] of Humility." The second exercise deals with the Ignatian election—the matter to be considered, the times for making it, and the methods. Even though the election plays its own essential role in the movement of the Second Week and in the director's sensing of its completion, I want to consider it as a part of our later treatment of discernment.

Humility, as we have experienced in the "Two Standards" meditation, is the virtue of identity for Jesus. Humility, living true to oneself, is Jesus living his truth—being true to his identity as Son of God. Extending over some days as we enter into our prayer about the public life of Jesus, Ignatius proposes this exercise to enable us to ruminate about how closely we identify with Jesus. How much do we want the truth of Jesus' life to be embodied in our own lives? Remembering allows us to associate the second degree with the Principle and Foundation consideration. To what excesses will we let love lead us? Like love songs that speak in metaphors of excess, so Ignatius paints a picture of the third manner of humility. A purely rational approach does not understand this third manner; only a lover's imagination can begin to grasp it and let it become the dynamic of one's life. After a time of rumination, Ignatius suggests that the retreatant begin to pray for the grace of this identity or at least for the desire for such a grace.

The Ignatian election, which deals specifically with life choices or decision making about a reform of one's life, becomes another occasion for using imagination and not just rationality. Although both the election activity and consideration of humility are outside regular prayer periods, the sense of completing the Second Week, or to put it another way, the judgment of receiving the grace of the Week, is readily made in terms of our response to the third manner of humility or to the resolution about our specific and embodied way of following Christ. How a Week is determined as being completed (since there is no set number of days) is a matter of imagination upon the part of both the retreatant and the director. The retreatant is trying to report to the director where God's grace seems to have led, and the director is attempting to hear from the retreatant how the grace prayed for and the grace received come together for future direction, following God's lead. No one grace can be identified as *the* gift of a Week of the Exercises. The continuing movement of the retreat flows from the imaginative interchange between the retreatant and the director.

The Third Week

Ignatius appears to be aware that our memory of the events of Jesus' passion and death can be an obstacle in the Third Week. He shows this awareness by his addition of three more points for each prayer period. Ordinarily the points act as particular areas of the matter under consideration that focus our attention. When Ignatius presents the material for the events from the Last Supper through the burial of Jesus, he adds three points, all of which deal with our getting inside the mystery and not just staying with external happenings. We pray for the grace that Christ will let us share his feelings as together we contemplate these days when he accomplished his greatest work, the work of redemption that his Father had given him to do. Each of the added Ignatian points stresses this interiority with Jesus. The grace of compassion is often described as the summary gift sought in the Third Week. Granted that the grace of God is most essential, the power of imagining is what allows us to grow in compassion. It is the most precious of graces in the Third Week because it signifies a wholly new intimacy and closeness to Christ. Just as the movement caught up in our deepening relationship with Christ is quite different from the movement from the First Week to the Second, so too do we find a similar kind of movement in intimacy between the Second Week and the Third. The Third Week has little to build on if an appropriate Second Week grace has not been received. But the Third Week grace of intimate relationship with Jesus goes well beyond the Second.

The Fourth Week

In a similar way the Fourth Week has nothing on which to build if some Third Week grace of compassion has not been received. For in the Fourth Week Ignatius wants us to pray for the grace to let Christ enter us into his joy of victory. We may find it difficult to experience the consolation that the risen Jesus offers us. The world looks so much the same after his resurrection; we seem to struggle in many ways despite our being baptized into Christ. How do we experience the risen Jesus and the power of his resurrection in our life? If we have known the precious gift of compassion from the previous Week, then we realize that in a similar way Christ stands with us in every life situation. Christ does not save us from life's trials, but he supports us with his consoling power. Our experience of compassion is reversed as we drink in the presence of our compassionate God of consolation—One with us, our Emmanuel.

Again Ignatius provides the way to realizing this new relationship with God. In addition to the usual three points of a contemplation, he now adds two additional points. By these points Ignatius draws our attention to the divinity shining out in the risen Jesus and his role as consoler that identifies his way of acting. Through the usual contemplative prayer dealing with the mysteries of the risen life of Jesus, Ignatius adds the image of a compassionate, consoling God. This image provides a deepening relationship between God and ourselves, sung, as it were, in a whole new key. This deepened relationship is further clarified in the last structural piece of the Exercises.

The final exercise of the Fourth Week is titled "The Contemplation to Attain the Love of God." Various commentators have pointed out that the four points of this contemplation roughly recall our experiences of the Four Weeks. That the matter of the prayer is not new material allows for this prayer to be truly a contemplation. We easily can gaze upon what is now familiar to us.

The newness comes from the imaginative way that Ignatius frames this prayer exercise. For the first time he offers two preliminary notes, rationally presented, coming from remembered human experience of loving. Building on the factual character of these preliminary notes, we see God pouring out love in such limitless ways that we are left gasping to make a response. The creativity of the prayer colloquy response, originating with Ignatius, lies in its careful selection of what we can share of something we might be able to call our own. Since we have imbibed from the Principle and Foundation that everything we have is a gift from God, what do we, as lovers, have to share with God except what he has already given to us? The "take and receive" of the Ignatian prayer response does not mean a "giving away," because we remember from our preliminary note that lovers share what they have. So we humans can *share* with God our potential for making ourselves who we are—our liberty. We can share with God our memory because what we remember is truly ours—*our* memories—and so we can share it with God in love. We can share our understanding because what and how we understand is unique, and we share this uniqueness with God. Finally we share our will because our will signifies so much of what we want, and so we offer our wants and our choices to God out of a sharing of love.

This prayer is Ignatius's imaginative creation for how we share as lovers. He suggests that we can respond to each point of the contemplation in the way that love moves us, and he offers his prayer response only as a model. He calls us to use our imagination to speak out what and how we as lovers can share with our loving God. The Ignatian prayer retains its classic popularity as a response because it has cut to the quick of imagining what we have to share with God. However we express our response, we are entering more fully into God's way of loving. From such a pervasive contact with God, we are setting forth as contemplatives in action—this will be the movement of our lives. We have made the Ignatian dynamic our own.

Truly the Ignatian Exercises do not have a closure or ending. The dynamic present in the retreat itself becomes the dynamic of human living in Christ. The interplay of remembering and imagining is the dynamic of the Exercises made visible to the retreatant. That dynamic is what continues to empower and vitalize the person who lives an Ignatian spirituality. Let us now consider one aspect of this spirituality that plays an especially important role in our everyday lives with God.

Discernment

The Rules for Discernment and the Election process that makes use of them are integral parts of the book of the *Exercises* yet, at the same time, gifts to spirituality independent of the retreat. Ignatius's gift to the process of discernment of spirits and to the process of decision making is his emphasis on the interplay of remembering and imagining.

From Ignatius's first awareness of the different spirits moving within him, as he relates in his *Autobiography,* remembering plays a necessary role. In making the comparison between one feeling and its source and another and its source, we must use our memory. Ignatius realized that what first had delighted and excited him in thinking about worldly success left him dry and dissatisfied. When he thought of imitating the saints and going to Jerusalem, he was not only consoled in the midst of such thoughts, but after putting them aside he remained satisfied and joyful. "Little by little he came to recognize the difference between the spirits that were stirring, one from the devil, the other from God."[3] It is this kind of experience that roots the Ignatian rules for discernment more in the affective human makeup than in the rational, calling upon a balance of memory and imagination.

Although the Ignatian discernment rules are not restricted to use in a retreat, I think it important to note that they are originally located within the retreat context. Because of the contemplative way that Ignatius was putting the retreatant into contact with the Jesus of the Gospels, he presumed that by the grace of God the retreatant was absorbing Jesus' way of acting and his way of coming to a decision. Jesus, then, becomes the paradigm for our own way of living and making choices. Just as the criterion for Jesus was always what enhanced his relationship with God, so too for us there can be no other criterion. God speaks a language within our very being about what enhances or detracts from this relationship. Not surprisingly, we understand this language as spoken through our affections. Learning to hear and understand this language of God is the Ignatian art of discernment.

As a result, rationality is not the focus of Ignatian discernment. Because Ignatius describes a third time of election in which one of the two ways is a listing of pros and cons, the tradition that Ignatian discernment is merely rational and methodical has been overemphasized. Besides the three preparatory points emphasizing memory, understanding, and imagination, and besides the fourth and fifth points with their methodical listing of advantages and disadvantages, we need to pay attention to the final point instructing us to bring our rational decision and offer it to God, praying insistently that God confirm it. How does God confirm this decision in the Ignatian approach? God confirms by consolation, and so once again we are led to hear and understand the language of God. Within this same third time, Ignatius offers a second way and gives four rules and a note. All four rules deal with imagination: (1) imaging my choice and how it affects my love of God; (2) imaging how I would counsel others if I want only their greater good; (3) imaging how I would want to have chosen as I take account of myself on my deathbed; and (4) imaging how I would want to stand before the judgment seat of the Lord in regard to this choice. The note reemphasizes that the decision that seems clear to me from this exercise should be offered to God for his confirmation just as was called for after the first way. Again confirmation is by consolation.

Memory plays an important role in discernment because we need to make comparisons between the experiences of consolation and desolation, and also because we need to measure this consolation experience against a previous one so that we can more easily assess its legitimacy. The use of imagination may be considered more subtle in that every choice or decision is made in hope, since what happens on account of our decision is not yet seen because it lies in the future. The first time of choice in Ignatian discernment identifies an undeviating consolation that empowers one to make a choice unhesitatingly because God is so clearly involved. Ignatius, of course, refers to Saul's decision on the road to change from being a persecutor of Christians to being the apostle Paul and to Levi's decision to abandon his tax booth to become the apostle Matthew. In the second time of election Ignatius describes the alternating feelings of consolation and desolation in the face of making a decision. Once again memory and imagination are deeply involved in whatever the Ignatian "time" may be for us.

For Ignatius, then, discernment always depends on the careful balancing of memory and imagination—our sensitivity to the movement of God's grace linking our past and future in view of a deepening relationship with God.

Other Rules

Besides discernment, Ignatius includes Ways of Praying and other rules in his text. Although I could point out the consistent interplay of memory and imagination throughout the remainder of Ignatius's *Spiritual Exercises,* I want to call our attention briefly to only two sets of rules. In presenting "rules" in the Exercises, Ignatius intends a measure or guideline for living out and deepening our relationship with God through some specified activity. For example, in his Rules for Eating that follow the Third Week text, the basic rule is the fifth rule, calling upon our imaging Jesus sitting at the table and eating with his disciples. All the other reasonable or prudential manners of acting are meant to be informed by this guideline, which is the fruit of our imagination. In a similar way, in the seventh rule of the Rules for Administering Alms, Ignatius suggests that we need to keep our eyes fixed on Christ our Lord, who is "our model and rule." Ignatius mentions saints in history who may give us other models, but he remains consistent with his reliance upon contemplative imagining for deepening our relationship with Christ and acting as he acts—whatever the activity.

An Apostolic Spirituality

From this study of the text of the *Exercises*, I intended to make clear that the keys to the dynamism integral in the apostolic spirituality identified as Ignatian are found in the movements of remembering and imagining. This spirituality finds its strength in reflection that gives us a foundation from the past to build upon. As a complementary movement, imagination opens this spirituality to the future; in this movement Ignatian spirituality finds its continuing creativity.

The call to us in the church today is to find a home in a spirituality that energizes us for a new evangelization, that helps us grow as discerning people, that enlivens us as contemplatives in action. Ignatian spirituality, with its proper balance of remembering and imagining, holds forth this promise to us.

Endnotes

1. John 1:3. All scriptural citations taken from the *New Oxford Annotated Bible with the Apocrypha: Revised Standard Version,* (Oxford University Press: New York, 1977).

2. For example, Matt. 28:16–20.

3. Ignatius of Loyola, *A Pilgrim's Testament,* trans. Parmananda R. Divarkar (St. Louis, Mo.: Institute of Jesuit Sources, 1995), 8.

Intellectual Conversion: Jesuit Spirituality and the American University

Joseph A. Tetlow, S.J.

For at least three decades, many of those living and working in Catholic colleges and universities have been aware of two causes for concern about their institutions. First, they learned that church-related colleges and universities, following a historical pattern in American higher education, have tended to drift into total secularity. Yale drifted away from the Congregationalists, for instance, as did King's College (Columbia) from the Episcopalians and Brown from the Baptists. And second, as large secular institutions gained the upper hand, religious institutions realized that they would not survive unless they embraced their true identity. As a consequence of these realizations, administrations and boards slowly found ways to insist on the identity of their institutions. Sometimes boards took the initiative, and sometimes administrators. Historically, then, Catholic institutions throughout the country began insisting on their Catholic identity three decades before *Ex Corde Ecclesiae*.

Jesuit institutions began insisting on their Jesuit identity through a strategic planning process (1973–1975), involving five university-trained men and costing perhaps three-quarters of a million dollars.[1] The earliest motivation of faculties, administrations, and boards was, quite candidly and professedly, survival. But the institutions have developed a more positive stance toward their identities as they have realized that their institutions actually do stand in living religious traditions of learning.

More recently, the religious and laity who conduct church-related institutions of higher learning have begun recognizing that the issue of identity presents a number of challenges. While the political challenges revolve around issues of tax exemption and accepting government monies, the theoretical challenges derive from issues of academic freedom and the liberty of inquiry. The institutions themselves can handle these challenges. A few, however, have come to recognize a new challenge that they cannot handle alone. This is the challenge of standing in a religious tradition, which means standing in a relationship with a church, a denomination, or a religious order. Who has been paying attention to this second partner?

Merrimon Cuninggim flagged this particular challenge a quarter of a century ago. Concluding the National Council of Churches' multi-year study of church-related institutions and institution-related churches, he wrote, "To be church related, a college must know how it wants to be so related and to complete the reciprocal arrangement, the church must know why it wants connections with its colleges."[2] He was raising critical questions. Why would churches or religious orders want to have institutions of higher learning today? They must have a reason. They have to show an active interest in the institutions they sponsor, or they will find that they have no institutions to sponsor. Their institutions can always go the way Yale, Princeton, and Brown have gone, which may not seem too dire. But they may also go the way scores and even hundreds of others have gone—they are gone and no longer remembered at all. This possibility catches the attention.

This essay focuses on one religious order: the Society of Jesus. It asks why the Jesuits have kept their connections with their twenty-eight American colleges and universities.[3] The principles and conclusions of this essay reach beyond the Jesuits' specific interests, however, and should be readily adaptable by any religious sponsor of higher learning. For what I detail here recounts the history of one group's dynamic interaction, during four centuries of great intellectual and cultural shifts, with the purposes and paradigms of institutions of higher learning. All religious groups shared in the history of that interaction as all moved away from the absolutes of scholasticism and of rationalism. In the largest sense, the "intellectual conversion" that I talk about here instantiates the later stages of the shift from modernism to postmodernism. We are all going through that shift, replacing earlier, more provincial mind-sets with newer global ones. As Albert Borgmann explains, "For each of the modern principles a counterpossibility is emerging: information processing in place of aggressive realism, flexible specialization instead of methodical universalism, and informed cooperation rather than rugged individualism."[4] Reduced to an intellectual imperative, the demand made by this shift is that we listen to one another intelligently and compassionately—a new habit in academia.

The Beginning in *The Spiritual Exercises*

This paragraph from Ignatius's sixteenth-century Spanish handbook is a good introduction to the Jesuit story:

> Presupposition: Every good Christian is more ready to find a correct meaning in a neighbor's statement than to reject it as erroneous. If we cannot construe the statement in some orthodox sense, we ask how he meant it. If he meant to say something wrong, then we try to correct him, moved by love. If this is not good enough, then we try every feasible way to bring our neighbor to some correct meaning in the statement so as to save it (the statement). [22][5]

This "Presupposition" took shape as Luther's German Bible circulated through Germany, as Protestants created their first university in Marburg and as the Confession of Augsburg galvanized the Schmalkaldic League against Charles V and the Catholics. It was written in Paris in the 1530s, a period when academic characters and careers were frequently destroyed in bitter theological wrangling. It was published and printed for the first time in Rome during the 1540s, as Pope Paul III established the Roman Inquisition.

The paragraph is the first to appear after the title of Ignatius of Loyola's *The Spiritual Exercises.* Though it has been given little attention, it marks an intellectual reorientation of startling reach, a shift away from the relentless disputation of its time and ultimately toward the perspectivalism of ours.[6] In Ignatius's day this reorientation, though adopted by a few humanists, remained quite foreign to devoted churchmen. It was particularly foreign and even keenly suspect to the Christian academic mind then consumed with polemic. The reorientation that Ignatius's paragraph enunciates, furthermore, was not merely declared in the paragraph and then ignored; rather, as can be readily shown, it permeated the entire experience of the Exercises. And since all agree that the experience of the Exercises has somehow animated Jesuit higher education in and from its inception, this intellectual reorientation must figure in it, too. So we would expect to find it epitomized in the *Ratio Studiorum* of 1599, the Magna Carta of Jesuit education.[7]

And so it is, but in an odd way: the *Ratio* shows tremendous respect for secular principles and procedures but offers no religious or spiritual rationale, no philosophy of education. Most readers are as surprised by this lack in the *Ratio* as Gertrude Stein was by Oakland, of which she said, "There is no there there." Those who have studied the *Ratio,* as have John Donahue and George Ganss, agree: The religious or spiritual rationale for Jesuit education is not enunciated in the *Ratio,* where it might be expected; rather, it is explicated in the Jesuit *Constitutions,* and it lies ultimately in the ongoing experience of the Exercises.[8]

So if we want to know the religious or spiritual rationale of Jesuit education, we must start with the *experience* of the Spiritual Exercises, the experience of either thirty days of silent prayer or months of daily guided prayer in ordinary life.[9] The Spiritual

Exercises elicit the experience of a fivefold conversion: religious, moral, intellectual, affective, and sociopolitical. Similarly, Jesuit institutions of higher education aspire to the complete conversion of the whole person, to *pietas*.[10] The culture of these institutions is meant to support and even promote these several conversions. The educational dynamic that specifies a Jesuit university is the integrating intellectual conversion of the students, which can be realized only by a faculty who have experienced this same intellectual conversion.

In this paper I start by giving a sketch of the five conversions elicited by the Spiritual Exercises; second, I explore intellectual conversion in the Spiritual Exercises; third, I attempt to recover *conversion* as a usable word, drawing from theologians Bernard Lonergan and Donald Gelpi; fourth, I probe the connection through intellectual conversion of the Spiritual Exercises and higher education. Finally, these reflections illuminate some of the crucial questions we face: What establishes a university in the Jesuit tradition? How can we maintain this tradition? What does the core curriculum contribute? And the major? How do agnostics, atheists, Jews, and non-Catholics become colleagues to the Jesuits? For that matter, how do Jesuits become colleagues? Beyond housing and fundraising, what does the administration and staff contribute to Jesuit education?

The Spiritual Exercises and Complete Conversion

Historically and currently, experiencing the Spiritual Exercises means experiencing the invitation to a measurable reordering of the whole self.[11] Dorothy Day had experienced this; for her, meeting the Exercises had the same outcome as meeting Emerson had on Whitman: the opening of a new horizon and the freedom to enact her most authentic desires. That reordering still happens.

Recently in Cleveland, a woman who had made the Exercises in their simplest form assessed her experience: "My life has not been the same."

Conversion is a good word for this experience, provided we can separate the common meanings, which include changing the church you belong to or going through a temporary (recurrent) emotional religious experience. For our purposes, *conversion* means finding a new horizon for conscious action or, alternatively, taking a new kind of personal responsibility in one of the realms of experience. In the experience of the Exercises, this conversion has five moments.

1. **Moral conversion.** The first "exercise" is a freshly conceived examination of conscience. For the person whose moral cognition is conventional—someone who, in Ignatius's words, "wishes no further help than some instruction and the achievement of some peace of soul" [18]—this conversion will lead to a somewhat more orderly and purposeful moral life. For the more adept or desirous, the first exercise opens a wider moral horizon; it establishes as a moral principle his or her personal relationship with Jesus Christ. This raises a new horizon, evident in the first colloquy, the conversation with the Lord at the end of the first hour of prayer that the exercitant is directed to make. Standing beside Jesus on his cross, I ask how he came to be there and I here: "What have I done for Christ? What am I doing for Christ? What might I do for Christ?" [53].

2. **Religious conversion.** This moment is perhaps best instantiated by the experience of the foundational relationship of creature to Creator. Ignatius hoped that during the earliest days of the thirty-day retreat, each exercitant would have the religious experience of ongoing creation that he himself famously had at the river Cardoner. This mystical experience entails a

turning away from the belief in a harsh accountant-God or a distant watchmaker-God to the acceptance of a God who acts moment by moment in the self and the world.

3. **Sociopolitical conversion.** The Exercises have always elicited this sort of conversion. Historically, those who experienced it joined the social groups—*compagnie*—created by the first Jesuits to help orphans, prostitutes, dispossessed Jews, nobility, and eventually their students. The experience itself urges reasonable norms for voluntary giving and for the use of food, and inculcates a foundational attitude toward wealth. By drawing exercitants to Jesus Christ who chose to live poor, the experience often spins out a preferential option for the poor [116, 210f, 337f, 189].

4. **Affective conversion.** Not surprisingly, the Exercises elicit the reordering of emotion and appreciative awareness. They invite a person to feel the grand new horizon of a plan "to conquer the whole world and all its enemies," as Ignatius has Jesus say in "Call of the King" [95]. They invite him or her to say to God the Gift-Giver, in a contemplation aimed at learning to love the way God loves, "Take, Lord, and receive all my liberty, my memory, my understanding, my entire will. . . . Give me Your love and Your grace; for me, that is enough" [234].

5. **Intellectual conversion.** The four conversions outlined above—moral, religious, sociopolitical, and affective—would achieve little if they were not ongoing. Consequently, it is hoped that even the less successful leave the Exercises with some "systematic method for amending and reforming the lives that they lead in their particular state" [189]. Among the more gifted and more desirous, that order and that system necessarily implicate an intellectual reorientation or conversion.

Intellectual Conversion in Spiritual Exercises

The Spiritual Exercises do not teach or promote doctrine as did Calvin's *Institutes,* another handbook of Christian living. In his first instruction to the spiritual guide, Ignatius warns against lecturing or instructing. Let the individual find things out alone, "for it is not knowing a lot, but grasping things intimately and savoring them that fills and satisfies the soul" [2]. Again, the Exercises do not initiate a person into a formal spiritual community, as does Benedict's *Rule.* Just as the director should not teach or instruct, neither should he or she urge an exercitant to one kind of life rather than another; it is the director's duty to "remain like a balance" [15] and be ready to help the exercitant through any choice of lifestyle he or she may make.

In Ignatius's day, spiritual counsel tended to guide younger men and women into preexisting patterns of life. The direction given during the making of the Spiritual Exercises does not aim at this formation. Rather, Ignatian direction aims to open anyone, man or woman, to one's own authentic desiring—that is, the desiring least influenced by fashion or shaped by someone else's wishes—by which one may find God's hopes in oneself and in one's life world. This nondirectiveness has been obscured for some by the book's continual and minute instructions on what to desire. The phrase *"lo que quiero"* ("what I want") appears more than any other in Ignatius's book. He tells the exercitant what to desire; for example, "to know him [Jesus of Nazareth] more clearly, love him more dearly, follow him more nearly" [104]. But this directiveness is superficial, for Ignatius also expects the one who is making the Exercises to infuse these formulaic petitions with intimately personal content so that in every prayer, "I beg to have what I more actively long for in some of my special interests" [199]. In everything, the individual's special interests stand foremost, for "God gives each individual a feel for what suits him" [89]. Nevertheless, this nondirectiveness is effective only if the person is intellectually convinced that God the Creator deals "directly with the one being created and the one being created directly with the Creator" [15].

The powerful idea that God deals directly and constantly with each individual is one that demands intellectual gifts that are perhaps not entirely ordinary. The Exercises do in fact demand lively and even instructed intelligence, otherwise they offer a fine prayer experience that is over when it's over. It is important to insist on this point. The intellectual conversion in the Spiritual Exercises calls for the acquisition of the following: first, a set of new religious concepts; second, a fresh appreciative awareness of the self; and third, a systematic way of thinking. Take these in turn.

1. **New religious concepts.** Ignatius charged traditional ideas with new definitions. For instance, he carried the traditional concept of "disordered affects" beyond morality and into metaphysics: disordered feelings and desires are not only a morally urgent reality; they skew our desiring at the sources of our being [21]. He took the scholastic notion of "indifference" beyond the idea of mere diffidence and made it stand for an eager, self-contained searching. *Consolation* and *desolation* may retain their ordinary reference to feelings, but in Ignatius's usage they come to include much more as alternate conditions of spiritual freedom and behavior. These are new concepts.

2. **A fresh appreciative awareness of the self.** Ignatius directs the exercitant to ask right at the start "that I might have a deep understanding of my sins from within, and feel revolted by them," to have an understanding of the disorder in sin itself, and to have an understanding of the disorder in his or her life-world [63]. The insistence here on *understanding* seems to presage current cognitive therapies that are based on the conviction that our ideas determine the shape of our behavior. Ignatius surely thought that they did, to a considerable extent. He also recognized how behavior

shapes desiring. This understanding feeds into his rarely understood principle of *agere contra:* when you want something in a way you feel is clearly excessive, you are free to beg for its opposite and for freedom [157]. But no one can beg to be free from an urgent, self-defining desire or conviction unless one has come to see the self as distinct from that desire or conviction. To practice this principle of *agere contra*, one needs to understand that one is not identified as or even with the desire or conviction, that one *is not* this concrete desire or conviction, but rather that one *has* the desire or conviction. Implied here is a mature level of appreciative self-awareness.[12]

3. **A systematic way of thinking.** Ignatius's deepest intellectual achievement—a fresh systematic way of thinking—lies in the discernment of the spirits, his way of interpreting spiritual experiences, which Hugo Rahner claims is his real genius. At some point, Ignatius knew, an exercitant will feel "a need to understand his other experiences of desolation and the wily maneuvers of the enemy, and of consolations as well" [8]. Once this feeling has been identified, the director gives "Norms Followed in Discerning Spirits" [313f]. These norms form an intellectual framework. They do indeed create an interpretation of experience; they also create a new horizon within which to experience, a concrete way for the individual to take responsibility for his or her own spiritual experience. "In all of the Spiritual Exercises included here," Ignatius wrote, "we set our minds in motion to comprehend." Ignatius helps us comprehend by describing patterns of desiring, giving a paradigm for growth in humility, and setting out standards for deciding [3, 136f, 181]. One way to reach decision, Ignatius suggests, is to think of the pros and cons on both sides of the option—a fairly sophisticated intellectual habit of thought [181].

These few indications might suggest how the Presupposition [22], cited at the beginning of this essay, has wide ramifications in the total experience of the Spiritual Exercises. It grounds a new relationship between director and spiritual disciple, a relationship that is open and risk filled. It grounds the Exercises' moral, religious, affective, and sociopolitical conversion, and in a singular way, its intellectual conversion. This intellectual conversion entails fresh concepts, fresh self-appreciation, and above all, the adoption of a strong intellectual system capable of supporting continued growth.

A Realistic and Usable Description of Conversion

Why bother to call this conversion? Here is my third point. Most of us feel about the word *conversion* the way Paul Tillich felt about the word *spirituality* thirty years ago: it is no longer usable. Tillich was only temporarily correct. The word *spirituality* is so useful a term that it has emphatically come back. If more adequately defined, *conversion* may also escape its temporary uselessness. At any rate, it is a necessary concept in the historical development detailed here.

Bernard Lonergan said, "By *conversion* is understood a transformation of the subject and his world."[13] It is a change of course and direction. It normally works out in a long process but may be concentrated into "a few momentous judgements and decisions." Lonergan summarized his description with an image: conversion is finding or accepting a new horizon within which to apprehend, judge, and act. Horizons, he wrote, "are the sweep of our interests and of our knowledge; they are the fertile source of further knowledge or care; but they are also the boundaries that limit our capacities for assimilating more than we already have attained."[14] Lonergan was interested more in objectifying conversion in its totality and less in its subjective process. In this discussion, we need to pay more attention to the *process,* since great conversions are constructed of many smaller conversions. We find new horizons continually throughout life, even in our most intimate relationships.

When I was nineteen, I spent two weeks in the swamps of Louisiana enjoying what was billed as a summer vacation for young Jesuits. While avoiding the withering sun, I listened for the first time to classical music: Schubert's *Unfinished,* Fauré's *Requiem,* Mozart's *Jupiter.* I had heard this music before, but I had never listened to it. The experience changed forever the way I hear music and the way I appreciate beauty. Even the swamps began to look beautiful, surely a shift in horizon.

In *Method in Theology,* Lonergan recognized three conversions: religious, intellectual, and moral. He later acknowledged a kind of affective conversion. He also pointed out that intellectual and moral conversions need not be religious but can be entirely secular. They may be religious—G. K. Chesterton's intellectual conversion led him into the Roman Church, and Dan Berrigan's moral stance of pacifism is utterly Christian—but neither need to be religious. This is crucial: a young man or woman can go through an intellectual conversion that is not motivated or affected by religious belief or conviction. In that intellectual conversion, he or she may decide to take responsibility for religious beliefs and practices, but that is a further conversion. Intellectual conversion is more likely to occur in institutions where both intellect and faith are held in honor.

Donald Gelpi's explorations of foundational theology—precisely the theology of conversion—help our understanding. In *Committed Worship,* he defines conversion as "the decision to pass from irresponsible to responsible behavior in some distinguishable realm of human experience."[15] He considers that human experience falls into five "distinguishable realms": religious, intellectual, moral, affective, and sociopolitical. When a person takes responsibility—say, for habits of thought about another race—and gives an account to himself or herself of where the thoughts come from and whether the images are valid, that person has gone through an intellectual conversion. Conversion, however, does not proceed merely within the person. Gelpi makes a strong case for the idea that conversion entails community in one way or another. We give an account to ourselves, but that account unavoidably entails giving an account to others. Ignatius's conversion was fueled by books—the dialogue of the learned community—but he was called on nearly a dozen times to give an account of himself to the community of the church. He felt driven to give others an account of what God had done in himself. That his conversion in its own dynamic functioned as a public act in the church makes it possible to understand his *Spiritual Exercises*. They did not and cannot thrive as dead text; they thrive only in a community of memory in which one generation passes, not the *book*, but the *experience* on to the next, individual by individual.

Conversion, then, can be religious, moral, intellectual, affective, or sociopolitical. Religious conversion requires faith; but intellectual, moral, affective, and sociopolitical conversion can be entirely secular. All of them go forward in community. Now, what have they to do with the community of Jesuit higher education? Or, more precisely, how are the Spiritual Exercises connected with Jesuit education?

Spiritual Exercises and Jesuit Education

Robert Schwickenrath figured in 1904 that the principal connection between the experience of the Spiritual Exercises and the experience of Jesuit higher education was the Jesuits, the men formed by Spiritual Exercises.[16] Francis P. Donnelly argued in 1934 that it was a set of behavioral principles that informs both the Exercises and Jesuit education: subordination of means to the end, repetitions of various types, and so on.[17] In 1954, George Ganss found fifteen principles flowing from the Spiritual Exercises through the Jesuit *Constitutions* into Jesuit education: self-activity, adaptation, reasoned outlook on life, and so on.[18] In 1963,

John Donohue figured that "some distinctive Jesuit outlook had quite likely shaped Jesuit schools" through the centuries, which he thought might include "a vital spirit" and "certain fundamental persuasions, attitudes, and commitments."[19]

However they describe the connection between the Exercises and education, every authority insists that Jesuit education has steadily balanced the two great forces of religion and learning—forces that were just beginning to separate as Jesuits became involved in education in 1548, but which in modernity have become inimical.[20] The Jesuits made a serious and characteristic effort to keep the two in a balanced relationship. The balance is made normative in the earliest drafts of the *Ratio Studiorum* on the grounds that *pietas* not fortified by learning is no good to self or neighbor.[21] Ganss, like other authorities who insist on what we used to call critical thinking, considers "the focus of integration for all the other elements in [the Jesuit] system" the fundamental demand that the student think his way through "to his own personal conviction."[22]

There is a public issue here, too. The earliest Jesuits subscribed to the optimistic Renaissance belief in "the power of education to form and reform the *mores* of individuals and entire societies,"[23] a socially conservative attitude toward education that underlies current American critiques of education. As John O'Malley has shown, the Jesuits moved into education convinced "like their contemporaries ... that humanistic studies formed upright character, *pietas*."[24] Now, when the Jesuits brought their *Ratio* to the United States in the eighteenth century, they found an already established collegiate culture. That culture, too, was based on *pietas*. It was church related, extensive (as many as 100 of the first 120 colleges founded in the colonies were church related), and confessional. Harvard's original motto was *Veritas Christo et Ecclesiae;* King's College (renamed Columbia in 1784) announced as its chief aim "to teach and engage [the young] to *know God* in *Jesus Christ.*"[25] The early American *pietas* was promoted for the sake of a learned clergy and laity, but it is interesting to note in passing that it was related to a characteristic balance in the new nation's education. The balance appeared in the federal government's Northwest

Ordinance of 1787, which declared that "religion, morality, and knowledge being necessary to good government and the happiness of mankind, schools and the means of education shall forever be encouraged."[26]

Georgetown, the first American Jesuit college, adapted to that established collegiate culture.[27] Led by that culture as well as by the experience of the Spiritual Exercises, the Jesuit colleges promoted *pietas*. But Jesuits also found the culture's insistence on intellectual vigor particularly amenable (it is crucial to remember that the first Jesuits had been university men who cherished academic excellence). Jesuits have never stopped. The present General, Peter-Hans Kolvenbach, said in 1985, "Ignatius knew perfectly well that a college is a college and a university is a university. They have their own purposes and are not opportunities that are favorable to evangelization or the defense of the faith."[28] From the first expression in the Presupposition on defending your neighbor's propositions [22], the genius in Jesuit education had been to respect the independence of human reason. Jerome Nadal, probably the greatest of the early Jesuit apologists, promoted all over Europe the conviction that Jesuits aimed at cooperating with and serving—not dominating—both God and nature. They wanted to do this "in Christ."

In America, this did not mean in the first instance teaching religion or theology. It is altogether instructive that Georgetown added a seventh year to the European *Ratio*'s six-year program. For what? So that students could study *philosophy*. For the first century and a half of their institutions' existence, Jesuits taught their students more philosophy than religion. They did not start teaching theology seriously until well into the twentieth century, by which time theology had become important to intellectual conversion. American Jesuits themselves were challenged in their conservative ultramontanism by the combined emergence of fresh anti-Catholicism and the movement that became Fundamentalism. How could they hold on to Catholic doctrine without falling into a slough of fundamentalism? How could they stand by the pope while standing by the American flag? Intellectually, the Jesuits who taught in seminary, college, and university had to distinguish their convictions and creedal statements from their selves. They had to see this as the case: Not that they were Ultramontanists, but that they *held Ultramontanist convictions and ideas.*

This is the shift that Robert Kegan describes as "the fourth order of consciousness."[29] Recognizing concomitant issues in morality, affectivity, aesthetics, and religious experience, the shift should nonetheless be thought of primarily as an intellectual conversion.

Intellectual conversion can be summarized as a triple turning:

- First, it is a turning away—from mindless conviction and prejudice, blameworthy ignorance, and resolute certitude about unreflected-upon ideas. It must include rejecting thoughtless conformity with parents' conservative or liberal ideas, say, of feminism; criticizing socially acceptable ambitions, say, of accumulating wealth; and repudiating merely politically correct ideas, say, of the corruption of political campaigning. In short, explanations that end with "That's just the way things are."

- Second, intellectual conversion means turning to. This means taking responsibility first of all for the ideas and convictions that drive life. One can decide that one will no longer think absurd the arguments against capital punishment and begin to hold the idea that capital punishment is mistaken or immoral. The conversion finally matures into a practiced judgment about evidences—the habitual judgment whether data, or a statement, or a decision is certain or probable, fixed or fluid.

- Finally, a third turning. In a complete intellectual conversion, people reach awareness of working with a system, and perhaps of adopting a recognizable system or method in intellectual work. For decades, Jesuits in higher education did what they could to invite their students to adopt the natural-law system of neo-scholasticism. Many of their most characteristic graduates have continued to think (and write) in that system, and some of them blame Jesuits for abandoning it or watering it down.

Obviously, ideas are not about nothing, and intellectual conversion touches on the other realms of human experience—religious, moral, affective, and sociopolitical. A conversion in any realm is likely to affect all the other realms of human experience. For people—not parts of people—turn away from the experience of certain attitudes, paradigms, and behaviors to a new horizon of thought and to deeper responsibility for themselves. From the beginning, this holistic approach to conversion was embraced by the American church-related colleges. Typically, though with varying emphases, the institutions have hoped for the complete conversion of their students.

For some recent decades until the nineties, Catholic and other church-related institutions have hesitated to proclaim or even admit this agenda. For several reasons, this has been understandable. Religion has earned or has been given a bad name. Increasingly during the past century, coverage by the press and other media has been resoundingly negative in both context and in tone. It still is. Science, able to live oblivious to its own lapses and absurdities, cannot bring itself to see that religious thought has evolved. And professionalization (undeniably fruitful) has required the separation of philosophy from ethics and science from religion.

Above all, "conversion" has been transmuted into something that happens to the grotesques in Flannery O'Connor's story "A Good Man Is Hard to Find." Conversion is associated typically with Jim Jones's Jonestown and with the Branch Davidians of Waco, Texas.

Until we can talk about conversion again, we might refer to our purpose in the Jesuit university as "foundational humanism." "Humanism" because we invite and intend the holistic maturation and fulfillment of each person—religious, intellectual, moral, affective, and sociopolitical—not in conformity to a preset pattern, which is not our tradition of spiritual direction and is contra-indicated by paragraph 22, but in conformity with each person's authentic history. "Foundational" because students must take responsibility for themselves in each of these realms; they must account for their ideas, convictions, and behaviors; and they must discover a "systematic method for [continually] amending and [always] reforming the lives that they lead in their particular state" [189].

Some Crucial Questions

All of this hardly leaves my thesis on Jesuit higher education and intellectual conversion cooly incontrovertible. Let me, perhaps recklessly, heave fuel on the fire by naming some of the consequences of accepting it.

Thesis: The role of the administration and staff is to shape the university's culture so as to invite each student to intellectual openness. In Catholic colleges and universities, this role includes maintaining what must be called a "Christian context of inviting openness." We will as a matter of course be glad to have people come to Jesus Christ.[30] However, we will seriously try to find the truth in every religious and secular proposition, not in the one who proposes it [22]. Our official stance is that the proposer has already been saved by Someone Else.

Thesis: The non-Catholic, the agnostic, and the atheist among us have an integral role to play in this intellectual conversion. They need to contribute, from their own grounds, not only to students' sociopolitical, affective, religious, and moral conversions but also to students' intellectual conversion. All Catholic universities stand for the conviction that there are purely rational grounds for the common good, grounds that must be explored and consciously affirmed by those who are given the gift of higher learning. In any sound analysis, it can be seen that religious conversion at the university level—far removed from the ravages of fundamentalism or the escapism of privatized religion—requires a plurality of authorities. For sharpened intellects, a truly universal church cannot have the bland taste of vanilla tapioca pudding.

Thesis: The function of the core curriculum is less to introduce students to areas of study to which they have already been introduced than to give them a preliminary experience of the systems of thought and of the methods of research and conclusion in each of the areas of study. How do we get ideas in this and that area? How do we order and validate them? How do we respond to these experiences with system? The function of the major in Catholic universities is not merely preparation for a profession, but rather the more serious intellectual pursuit of thoroughly adopting the procedures of one area of learning to the point of developing a maturing sense of system and of system's limits.

Thesis: Intellectual conversion does not entail selling ideas—that is proselytizing. Intellectual conversion does, however, entail giving explanations—faculty members do not just describe, they explain. They point not only to the significance of things but to their meaning as well. Description alone might possibly approach value-neutrality, though Heisenberg's uncertainty principle makes that doubtful even in science, where description is supposed to be totally objective.

Those who explain things and give a meaning to them need to be quite conscious that their explanations necessarily entail some normativity. All real explanation explores and exposes the tendencies and laws in things—in a word, the norms in them. In any university, perhaps, explanations are given—that is expected at the level of doctoral work. In a Jesuit university, tradition requires that explanations be given all the way to the reasons why they are held and expounded, and even to the reasons why they are less suasive. This is giving the pros and cons on both sides [181], which is not a jest but a serious means of examining one's deeper motivations. Giving pros and cons on both sides of an issue is an intellectually demanding exercise. No one can be free enough to do this without having gone through the intellectual conversion of recognizing that "our predispositions and longings may be as misguided as our ideas."[31] This conversion means being open about one's explanations—open both as a source and as a receiver. Open to tell and to listen.

Back to that radical paragraph 22. By being faithful to the Jesuit tradition, every good faculty member and administrator in a Jesuit institution is more ready to find a correct meaning in a peer's statement than to reject it as erroneous. We correctly ask this even of students. In a Jesuit institution, political correctness does not suffice in any matter. In a Jesuit institution that is living up to the tradition in good measure, explanation will go all the way to the famous concluding remark in medieval academic debates: *Et sic stat thesis, salvo meliore judicio.* The thesis in question has been established, unless there should be a better judgment about it. Josiah Royce called this "contrite fallibilism" and considered it a crucial condition of community. It is surely the condition of any functioning community of intellectuals. It is certainly one of the conditions that must be met if a university is to be genuinely Jesuit.

So say I, contritely, *salvo meliore judicio.*

Endnotes

1. John W. Padberg, et al., *Project 1: The Jesuit Apostolate of Education in the United States* (Washington, D.C.: The Jesuit Conference, 1974). The research team early on rejected as a "mistaken impression" that manpower and money posed the main problems to Jesuit institutions. They were "convinced that the major problems facing American Jesuits" involved vision, goals, and the structures that would support them. See no. 2, "Introduction," v.

2. Merrimon Cuninggim, "Essentials of Church-Relatedness," in *Church Related Higher Education,* ed. Robert Rue Parsonage (Valley Forge, Pa.: Judson Press, 1978), 84.

3. As the Second Vatican Council finished its work in 1965, the Jesuits' highest governing body decreed that "the Society should have its own educational institutions where resources and circumstances permit" for the sake of "synthesizing faith and culture." *General Congregation Thirty-One,* ed. John W. Padberg, S.J. (St. Louis, Mo.: Institute of Jesuit Sources, 1977), decree 28, no 5.

4. Albert Borgmann, *Crossing the Postmodern Divide* (Chicago: University of Chicago Press, 1992), 65.

5. Ignatius of Loyola, *Spiritual Exercises,* trans. with commentary Joseph A. Tetlow, S.J. (New York: Crossroad, 1992). Hereafter, references to *Exercises* are made within the text by bracketed paragraph numbers.

6. Commentators who remark on the historical context attend exculsively to the Inquisition. See Herve Coathalem, *Ignatian Insights: A Guide to the Complete Spiritual Exercises,* trans. Charles J. McCarthy, S.J. (Taichung [Taiwan]: Kuangchi Press, 1971). Most simply insist on the Presupposition's relevance today. See Santiago Arzubialde, S.J., *Ejercicios Espirituales de S. Ignacio: Historia y Análisis* (Bilbao-Sanatander: Sal Terrae, 1991).

7. *The Jesuit Ratio Studiorum of 1599,* trans., intro., and notes, Allan P. Farrell, S.J. (Washington, D.C.: Conference of Major Superiors of Jesuits, 1970). Farrell had written the most complete study of the development of Jesuit education, *The Jesuit Code of Liberal Education* (Milwaukee, Wis.: Bruce, 1938).

8. John W. Donahue, S.J., *Jesuit Education: An Essay on the Foundations of Its Idea* (New York: Fordham University Press, 1963), 20–21, 165ff. George E. Ganss, S.J., *Saint Ignatius' Idea of a Jesuit University* (Milwaukee, Wis.: Marquette University Press, 1954), 19:194–207.

9. The most recent summary statement of the first Jesuit rationale in education begins with the experience of colleagues in Jesuit institutions. *Go Forth and Teach: The Characteristics of Jesuit Education,* Final Report of the International Commission on the Apostolate of Jesuit Education (Washington, D.C.: Jesuit Secondary Education Association, 1987).

10. No change here. In 1995, General Congregation Thirty-four agreed on this point: "A Jesuit university must be outstanding in its human, social, spiritual, and moral formation, as well as in its pastoral attention to its students and to the different groups of people who work in it or are related to it." *Decrees of General Congregation 34* (Rome: Curia of the Superior General, 1995), decree 17, no. 11.

11. Gilles Cusson, S.J., *Pedagogie de l'experience spirituelle personelle Bible et Exercises Spirituels,* 3rd ed. (Montreal: Les Editions Bellarmin, 1986). English translation by Mary Roduit, R.C., and George Ganss, S.J., *Biblical Theology and Spiritual Exercises* (St. Louis, Mo.: Institute of Jesuit Sources, 1988).

12. See Robert Kegan, *In Over Our Heads: The Mental Demands of Modern Life* (Cambridge, Mass.: Harvard University Press, 1994), particularly chap. 8.

13. Bernard J. F. Lonergan, *Method in Theology* (New York: Herder and Herder, 1972), 130.

14. Ibid., 347.

15. Donald L. Gelpi, S.J., *Adult Conversion and Initiation,* vol.1 of *Committed Worship: A Sacramental Theology for Converting Christians* (Collegeville, Minn.: Michael Glazier, 1993), 17.

16. Robert Schwickenrath, S.J., *Jesuit Education: Its History and Principles Viewed in the Light of Modern Educational Problems* (St. Louis, Mo.: B. Herder, 1904), 92.

17. Francis P. Donnelly, S.J., *Principles of Jesuit Education in Practice* (New York: P. J. Kennedy and Sons, 1934), 46.

18. Ganss, *Ignatius' Idea,* 185.

19. Donohue, *Jesuit Education,* xvi.

20. Richard Tarnas, *The Passion of the Western Mind* (New York: Ballantine Books, 1991), 298–324.

21. See Farrell, *Jesuit Code,* chap. 10.

22. Ganss, *Ignatius' Idea,* 186. Most recently, historian David O'Brien argued that Catholic education "aims at graduating persons who have

made their religious and moral commitments intelligible." David J. O'Brien, "Jesuit Si, Catholic . . . Not So Sure," *Conversations* 6 (fall 1994): 4–12, 9.

23. John W. O'Malley, *The First Jesuits* (Cambridge, Mass.: Harvard University Press, 1993), 210.

24. Ibid., 212.

25. Joseph A. Tetlow, S.J., "The Jesuits' Mission in Higher Education: Perspectives and Contexts," *Studies in the Spirituality of Jesuits*, vol. 15, no. 5 (November 1983), 9.

26. Interestingly, this citation appears even in the coffee-table book, *Chronicle of America*, ed. John W. Kirshon (New York: Prentice Hall, 1991), 191.

27. American colleges became universities and comprehensive colleges roughly a century after Georgetown's founding. At least according to their prospectuses, however, most *colleges* remain dedicated to the holistic education of the student. I speak here about that collegiate education, aware that there are differences among four-year institutions, liberal arts colleges in comprehensive colleges, and in true universities.

28. Peter-Hans Kolvenbach, "The Jesuit University Today," address to the Presidents and Rectors of Jesuit Institutions of Higher Education, Frascati, Italy (5 November 1985), 14. Privately circulated.

29. Kegan, *In Over Our Heads*, 91–96.

30. The official statement of the Society's aims in this remains one made by General Congregation Thirty-one in November of 1966. The Society "aims to provide non-Christians with a humanistic formation directed towards the welfare of their own nation and, at the same time, to conduct them by degrees to the knowledge and love of God or at least to the acceptance of moral, and even religious values" (decree 28, no. 7).

31. Roberto Mangabeira Unger, *Passion: An Essay on Personality* (New York: The Free Press, 1984), 102.

Soul Education:
An Ignatian Priority

Howard J. Gray, S.J.

INTRODUCTION

ROWAN WILLIAMS, IN HIS STUDY OF TERESA OF ÁVILA, suggests that mysticism is perhaps less a state of prayer than a worldview, a way of interpreting life rather than an ecstatic removal into a higher life.[1] He is not denying that mysticism is an event, but he is calling attention to another way of looking at union with God. Recently, there has been a recovery of Ignatian spirituality as a hermeneutic, a way of interpreting life, rather than an inspiration for work, or a spur to dedication, or a discerning way to critique life.[2] I want to approach the topic of Ignatian spirituality and its relationship to higher education, a topic that John Padberg has spent his life exploring and communicating, by adapting Williams's worldview approach and aligning myself with those who see this spirituality as an interpretative prism. Therefore, I begin with the familiar expression of purpose that introduces the Ignatian *Constitutions* of the Society of Jesus:

> The end of this Society is to devote itself with God's grace to the salvation and perfection of the members' own souls, but also with great diligence to labor strenuously in giving aid toward the salvation and perfection of the souls of their fellow men [and women].[3]

In his translation of the *Constitutions,* the late George Ganss, a man to whom the contemporary Society of Jesus owes a deep debt of gratitude, notes that *animas* in Ignatius's Spanish means "the person," first the men of the Society and their entire selves, and then the persons they serve—men and women in their total reality.[4] Ganss insists that this understanding of Ignatian vocabulary corrects the misunderstanding of those who read Ignatius as having "an exaggerated dualism or even Neoplatonism in his thought."[5]

Years ago when I first read Ganss's note, I found it a liberating insight. In time this fairly modest reflection opened up a way of viewing Ignatian spirituality and its enterprise that explained its reverence for the human. Simply put, the Ignatian instinct is to help people become fully alive. I would like to continue to explore this "soul education," this way of reading spirituality as exploring how people can become as fully present to their humanity as possible. In this view God is the ground and the goal of human life. This reflection has three parts: (1) Ignatian education is about appropriation, (2) Ignatian education is about the social ramifications of learning, and (3) Ignatian education reconciles a plurality of experiences within a Catholic commitment.

Ignatian Education and Appropriation

As a ten-part program detailing Jesuit formation, communal life, and work, the Jesuit *Constitutions* represent the last great work of Ignatius. Composition of the *Constitutions* engaged his energies from 1547 to his death in 1556. Consequently, this in-house document offers an important commentary on Ignatian spirituality in dialogue with its culture—ecclesiastical and secular. But to illustrate how to enter into this world, I want to use a reflection by a non-Jesuit, the novelist Larry Woiwode. In his memoir, *What I Think I Did,* Woiwode recalls how when he was twelve he loved to walk around his town, "outside my habitation—in the gap of a railroad line along a dirt track that led through pastures or rows of clattering corn to a woods . . . halfway between my parents and the lake."[6] Woiwode recounts that on these walks,

> The chill of presence slithered over me as if I were shedding leaves myself and I looked up. It was the presence of God, I thought, as I watched the trees sway as if ascending the sky. . . . One presence was here, I knew, as I turned with my face raised, in the trees and sky, and in the earth that held me as I turned. The presence has put all this in place to instruct me about myself and the complications of the love I felt for Him. I had been told to love Him but the words of the language I knew couldn't reproduce the language pouring from everything here with a familiarity I couldn't define. I was given a glimpse of it when I read, "The heavens declare the glory of God. . . . Day unto day utters speech . . . no speech or language where their voice is not heard . . . since the creation of the world His invisible attributes are clearly seen. . . . All things were created through Him and for Him . . . and in Him all things consist."[7]

Woiwode's youthful encounter stayed with him because it represented his appropriation of all he had been taught by his parents, pastors, nuns, and nature. This is what I mean by soul education: the personal appropriation of teaching, experience, and insight that mark what one business ethician calls "a defining moment" of one's life.[8]

It has gradually dawned on me that the reading of Ignatian texts as a way to enter into a tradition has severe limitations. The reason lies, I believe, in the hermeneutic used to explore and to explicate the text. If the Ignatian tradition is only an object of inquiry, it resists what it is supposed to do. Let me use an example to illustrate this point.

In the summer of 1997 a remarkable group of scholars assembled at Boston College to focus their expertise and energies on the topic "The Jesuits: Cultures, Sciences, and the Arts, 1540–1773." At the closing session of this conference Michael Buckley and Luce Giard offered an important addendum to the proceedings.[9]

While the scholars had illumined *what* the early Jesuits had accomplished, they had avoided or neglected the question of *why* Jesuits had engaged their cultures of Europe, Asia, Latin America, and Africa. Jesuits' presence in mathematics, science, music, and art of their day presumed an inspiring presence that initiated their search and sustained its progress. Like Larry Woiwode the early Jesuits lived not only out of an intellectual curiosity to know or an artistic drive to create but out of a religious pilgrimage toward meeting the God in whom all things consist.[10]

Consequently, the goal of Ignatian tutelage, as it had been codified in the texts of the *Exercises* and the *Constitutions,* is not information but appropriation, an integration into the very activity of God within created reality. This goal has important ramifications for how one approaches the reading of Ignatian texts.

First, the textual tradition (i.e., the way most people in higher education enter into the Ignatian tradition) is and must be open to literary, historical, and theological analysis and critique: What do these words mean in terms of their cultural matrix? This critical reading will not yield the meaning of the text but only a *reading* of the text, a way of controlling the data and integrating this data into an intellectual mind-set antecedent to the reading. For example, in part 7 of the *Constitutions,* there is a section that attempts to describe the internal dynamic that, ultimately, operates within the Jesuit community to sustain its union even as its membership is dispersed throughout the world in various ministries.

The chief bond that cements the union of the members among themselves and with their heads is on both sides—the love of God our Lord. For when the superior and the subjects are closely united to His Divine and Supreme Goodness, they will very easily be united among themselves "through that same love which will descend from the Divine Goodness and spread to all other people" and particularly to the body of the Society.[11]

What this important section from the *Constitutions* asserts is that in proportion as Jesuits link themselves to God so will they be united to one another and to their General Superior. This union with God, in turn, generates love in the people for whom they work as well as for the members of the Jesuit community.

This text can be parsed, analyzed, and read within the context of a wider and older religious tradition that acknowledges the power of conviction and the socialization of an ideal. But that reading stays outside the experience of that union. When teaching this text to a group of Jesuits, for example, my presumption is not only that they will understand its terms but that they will want to incorporate its meaning into how they live and work. Their Jesuit hermeneutic, then, is not understanding but appropriation.

When we desire more participation in the distinguishing characteristics of Jesuit education, we must ask ourselves if we can really achieve this appropriation of a textual tradition. Do we have a right to ask this?

This is not an insignificant query. Can you invite non-Jesuits, non-Christians, nonbelievers into a tradition that asks for appropriation, a reading of the textual tradition that presumes you want to enter into its experience? Can non-Jesuits understand truly the Ignatian purchase on how community works as a gift from God: to be united "through that same love which will descend from the Divine Goodness and spread to all other people"?[12]

I would say yes for three reasons. First, the Ignatian tradition presumes that prior to any person's assimilation into the tradition, God has been active in that man's or woman's life.[13] Second, the activity of God is within the specifics of a man's or woman's personal history, temperament, talents, graces.[14] Third, God works in all toward good, not evil; toward consolation, not desolation; toward building up justice, faith, hope, confidence, human freedom, and productivity.[15]

How, then, practically speaking, can people outside the tradition participate in that tradition? In the *Constitutions* there is an Ignatian strategy designed to help novices in the Order assimilate a process by which they can find how God dwells in their lives and works. What is remarkable is that this process, as a process, does not demand that one be a Catholic, much less a Jesuit. It is soul education, a process that invites novices—people learning how to be Jesuits—to trust their experience as a source of revelation and direction. The process does call for a certain psychological focus that includes self-composure and openness.[16] It suggests three activities: be attentive to the reality about you, reverence what you encounter, and appreciate how this kind of presence leads to revelation, what Ignatius calls *devotion* and what Woiwode has described as "the presence of God."

Whether one is a teacher or a counselor, an administrator or a plant manager, this ability to focus so that "the other" is truly present to him or her, and then to reverence the reality that one has discovered, leads to another discovery, that of a presence, a reality that invites appropriation. Such appropriation represents an acceptance that can, finally, only be called love. The point is that whether the professional work is coaching, research, or academic planning, what the Ignatian tradition offers is not a time-consuming addition to an already heavy workload. Rather it is a way of proceeding within one's profession, a style of professional alertness and dedication. It is a process that enables a person to become "a soul," someone trying to live in mutuality with or openness to all other realities.

One can verify the presence of this activity by the threefold criteria I outlined earlier. First, what I have appropriated comes from who I am and the way God has worked within me. Second, what I have appropriated is in harmony with my personal history, psychological makeup, or grace. Third, what I have appropriated leads toward something good for me, for my work, for the community.

The Ignatian tradition does not indoctrinate nor does it enforce; it invites a willingness to appropriate reality into a person's life. It is an education of soul, of becoming more humanely alert and responsive to the world about you. What you accept accepts you too.

Ignatian Education and the Social Ramifications of Learning

While the recent emphasis of the Jesuit Superior General, Peter-Hans Kolvenbach, has been on the role of higher education in forming a social consciousness, this emphasis is not new.[17] From its inception the Society of Jesus has focused on "the care of those souls for whom either there is nobody to care or, if somebody ought to care, the care is negligent. This is the reason for the founding of the Society. This is its strength. This is its dignity in the Church."[18] This dictum was coined by one of the giants among the early Jesuits, Jerome Nadal, and developed from Ignatius's mystic experiences at Manresa, the small town where for almost a year he underwent an intense self-scrutiny and graced reorientation of his life. At Manresa, Ignatius composed most of the text of *The Spiritual Exercises* and there moved away from a life of solitude toward a life of pastoral service. His expression of this shift was direct and simple: he had been called by God "to help people."

In *The First Jesuits*, John O'Malley provides an overview of how many of these pastoral works—albeit inspired by a fundamental mission to preach and to teach the Word of God—included prominently the implementation of the Word of God, particularly in the care of the poor, the unlettered, those in prison and hospitals, and prostitutes.[19] The contemporary Jesuit emphasis on social justice as a constitutive element in the life of faith is, therefore, not an innovation. This emphasis on social justice and solidarity is in continuity with the foundation and original mission of the Society of Jesus. More important, this commitment is an expression of its apostolic integrity. By *apostolic integrity* I mean that the work of contemporary Jesuits finds its deepest religious instincts in the prophetic teaching of Jesus about the dignity of the poor, the widow, the orphan—the social and religious outcasts of his day. To preach and to teach the gospel of Christ, to translate its significance to our postmodern world, to confront some of the economic and social fallout from globalization—this has to be part of the professional awareness within every Jesuit work, but especially in higher education.

Father Kolvenbach's Santa Clara presentation sparked enthusiasm and, for many of us, suggested a most fruitful area for renewed cooperation within our institutions. But what I want to focus on is that this call to social action touches the soul (i.e., the animation of men and women) in the work of higher education.

My experience is that the significant core of faculty and staff who are proactive in developing the Ignatian tradition within their institutions can also hear this call to social justice and solidarity with some frustration. Their scholarship and research, their teaching and departmental responsibilities, their counseling and advising absorb time and energy. Their own family commitments demand—also in the name of justice and solidarity—energies and attention that leave scant time or energy to undertake works that directly help the poor, comfort the marginalized, and confront the oppressors. Consequently, guilt and fatigue rather than dedication and inspiration become the dominant reactions to the summons to social justice and solidarity. I do not think that it is Ignatian to make good people feel guilty about what they cannot do. This concern has led me to reconsider how to integrate social justice into the life of the university.

First, the service programs that our students undertake, the efforts to integrate academic courses with field experiences involving social justice (e.g., Boston College's Pulse Program), and the volunteer work that students, staff, and faculty support—these are genuinely both education and social justice. Second, we influence social action among our students by offering them the opportunity to devote a year or more to postgraduate service in a program like the Jesuit Volunteer Corps (JVC) or in a Nativity-type inner-city school. Third, the teaching and scholarship that explore the ramifications of economic justice or the common good or the dignity of the human person are indispensable to the unique contribution that a university as a university makes toward the mission of social justice. Fourth, the ethical environment of a university community—the way we hire, promote, and pay; the way we deal with one another; the civility and care that we extend to our colleagues—is either an ethos of justice or one of neglect or even injustice. This litany of activities demonstrates the social-justice commitment of our universities. This commitment should give us all a deep sense of consolation. But what I want to suggest is that within the mainstream tasks of teaching and research, counseling and advising, there runs a current of spiritual energy—grace, if you will, or manifestations of soul—that we also need to acknowledge, cherish, and develop. The risk is that in looking for "the more" beyond us, we lose "the more" that lies deeply within what we already do.

In the introduction to that part of the Jesuit *Constitutions* that deals directly with education, Ignatius proposes three constitutive elements in the formation of an effective Jesuit: he must have solid learning, be able to communicate what he has learned, and live and work in such a way that he gives "good example."[20] These same three characteristics should also inform the kind of education that Jesuits offer.

In the first part of this essay I emphasized the mutuality of Ignatian spirituality. Whatever one gives, one also receives, or better, it is impossible to donate without becoming a beneficiary. In guiding someone through the Spiritual Exercises, in preaching or counseling or teaching, you discover what God wishes you to learn as well. The unspoken reality is relationship, and its recurring symbol is conversation, the dialogue that creates a climate of mutual donation.[21]

In our work in the classroom, in student services, in research, we are all laboring for sound learning, to make truth, wisdom, and competency come to life. The culture of a university is learning. In the Ignatian tradition this process is sacred. For in the act of learning mathematics, Shakespeare, economics, or chemistry, something about the way God works within knowledge touches the soul and enlivens our humanity. And in the act of communicating our knowledge, skills, or care, in our conversation and generosity, God reveals. And in the integrity to our various professions, we present ourselves as stewards of God's continuing care of the world.

As educators we need to exercise that attention, reverence, and devotion to ourselves. We need some moments to possess what we profess, to cherish its meaning for us, to recognize something greater than ourselves that makes learning happen.

In a university culture there are many traditions that form our common consciousness. But in the process of being true to sound learning, in the asceticism of effective communication, and in the integrity of professing our commitment to the young generations before us, we witness that a university, finally, carries its own justice within its own soul and creates its own solidarity.

Ignatian Education Reconciles a Plurality of Experiences within a Catholic Commitment

The papal document *Ex Corde Ecclesiae* and its application in the United States have occasioned a number of reflections. My intention is not to summarize these reactions but to present my own take on the focus these documents have invited. First, the decree and its application in the United States present a genuine issue. How does a university that claims a faith tradition as an essential component in its mission implement that faith component? Moreover, how does the university fulfill this mission in a secular and pluralistic academic and cultural climate? Finally, how does a university implement this mission with a concomitant fidelity to academic freedom and to ethical and professional priority within U.S. higher education? I am not arguing about *how* the church documents answer these concerns; I am saying that there is an issue of identity and integrity for universities that claim a Catholic tradition. Second, any implementation of the Catholic character of a university steers a prudent course between enforcement and neglect. Third, and to my mind most important, how does one read and communicate the term *Catholic?*

Similarly, there are issues surrounding the pluralism that characterizes higher education in the United States. First, pluralism cannot be reduced to a bland tolerance that stands for no real personal or professional convictions. Neither can pluralism mask a clever delaying tactic, such as waiting for the right political moment to suppress all opposition. Pluralism has to be an ethical relationship, some mutual commitment to the good that can be obtained precisely because there are different opinions. I do not claim that I can satisfactorily treat these issues here, but I think that they must be on the agenda of every university community. The Ignatian purchase of being "Catholic" is complex. On the one hand, for Ignatius Catholicism was the way to God. He could only have been a Roman Catholic; that was his birth identity, his culture, his context for contemplative reflection and for energetic action.[22] But what is remarkable is that he placed in the forefront of this faith the experience of God, unique to each individual, and yet a source of union among people.

In *The Spiritual Exercises* Ignatius repeatedly underscores both the individual's right to find God in his or her own way and the duty of the one who guides this experience to maintain a respectful distance to avoid interfering in this personal encounter with God.[23] For Ignatius every individual has the right to his or her soul and to discover God for her- or himself. The church was a privileged guide in this journey of finding God, but Ignatian spirituality is not "churchy."[24] For Ignatius God could be found in all things, but only if one first found "all things." This is my reason for insisting on that part of the Jesuit *Constitutions* that presents attention and reverence as prior to devotion, i.e., the integrity of being present to the creature is the only way to honor the Creator. This Ignatian regard for individual experience has at times been misrepresented as isolation from the social. It is far from this distortion. The Ignatian regard for individual religious experience originates from an esteem for human freedom and liberality.[25] Freedom for Ignatius is the power to donate, not simply to act. And liberality is the ability to act generously for something greater than oneself. For Ignatius, one discovers one's soul only when one freely donates one's life to something greater than oneself. Ignatius called this *an election,* a choice to be a particular kind of self, to orient one's life with an abiding commitment to do something good and enduring.

Note how inherent in this Ignatian process is the assumption that there are many ways to God. Experience emerges out of individual histories; is contextualized by one's talents, culture, and graces; and is communicated by a personal set of symbols and rhetoric. It is for all these reasons that Ignatius insists on the principle of adaptation within the Spiritual Exercises, i.e., fitting the movements, presentations, and strategies of this program to people.[26] In brief, Ignatius believed that people should be helped to encounter, not to perform.

This is the point where the Ignatian tradition and religious pluralism become tricky. Ignatius does not give us an adequate model for the kind of ecumenism and plurality we honor in today's university community. But Ignatian spirituality provides the tools to assemble a model that reflects our theological and academic values. And the principle that allows us to reassemble these Ignatian tools to construct this model is that of adaptation, fitting general principles or communal strategies to individual reality.[27]

My view is that Catholicism can been seen in two ways, much as law can be understood in two ways. *Law,* as *lex,* can mean the codes that govern conduct within a society.[28] But *law* can also mean *jus,* human rights, the fundamental human desires for a home, for personal security, for food and education, for human dignity. So, too, to be a Catholic can mean living within those social codes that define the publicly believing body: codes of formal belief, such as the divinity of Christ; codes of conduct, such as prohibitions against the taking of innocent life; and codes of worship, such as the rituals that guarantee legitimate Catholic celebration of the Eucharist. Living within these social codes is an important way to be an authentic Catholic. In his "Rules for Having the Right Attitude toward the Church," Ignatius promotes this understanding of being a Catholic. However, the main thrust of *The Spiritual Exercises* and even the *Constitutions* is to facilitate the context for the discovery of God. For Ignatius, to be a Catholic is to find how the human and the divine come together. The figure of Jesus is central to his prayer not only as the privileged object of devotion but also as the exemplar of action. It is this sense of Catholic tradition that most resonates with the pluralism of the university. The Ignatian tradition invites people to find their way to being the divine and the human together.

Let me be very clear here. To be Catholic is to live an authentic union with the institutional church. But to be a Catholic is also to live an authentic union with God, the only final Absolute. Ignatius made that distinction and so must we. The end of belief, of ethical conduct, and of worship—of keeping the law—is to find the love that guides all law.

To dedicate oneself to an educational process like Ignatian/Jesuit higher education is to take risks. Martin Marty, a major contemporary academic figure, puts it this way:

> Those who favor one or another expression of religion have to take their risks with its exposure on the academic front. But they will have seen those who advocate study of it and who study it well to be servants of a public scene in which educators and educated alike will deal more fairly with the reality around them than they did when too readily the academy reduced our society to the conception of being a secular one. Humans as individuals and in society are too full of passions, of intelligence, of mystery to be properly characterized as members of such a reduced society.[29]

Jesuit higher education, which has been so much a part of John Padberg's Jesuit career, possesses a proud and fruitful tradition of religious seriousness and academic pluralism. *And* is the operative word here. Ignatius loved doublets: "both . . . and" or "yes . . . but." Living like this is risky business, but that is what every great university community strives to become—a community where risk is a way of life.[30]

Endnotes

1. Rowan Williams, *Teresa of Ávila* (London: Continuum, 2000), 143–73.

2. This is significant in the work of John W. O'Malley, S.J. in *The First Jesuits* (Cambridge, Mass.: Harvard University Press, 1993) and in "The Historiography of the Society of Jesus: Where Does It Stand Today?" in *The Jesuits: Cultures, Sciences, and the Arts 1540–1773*, ed. O'Malley, et al. (Toronto: University of Toronto Press, 1999), especially 27–29.

3. *The Constitutions of the Society of Jesus*, trans. and introd. George E. Ganss, S.J. (St. Louis, Mo.: The Institute of Jesuit Sources, 1984), [3].

4. *Constitutions*, [10], 77–78.

5. *Constitutions*, [10].

6. Larry Woiwode, *What I Think I Did* (New York: Basic Books, 2000), 133.

7. Ibid., 135.

8. Joseph L. Badaracco Jr., "The Discipline of Building Character," in *Harvard Business Review on Leadership* (Boston: Harvard Business School Press, 1998), 89–113.

9. "Reflections," in O'Malley, *The Jesuits: Cultures, Sciences, and the Arts*, 707–12, 713–16.

10. Howard J. Gray, S.J., "What Kind of Document," in *The Way Supplement* 61 (spring 1988), 24–25.

11. *Constitutions*, [671].

12. Ibid.

13. I take this both from the first twenty annotations from *The Spiritual Exercises*, trans. George E. Ganss, S.J. (St. Louis, Mo.: The Institute of Jesuit Sources, 1992) and [22] from the General Examen in the *Constitutions*.

14. *Exercises*, #18.

15. *Exercises*, #332, 335.

16. *Constitutions*, [250].

17. Peter-Hans Kolvenbach, S.J., "Faith, Justice, and American Jesuit Higher Education," in *Studies in the Spirituality of Jesuits*, 31/1 (January 2001), 13–29.

18. In O'Malley, *The First Jesuits*, 33.

19. O'Malley, "Works of Mercy," in *The First Jesuits*, 165–99.

20. *Constitutions*, [307].

21. Howard J. Gray, S.J., "Contemporary Jesuits as Friends in the Lord," in *Review of Ignatian Spirituality*, vol. 29, iii, n. 89 (1998), 41–56.

22. Jose Ignacio Tellechea Idigoras, *Ignatius of Loyola: The Pilgrim Saint*, trans. Cornelius M. Buckley, S.J. (Chicago: Loyola University Press, 1994).

23. *Exercises*, #15.

24. O'Malley, *The First Jesuits*, 284–328.

25. Michael J. Buckley, S.J., "Freedom, Election, and Self-Transcendence: Some Reflections upon the Ignatian Development of a Life of Ministry," in *Ignatian Spirituality in a Secular Age*, ed. George P. Schner (Waterloo: Wilfrid Laurier Press, 1984), 65–90.

26. *Exercises*, #18.

27. Ibid.

28. Howard J. Gray, S.J., "Being Catholic in a Jesuit Context," in *America*, 20 May 2000, 23–26.

29. Martin Marty, *Education, Religion and the Common Good* (San Francisco: Jossey-Bass, 2000), 139–40.

30. This paper was first delivered as a talk at Saint Louis University on 26 February 2001.

PART II: STYLE

The Florentine Reformers and the Original Painting Cycle of the Church of S. Giovannino

Gauvin A. Bailey

ALTHOUGH THE JESUITS RANK AMONG THE MOST important art patrons of the late Renaissance, they had a much greater presence in Rome and other parts of Italy than they ever did in Florence, the birthplace of the very humanism they championed around the world. Perhaps the memory of Savonarola (1452–98) was too strong for these charismatic preachers to be welcomed by the suspicious Medici Grand Duke Cosimo I de Medici (1519–74) when they first arrived in 1546. Even after their relations with the Medici improved they could never compete with the more established Florentine orders such as the Dominicans, Franciscans, and Augustinians, whose giant churches dwarfed the Jesuits' own foundation. Yet the Jesuits' artistic ties with Florence were very strong. Two-thirds of their painting commissions in Rome were done by Tuscan artists, and the various reformist styles the Society promoted in the 1580s and 1590s were primarily Florentine in origin. Artists such as Niccolò Circignani, Antonio Tempesta, Agostino Ciampelli, and Andrea Commodi helped define Jesuit taste, together with other Tuscans such as Giovanni de'Vecchi, Ventura Salimbeni, Antiveduto della Gramatica, and

Matteo da Siena. Especially in the later 1580s and 1590s, many of these painters worked in a devout style that departed from the artificialities and coldness of Florentine *Maniera* and sought a greater naturalism, solemnity, and appeal to the emotions, as well as a stable clarity of composition which derived from Raphael and High Renaissance classicism. In a forthcoming book I have suggested that it was precisely these qualities that made the Jesuits choose these artists.[1]

Nowhere is their enthusiasm for Florentine reform painting more evident than in their Church of S. Giovannino in Florence [Fig.1], an important monument of Jesuit art patronage whose original decorations have never been studied before.[2] Since its paintings and stuccoes were finished as many as ten years before those of the Roman Gesù, the Church of S. Giovannino is also one of the earliest demonstrations of Jesuit attitudes toward the arts.

Fig. 1. S. Giovannino, Florence, exterior *(photo courtesy of author)*

The Jesuits were in Florence as early as the 1540s, but their cold reception from the ducal family kept them from gaining a permanent foothold until 1551, even though they enjoyed popular approval.[3] Thanks to the political tact of Father General Diego Laínez (1558–65) and to the personal support of Grand Duke

Cosimo's consort Eleonora of Toledo, the Jesuits were able to found a college in a private house near the Church of S. Spirito and began holding classes there in 1552. They soon gained the favor of influential patrons, including the Medici, and in 1554 Cosimo granted them the ruined Trecento church of S. Giovanni Evangelista (S. Giovannino), located in a prestigious area of the city next to the former Medici family seat, backing onto the Piazza S. Lorenzo and close to the Duomo. However, owing to financial problems and declining enrollments, the Jesuits considered closing the school in the early 1560s.[4]

The man who came to the rescue was to have an unusually profound effect not only on the financial well-being of the foundation but also on its physical appearance. Bartolomeo Ammannati (ca. 1510–92), the architect and sculptor to the Granducal Court, was the most celebrated follower of Michelangelo and is best known as the designer of the new Palazzo Pitti and Ponte SS. Trinità in Florence.[5] Ammannati went through a spiritual conversion late in life, which was expressed in a famous letter he wrote in 1582 to the Accademia del Disegno (Florentine Academy) discouraging the use of nude figures in art. Ammannati felt an affinity with the Society of Jesus as early as the 1570s, and it was through his efforts that Cosimo granted the Jesuits the site of S. Giovannino.[6] Ammannati not only designed the new building for free but was its main benefactor, together with his wife the poet Laura Battiferri. He even selected the altar of St. Bartholomew for his own tomb [Fig. 2].[7] Thanks to his initial act of support, the College of S. Giovannino went on to become an important center for the diffusion of Jesuit spiritual formation, catechism, and culture.

Although the foundation stone for the new S. Giovannino was laid as early as 1579, it was not really begun until 1581, since the Jesuits were more concerned at first with the college buildings. Under Ammannati's direction and patronage (he had spent 12,000 scudi by 1584), a team of Jesuit and non-Jesuit masons, stucco workers, and artists spent the next seven years building the main body of the church over the foundations of the medieval structure.[8] The newly appointed Jesuit superior, Father General Claudio Acquaviva (1581–1615), wrote enthusiastically about the plan

Fig. 2. S. Giovannino, Florence, Apostles Chapel and tomb of Bartolomeo Ammannati (1592) *(photo courtesy of author)*

in 1582: "I have seen [the plan] with much satisfaction, and it seems to us that the whole is very well understood, and orderly, and that it will be a fitting work for your efforts."[9] Acquaviva did not have the misgivings he famously expressed about Ammannati's design for the college façade facing Piazza S. Lorenzo, whose top floor loggia and Jesuit emblem he considered too extravagant.[10] At least some of the walls were completed in March of 1583, since the account books start to list payments for whitewash at that time, and the roof was put on in May of 1584, when a carpenter was paid one florin, ten soldi "to cover the roof of the church."[11]

From the start Ammannati was concerned about the subjects that would be painted inside the new church, so much so that Acquaviva advised him in the same letter to worry about building the church first: "As for the histories which might be painted in these spaces, may it please the *Signore* that you finish the rest of the church as soon as possible, as one will be able to find these without difficulty."[12] The façade, left unfinished when Ammannati died in 1592, was completed only in the mid-seventeenth century by the Granducal architect Alfonso Parigi il Giovane, who also replaced Ammannati's original wooden pitched roof with a much higher vault between 1655 and 1656. This vault was painted in 1757 with the *Apocalyptic Vision of St. John* by Agostino Veracini.[13]

The original 1575–76 plan of S. Giovannino called for a single-aisled church with shallow Florentine-style side chapels, an arrangement that allowed for large congregations and good acoustics for preaching, a concern it shared with the Gesù in Rome [Figs. 3, 4].[14] Like many mid-sixteenth-century Roman churches, the apse was framed by a triumphal arch motif at the east end of the church—a statement of Christian victory.[15] Each side chapel was enclosed in a niche and included a main altarpiece framed by pilasters and a pediment, a pair of narrow rectangular or oval frescoes on the sidewalls, and an equally shallow vault above. The two chapels flanking the altar (fourth left and right) are higher, breaking through the entablature and resembling transepts. The side chapels took up much less space than their equivalents at the Roman Gesù, and consequently their potential for decoration was more limited.[16] Between the chapels were smaller niches holding plaster statues, and above and below these were additional panels, in fresco above and oil below. Other than the high altar, the rest of the church was plain and sober with its gray *pietra serena* stone, a much simpler affair than most of the Jesuits' Roman commissions and clearly calculated to present the image of humility and deference that was so crucial to their well-being in Medici Florence.

Fig. 3. S. Giovannino, Florence, interior *(photo courtesy of author)*

The Non-Jesuit Artists

This austerity and sobriety played into their choice of artists as well, many of whom were from that group of painters Sydney Freedberg has called "The Florentine Reformers." Santi di Tito (1536–1603) was the leader of this movement, and although he himself did not contribute to the decorations of S. Giovannino, many of his pupils and followers did.[17] Beginning in the 1560s, Santi adopted a radically prosaic style, which sought the kind of

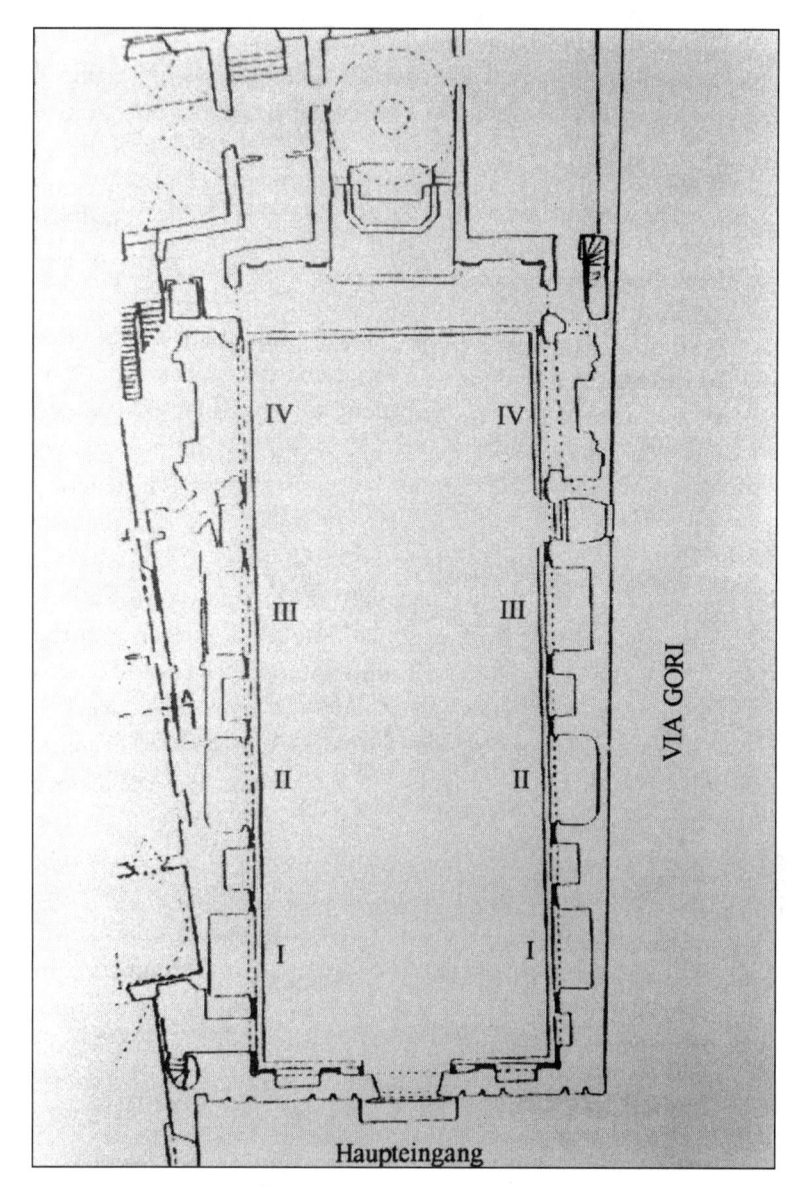

Fig. 4. S. Giovannino, Florence, plan *(courtesy of Father Gualtiero)*

simplicity and naturalism called for by churchmen during and after the Council of Trent (1545–63). He was reacting against the courtly style of *Maniera*, a late branch of Mannerist painting prevalent especially in Florence, which emphasized virtuosity and grace over naturalism and was characterized by dancelike artificial figures, a cold light, a general flattening of space, busy decorative detail, and repetitiveness. Santi's main models were Raphael (1483–1520) and Andrea del Sarto (1486–1530), and his mixture of realism and muted emotion with a hint of *Maniera's* idealized grace gave him great success in the new religious climate of late cinquecento Florence.

Many of the artists who worked on the side chapels at S. Giovannino shared Santi's vision of visual honesty and clarity of communication, the painterly equivalent to preaching. Domenico Cresti, called "il Passignano" (ca. 1558–1638), combined Santi's naturalism with the rich, saturated colors and shading of Venetian painting.[18] He was also influenced by the direct, academic manner of the Zuccaro brothers, a style he encountered in Rome, where it was favored by the Jesuits. Passignano made many contributions to Florentine church interiors, most notably the frescoes in the Salviati Chapel in S. Marco. Jacopo Ligozzi (1547–1627) also brought a new awareness of Venetian painting to Florence.[19] A native of Verona, Ligozzi worked from 1577 for the Medici court, where he specialized in both large-scale works, such as the history paintings he executed for the Salone dei Cinquecento at the Palazzo Vecchio (1591–92), and miniature paintings, including scientific watercolors of birds and animals. Ligozzi left many important religious works in such places as the Church of the Ognissanti, S. Maria Novella, S. Croce, and Sts. Annunziata in Florence, as well as in Lucca, S. Gimignano, and the Casentino. The older Michele Tosini (Michele di Ridolfo del Ghirlandaio, 1503–77) was head of one of Florence's leading painting workshops, and in the 1550s he promoted the *Maniera* style of Giorgio Vasari and Agnolo Bronzino, with its emphasis on Michelangelo's figure type.[20] With S. Giovannino, however, Tosini returned to a more traditional kind of composition inspired by the Florentine reformers and early sixteenth-century painters such as Andrea del Sarto, who aimed at greater legibility and simplicity. His best known works are at the Badia di Passignano and the Church of the Madonna della Quercia near Viterbo.

Another reformist painter who worked on S. Giovannino was Francesco Curradi (1570–1661), a Florentine whose style has been compared to those of Santi, Ligozzi, and Passignano.[21] Curradi used darker shading, articulate compositions, and increased naturalism to communicate messages of simple devotion, while never abandoning the courtliness and rigidity of *Maniera* painting. Curradi's work can be seen at the Duomos in Volterra and Pisa, and Casa Buonarroti in Florence. Bernardino Barbatelli Poccetti (1548–1612) was another key painter in the Florentine reform movement.[22] A student of Michele Tosini and of Buontalenti, Poccetti executed several important fresco cycles in Florence, including the Palazzo Capponi, the Oratorio della Confraternità della SS. Annunziata (S. Pierino), the Cappella Canigiani in S. Felicità, the Chiostro Grande at S. Maria Novella, and the Certosa del Galluzzo. Although his style at first was heavily influenced by Vasari, in the later 1580s he fell under the sway of the Florentine reform movement. His later paintings embraced a greater humanity and a more natural use of light and space, while maintaining the decorative quality of line for which he was celebrated in his youth.

The other five known artists who contributed to the decorations at S. Giovannino were not, strictly speaking, part of the Florentine reform movement. Although their style had strong ties with the *Maniera*, they diluted its coldness and complexity with an increased naturalism and shading inspired by Santi and his colleagues, with whom they shared a similar vision of the function of sacred painting. By far the most famous was Alessandro Allori (1535–1607), the adopted son of Agnolo Bronzino and the main champion of his style after the latter's death in 1572.[23] Like Santi, Allori began in Bronzino's workshop and later worked in Rome. In the 1570s he became the chief painter to the Medici court, executing such Granducal commissions as the Room of Leo X in the Villa Medici in Poggio a Caiano. He was such a prolific painter of altarpieces that few Florentine churches do not display his work. His paintings have the statuesque figures and rigidity of *Maniera*, but they are often set against backgrounds of compelling naturalism, and their heightened shading gives them greater emotional warmth. Allori's pupil Giovanni Bizzelli (1550–ca. 1612), who studied in Rome as a youth and worked on the ceilings of the new Galleria degli Uffizi (1581–82), promoted Allori's warmer, more atmospheric brand of *Maniera* into the next generation.[24] Lorenzo dello Sciorina (ca. 1535–98) belonged to Santi's generation and like him studied with Bronzino. He and Santi shared several projects, including the decorations for Michelangelo's funeral in 1564, the Studiolo in the Palazzo Vecchio, and the great cloister of S. Maria Novella.[25] Sciorina painted in a style very close to that of Allori, based on a *Maniera* figure type and with something of *Maniera's* stiffness and artificiality. But like so many of his contemporaries, Sciorina deepened the shading to give his religious pictures a sense of solemnity and humanity that was lacking in much of Bronzino's work.

The artist whose style differs the most from the rest is Francesco Da Ponte Bassano (1549–92). The son of the celebrated Venetian master Jacopo Bassano, his commissions include the Palazzo Ducale in Venice, S. Luigi dei Francesi in Rome, and the main altar of the Trinity Chapel at the Roman Gesù, a work that brought him considerable renown in that city.[26] Bassano's work is characterized by the moody darkness and sharp highlights of his father and late Titian, and his scenes are thronged with crowds in the grand manner of Titian's work for Charles V of Spain. His paintings share an emphasis on shadow with the Florentine reformers, but they are often so murky that certain passages resemble a photographic negative.

By obtaining private patronage, the Jesuits were able to hire celebrated professional artists like these to decorate the side chapels in S. Giovannino. As was common in both Jesuit foundations (like the Gesù in Rome) and non-Jesuit churches, well-to-do local families purchased the right to use side chapels as family memorials or tombs and paid for their decoration. These noble patrons included Francesco Guadagni, Alfonso de' Pazzi, Antonio Suarez, and the daughter of Bandino degli Alessandri.[27] In Rome, however, the Jesuits usually had complete control over the hiring and payments of the side chapel artists so that their contracts and payments were handled by a Jesuit building master and appear in

Jesuit account books.[28] By contrast, at S. Giovannino there are virtually no references to the side chapels in the accounts, and the Jesuits seem to have allowed patrons much more freedom in choosing and hiring artists. This more open approach to patronage did not mean that the Jesuits were any less interested in which artists were hired. The stylistic affinities of the painters who worked on S. Giovannino suggest that the Jesuits consulted closely with their patrons and approved their choices before the hiring took place. Jesuits also seem to have dictated the iconographic programs of the chapels before the patrons were invited to purchase the rights to them. As we will see, the iconographic program at S. Giovannino bore significant similarities to that of the Roman Gesù.

The Jesuit Artists

But there was much more to S. Giovannino than the side chapels. For the paintings in the nave, vault, and tribune, the Jesuits had to rely on the generosity of Ammannati and their own meager funds. As in similar situations in Rome, Jesuits engaged some less expensive artists for this work, usually younger men. But the brunt of the work fell on the Jesuits' own artists. Most Jesuit artists were brothers, or *fratelli coadiutori*, men who joined the Society but did not aspire to the priesthood. Usually from artisanal backgrounds, Jesuit brothers provided the backbone of the building organization, acting as carpenters, masons, and stucco workers, as well as cooks and gardeners. Among the brother artists active in Rome in the last decades of the cinquecento were Giovanni Battista Fiammeri, Rutilio Clemente, Bartolommeo Tronchi, Giovanni di Benedetti, Giulio Cesare Fioravante, Bernardo Melcetti, and Matteo and Gisberto Gisbert—men who never signed their work but whose names are preserved in Jesuit personnel catalogues.[29] They were called in to paint and stucco buildings for which the Jesuits could not find sufficient private funding or whose only audience would be other Jesuits. Such was the novitiate of S. Andrea al Quirinale, a foundation exclusively for Jesuit eyes, which was painted in the

1590s and early 1600s by Clemente, Fiammeri, and the Gisbert brothers. Most of the decorations in the nave of S. Giovannino were the work of Jesuit artists, including Fiammeri, Clemente, and Tronchi, as well as stucco workers and carpenters who had also worked on the Jesuits' Roman projects.[30] Although there is no mention of it in past scholarship, Jesuit architect Father Giuseppe Valeriano also worked briefly on the paintings in S. Giovannino.

The senior Jesuit artist at S. Giovannino and the manager of the entire decorative project was the Florentine sculptor and painter Giovanni Battista Fiammeri (ca. 1543–1617). Fiammeri helped conceive and paint many of the first Jesuit iconographic cycles in Rome; he also designed the final series of illustrations for Jerome Nadal's *Evangelicae Historiae Imagines* (Antwerp, 1593), an influential illustrated Gospel that was copied literally around the world.[31] Known during his youthful career as "Battista di Benedetto," Fiammeri is often mistaken for Valeriano in the literature and remains almost entirely unknown to scholars today. Milton Lewine even refers to a painter called "G. B. Valeriano called Il Fiammeri," and Michael Keine recently made the same mistake, claiming that Giovanni Battista di Benedetto Fiammeri is not to be mistaken with "the painter and architect Giovanni Battista Fiammeri (l'Aquila 1530–Roma 1606), later a Jesuit with the name of Giuseppe Valeriano."[32] Yet Fiammeri was well known at the time. Vasari mentions him in his *Lives of the Artists* as one of the more promising young pupils of Ammannati, whose sculpture is "in nowise inferior . . . to any other of the young sculptors who are Academicians, whether in genius or judgment."[33] Giovanni Baglione also included an entry on this "lively flame" *("viva fiamma")* in his *Lives of the Painters,* praising him for "reducing the superfluous from the stone, reducing the form of the bodies to the idea of artifice, conforming to and using measurement, but accompanied by the judgment of his eye, he gives proportion and grace to ornaments and figures; and he was a fine sculptor."[34]

Fiammeri probably came from a Florentine family and seems to have been the cousin of Giulio Parigi (1571–1635), another artist who worked on S. Giovannino.[35] A certain "Lisabetta Fiameri" may have been Fiammeri's sister-in-law or stepmother, and the artist may also have had a younger brother, since a Lorenzo Fiammeri made his final vows as a Jesuit eight years after Giovanni Battista.[36] Fiammeri was apprenticed very young; he was already present in Ammannati's shop in 1557, when he was in his early teens.[37] He was a member of the Florentine Accademia del Disegno from its very beginning in 1563, and for eight years he participated in its government.[38] Upon Michelangelo's death in 1564, Fiammeri executed a colossal artificial marble allegorical statue of the Arno to adorn his funeral bier at S. Lorenzo in Florence. He also assisted Ammannati on his Neptune fountain in the Piazza della Signoria (begun 1575), executed designs for the Villa Medici in Rome with Ammannati (1576), and was commissioned to carve one of the three statues that adorn Vasari's Tomb of Michelangelo at S. Croce, despite the fact that in the end Ammannati did not give his consent, remarking that "[Fiammeri] could be employed in other tasks which he was working on, which are also numerous and important."[39] Although none of his early sculptural work survives, a couple of delightful sketches in sanguine of projects for fountains—one of which closely follows the lower structure of Ammannati's Neptune fountain—can be seen at the Uffizi. Typical of a young sculptor working in the Ammannati circle, the drawings use shading at the expense of line and adopt an elongated form of Michelangelo's body type.[40] Fiammeri left the world of the Florentine Academy behind him in May–August of 1575, when he stepped down from his position as *Infermiere* to enter the Society of Jesus. When he left, he paid his dues to the academy in advance through May 1577.[41]

Fiammeri joined the Society of Jesus on the 3 March 1576, entering the novitiate of S. Andrea al Quirinale.[42] He was usually in residence at the Collegio Romano, except for the years 1586–88 and 1591 when he was working again in Florence on the College of S. Giovannino. Although Fiammeri's true calling was sculpture, he turned almost exclusively to painting when he entered the Society of Jesus, since the Jesuits needed this less expensive medium to cover their ever-expanding wall space. The catalogues list him variously as a "quite talented painter," a "painter and sculptor of statues," and in one case as "skilled at painting and engraving images."[43]

Seventeenth-century art critic Giovanni Baglione remarked that Fiammeri painted "many things" for the Jesuits after joining the Society, "and he was especially praiseworthy in making *cartelle* with various sorts of shading and with various caprices, and beautiful eccentricities, as indeed one can see throughout the College, and in the House of the Gesù, and in other places of that Society."[44]

Fiammeri pronounced his final vows in the Professed House at Rome on 15 August 1587, during one of his brief sojourns there while working on the Florence college.[45] Although biographers and art historians tend to refer to him as "Padre Fiammeri," he remained a brother throughout his life, as did the late seventeeth-century painter Andrea Pozzo, who is still regularly referred to as "Padre Pozzo." In Fiammeri's later years the Jesuits kept him busy with various design projects, as Baglione tells us: "And always for the Society he was working now on one thing and then on another, because he was skilled in everything to do with the profession of *disegno*."[46] Fiammeri died on 23 August 1617 in Rome, three years before Lorenzo Fiammeri, who died at Viterbo.[47] Throughout his career as a Jesuit painter, he received accolades from fellow Jesuits, especially from Acquaviva, who demonstrated a great respect for Fiammeri.[48]

Fiammeri's main assistant at S. Giovannino was the *perugino* Rutilio Clemente (1558–1643), who had the kind of peripatetic career typical of the early artists of the Society, dividing his time among several of the Jesuit complexes in Rome, Florence, and Perugia. He entered the Order at S. Andrea in 1579 and lived with Fiammeri at S. Giovannino between 1586 and 1588.[49] Among Clemente's better-known works are the tribune arch in the Gesù in Perugia, with a scene of *Christ in Benediction among Angels*, as well as two tondos in chiaroscuro of *Joseph's Dream* and the *Adoration of the Child*.[50] He is also responsible for much of the interior decoration of the Jesuit church at Tivoli, which was finished in 1599 and praised by Acquaviva in a letter.[51] Although primarily a painter, Clemente was also listed in the Jesuit catalogues as a sculptor, *stuccatore*, architect, and gilder.[52] Between December 1593 and 1599 he worked on the Roman novitiate and its church of S. Vitale.[53] In the realm of sculpture, Fiammeri and Clemente were assisted by the Florentine Jesuit woodworker Bartolommeo Tronchi (1529–1604). Tronchi executed the magnificent ceiling (mostly destroyed in a fire in 1989) and a wooden crucifix at the Gesù in Perugia; he also made tabernacles for SS. Annunziata, the Jesuit church in Nola, and the Gesù in Rome, where he created the angels in the high altar area.[54] Known as a sculptor as well as a carpenter, Tronchi entered the Society at the age of twenty-nine.[55] In 1586 he left 50 Roman scudi to the Banco di Guadagni in Florence to be administered by the Jesuit college of S. Giovannino as a trust fund for his nieces Domenica and Francesca.[56]

Although it seems he only contributed briefly on two occasions to the decorations, by far the best-known Jesuit artist to work at S. Giovannino was the frenetically overworked architect and painter Giuseppe Valeriano. Valeriano has achieved something of a cult status in the literature as the embodiment of Counter-Reformation intolerance and has been the subject of several studies in the past fifty years, mostly focusing on his role as an architect.[57]

Born in Acquila in 1542, Valeriano may have studied with his compatriot, the painter Pompeo Cesura, who worked in the style of Michelangelo.[58] In his early career as a professional artist he worked in *Maniera* circles, where he championed the Michelangelo figure type with its exaggerated musculature, large figures, and twisting poses, as well as the cold colors and polished surfaces of Florentine *Maniera*. These features can be seen in Valeriano's first attributable painting, an *Ascension* in the Church of S. Spirito in Sassia (before 1572).[59] However, from the very beginning Valeriano shows a sympathy for a darker, somber tonality pioneered by Sebastiano del Piombo (ca. 1485–1547), paralleling the stylistic shift introduced by the Florentine reformers.[60] The clarity of symmetry, the simplicity of the drapery and setting, and the emotional levity of his figures made his paintings accessible to ordinary people.[61] This aspect of Valeriano's style is best seen at the Chapel of the Madonna della Strada at the Gesù, which Valeriano painted in 1586–88, at exactly the same time as the S. Giovannino decorations.

Valeriano joined the Society around 1572 and rapidly rose in prominence to become the Jesuits' chief architect and building inspector, traveling through Portugal, Spain, Italy, and the north to inspect and design Jesuit foundations. Pietro Pirri notes how little time he had for painting between 1580 and his death in Naples in 1596: "These [building projects] accumulated ever more each year and Valeriano was reduced in the end only to making sketches that other artists would paint."[62] He was also plagued by ill health, as letters as early as 1580 and 1581 attest.[63] Nevertheless, Valeriano made the decision in 1582 to become a priest, even though it meant he would spend most of his time studying and could only work on things like a "beautiful icon for the church . . . for two or three hours in the morning."[64]

Chronology of the Decorations of S. Giovannino

Although most of the paintings at S. Giovannino have been dispersed and many of them are lost, we can reconstruct the church's original appearance from archival and published sources. Paintings and stuccoes in the main body of the church were executed mostly between 1586 and 1588, with some additional stuccowork in the early 1590s, most of which was finished when Ammannati died in 1592. Most, if not all, of the side chapels were also completed in the 1580s and early 1590s; some of them, however, had their dedications changed in the early seventeenth century, and several of the first paintings had already been replaced at that time. S. Giovannino underwent a surprising number of renovations in the seventeenth and eighteenth centuries—even before it was taken over by the Scolopian fathers in 1775—affecting virtually every chapel. Originally, the nave had fresco panels above the entablature of the scenes of the Passion, life-sized stucco figures of the apostles in niches in the wall between the chapels, and small oil panels showing the martyrdoms of those same apostles below the statues. The Jesuits had pioneered martyrdom cycles such as this just a few years earlier in Rome, in places like S. Stefano Rotondo and S. Tommaso di Cantorbery (early 1580s).[65] Such imagery was especially favored by the Society as a way of celebrating the triumph of early Christianity and also to prepare Jesuits and other young Catholic men for the trials of ministry.

Fiammeri, the director of the decorative program, is first mentioned in October of 1586, when he purchased pigments for the paintings, a task he continued to perform until late 1587.[66] As is traditional for Jesuit brother painters, Fiammeri was never paid for his labor, only for supplies. In contrast to what scholars have said in the past, he did not stay in Florence the whole time but made a number of trips back to Rome, including those in February 1586 and April–May of 1587, as well as another trip to Florence in late 1591 after he had moved to Rome again permanently.[67] Fiammeri probably contributed to the fresco panels of Christ's passion and the oil panels of the martyrdoms; he likely also had a hand in the stucco apostles, since he was an expert in stuccowork and made four *Church Fathers* on a similar scale for the Roman Church of S. Vitale at the end of the next decade.[68] Fiammeri was joined by Valeriano for a brief period in January 1586, when the accounts record that the Florentine painter spent a single scudo "to buy paints" for his colleague.[69] Valeriano is mentioned again two years later when he spent twenty-one florins on varnish *(lacca)*.[70] Perhaps the more senior Jesuit came in to inspect Fiammeri's work, or maybe he just happened to be in town. Fiammeri's assistant Rutilio Clemente started buying pigments for the church in August of 1586 (two months before Fiammeri), and worked there until September of the next year when he went to decorate the Abbey of Chiaravalle, a property in the Marches belonging to the Collegio Romano.[71] Clemente likely also contributed to the Passion and martyrdom panels. The last Jesuit artist mentioned in the account books is Bartolommeo Tronchi, who traveled between S. Giovannino and Rome in January of 1586 and May of 1587. Although records do not specifically state that Tronchi worked on the decorations, it is very unlikely that he would not have, since Jesuit artists were few and far between.[72]

Five professional painters also helped the Jesuits with decorations in the main body of the church. All inexpensive, they are entirely unknown today with the exception of Parigi, who worked for so little because he was young and related to Fiammeri. The first such artist mentioned is one "Giuseppe the painter," who was hired between November and January 1586 (the Florentine New Year was March 25) at a rate of fifteen florins a day for about forty-two days.[73] This amount was very low, and either the artist was a novice willing to work for very little or he worked at a low rate out of charity, something not uncommon among artists working on Jesuit projects in Rome. In Rome the Jesuits tended to pay younger artists by the day *(giornata),* while more established artists received a lump sum in installments.[74] Another unknown painter called "Mastro Antonio" was responsible for stuccowork that he carried out over two months in August and September of 1588 for about eighty-six florins.[75] He may have been Antonio Mariani, a painter listed in the records of the Accademia del Disegno in 1583 and 1586.[76]

Fiammeri's cousin Giulio Parigi worked on the project for four months, between January 1591 and April 1592. Son of the Florentine architect Alfonso Parigi il Vecchio, Giulio was Ammannati's grandnephew and a pupil of the *Maniera* sculptor and architect Bernardo Buontalenti (1523–1608).[77] A court favorite, Giulio was drawing master to the Grand Duke's sons and was especially popular as an architect and designer of *apparati* for court spectacles (he did the *Scena di Mare* for the Carnival of 1612). Nevertheless, Parigi made a reputation for himself as a painter, especially of landscapes. At S. Giovannino, Parigi was first employed in the college building itself, where he was paid a single scudo for "painting four Jesuses" for the refectory (possibly frescoes of a *Last Supper, Wedding at Cana, Miracle of Loaves and Fishes,* and *Christ Succored by the Angels in the Desert,* all of which subjects adorned the refectory of the novitiate of S. Andrea in Rome).[78] The refectory was located immediately adjacent the church, on the left-hand side of the tribune. Parigi's final contributions to S. Giovannino were the paintings behind the ciborium and altar in the apse, the "manufacture" of a St. Peter and St. Paul, and the manufacture and painting of the "tomb," presumably that of Ammannati, who had died that very month, for which he was paid the humble sum of two scudi.[79] The *Saints Peter and Paul* images were either part of the earlier series of stucco statues in the nave niches or two of the oil paintings of the martyrdoms of the apostles originally located below the stucco statues.[80] Baldinucci has attributed three of these lost panels to Florentine reformers Andrea Boscoli, Giovanni Nigetti, and Anastasio Fontebuoni, but I doubt that men of this stature would have been hired to paint in the nave, and nowhere are they mentioned in the accounts.[81]

Other unknown minor painters include Andrea Poiana, who painted scenes over the church's reliquary—presumably lives of the saints—between February 1594 and May 1595, when he was paid a comparably handsome sum of 4 scudi.[82] According to Ferdinando Del Migliore, the relics were located under the high altar, so this decoration was probably in the tribune area.[83] All we know about Poiana (elsewhere spelled "Piana" and "Puiana") is that he served in the Accademia del Disegno in 1587 and 1594.[84] The last professional painter to work on the main body of the church was a certain Jacopo Cigoli, presumably from the same town as his much more famous contemporary Ludovico Cardi ("Il Cigoli," 1559–1613), who executed a painting of St. Matthew for the church in September of 1596, for which he was paid a decent eight scudi.[85] This *St. Matthew* was probably another one of the small oil panels of the martyrdoms of the apostles.

Between the gallery openings and above the entablatures are ten fresco panels of the passion of Christ flanked by quartets of angels, including (clockwise from the door) the *Transfiguration, Last Supper, Agony in the Garden, Ecce Homo, Crucifixion, Deposition, Resurrection, Three Marys at the Tomb, Doubting Thomas,* and *St. John's Vision of the Apocalypse.* They are dark and somber paintings (two of them are night scenes), and the number of figures is reduced to the bare minimum. These paintings have never been studied because, in one scholar's words, "the paintings cannot be seen, much less studied, in their darkened condition and inaccessible location."[86] Yet the eighteenth-century chronicler Giuseppe Richa assigns them to a wide variety of luminaries, including Passignano, Santi di Tito, Alessandro Fei, Jacopo Ligozzi, Curradi, and even Bronzino.[87] His late-seventeenth-century colleague Fernando Del Migliore assigns them all to Alessandro Fei (1543–92), while Gaetano Cambiagi, another eighteenth-century writer, attributes them to Cammillo Cateni.[88] Jack Spalding found the inconsistency of these attributions "rather unconvincing," given that the sources differ. I agree with Spalding, especially since there is no mention in the account books of any of these artists working on the nave decorations.[89] Recently I was able to study these paintings in decent light and determined that they are not all by the same artist. I was also able to identify the *Transfiguration* as the work of Giuseppe Valeriano, with his unmistakable starchy drapery with bevelled edges and elongated figures. The overall composition and figure of Christ strongly recall Valeriano's *Ascension* at S. Spirito. I see no reason to doubt, given the archival references mentioned above, that the other paintings are by Fiammeri and Clemente. The *Last Supper*, with stockier, more solid figures like those used by Fiammeri at S. Vitale, also echoes the basic composition of Fiammeri's *Last Supper* images in Nadal's Gospel (plates 102, 103).[90]

The first phase of the sculptural work in S. Giovannino took place between November and December 1586, when the account books record payments for metal and wood frameworks (for plaster statues) and carbon.[91] In April 1587 a certain "Giovanni the Painter" (possibly Giovanni Bizzelli) carved four rosettes for the baldachino over the ciborium, for which he received seven florins, eight soldi.[92] The last sculptural work to be done was a series of stucco angels made after Ammannati's death between September 1592 and June 1593. Agostino Magnano made the metal frames, which were gilded by Detio Pignotti.[93] These may be the angels found in some of the chapel vaults, but more likely they are figures in the nave that were removed in the seventeenth-century renovations. The plaster apostles that are there today were done in the eighteenth century by Giuseppe Cateni, although Filippo Baldinucci notes an earlier series of stucco apostles, which he attributes to Ammannati himself.[94] Richa assigns this earlier series to Bartolommeo Carducci (ca. 1580), although I believe it more likely to be the work of Fiammeri, since Carducci is never mentioned in the account books and stucco sculpture was Fiammeri's specialty.[95]

The chronology of the side chapel decorations is much harder to determine, since they barely appear in the account books, and we are forced to rely on early printed sources. However, we do know that they were begun around 1583, and the altarpieces probably date from after January 1587 (1598 outside the Florentine calendar), since in that month Mastro Francesco, the carpenter, was paid for a frame *(telaio)* on which to stretch the canvases.[96] The first chapel on the right (Fig. 4; I), dedicated to the Passion, originally had an altarpiece by Passignano showing *St. Veronica Handing the Veil to Christ*, which was replaced around 1610 by a portrait of St. Francis Borja by an unidentified Roman painter.[97] On the lateral walls are four highly damaged and darkened fresco panels from the original sixteenth-century decorative cycle showing the *Agony in the Garden* and *Christ before Pilate* on the left and the *Taking of Christ* and *Crowning with Thorns* on the right. The fine stuccowork in the vault also dates from the sixteenth century. The altar there today is a *Crucifixion* by Michele Tosini; it was originally in the fourth chapel on the right and later the High Altar.

The second chapel on the same side (Fig. 4; II) was devoted to St. Catherine in particular and martyrdom in general. Francesco Bassano's canvas was of the *Martyrdom of St. Catherine*.[98] Like so much of Francesco's work, this canvas features a crowded scene dominated by an almost oppressive darkness, picked out by dramatic highlights. At the bottom we see Catherine's executioners heaped into a murky and seemingly lifeless mass, with the saint herself standing out as a burst of light in the middle ground. An equally bright angel bursts into the scene from above, bearing the palm and crown of martyrdom and proclaiming the triumphant theme of the painting. It is a positive and optimistic image, quite distinct from the gorier scenes of martyrdom featured in most of the Jesuits' Roman cycles. Although Bassano's contract and payments do not survive, his altarpiece must have been executed before 1591, when the artist threw himself from a precipice and died a slow and miserable death over the course of eight months.[99] It was accompanied on the sidewalls by frescoes by Poccetti of the life of St. Catherine.[100] Bassano's painting, acquired by Francesco II de'Medici, was also replaced in the late seventeenth century by Jesuit imagery. First it was switched with a painting by Giuseppe Nasini (1657–1736) of St. Aloysius Gonzaga (1568–91), a Jesuit youth who was one of the Jesuits' most popular figures in that century. This painting was then replaced by one by Ottaviano Dandini showing Aloysius together with Stanislas Kostka (1530–68), another Jesuit youth who served as a model for Jesuit novices and students, probably around the time of their joint canonization in 1726.[101] This eighteenth-century renovation also included the frescoes on the sides of the chapel, which were repainted to show *St. Maria Maddalena de Pazzi Seeing St. Aloysius in a Vision* and *St. Stanislas Receiving the Eucharist from Angels*, as well as a vault of angels and false architectural ornament above.[102] The altarpiece was replaced in 1936 by an image of *St. Pompilio*, patron of the Scolopian fathers, by A. del Zardo.

The third chapel on the right (Fig. 4; III) was dedicated to a female saint, St. Helen, and featured an altarpiece either by Bizzelli or Lodovico Buti (1550–1611) of *Saint Helen Adoring the Cross*. Buti was another student of Santi di Tito who worked in the reformist style and left works in the Chiostro Grande at S. Maria Novella and the Church of the Ognissanti.[103] The altarpiece, and presumably the chapel, was paid for by the noble Morelli family in memory of Girolamo Morelli.[104] It is one of the few that we can date precisely, since seventeenth-century art historian Filippo Baldinucci claims it was painted in 1587. Baldinucci also tells us that Bizzelli was paid sixty scudi for the work, an amount that shows us how little the painters of the main body of the church were paid by comparison.[105] That painting, too, was removed, and in the eighteenth century it was hung on the sidewall of the tribune, together with a *St. Jerome* by Ligozzi (both are now in the nearby residence—the Bizzelli in the porter's lodge and the Ligozzi on the third floor).[106] Bizzelli's canvas has the emotional vigor and sturdy, monumental figures of early baroque painting. Helen kneels on the right before a towering image of the cross, presented at a dramatic angle and reflected below by a smaller cross on a diagonal. Bizzelli's dramatic diagonals, as well as the shimmering surfaces of the garments, the atmospheric landscape, and Helen's Titian-like figure, betray the influence of Venetian painting. The *St. Helen Adoring the Cross* was replaced by a painting of *St. Francis Borja* at the time of his canonization in 1726 (Richa claims it was the same one that was in the Passion Chapel, which would make sense). This painting was then replaced by a portrait of Nicholas of Bari, by Giovanni Domenico Campiglia from Lucca, and the sidewalls were painted with oval canvases of *St. Francis Borja* and *St. Giuliana Falconieri* by Agostino Veracini (1699–1762).[107] These latter two frescoes were funded by Marchese Domenico Arnaldi, who also provided the marble for the chapel. Some original sixteenth-century stuccowork and paintings with triads of angels survive in the vault.[108]

The last chapel on the right (Fig. 4; IV) was originally dedicated to the Crucifixion.[109] I strongly suspect that the altarpiece of the Crucifixion now in the first chapel on the right (and in the eighteenth century located behind the high altar) was originally in this chapel.[110] Incorrectly attributed for years to Girolamo Macchietti (1535–92), the painting is most likely by Michele Tosini.[111] Typical of reformist painting at the time, Tosini's canvas features the elongated bodies and tiny heads of *Maniera*, which he softened by a blurring of outlines *(sfumato)* and setting them against a shadowy and sober setting so that the figure of the Madonna barely emerges from the darkness. The figures' lightness suggests a mystical vision, and pious fervor ripples through their garments with an electric charge. The chapel's dedication was changed in 1622 to commemorate the newly canonized St. Francis Xavier, and a large altarpiece of *St. Francis Xavier Preaching to the Indians* was commissioned from Curradi, which remains in place today. A grandiose celebration of Jesuit mission enterprise, Curradi's canvas shows Xavier with arms raised and cross held aloft before an exotic crowd made up not only of Asian figures wearing luxurious fabrics but also—in a standard misunderstanding of the word "Indian"— American Indians with feathered headdresses (Francis Xavier never traveled to the Americas).[112] The scene is set against a crowd representing all of humanity: men and women, rich and poor, European and non-European. Especially wonderful is the Ottoman fabric worn by the man on the lower right, with its exquisitely detailed tulip pattern. The latest additions to the chapel were some new colored marbles, a jewel-like *pietre dure* tabernacle added around 1700 by Grand Duke Cosimo III (1642–1723), and lateral frescoes by Bamberini showing a vision of *St. Francis as a Pilgrim* and *St. Francis Embracing the Cross*.[113] At about the same time, Cosimo III sent luxurious colored-marble revetments to decorate St. Francis's tomb in Goa, India.[114] The chapel is now the location of the tomb of early Christian martyr S. Fiorenzo, whose body was placed there for the papal jubilee in 1700.

The fourth chapel on the left (Fig. 4; IV), directly across from the Chapel of St. Francis Xavier, was the Chapel of St. Ignatius. Unlike the one opposite, this chapel may not have been dedicated at all before it was assigned to the founder of the Society of Jesus upon his canonization in 1622.[115] Curradi painted a canvas showing the *Vision at La Storta* to accompany *St. Francis Xavier Preaching to the Indians,* but it has since been replaced by an eighteenth-century painting of St. Ignatius by Antonio Puglieschi (1660–1732), with oval laterals by Bamberini.[116] All of the original decorations are now lost.

The third chapel on the left (Fig. 4; III) was originally dedicated to the Nativity and had an altarpiece of the *Adoration of the Shepherds,* until quite recently attributed to Santi di Tito. But recent restoration work has uncovered the signature of Lorenzo dello Sciorina—a reference already found in Richa—and the date of 1587.[117] The panel, now in the church of S. Felicità, was commissioned by Marchese Gabbriello Riccardi, of the family who bought the Medici Riccardi Palace across the street, who paid Sciorina the princely sum of 120 scudi for his work.[118] Although his canvas retains the artificial figure type of Bronzino, especially in the elongated hands and balletic poses, the artist reduces the number of figures and places them in a central, balanced composition. He also uses strong shading, allowing the eyes to focus on the protagonists, who are highlighted with bright colors—the shepherds with gold, red, and pink, and the Madonna with a brilliant rose-colored gown. These movements toward simplicity and legibility give this work a very different spirit from the *Maniera*. A certain Francesco Bronconi, a complete unknown, was paid more than seven scudi in the same year of 1587 for "a panel which is painted of the Madonna," which may have been one of the lateral panels in the same chapel.[119]

The Jesuits then switched the dedication of the Nativity Chapel to the Immaculate Conception, and Curradi was hired around 1622 to paint the altarpiece, now in the third-floor stairwell of the residence.[120] Like the Tosini *Crucifixion*, Curradi's *Immaculate Conception* is energized by fluttering drapery and a soft *sfumato*. The simple, symmetrical composition shows a very young Madonna on a moon above with figures of David and Solomon below, holding inscriptions of their prophecies. The naïve Madonna figure, which recalls late medieval imagery, is close to a version of the scene by Scipione Pulzone (ca. 1550–88), an artist who worked at the Gesù in Rome, in the Chiesa dei Cappuccini in Ronciglione.[121] Curradi's painting was replaced after the late eighteenth century with a 1694 painting by Antonio Franchi (1634–1709) of the Scolopian patron S. Giuseppe Calasanzio, which had been in the second chapel on the left since 1775 and had originally come from the Church of S. Maria dei Ricci.[122] The ovals showing the *Virgin Mary as a Child* on the right lateral wall and the *St. John the Baptist as a Child* on the left wall are the work of Pier Dandini (1646–1712).[123]

Ammannati himself was the patron of the second chapel on the left (Fig. 4; II), dedicated to St. Bartholomew, which became the location of his tomb in 1592 [Fig. 2]. The altarpiece of *Christ and the Woman of Canaan*, signed by Alessandro Allori and painted for the price of 130 scudi shortly after Laura Battiferri's death in 1589, is one of the few original paintings in place today.[124] It contains portraits of its patrons, including Ammannati, who appears as St. Bartholomew standing on the right, and Laura, who stands just below him, holding a book.[125] Allori departs from *Maniera* style by using darker colors and the atmospheric landscape of Venetian and Northern European painting, with naturalistic details like the flowers and the fishpond in the foreground. The mood here is one of devout sobriety. Three preparatory drawings that survive in the Uffizi show that the artist experimented with more crowded compositions before arriving at this extremely focused and balanced solution. On the sidewalls of the chapel were five scenes of the martyrdom of St. Bartholomew by Bernardino Poccetti, and below the altar was a *predella* (now missing) by the otherwise unknown Giovanni di Rafaello, who received four florins for his work.[126] After the church was taken over by the Scolopian fathers, the dedication was changed to St. Giovanni Calasanzio, and the Franchi altarpiece now in the third chapel on the left was located here. The Allori was in the first chapel on the right until sometime after 1940, when it was returned to its original home. Nevertheless, the lateral walls still have eighteenth-century ovals of the life of St. Giovanni, and there is now another Zardo painting from 1936, an oval showing the *Madonna Helping Souls in Purgatory*.

The first chapel on the left (Fig. 4; I) is the earliest chapel dedicated to angels in a Jesuit church. The most famous is the one at the Gesù in Rome, decorated after 1596 by Federico Zuccaro.[127] The entire chapel at S. Giovannino was painted by Jacopo Ligozzi, and everything but the altarpiece was executed between 18 August 1593 and 13 April 1595, although "a very devout person" gave additional money for the decorations in January of 1595 (1596 outside of Florence).[128] Richa and Del Migliore record that the canvas there today replaced an earlier one signed by Ligozzi and dated 1593, which depicts *St. Jerome Succored by an Angel*, a marvelous picture later hung on one of the lateral walls of the high altar and now on the third floor of the residence.[129] A mystical image dominated by an emotional sweetness, the canvas shows the aged Jerome being helped in his meditation upon the cross by a young angel, who gingerly lifts him off the ground. Darkness prevails throughout the picture, pierced only by a sunburst with three cherubs above, the brilliant golds and blues of the attendant angel, and Jerome's blood-red cloak. The most interesting part of the altarpiece is the group of incredibly detailed and naturalistic still-life elements found in the lower part of the canvas, including a meditative image of the Madonna, a skull, books, a basket of fruit, and a flask of water. These images testify not only to Ligozzi's skill at miniature painting but also to the increased naturalism in Florentine reform painting in general. The subject of Ligozzi's painting is a change from the original dedication to the Annunciation recorded in Ammannati's plan.

Angelic intercession was very important to leading Jesuits such as Ignatius and Claudio Acquaviva. The cult of the Guardian Angel, which had been growing since the fifteenth century, was especially promoted by the Society, particularly at the turn of the century with the publication of Robert Bellarmine's *Meditazione sopra gli Angeli Santi* and the *Trattato dell'angelo custode* by Francesco Albertini, S.J. (1612).[130] The S. Giovannino Angels Chapel treats subjects that were later repeated at the Gesù, including *Jacob's Ladder* on the left [Fig. 5], the *Fall of the Rebel Angels* on the right, and an altarpiece devoted to the *Seven Archangels*, without their controversial apocryphal names but with their symbols, as in a version by Ventura Salimbeni at the Duomo in Pisa. Stylistically, the *Seven Archangels* is consistent with various versions of the image painted in the second half of the sixteenth century in Rome and elsewhere.[131]

We have no record of the original subject of the high altar, which is now adorned only with a wooden crucifix but earlier in this century boasted an elaborate eighteenth-century altar frame with twisted Solomonic columns and angels at the top.[132] Even the altar itself is not original, dating from just before 1713 and built after plans by Carlo Andrea Marcellini.[133] In the eighteenth century, Michele Tosini's altarpiece of the Crucifixion was positioned behind the high altar, which as I have already mentioned probably came from the fourth chapel on the right. I suspect that the high altarpiece was originally intended to be a *Circumcision*, the subject of Girolamo Muziano's high altarpiece at the Gesù and of those in several other Jesuit churches, such as the Gesù at Lecce. The main evidence is that the St. Francis Xavier altar was originally dedicated to the Crucifixion, the same dedication as one of the two transept chapels at the Gesù in Rome, the other of which was devoted to the Resurrection. Although, as we have seen, there is no record of the opposite chapel's original dedication at S. Giovannino, it might well have been the Resurrection, resulting in an iconographic triad identical to that at the Gesù.[134] At the Gesù, as here, the dedications of the two transept chapels were changed in the seventeenth century to St. Ignatius of Loyola and St. Francis Xavier.

Fig. 5. Jacopo Ligozzi, *Jacob's Ladder* (ca. 1593). S. Giovannino, Florence, Angel's Chapel *(photo courtesy of author)*

S. Giovannino was one of the first completed Jesuit church interiors in Italy, predating even that of the Gesù in Rome. Many of the same Jesuit artists who worked on the Roman commissions contributed to S. Giovannino, and even though none of the church's professional artists worked for the Jesuits in Rome, their style had much in common with the Tuscan artists who did. Enthusiasm for an honest, devout manner of painting, with simple compositions, legible subjects, and emotional warmth characterized Jesuit decorative projects throughout central Italy. The affinity between S. Giovannino and the Roman churches also includes iconography. Several of the chapels in the Florentine church shared dedications with the original Gesù so that both churches had a Passion Chapel, an Angels Chapel, a Martyrs Chapel, and a Nativity Chapel, as well as a chapel devoted to the apostles (to St. Bartholomew in S. Giovannino and to Sts. Peter and Paul in the Gesù). Furthermore, in both the Gesù and S. Giovannino the chapels flanking the altar were dedicated to the Crucifixion and probably also the Resurrection; in both churches these dedications were changed in the early seventeenth century to commemorate the Jesuits' two new saints: St. Ignatius of Loyola and St. Francis Xavier. S. Giovannino also resonates with earlier Roman Jesuit commissions, such as S. Stefano Rotondo, S. Apollinare, S. Tommaso, and S. Vitale—all of which featured a martyrdom cycle, an iconography begun by the Jesuits in the early 1580s and especially promoted by them. Although there is certainly no "Jesuit style" at work here, these foundations in distant cities demonstrate a remarkable unity of purpose and iconographic harmony, proving that the Society was much more conscious of the role of style in the visual arts than it has been given credit for.[135]

Endnotes

1. Gauvin Alexander Bailey, *Between Renaissance and Baroque: The First Jesuit Paintings in Rome, 1564–1610* (forthcoming).

2. Much work has been done on the architecture of this church because of its connection with a man of the stature of Bartolomeo Ammannati. See Vieri Franco Boccia, "La chiesa di San Giovanni Evangelista a Firenze," in *Architetture della Compagnia Ignaziana nei centri antichi Italiani*, ed. Giuseppe Rocchi Coopmans de Yoldi (Florence, 1999), 105–10; Pietro Matracchi, "Il Collegio di S. Giovannino a Firenze," in Yoldi, *Architetture*, 111–17; Mario Bencivenni, *L'architettura della Compagnia di Gesù in Toscana* (Florence, 1996), 29–44; C. Carmagnini and P. Matracchi, "Il Collegio di S. Giovannino in Firenze," *Richerche* 18 (1986), 299–347; Michael Keine, *Bartolomeo Ammannati* (Milan, 1995), 136–45; Michael Keine, "Bartolomeo Ammannati e i Gesuiti," in *Bartolomeo Ammannati: Scultore e architetto*, Niccolò Rosselli Del Turco and Federica Salvi (Florence, 1995), 187–94; Richard Bösel, *Jesuitenarchitektur in Italien* (Vienna, 1985), 78–89; Pietro Pirri, "L'architetto Bartolomeo Ammannati e i Gesuiti," *Archivum Historicum Societatis Iesu* XII (1943), 5–57; Mazzino Fossi, *Bartolomeo Ammannati architetto* (Florence, 1964), 127–40; Walter Paatz, *Die Kirchen von Florenz II* (Frankfurt, 1940), 319–43; Arnaldo Cocchi, *Le chiese di Firenze I* (Firenze, 1903), 265–66.

3. Matracchi, "Il collegio," 111; Gilberto Aranci, *Formazione religiosa e santità laicale a Firenze tra cinque e seicento* (Florence, 1996), 45–47; M. Scaduto, *Storia della Compagnia di Gesù in Italia* (Rome, 1964), 3:139–41, 577–79. I would like to thank David Rosenthal for bringing the Aranci source to my attention.

4. Bencivenni, *L'architettura*, 29.

5. Keine, *Ammannati*, 141.

6. Fossi, *Ammannati*, 127–29.

7. Archivio di Stato di Firenze (ASF) Comp. Rel. Sopp. 990, #74, 154b–55b.

8. Keine, *Ammannati*, 141; Paatz, *Kirchen von Florenz*, 320.

9. "Si è ricevuta la sua de 24 di giugno, con il disegno ... l'habbiamo visto con molta sodisfattione, et ci pare che il tutto sia molto ben inteso, et ordinato, et che riuscirà opera degna della fatiga sua," (Acquaviva to Ammannati, from Rome, 12 August 1582). ASF Comp. Rel. Sopp. 1064, #335. The letter was later published in Filippo Baldinucci, *Notizie dei Professori del Disegno da Cimabue in qua* (Florence, 1846), 2:392–93.

10. Keine, *Ammannati*, 142; Pirri, "Ammannati," 27.

11. The first reference to whitewash *(gesso)* dates from 13 March 1583, and the roofer was paid on 26 May 1584: "E più y.[florins] una e B.[soldi] 10 per un opera d'un faligname che servi a coprir il tetto della chiesa, 0.1.10." ASF Comp. Rel. Sopp. 1064, #335.

12. "Intorno all'historie che si potrebbono dipinger in quelli spatii, piaccia al S.re che si spedisca così presto il restante della chiesa, come queste si troveranno senza difficoltà," ASF Comp. Rel. Sopp. 1064, #335.

13. Bösel, *Jesuitenarchitektur*, 82; Paatz, *Kirchen von Florenz*, 320, 328.

14. Boccia, "La chiesa," 105; Bösel, *Jesuitenarchitektur*, 88.

15. See Milton Lewine, "The Roman Church Interior, 1527–1580" (Ph.D. diss., Columbia University, 1960).

16. Nowhere here do we get the kind of iconographic complexity that was a key feature of the Gesù chapels. See Bailey, *Between Renaissance and Baroque*, chaps. 6 and 7.

17. Jack Spalding, "Santi di Tito" (Ph.D. diss., Princeton University, 1976), 36ff.; Freedberg, *Painting in Italy*, 620; Gunter Arnolds, *Santi di Tito, pittore di Sansepolcro* (Arezzo, 1934); Baldinucci, *Notizie*, 2:534–44.

18. Passignano lived in Venice 1581–89. See Freedberg, *Painting in Italy*, 625–26; Baldinucci, *Notizie*, 3:439ff.

19. *La Pittura in Italia: Il Seicento* (Milan, 1988), 2:786–87.

20. Ibid., 2:855–56.

21. Ibid., 2:706–08; Baldinucci, *Notizie*, 4:173–74.

22. *La Pittura in Italia: Il Cinquecento* (Milan, 1988) 2:807; Freedberg, *Painting in Italy*, 626–27.

23. S. Lecchini Giovannoni, *Alessandro Allori* (Turin, 1991); *La Pittura in Italia: Il Cinquecento*, 2:622–23.

24. *La Pittura in Italia: Il Seicento*, 2:642–43; Baldinucci, *Notizie*, 3:666–67.

25. Spalding, "Santi di Tito," 475–76; *La Pittura in Italia: Il Cinquecento*, 2:699.

26. *La Pittura in Italia: Il Cinquecento*, 2:693; Edoardo Arslan, *I Bassano* (Milan, 1960), 1:183–226.

27. Ferdinando Leopoldo Del Migliore, *Firenze città nobilissima illustrata* (Florence, 1684), 192.

28. Bailey, *Between Renaissance and Baroque,* chaps. 6 and 7.

29. Ibid., chap. 1.

30. Fiammeri and Clemente were accompanied by the gilder Vincenzo Maria, the sculptor Bartolommeo Tronchi, and the carpenter Antonio de Sanctis (Archivum Romanum Societatis Iesu [ARSI] Rom. 53, 108b; Pirri, "Ammannati," 22). See also ASF Comp. Rel. Sopp. 1000, #111, 87b, 89a, 96a.

31. Gauvin Alexander Bailey, *Art on the Jesuit Missions in Asia and Latin America, 1542–1773* (Toronto and Buffalo, 1999), especially 93, 98–99.

32. Lewine, "The Roman Church Interior," 252; Keine, *Ammannati,* 169, n. 9.

33. Vasari calls him "Battista di Benedetto, . . . a youth who has already given evidence of future success, [and who] was also the disciple of Ammannato; his many works produced thus early show him to be in nowise inferior to the above mentioned Andrea [Calamec of Carrara], or to any other of the young sculptors who are Academicians, whether in genius or judgment." (Italian text: "E Batista di Benedetto, giovane che ha dato saggio di dovere, come farà, riuscire eccellente, avendo già mostro in molte opere che non è meno del detto Andrea, nè di qualsivoglia altro de'giovani scultori accademici, di bell'ingegno e giudizio.") *Vasari's Lives of the Painters, Sculptors, and Architects V,* ed. Mrs. Jonathan Foster (London, 1883), 489; *Le Vite de' piu eccellenti pittori, scultori, ed architettori scritte da Giorgio Vasari VII,* ed. Gaetano Milanesi (Florence, 1881), 626.

34. "Che levando il superfluo alla pietra, riduce le forme de' corpi all'Idea dell'artifice, conformi; & usando la misura, ma co'l giuditio però dell'occhio accompagnata, comparte a gli ornamenti & alle figure proportione, e gratia; E su egli buon scultore." Giovanni Baglione, *Le vite de' pittori scultori et architetti* (Rome, 1642), 98.

35. The account books for the Florence college include a reference dated June 1592 to a small trust placed by "M.a Lisabetta Fiameri vedova" and delivered by "Giulio Parigi suo nipote" for 40 Florentine lire. This amount was to be invested with the Collegio Romano in Rome as a dowry for her daughter (ASF Comp. Rel. Sopp. 990, #74, 3b).

36. ARSI Ital. 40, 422a. For the reference to "Lisabetta Fiameri," see n. 35.

37. Fiammeri witnessed a receipt for a loan from Ammannati to Giovanni Figiollo di Francone dated 26 June 1557: "Io basista di benedetto fui presente a quanto di sopra si chontiene" (ASF Comp. Rel. Sopp. 1036, #240, 102a).

38. ASF Accademia del Disegno 24 (Giornale di Negozi, 1563–71), 2a, 9a, 21a; Accademia del Disegno 25 (1571–73), 11b, 25b; Accademia del Disegno 101 (Entrate e Uscite, 1562–85), 5a, 14b, 20b, 24a, 29a, 32a, 33a, 36b; Accademia del Disegno 123 (Entrate e Uscite, 1568–77), 7b, 8a, 27a, 28a, 53b, 54a. For a recent history of the Florentine Academy, see Karenedis Barzman, *The Florentine Academy and the Early Modern State* (Cambridge, 2000).

39. The references to these two commissions are in three letters, the first from Don Vincenzo Borghini to Duke Cosimo de' Medici (Pisa, 4 November 1564); the second from Giorgio Vasari to Duke Cosimo (Pisa, 5 November 1564); and the third from Borghini to the Duke (Pisa, 29 December 1564) (ASF Cart. Med. Un. 510, 586a, 1486a). The full texts are published in Karl Frey, *Der literarische Nachlass Giorgio Vasaris* (Munich, 1940), 2:116–23, 138–89. See also Pirri, "Ammannati," 25–26; Keine, *Ammannati,* 161.

40. Annamaria Petrioli Tofani, *Gabinetto disegni e stampe degli Uffizi: Inventario 2. Disegni esposti* (Florence, 1987), 924e; M. B. Wadell, *Evangelicae Historiae Imagines: Entstehungsgeschichte und Vorlagen* (Göteborg, 1985), Abb. 228.

41. ASF Accademia del Disegno 25, 11b. Fiammeri's name is crossed out and substituted by that of Domenico di Francesco di Siena. In the book of Entrate e Uscite, Fiammeri pays his dues in advance up to May 1577 in a lump sum in 1575, the year before he entered the novitiate (ASF Accademia del Disegno 123, 27a, 28a, 53b, 54a).

42. The register of new novices from 1576 reads: "Gio. Batt.a Fiammiero Fiorenza 3 Marzo" (ARSI Rom. 169, 12a). Another notice of new novices for 1576 reads: "Giovanni Battista Fiammeri Fiorentino. Pittore assai valoroso. 3 Marzo" (ARSI Rom. 162 I, 45b).

43. The catalogue entries read: "[1579] Io. Baptista Flamerius/ Florentinus/Annorum 33/Sanus/admissus est Romae anno 1576/pictor/ coadjutor Formatus Temporalis"; "[1584] Gio: Batt.a Fiammeri/ Florentinus/1550/bonas/1576 in Febr./pictor"; "[1586] Gio. Batt.a Fiammere pittore"; "[1590] Jo: Bap.ta Flammerius/Florentinus/Annos 47/Satisfirma/Annos 14/ Pictor et statuarius sculptor" (ARSI Rom. 53 I, 38b, 63a, 105b, 165a; Pietro Pirri, "Intagliatori gesuiti italiani," Archivum Historicum Societatis Iesu 21 [1952], 37, n. 66; Carlo Galassi Paluzzi, "Note di Storia e d'arte su le cappelle e gli altari del Gesù," Roma VII [1929], 393); "[1600] pictoris officio fungitur, praeterea nihil" (ARSI Rom. 54, 129b, 263a; Pirri, "Intagliatori," 37, n. 66); "[Fiammeri is] aptus ad pingendum et imprimendas imagines, et sculpendas in aere . . . mediocris iudicii et prudentiae: habet aliquam experientiam. Collericae

complexionis" (ARSI Rom. 55, 57a; Pirri, "Intagliatori," 37, n. 66). For references to Fiammeri in his old age, see ARSI Rom. 55, 16b; Rom. 78, 42a; Rom. 143, 120.

44. "E particolarmente era bravo in far cartelle di diversi sorti di charo, e scuro con varii capricci, e belle bizzerrie, sì come se ne mirano per il Collegio, e nella Casa del Giesù, & in altre luoghi di quella Compagnia" (Baglione, *Le vite de' pittori*, 98).

45. His final vows read: "Io Giovanbattista Fiammeri prometo all'omnipotente Dio in presentia della Beatissima Vergine sua madre Maria, et di tutta la corte celeste, et a voi Reverendo Padre Preposito vener.e dalle Compagnia di Giesù che tenete il loco di Dio, et à Vostri successori perpetua povertà, castità et obbedenzia secondo il modo espresso nelle lettere Appostoliche, et constitud.e di detta Compagnia. In Roma nella Chiesa della Casa Professa di detta Compagnia à dì 15 d'Agosto 1587" (ARSI Ital. 40, 211a).

46. Baglione, *Le vite de' pittori*, 98.

47. "[1617] Joan: Bap.a Flammerius ibid [Rome] 23 Aug."; "[1620] Laurentius Fiammerius Viterbij—20 Sept" (ARSI Hist. Soc. 43 [Defunti], 6b, 7a).

48. ARSI Rom. 13 I, 120a 176b, 177b; Rom. 13 II, 250a, 390a; Pirri, "Ammannati," 27–28, 50, 52.

49. The following are some listings for Clemente from Jesuit annual catalogues, listing such things as his name, origin, birthdate, health, date of entry into the Society, and profession: "[1584] Rutilio Clemente/ Peruginus/ 1558/ mediocres/ 1579/ pictore, stuccatore, scultore & orifice ora ista excravit" (ARSI Rom. 53 I, 65a); "[1590, Roman College] Rutilius Clemens/ Perusinus/ 32/ mediocres/ 1579/ Ae dieri emptoris pictoris" (ARSI Rom. 53 I, 151a); "[1594, S. Andrea] Rutilius Clemens/ Perusinus/ mediocres/ 14.6.Xbris 1579/ Pictor/ Coad. form. Xi. 9bris 1596" (ARSI Rom. 53 II, 188b); "[1597, S. Andrea] Rutilius Clemens/ Perusinus/ Pictor/ Nat.s An.o 1558/ adm.s 6 Decembris 1579/ Ex.a pictor/ Coad. Form. Xi 9bris 1596" (ARSI Rom. 53 II, 258a, 301a). His obituary is listed in the book of deaths from 1640–49: "Rutilius Clemens Perusiae 26 Februarij 1643 Romanae" (ARSI Hist. Soc. 47 [Defuncti, 1640—49], 62a.) See also Pirri, "Ammannati," 25, who cites other records, but says he died in Perugia.

50. Serafino Siepi, *Descrizione topologico-istorica della Città di Perugia* (Perugia, 1722), 1:412; ASPer, Perugia II 167 5; Annibale Mariotti, *Memorie storiche delle Chiese della Città di Perugia, 1819*, 191–206.

51. The foundation stone of the Jesuit church at Tivoli was laid on 8 July 1582 (ARSI Rom. 12 II, 100b). However, the paintings were not executed until late in the following decade. On 18 February 1599, Acquaviva wrote in a letter to Sebastiano Sicinio that he was pleased with the work Rutilio Clemente did at the church: "Mi rallegro poi che il nostro fratello Rutilio habbia fatto buon effetto alla sua cappella il tutto sia a gloria del Signore da cui prego a V.S. grand'abondanza di gratia et ogni felicità" (ARSI Rom. 14 II, 403a).

52. For example, ARSI Rom. 53 I, 63a, 65a.

53. "[27 December 1593] b. 10 pagati al fratello Rutilio per comprare cerchi, b. 10 . . . [19 January 1594] deve dare per tre moneta pagati al battiloro, per l'oro dato al frattello Rutilio Clementi per le pitture, scudi 3; [11 February 1594] Scudi 2 sinò a dì 11 detto al F. Rutilio per comprare di colori per le pitture, scudi 2; [13 April 1594] b. 90 pagato conto Rutilio Clementi fino al primero del presente disse per pagare colorj, b. 90" (ARSI FG 866 A, no folio numbers).

54. Pirri, "Intagliatori," 4–10. On Tronchi's ceiling for the Gesù in Perugia, gilded and painted in 1574, see the description in the 1819 manuscript gazetteer of Perugia by Annibale Mariotti, *Memorie storiche delle Chiese della Città di Perugia* (ASPer, Perugia II 167 5, 205), and Serafino Siepi, *Descrizione Topologico-Istorica*, 1:407.

55. The personnel records list him as follows: "Bartolomeo de Tronchi da Brozzi fiorentino d'età di 40 anni, sono 11 anni che entrò nella Compagnia in Roma, fece i voti dapoi l'entrata, fu fatto coadiutore temporale formato sono da 3 anni, falegname, intagliatore, et ha buon dissegno di questa arte, di sanità mediocre et mediocre forze"(ARSI Hist. Soc. 41, 89a). See also Pietro Pirri, *Tristano,* 245; and Pirri, "Ammannati," 22–23, n. 51.

56. ASF Comp. Rel. Sopp. 978, #52, 34a; Comp. Rel. Sopp. 999, #104, 91a, 91b, 233a, 234b, 238a; Comp. Rel. Sopp. 998, #98, 112b.

57. Maria Calì, *Da Michelangelo all'Escorial* (Torino, 1980), 283; Federico Zeri, "Giuseppe Valeriano," *Paragone* 61 (1955): 35ff.; A. Rodríguex Gutiérrez de Ceballos, "Juan de Herrera y los jesuítas Villalpando, Valeriani, Ruiz, Tolosa," *Archivum Historicum Societatis Iesu* 23 (July–December 1966): 287ff.; Gutiérrez de Ceballos, *Bartolomé de Bustamente y los origines de la arquitectura jesuítica en España* (Rome, 1967); Pietro Pirri, *Giuseppe Valeriano S.I. architetto e pittore 1542–96* (Rome, 1970). A major reassessment of Valeriano's architectural work is currently being undertaken by Maria Ann Connelli *The Gesù Nuovo in Naples: Politics, Property, and Religion* (forthcoming).

58. Pirri, *Valeriano*, 1–3.

59. Federico Zeri, *Pittura e controriforma*, 49–50; Calì, *Da Michelangelo*, 283.

60. Valeriano's Christ figure very closely follows that of Sebastiano's own *Ascension* at S. Pietro in Montorio. See Baglione, *Le vite de' pittori*, 83.

61. Calì, *Da Michelangelo*, 284.

62. Pirri, *Valeriano*, 225, 228.

63. The first letter is from Claudio Acquaviva to Valeriano, written upon receipt of two of his letters on 26 October 1580: "Habbiamo ricevuto le due vostre lettere, et ci siamo rallegrati intendere per esse il miglioramente di vostra sanità, la quale preghiamo Dio Nostro Protettore vi vistosi ... M'è piaciuto intendere le buone qualità di quel curato, di cui mi scrivete, et lodo il desiderio, che nella vostra mostrate del suo aiuto spirituale per mezzo di nostri essercitij" (ARSI Rom. 12 II, 85a). The second is from Father Manareo to Valeriano from Recanati on 4 January 1581: "Mi son rallegrato nel Signore d'intendere dalla vostra lettera il commodo viaggio che havete havuto, et insieme che vi trovate consolato nell'animo et con sanità nel corpo. Spero che cotesta aria vi habbia ad aiutare e ricoverare interamente la sanità. Et per questo rispetto mi pare, che vi tratteniate più presto costì, che in Loreto, per la strettezza grande che hanno di luogo; stimo che quell'aria non vi sarebbe così giovevole. Intanto potrete andarvi rinfrescando le cose della lingua, et insieme fare qualche essercitio intorno alli casi, perché per profittarsi bene della pratica è necessario prima havere li principii della scienza, et al suo tempo poi non si mancherà darvi aiuto ancora in questo. Mi fu caro che si rimandesse consolato il vostro cugino. Et con questo mi raccomando alle vostre orationi" (ARSI Rom. 13 I, 29b; Pirri, *Valeriano*, 256–57).

64. In a letter of 21 November 1580, Father Oliveiro Manareo described Valeriano's regime to the vicerector of Recanati, Giovanni Giorgio: "Viene il fratello Gioseffo Valeriano, del quale già scrissi a V.R. l'esercitio suo è di pingere, et ha in ciò buona mano. Ma perché il P. Generale di buona memoria disegnò farlo sacerdote et il P. Vicario sta nel medesimo, conviene ch'egli attenda agli studi della lingua et de' casi. Pertanta basterà che in pingere qualche bella icona per le chiese si occupi due o tre hore del giorno, come egli s'inclinarà, et il resto del tempo V.R. glie lo lasci libero, procurando che alcuni de' nostri costì l'aiuti. E glie lo racommando" (ARSI Rom. 13 I, 16a; Pirri, *Valeriano*, 256).

65. See Gauvin Alexander Bailey, "The Jesuits and Painting in Italy, 1550–1690: The Art of Catholic Reform," in Franco Mormando, ed., *Saints and Sinners: Caravaggio and the Baroque Image* (Boston: 1999), 151–78.

66. "[7 October 1586] E più giuli 10, et mezzo tanti sono dati al F. Gio. Batt.a Fiammeri p. comprare colori p. il P. Valeriano, [scudi] 1.0 . . . [3 December 1586] ho dato al F. Gio. Batt.a pittore p. comprare colori p. le statue . . . [23 December 1586] ha dato il P. R.re al d. Fr.llo [Fiammeri] p. comprare gesso, et colori y. 5 . . . [2 February 1586] ho dato al F. Gio. Batt.a Fiammeri p. viatico quando si è partito di qui per Roma giuli trenta, [scudi] 2.6.0 . . . [8 April 1587] . . . la partita di sopra det. F. Gio. Batt.a Fiammeri non se gli deve mettere à conto in po. si nota qui, et di questi giulii 25 si cavaro giuli 10 1/2 restano giuli 14 1/2 , [scudi] 1.2.13.4 . . . [22 September 1587] ho dato . . . et più dati al F. Gio. Batt.a Fiammeri p. comprare colori . . . in tutto [florins] 99" (ASF Comp. Rel. Sopp. 999, #104, 238a; Comp. Rel. Sopp. 1000, #111, 95b, 96b, 102a).

67. "[3 December 1591] Al Fratt.o Gio. Batt.a Fiameri à di detto scudi cinque, gli furono dati per suo viatico per andare à Roma, [scudi] 5. . . . [4 January 1591] Al P. Rettore à di detto scudo uno disse haverli dati al F. Gio. Battista Fiameri à conto del viatico quando andò à Roma, [scudo] 1" (ASF Comp. Rel. Sopp. 990, #74, 151a-b).

68. See Bailey, *Between Renaissance and Baroque,* chap. 5.

69. "[4 January 1586] ho dato al F. Gio. Batt.a Fiammeri per comprare colori p. il P. Gioseffe Valeriano, [scudo] 1.0" (ASF Comp. Rel. Sopp. 1000, #111, 96b).

70. "[7 September 1588] et più dati al P. R.re y. 21 quali sono p. comprare lacca mandata à domandare dal P. Gioseffe Valeriani . . . [9 September 1588] spesi p. il P. Gioseffe Valeriani in tanta lacca y. 21.4, scudi 3" (ASF Comp. Rel. Sopp. 1000, #111, 106b; Comp. Rel. Sopp. 999, #104, f. 238a).

71. "[21 August 1586] A 21 di d.o ho dato al Fr.llo Rutilio p. comprare colori y. [florins] 3.6.8, [scudi] 0.3.6.8 . . . [16 September 1586] A di 16 ho dato al F. Rutilio p. comprare colori y. 1.8.4 . . . [10 March 1586] ho dato al F. Rutilio p. comprare colori y. 3.6.8 . . . [7 April, 1587] ho dato al F. Rutilio per compare colori giuli cinque, [scudi] 0.3.6.8 . . . [24 September 1587] ho dato al F. Rutilio p. comprare colori p. portare all'Abbatia del Coll.o Rom.o y. 10, et p. opere 3 di Ms Muratore à B. [soldi] 35 il di, et opere 3 di manuale à b. 18 p. la facciata di fuore, [scudi] 2.3.19 . . . [26 September 1587] ho dato p. viatico al F. Rutilio Clemente quando si è partito di questo Coll.o per ire all'Abbatia di Chiaraualle giuli 25 et p. un opera di manuale, b. 15, [scudi] 2.3.6.8" (ASF Comp. Rel. Sopp. 1000, #111, 92b, 97a, 98a 102a, 102b).

72. "[7 January 1586] al F. Bart. Tronchi p. fare accomodare li scarpelli, [scudi] 0.1.0 . . . [9 May 1587] ho dato al F. Bart.o Tronchi quando si è

partita di questo Coll.o per Roma per il suo viatico, et vettura del cavallo scudi 5 et baiocchi 10 alla romana, [scudi] 4.5.0 . . . [19 May 1587] E più deve havere scudi 4 alla romana p. haverli dati al detto Fratello p. viatico quando è venuto à Fiorenza à di 29 di Maggio 1587 che sono alla fiorentina, [scudi] 3.5.13.4" (ASF Comp. Rel. Sopp. 1000, #111, 99a; Comp. Rel. Sopp. 998, #98, 112a).

73. "[29 November 1586] ho dato à Joseph Pittore p. op.e 6 à b. 15 il giorno y. 4.10, [scudi] 0.4.10 . . . [6 December 1586] ho dato à M.o Vinc.o nostro per comprare colori y. sette, et al d.o p. dare à Gioseffe pittore per 6 giornate à b. 15 il giorno, y. 4.10 in tutto, [scudi] 1.4.10 . . . [6 December 1586] E più il P. R.e ha dato al d.o [Gioseffe pittore] y. 6, et à M.o Gio. Batt.a p. comprare colori y. 2 in tutto, [scudi] 1.1.0 . . . [13 December 1586] ho dato à Joseffe Pittore per opere cinque di cinque giornate y. 3.15, [scudi] 0.3.15 . . . [16 December 1586] ho dato al F. Vinc.o y. due 13.4 per comprare colori, [scudi] 0.2.13.4 . . . [20 December 1586] ho dato al F. Vinc.o per dare à Gioseffe pittore p. sei giornate y. 4.10, [scudi] 0.4.10 . . . [23 December 1586] ho dato al F. Vinc.o p. dare à Gioseffe pittore per 3 giornate y. due b. 5 . . . [3 January 1586] ho dato al F. Vinc.o p. dare à Gioseffe pittore p. giornate 4 et mezzo y. quattro, un giulio à buon conto, [scudi] 0.4.0 . . . [10 January 1586] ho dato à Gioseffe pittore p. giornate cinque y. 3.1.8 et b. 13 et 4 haveva havuto à buon conto il sabbato passato, scudi 0.3.1.8" (ASF Comp. Rel. Sopp. 1000, #111, 95a-96b).

74. See Bailey, *Between Renaissance and Baroque,* chap. 6.

75. "[21 August 1588] ho dato à M.o Antonio pittore, p. la stuccatura delli Ap.i à buon conto y. 14 et y. 21 haveva havuto prima . . . [27 August 1588] ho dato y. 28 al d.o M.o Ant.o pittore à buon conto p. dette stuccature . . . [3 September 1588] ho dato al d.o Ms Ant.o à buon conto p. dette stuccature y. 12 . . . [7 September, 1588] ho dato . . . et più p. il resto à Ms Ant.o p. le stuccature y. XI" (ASF Comp. Rel. Sopp. 1000, #111, 106b).

76. ASF, Accademia del Disegno 26, 33a; Accademia del Disegno 27, 75a.

77. *La Pittura in Italia: Il Seicento* 2:836–7; Baldinucci, *Notizie,* 4:122–45.

78. "[11 January 1591] A Giulio [Parigi] pittore . . . scudo uno, gli fu dato p. il colore et pittura di 4 hiesù p. il refettore, p. un festone et portatura di dette robbe, scudo 1" (ASF Comp. Rel. Sopp. 990, #74, 151b). For S. Andrea, see Bailey, *Between Renaissance and Baroque,* chapter 2.

79. "[March 1592] A Giulio Parigi pittore sino a di 31 di gennaio scudi tre per ordine del P. Rettore, scudi 3 . . . [12 April 1592] A Giulio Pittore a di detto B. sei et d.[enari] otto p. una libra di candele p. il sepolcro, scudi

0.6.8 . . . [19 April] A Giulio Parigi pittore a di detto scudi dua sono per resto d'haver dipinto dietro al ciborio, l'altare, della fattura di S. Pietro et S. Paolo, fattura et pittura del sepolcro, et di tutto quanto havesse à fare con il nostro Coll.o et Chiesa sino al di presente, et vi ha fatto riceuta nel nostro libro delle riceute, scudi 2" (ASF Comp. Rel. Sopp. 990, #74, 173b, 175a).

80. These scenes of martyrdom are illustrated in an elevation by Ammannati (Keine, *Ammannati*, 140) and are mentioned in Del Migliore (Del Migliore, *Firenze*, 192).

81. Baldinucci, *Notizie*, 3:73–74, 676; 4:33. See also Paatz, *Kirchen von Florenz*, 333.

82. "[May 1595] A M.o Andrea Poiana sino a di 3 di febraio 1594 scudi quattro gli furono dati p. pagamento d'una di quelle storie sopra li reliquarij della Chiesa, p. ordine del P. Fabriano Rettore in quel repo. Et il P. Ludovico promise renderli et poi non gli ha voluto mai pagare, scudi 4" (ASF Comp. Rel. Sopp. 990, #74, 205a).

83. Del Migliore, *Firenze*, 193.

84. ASF Accademia del Disegno 27, 75a, 60b.

85. "[19 September 1596] A Jacopo Cigolli pittore a di 19 detto scudi otto sono p. un quadro di S. Matthia p. la nostra chiesa, [scudi] 8" (ASF Comp. Rel. Sopp. 990, #74, 222b).

86. Spalding, "Santi di Tito," 508.

87. "finalmente tra' pilastri sopra il Cornicione, con emulazione, a fresco rappressentarono i Misterj di Christo il Passignano, Santi di Tito, Alessandro del Barbiere, Iacopo Ligozzi, il Curradi, ed il Bronzino," Giuseppe Richa, *Notizie istoriche delle chiese fiorentine* (Florence, 1757), 5:146. This has been accepted by later sources, including Cocchi, *Chiese di Firenze*, 1:265–66.

88. "Sopra il cornicione andante, s'alzano altri Pilastri schiacciati, corrispondenti a que' di sotto, che tramezzano altri quadri di pittura a fresco d'Alessandro del Barbiere," Del Migliore, *Firenze*, 192. Cambiagi writes: "Gli Apostoli delle Niccie sono di Cammillo Cateni" (Cambiagi, *L'Antiquario*, 25). Walter Paatz follows the attribution to Alessandro Fei for all of the paintings (Paatz, *Kirchen von Florenz*, 328).

89. Spalding, "Santi di Tito," 508.

90. Bailey, *Art on the Jesuit Missions*, especially 93, 98–99.

91. "[7 November 1586] per ferri per le statue di stucco y. dicianove.1.4, [scudi] 2.5.1.4 . . . [15 November 1586] per opere 3 di un falegname ha

messo p. li legni delle statue à giulij 2 il di et p. un lavorante pittore ho dato à M.o Vincenzo nostro giuli cinq. Somma in tutto [scudi] 1.0.6.8 . . . [31 December 1586] ho dato per una soma di carbone per le statue y. 8, [scudi] 1.1" (ASF Comp. Rel. Sopp. 1000, #111, 94b–95b).

92. "[8 April 1587] ho dato à Ms. Gio. pittore per l'oro, et manifattura di quattro rosoni p. il baldacchino sopra il ciborio y. sette. 6.8, [scudi] 1.0.68" (ASF Comp. Rel. Sopp. 1000, #111, 98a).

93. "[15 September 1592] A M.o Agostino Magnano a di detto y. tre sono p. resto di ferri per le mendole degl'Angeli della Chiesa nostra, [scudi] 0.3.0 . . . [5 June 1593] A Detio Pignotti indoratore a di 5 detto scudo uno à bon conto dell'indoratura degl'Angeli per la chiesa" (ASF Comp. Rel. Sopp. 990, #74, 164b, 178a).

94. Richa writes: "Le statue degli Apostoli nelle Nicchie alti più del naturale, che di presente si veggono lungo la Chiesa, sono di Gio. Cammillo Cateni" (Richa, *Notizie*, 5:148). See also Bösel, *Jesuitenarchitektur*, 82. Baldinucci mentions an earlier series, saying that Ammannati "fece di stucchi le grandi statue de' santi apostoli" in the church of S. Giovannino (Baldinucci, *Notizie*, 2:381).

95. Richa, *Notizie*, 5:146.

96. "[2 January 1587] ho dato à Ms Fran.co per 3 gelosie servero p. le finestre verso la strada delle camare di sopra, et un telaio p. li quadri di chiesa in tutto y. 11, [scudi] 1.4.0" (ASF Comp. Rel. Sopp. 1000, #111, 104a).

97. Del Migliore records: "Nella prima all'entrare a man ritta; una Veronica in atto di porger a Cristo portante la Croce, il Sudario, è Opera del Cavalier Domenico Passignani" (Del Migliore, *Firenze*, 193). Richa remarks: "Alla prima nell'ingresso a manritta eravi la tanto lodata Tavola del Passignano, che vi dipinse la Veronica in atto di porgere il sudario a Christo portante la Croce" (Richa, *Notizie*, 5:145. See also 146–47). Baldinucci also mentions Passignano's canvas: "E la non mai abbastanza lodata tavola del Cristo portante la croce, per la chiesa di San Giovannino de' padri gesuiti" (Baldinucci, *Notizie*, 3:439). So does Jacopo Carlieri: "In un'altra, che è la prima a mano destra, la tavola dell'Altare è del Passignano" (Jacopo Carlieri, *Ristretto delle cose più notabili della città di Firenze* [Florence, 1767], 19).

98. "Nella seconda vedevasi il martirio di S. Caterina, opera del Bassano" (Richa, *Notizie*, 5:145). For more on the painting, now in the Pitti Palace, see Arslan, *I Bassano*, 229.

99. Hibbard, "Ut picturae sermones," 44.

100. "Il Martirio di S. Caterina, è del Bassano Lombardo, e le due Storiette a fresco dalle bande de' fatti di essa Santa, del Poccetti" (Del Migliore, *Firenze*, 193).

101. "La seconda Tavola di S. Luigi Gonzaga, e S. Stanislao è Opera di Ottaviano Dandini" (Cambiagi, *L'Antiquario*, 24). See also Paatz, *Kirchen von Florenz*, 329.

102. Richa, *Notizie*, 5:146–47.

103. *La pittura in Italia: Il Cinquecento*, 2:658.

104. Del Migliore attributes the painting to Buti: "Il B. Francesco Borgia, è d'un Romano, messovi nel 1671. quando fù Canonizzato da Clemente X. in luogo d'una S. Elena di Lodovico Buti, che oggi è in Convento" (Del Migliore, *Firenze*, 193). Richa attributes the painting to Bizzelli: "e appresso veniva S. Elena, che adora la Croce santa, dipintura fatta fare dalla Famiglia de' Morelli, che giusta le Scritture comunicatemi, diedero scudi 60. a Tommaso [sic] Bizzelli, che la dipinse, e non a Lodovico Buti, come scrisse il Migliore" (Richa, *Notizie*, 145).

105. "Per gli eredi di Girolamo Morelli, nobile fiorentino, [Bizzeli] colorì l'anno 1587 la tavola della S. Elena che adora la croce, per la loro cappella, la terza a man destra, entrando nella chiesa de' padri gesuiti di S. Giovannino, della quale trovasi avere avuto per onorario scudi 60, e ch'ella fusse posta su, dopo essere stata ornata di stucchi e di pitture a fresco essa cappella, per la pasqua del Natale dello stesso anno 1587, dove è stata presso a cent'anni, e poi tolta via da quei padri, e postavi altra di S. Francesco Borgia, seguita che fu la canonizzazione di tal santo" (Baldinucci, *Notizie*, 3:666).

106. Gaetano Cambiagi wrote about the sidewalls of the high altar: "Nei due laterali il San Girolamo è di Giacomo Ligozzi, e la S. Elena del Bizzelli" (Cambiagi, *L'Antiquario*, 25).

107. Richa, *Notizie*, 5:147; Cambiagi, *L'Antiquario*, 25.

108. Walter Paatz assigns these to Bartolommeo Carducci (before 1585), based on Baldinucci's claim that Carducci executed the apostles, but I see no evidence to support this attribution. See Paatz, *Kirchen von Florenz*, 329.

109. The original dedication is visible on an autograph plan by Ammannati in the Archivio di Stato di Roma (Keine, *Ammannati*, 139).

110. Eighteenth-century guidebooks demonstrate that this painting was behind the high altar at the time. Gaetano Cambiagi, who incorrectly attributes it to Macchietti, writes: "Ne segue la Cappella maggiore, la di cui Tavola ove è espresso il SS. Crocifisso è di mano di Girolamo Macchietti,

nei due laterali il San Girolamo è di Giacomo Ligozzi, e la S. Elena del Bizzelli" (Cambiagi, *L'Antiquario,* 25). Carlieri, meanwhile, does not attempt an attribution: "L'Altar maggiore è stato modernamente rinnovato, la di cui Tavola di un Crocifisso, è di mano di eccellente Professore" (Carlieri, *Ristretto,* 19).

111. See Marta Privitera, *Girolamo Macchietti* (Milan: 1996), cat. E2.

112. Del Migliore writes: "Il S. Francesco Xeverio, che predica agl'Indiani, e Nazzioni Barbare, lo dipinse il Cavalier Francesco Curradi" (Del Migliore, *Firenze,* 193). Richa agrees: "Alla Quarta Cappella segue un S. Saverio in atto di predicare agl'Indiani, fattura del Cav. Curradi, il quale per le varie invenzioni di abiti bizzarri all'uso di que'Paesi, e per la moltitudine delle turbe nel quadro sì ben disposte, diedesi a conoscere per Pittore universale, e non solamente di Santi devoti, come alcuni lo criticavano" (Richa, *Notizie,* 5:145–46). Cambiagi says about Curradi's painting, "Dove . . . ha con straordinaria eccellenza rappresentato il detto Santo nell'atto di predicari agl'Infedeli" (Cambiagi, *L'Antiquario,* 25).

113. Richa, *Notizie,* 5:147.

114. See Gauvin Alexander Bailey, "Le style jésuite n'existe pas: Jesuit Corporate Culture and the Visual Arts," in John O'Malley et al., *The Jesuits: Cultures, Sciences, and the Arts, 1540–1773* (Toronto and Buffalo: 1999), 46.

115. The same plan by Ammannati, which shows that the St. Francis Xavier Chapel had been dedicated to the Crucifixion, does not indicate any prior dedication for the chapel of St. Francis Xavier (Keine, *Ammannati,* 139).

116. Del Migliore records: "Il Sant'Ignazio in atto d'estasi, avanti alla Vergine Maria, è Opera pur del Curradi, espostovi nel giorno solenne della sua Canonizazione, che seguì ne' 12. Marzo 1622. per Gregorio XV. Ludovisi" (Del Migliore, *Firenze,* 194). Richa writes: "Addirimpetto a questa, viene la Cappella di S. Ignazio, che vedevasi in estasi avanti a Maria, dipinto dal medisimo Curradi" (Richa, *Notizie,* 5:146). Cambiagi adds, "Trovasi dipoi la nobil Cappella di Sant'Ignazio tutta incrostata di marmi, ove è di mano del Puglieschi la bella Tavola di detto Santo" (Cambiagi, *L'Antiquario,* 25).

117. Claudia Ricci, *The Church of Santa Felicità in Florence* (Florence, 2000), 40–41; Spalding, "Santi di Tito," 474–75.

118. The confusion is based on Baldinucci's and Del Migliore's claim that Santi painted the altarpiece. Baldinucci writes about Santi: "Fra le quali s'anno vera una bella tavola per la chiesa di S. Giovannino dei padri gesuiti, in cui rappresentò la natività del Signore, con una gloria e molte figure

d'angelleti, il tutto condotto in sulla maniera d'Angolo Bronzino suo maestro. Questa bell'opera, alle quale era stato dato luogo nella cappella, che è fra'l pulpito, e quella di S. Ignazio, fu poi circa all'anno 1635 levata di quivi, e postavi in sua vece la tavola dell'immaculata concezione di Maria sempre Vergine fatta per mano del Cavalier Curradi, e quella di Santi (che è sopra legno) vedesi oggi dentro il collegio di quei padri, rimpetto appunto alla seconda scala principale" (Baldinucci, *Notizie*, 2:535–36). Del Migliore concurs: "La Concezione è del medesimo Curradi, figurata la Vergine in mezzo a due Profeti Reali, con i detti della Scrittura in certe Tavole, alludenti a quel Misterio, e questa è in luogo d'una Natività di Cristo, di Santi di Tito, che oggi è in capo alle Scale del Convento" (Del Migliore, *Firenze*, 194). Richa, however, disagrees, claiming: "E quì, benchè fuor di suo luogo, debbo notare un dubbio sopra la tavola della Natività di Christo, che si disse opera di Santi di Tito, quando ne' Libri de' conti fatti dal Pittore Lorenzo Sciorina al Marchese Gabbriello Riccardi leggesi come appresso 'E per la tavola della Natività di Nostro Signore, che più mesi fa si è messa in S. Giovannino alla vostra Cappella scudi centoventi, e quel che vuol Vo' Signoria'" (Richa, *Notizie*, 5:149).

119. "[3 July 1587] ha dato il P. R.re à Ms Fran.co Bronconi p. la tavola ch. si è depinta della Madonna scudi sette y. 3.10, scudi 7.3.10" (ASF Comp. Rel. Sopp. 1000, #111, 100b).

120. "Il quale [Curradi] effigiò pure a quella, che segue, la Concezione" (Richa, *Notizie*, 5:146). Cambiagi writes, "Nella prima delle quali ov'è l'Immcolata Concezione, è di mano del mentovato Curradi" (Cambiagi, *L'Antiquario*, 25).

121. Zeri, *Pittura e controriforma*, fig. 15.

122. I would like to thank Father Gualtiero for kindly providing me with the complicated recent history of these altarpieces.

123. Richa, *Notizie*, 5:147.

124. Del Migliore writes: "La Storia della Cananea, è Opera d'Alessandro Bronzino, e le due Storiette dalle bande a fresco, de' fatti di San Bartolommeo, del Poccetti" (Del Migliore, *Firenze*, 194). Richa adds: "E passato il Pulpito trovasi l'Altare della Cananea con tavola di Alessandro Bronzino, cui il nostro Ammannato pagò scudi 130 . . . Segue la Cappella dell'Ammannato, veggendovisi alle pareti le cinque Pitture del Poccetti allusive al martirio di S. Bartolommeo, ed alla tavola del Bronzino notisi essere stato ritratto l'Ammannato in quell'Apostolo appoggiato ad un bastone in atto di guardare la Donna, che sta dietro alla Cananea; che è l'effigie di sua moglie Laura Battiferri" (Richa, *Notizie*, 5:146, 147–48). See also Lecchini Giovannoni, *Allori*, 272–73.

125. Gaetano Cambiagi, incorrectly locating this painting in the first chapel on the right, describes the portraits: "Stà collocata un insigne Tavola di Alessandro Allori, ove ha rappresentato N. S. con alcuni Apostoli in atto di esaudire la Cananea, ed è da notarsi che quel Vecchio, che si appoggia al bastone, figurato per S. Bartolommeo è il Ritratto del medesimo insigne benefattore Architetto Bartolommeo Ammannati, che la fece fare" (Cambiagi, *L'Antiquario*, 24).

126. The account books list the payment to Rafaello, one of the few which concern the side chapels: "[29 April 1592] A Gio. di Rafaello dipintore à di detto y. quattro sono p. haver fatto le tre alla predella della tavola della Cap.la di Ms Bart.o Am.ti come appare nel Libro delle ricevute, [scudi 0.4.0]" (ASF Comp. Rel. Sopp. 990, #74, 156a).

127. Bailey, *Between Renaissance and Baroque,* chaps. 6 and 7.

128. The final payment for this work was just over 58 scudi: "[November 1595] A diverse scudi cinquantaotto y. cinque B. diciotto et d. otto, sono p. suppliamento delle spese fatte nella cappella degl'Angeli di nostra chiesa nel quadro, ornamento, stucchi, oro, etc., dal di 18 di agosto 1593, sino alli 13 d'aprile 1595 come si vede in un quinternuccio di tutte le spese fatte per detta cappella, scudi 58.5.18.8" (ASF Comp. Rel. Sopp. 990, #74, 212b). The final payments, totalling just over 54 scudi, are "[23 December 1595] Da una persona divota . . . scudi trenta restituici p. haverli io spesi p. lei nella Cappella degli Angeli che lei fa nella nostra chiesa, [scudi] 20 . . . [7 January 1595] Da una persona nostra divota . . . scudi trenta quattro y. tre et b. dieci restituici per haverli io spesi nella Cappella degl'Angeli che lei ha fatto fare nella pittura, ornamento, etc., [scudi] 34.3.10" (ASF Comp. Rel. Sopp. 990, #174, 24b).

129. Del Migliore records: "Gli Angioli son d'Iacopo Ligozzi Veronese; avanti vi stava un S. Girolamo pur del medesimo Maestro, collocato oggi in Convento" (Del Migliore, *Firenze*, 194). "E nell'ultima Cappella fu collocato il San Girolamo, che sviene, sostenuto da un Angiolo, dipintura mirabile di Iacopo Ligozzi Veronese . . . Nell'ultima Cappella manca il San Girolamo del Ligozzi, dedicata essendo inoggi agli Angioli: del Ligozzi però vi restano i due quadri a fresco, che sono la Scala di Giacobbe, e la cacciata di Lucifero" (Richa, *Notizie*, 5:146—48). Cambiagi simply credits Ligozzi with the main canvas of the Seven Archangels without mentioning his other work (Cambiagi, *L'Antiquario*, 25). For a recent evaluation of the Ligozzi canvas, see *Il seicento fiorentino: pittura* (Florence, 1986), 93–95.

130. See Pamela M. Jones, "The Power of Images: Paintings and Viewers in Caravaggio's Italy," in Mormondo, ed., *Saints and Sinners,* 32; and Alessandro Zuccari, "La Cappella degli Angeli," 612–13.

131. See Bailey, *Between Renaissance and Baroque*, chap. 2.

132. Compare the photographs in Bencivenni, *L'architettura*, 34, and Keine, *Ammannati*, 141.

133. Bösel, *Jesuitenarchitektur*, 82.

134. See Bailey, *Between Renaissance and Baroque*, chap. 6. The order is reversed at S. Giovannino, however, since the Crucifixion was on the left at the Gesù.

135. I would like to thank Father Gualtiero for his invaluable assistance in allowing me to study the paintings now in the Scolopian residence and for lighting the frescoes for me inside the church.

The International Jesuit Style: Evil Twin of National Styles

Evonne Levy

THERE WERE THREE POTENTIALLY SUBVERSIVE INTERnationalist threats to the burgeoning national interests of France and Germany in the nineteenth century: the Jews, the Socialists, and Jesuits. In these countries were cradles of the nascent discipline of architectural history—a handmaiden in the broad effort to define national identity—but architectural historians had to contend with only one of these groups. The Jews, marginalized throughout their history, had no single architecture identifiable as their own, and while Socialists had plenty of ideas about the role of architecture in reshaping society, theirs was a brand-new movement with no architectural tradition to which one could point.[1] Jesuits, however, had been building churches for three centuries, and their monumental church architecture was all too visible on the skylines of Paris, Munich, Vienna, Prague—most European cities with significant Catholic populations. With three hundred years of often distinguished architecture in the centers of European cities, with hundreds of churches and houses recognizably their own all over the world, the Jesuits did, indeed, have a coherent corpus of architecture. It is no wonder that when, in the mid-nineteenth century, historians and architects turned their attention to the early modern period after spending decades focusing on ancient and medieval architecture, they began to contend with the Jesuit corpus of buildings.

In the early 1840s the term "Jesuit style" was coined in German publications to describe this corpus.[2] It was, from the beginning, an overwhelmingly negative designation. Usually characterized by material excess, this Jesuit style was understood as the product of a corporate author, the Society of Jesus, whose method of handling form reflected the character of its manipulative inventors. The core of the idea of the Jesuit style is that it was imposed by Jesuits all over the world; it amounted to what I would call Jesuit architectural imperialism. The subject of scores of books and articles over the past one hundred and fifty years, the Jesuit style occupies a central place in the historiography of the baroque.

Here I wish to focus on the context and significance for art history of one key aspect of this rich and controversial subject, namely, the *international* dimension of the Jesuit style. In doing so, I wish to bring an issue from the history of political theory to bear on the historiography of this term. Political theorist Micheline Ishay has shown that nationalism and the related efforts to establish national identities in European countries (France and Germany in particular) in the nineteenth century emerged as a result of the failure of the liberal internationalism of the Enlightenment. Nationalism and internationalism, she argues, must be understood as having been intertwined throughout history with the "acute manifestation of one" exciting the "dialectical response of the other."[3] I believe that this observation helps us to understand the emergence and tenacity of the rubric Jesuit style. For just as nationalism and internationalism were continually feeding each other in political theory in this period, so in art history Jesuit style was fundamentally intertwined with the project of defining national styles. In other words, the international Jesuit style was useful in the nineteenth century because it provided among other things an anti-type to national styles.

Let me clarify my use of terms. Where the worldwide scope of Catholicism is concerned, *universalism* has historically been the appropriate term.[4] Indeed it is often forgotten that *Catholic* means *universal.* As Micheline Ishay has shown, the Western concept of universalism replaced the ancient Roman notion of cosmopolitanism, which described the solidarity—secular and individualist—among men of equal status across the Roman Empire.[5] With the decline of the Roman Empire, cosmopolitanism was replaced by universalism. The early Christian church sought to create a universal religion with a common God and a common fate for man, to be mediated by the church. Falling short of its ideal from the beginning, Christendom—the international sociopolitical counterpart to the nation-state—resembled an imperium more than a universal collective of men bound by love. It was during the Enlightenment that the failure of the church's universalism generated an alternative—internationalism—now based on universal reason and the rights of man. At the same time—and this is the difficult paradox that explains the shift from universalism to internationalism—the nation-state emerged as the only institution capable of guaranteeing those rights. Enlightenment internationalism collapsed under Napoleon's pursuit of a new imperium, helping to produce nationalist Romanticism in the wake of disillusionment all over Europe.

Ishay's analysis of the decline of internationalism and the rise of nationalism stresses the disillusionment—first with the church and then with the Napoleonic experiment—that accompanied the rise of nationalism. The nation was now to be defined by its historical and cultural traditions rather than by universal reason. This turn to the cultural and historical bonds between men stimulated disciplines, such as art history, that would play a critical role in the formation of national identity.

While the Catholic Church and the Jesuit order were perceived as threats to national unity and identity, it would oversimplify matters to either simply correlate or contrast the church with the nation, which in a sense replaced it. In pointing to *internationalism* as a critical aspect of nineteenth-century anti-Jesuitism, I am making a specific point. The rise of nationalism transformed universalism, translating it into new terms in relation to a newly configured set of concerns. The moment Catholic universalist ideology came into conflict with national political interests, universalism became, effectively, internationalism. Thus in referring here to Jesuit style as constitutively international, I am drawing a connection between the

Jesuit style episode in the historiography of art and the shift in European political aspirations from universalism to nationalism, which in turn made the internationalism of the Jesuits threatening.

To begin, how could a Jesuit style in architecture be conceived of? The idea was imaginable because of the unavoidable similarity of some Jesuit buildings, particularly their churches, to each other. Those who have debunked Jesuit style over the years have rightly pointed to dozens of Jesuit buildings that do not conform to Jesuit prototypes. But the designation persisted because of the numerous buildings that did aim to imitate other Jesuit buildings. The Church of the Gesù (Fig. 1) and the Society's administrative center, the Collegio Romano, both located in Rome, provided the most frequent prototypes.[6] But Jesuit churches in important regional centers like Milan, Vienna, or Krakow were imitated just as frequently in nearby cities.[7] And as soon as Jesuit architect Andrea Pozzo's two-volume treatise, the *Perspectiva pictorum et architectorum* (Rome, 1693–1700), was published and widely translated, his chapel and illusionistic ceiling designs were also widely imitated.[8] As many have pointed out, Jesuits did not impose a style of architecture on their own members or on anyone else. But there was a reason for these indisputable resemblances, and it lies at the core of the Jesuit style. Jesuits were motivated to replicate their own forms out of a desire—often deepened by distance from the Society's physical and spiritual center—to express affiliation. Thus while style (as understood in our century, but not in the nineteenth century when the designation first arose) has proven to be a misnomer today, there was indeed a "Jesuitness" to Jesuit architecture, a subject that I have taken up elsewhere.[9]

The term *Jesuit style* appeared virtually contemporaneously in France and Germany in the 1840s. The designation was put squarely on the map in 1845 in an entry under "Jesuitenstyl" in the ninth edition of the Protestant Brockhaus's *Conversations-Lexikon*. That entry, the first in a long string of subsequent refinements of the definition, established the parameters of Jesuit style.

> The Jesuit style in architecture and decoration designates the method of handling forms in Jesuit churches and houses that

Fig. 1. Church of the Gesù, Rome *(courtesy of Fordham University Press)*

had become preeminent since the middle of the seventeenth century. The Jesuits are as insincere in their architecture as they were in every other aspect of the spiritual life of the people; they wished only to impose their will on them. . . . The interiors of their buildings at times are decorated with heightened pomp, full of gilding and carving. . . . From the middle of the seventeenth century they reached the apex of church architecture and the degenerate Italian style would now be their own realm. . . . The great pomp of their church style with its inner poverty brought all of church architecture of the time down with it, following the lead of the Jesuits.[10]

There is much to say about this passage, the first extensive articulation of the Jesuit style that I have discovered was written by the Swiss cultural historian, Jacob Burckhardt.[11] He wrote at a moment of particularly heated debate in Switzerland (one that verged on armed conflict) over the presence of the Jesuits in Lucerne. At few moments in the history of art have concepts developed in such direct response to contemporary events. But here let me pick out the most important strands. First, the insincerity of Jesuits—their desire to control the viewer—is posited as a method of form making, and this approach, rather than any period-specific form, constitutes style. Second, the Jesuits are imagined as imposing their will through architecture. The key point for the argument I am advancing here is that the geographical *origin* of forms in Italy is subordinate to a political deployment of forms wherever the Jesuits built. Burckhardt argues that the Jesuits essentially took over the baroque, and by bringing down "all of Church architecture of the time" with them, he implies that they brought down the German people as well.[12]

I should emphasize that the notion of a Jesuit style did not originate in Italy. Especially in Rome, Jesuit buildings did not appear substantially different from any other Catholic architecture; there was no sense of a *foreign* architecture. The argument that Jesuit architecture is indistinguishable from any other has been used time and again in the twentieth century to dismiss the concept of Jesuit style.[13] But this dismissal misses the point of the designation. Jesuit buildings that rose in France and Germany alongside Gothic architecture *did* look different.

Such is the case of the Jesuit Martinskirche in Bamberg (Fig. 2), for example, which only vaguely resembles the Roman Gesù. But this building and many other examples like it—seen in their local context of Gothic churches and vernacular architecture (Fig. 3)[14]—pointed to the Germanness or the Frenchness of what was already there.[15] More to the point, because of political tensions surrounding the presence of Jesuits in those nineteenth-century German and French cities, Jesuit buildings—monumental and often on prime real estate—looked like the architectural embodiment of a foreign occupation. Especially after the Jesuits themselves were expelled from most European cities in 1773, their houses and churches still remained as a constant reminder that the Jesuits were working to reinstate themselves.

Though Burckhardt's encyclopedia definition may seem absurd today, it was politically exigent in the mid-nineteenth century. Two main strains of this context converge in the designation "Jesuit style." First, it emerged amidst a massive concern in mid-nineteenth-century architectural history to define national style.[16] The question of a national style was driven in part by contemporary architects

Fig. 2. St. Martin's, Bamberg *(courtesy of Getty Institute)*

asking what part of their architectural heritage they should be drawing upon. In a tract of 1828, German architect Heinrich Hübsch formulated the question that would be asked throughout the century: *"In welchem Style sollen wir bauen?"* ("In what style should we build?").[17] That architecture was both a symptom of and played a formative role in shaping national identity was a well-understood principle.

Fig. 3. View of Bamberg from Kurt Hielscher, *Deutschland: Baukunst und Landschaft* (Berlin: Atlantis, 1924).

The second strain, which forms the substratum for historicism in architecture, is the rise of political nationalism, to which I have already referred.[18] The Jesuits entered the story of nationalism in debates over the role their international Jesuit order should play in the public realm, i.e., primarily as influential advisers and as educators. It is difficult for us to recapture today the heat of these debates over the continued existence of the Jesuit order in nineteenth-century Europe. For many reasons anxieties were felt around the continuous activity of the antirevolutionary and Ultramontanist Jesuits. These priests, with their hold on schools and confessionals, had been (prior to their suppression in 1773) and remained (after their restoration in 1814) enormously influential in forming and sustaining European nations. One major reason for anxiety about the Jesuits was their very internationality—the perception that they were loyal to an international organization with its own territorial ambitions, rather than to a single nation. In the 1870s one anti-Jesuit writer aptly remarked that he feared the whole German clergy being trained by Jesuits "swore allegiance to their flag."[19] The phrase was not a casual metaphor.

France was slightly ahead of Germany in the virulence of its nineteenth-century version of anti-Jesuitism. From the late 1810s through the end of the century anti-Jesuitism was a constant theme, stimulating new rounds of expulsions following the complete suppression of the Society (1773) and its restoration (1814). Nineteenth-century anti-Jesuitism reiterated themes established in the seventeenth century, but political circumstances after the Revolution were obviously different. The broader French fear of Jesuitism at this time was channeled into debates over whether Jesuits should be allowed to run schools.[20] Should Jesuits, it was asked, be allowed to continue to form the views of a promonarchy, antirevolutionary youth? In France, cultural anti-Jesuitism climaxed around 1843–45. At this time Eugène Sue's anti-Jesuit conspiracy novel, *Le Juif errant*, caused a publishing sensation,[21] and two of the most influential intellectuals of the time, Edgar Quinet and Jules Michelet, delivered infamous anti-Jesuit lectures at the College de France that were widely translated and circulated throughout Europe.[22]

The Jesuit style was in the air in France precisely at this moment. It is no coincidence that the idea first issues forth from the pen of Léon Vaudoyer. A politically engaged architect in the circle of the socialist historian Edgar Quinet and Hippolyte Fortoul, Vaudoyer believed fervently in the potential that architecture held for the reform of society.[23] He first spoke of a Jesuit architecture in 1846 in an article on seventeenth-century French churches. He concurred with the Brockhaus entry in characterizing Jesuit architecture by its ornamental excess. He also made a precociously judicious assessment of Jesuit dissemination of its own architectural style. He did so first, surprisingly, in a discussion of a non-Jesuit church, St. Gervasius (a Gothic parish church with a new Vignolesque façade); then he applied it to the Jesuit church of St. Paul–St. Louis as well.

> The architectural style of this church is that which the Jesuits imported to all of the European countries where they established their order. This style is distinguished neither by its simplicity nor its correctness, but it is characterized by a great richness and does not fail to produce a certain effect.[24]

Within a few years, the idea was elaborated in another publication to which Vaudoyer likely contributed essays on the same churches in Paris about which was written:

> The imitations, more or less successful, of the works of Vignola, modified according to the country, sometimes in form, at others only in detail, as they passed under the hands of different architects, soon covered all Europe with buildings that betrayed a common origin. This kind of architecture, of which the principal type is the Jesuits' Church at Rome, begun by Vignola, and finished by Jacopo della Porta, his pupil, was distinguished by the name of *Jesuitical Architecture,* and it is characterized by certain peculiarities to be remarked in all the religious edifices erected at that epoch in the different cities of Europe, where members of that Company were established.[25]

Vaudoyer was the first to explicitly identify an Architecture Jesuitique as a set of forms, based on the mother church Il Gesù and imitated wherever the Jesuits went. Minor or even major variants between Jesuit prototype and its adaptation, cited by historians later as evidence of the bogusness of the term *Jesuit style*, are here deemed unimportant. It is understood that individual architects will reinterpret the paradigm. Rather, the essence of the designation Architecture Jesuitique is the shared point of origin and diffusion all over Europe of buildings with a corporate stamp. I limit my French examples to these. What I want to point out here is that the *international* character of Jesuit architecture was critical to the definition of the Jesuit style in both France and Germany.

In contrast to France, where anti-Jesuitism came from within Catholic circles, in nineteenth-century Germany the situation was more complex.[26] Since the Peace of Westphalia, Germany was divided along confessional lines into homogenous political units according to the principle *cuius regio, eius religio*, established in the sixteenth century. That principle remained in place even after the new system of states was created in 1815. In the drive to unify Germany in the second half of the century, resolution of the Catholic-Protestant problem was the preeminent concern of the Protestant administration of Prussia. The rise in the 1830s of a rigid and antiliberal Ultramontanism that recalled the Counter-Reformation Church provoked the Protestants. Bismarck's goal after unification was not to stamp out Catholicism, which played an important and positive role in the nationalist German Romantic movement that proved so important in developing a sense of Germany identity, but to rid Germany of a Catholic axis with Rome, a non-German power, a nation without a nation, the church universal. The German Catholic population had shrunk to a minority (from half of Greater Germany to a third of Lesser Germany) after the Prussian defeat of Catholic Austria in 1866. National liberals interpreted the moment as a Protestant defeat of the "Catholic Principle." With confessional divisiveness rising rather than declining, some Germans called for the establishment of a German national church.[27]

All over Europe the Jesuits had become so closely identified with the papacy that radical and reactionary Catholicism had become almost synonymous with the old term *Jesuitism*. In Germany, as elsewhere, Jesuits became the symbolic center of an extreme international Catholicism hostile to the kinds of compromises deemed necessary for German unification.[28] German anxiety over Jesuit influence in particular reached its climax in the late 1860s during the debates over the notorious papal Syllabus and the vote on papal infallibility (1869–70), both widely believed to have been promoted primarily by the Jesuits. The dangerous implications of infallibility—which forced Catholics to pledge loyalty to church over state—caused considerable alarm in Germany on the eve of unification in 1871. The definitive expulsion of the Jesuits in 1872 came as the climax to the Syllabus debacle and at the beginning of the government-driven anti-Catholic Kulturkampf that dominated German discussion of culture until 1887.[29]

Different as the developments of French and German nationalism were in relation to confessional issues, their national champions agreed on one thing: the desire to rid themselves of the Society of Jesus, an organization with its own dangerous interests as well as an undesirable alliance with the Catholic Church. In both countries these alliances threatened to disturb a fragile national coherence.[30] The Jesuit style, characterized by its internationalist dimension, initially found expression and continued to be useful, I believe, because it provided a foil to—and cast a desirable light on—national styles then under heated definition, discussion, and adaptation by contemporary architects.

The internationalist dimension of Jesuit style found its most forcible argument in Germany in Cornelius Gurlitt's three-volume history of European baroque architecture, which appeared between 1887 and 1889 and was the first study to explicitly reject the notion that Jesuits were responsible for the baroque.[31] These volumes marked the end of a period in German history that the volume on baroque architecture in Germany in particular reflected. Many considered 1887 to mark the end of the Kulturkampf, with the final repeal of the repressive laws aimed at Catholic priests. Bismarck's experiment had failed to unite the German people, but

Jesuits remained the enemy of Germany, and the anti-Jesuit law was not repealed.[32]

Gurlitt's volume on German architecture is everywhere marked by confessional politics. His treatment of the Jesuit style is symptomatic. As if expulsion of the Jesuits called for the expulsion of the Jesuit style, Gurlitt argued that Jesuitenstil had been superseded in art history because its qualities are in fact the characteristics of the style of seventeenth-century architecture in general.[33] There was, nonetheless, still a prominent place for the Jesuit style in Gurlitt's baroque, just as Jesuit presence, albeit symbolic, continued in German politics and intellectual life in spite of the absence of Jesuits. Indeed, the book begins with a chapter on the Jesuit style. Gurlitt argued that German Jesuitism was no different from Jesuitism in any other country. What was different was that Jesuitism was foreign to the German people, whose entire spiritual development in Protestantism was contrary to the spirit of Jesuit teachings. Where architecture was concerned, the Jesuits introduced a foreign way that was Italian (and at times Flemish) in form. For Gurlitt, as previously for Vaudoyer, the Jesuit style was neither entirely synonymous with Jesuit buildings nor definable by distinct Jesuit forms.[34] It referred, rather, to importation into Germany, Germanic lands, and elsewhere of non-German design. Gurlitt also wrote, for example, of a Huguenot style that shows the principle manifesting itself in the importation of other, foreign forms into Germany through immigration rather than institutional design.[35] In spite of the ubiquity of foreign influences in Gurlitt's account, the essence of the term *Jesuit style* as he defined it was the principle of an *imposition* of nonnative sensibility. Of course many continued to see the Jesuit style, not as a principle, but as a historical fact.[36] Gurlitt's baroque, divided into regions determined by confessional divisions, is a complex reflection of the political situation of Kulturkampf Germany.[37]

The Jesuit style has been declared dead many times since Gurlitt stated that it had been superseded. These serial deaths were due first to a rejection—as art historians became more concerned with individual stylistic trajectories than with institutional intentions—and second to amnesia of the cultural explanation of style that arose in the mid-nineteenth century. Historians are still declaring the Jesuit style dead today, which should make us suspicious that it may still be alive. It *is* alive because those who coined the term *Jesuit style* captured something essential about the ideological substance of Jesuit architecture.

The persistence of the designation is stunningly apparent in a startling postscript to the German historiography of Jesuit style, one which has not been previously noticed. The late paradoxical holdout on Jesuit style was Adolf Hitler, who, in one of his recorded evening conversations, made the following remark:

> When all's said, we should be grateful to the Jesuits. Who knows if, but for them, we might have abandoned Gothic architecture for the light, airy, bright architecture of the Counter-Reformation? In the face of Luther's efforts to lead an upper clergy that had acquired profane habits back to mysticism, the Jesuits restored to the world the joy of the senses.[38]

Hitler was neither an educated nor a cultured man, and this highly derivative remark is bereft of both originality and insight. He is merely sputtering forth truisms that any German or Austrian with a high school education might have been able to reproduce.[39] On the one hand he is echoing the view, famously articulated by Heinrich Heine in the 1830s, that while Luther advanced a spiritualism idealized as the true essence of German Christianity, Luther's Christianity had also shut down the senses and simultaneously shut down art. Heine, though, was no supporter of the Jesuits.[40]

In his praise for Jesuit architecture Hitler made two departures from well-known and highly prejudiced Nazi views: from the general Nazi antipathy for Catholicism and from the more specific position on Jesuit art. The Nazi view of Jesuit architecture, articulated by of one of Hitler's ideologues, Alfred Rosenberg, followed most of the art historical tradition that judged Jesuit architecture negatively for going *against* a German way of building.[41] What is so surprising is that Hitler saw this opposition as a rescue. In his glowing portrayal of the Jesuit architecture he followed closely the view of Alfred Ilg, a Viennese colleague of Riegl's who was a vocal proponent of the Jesuit style. Ilg had argued back in the 1880s that the Jesuits had (thank God!) invented the baroque themselves.[42] This politico-philological note aside (and there is more to be said about the Catholicity of Hitler's views of architecture), I cite this remark because it is symptomatic of the political nature of the designation *Jesuit style*. Even though the term *Jesuit style* had been tossed out by art historians decades before the rise of National Socialism, it is clear that it remained a powerful idea. It is not surprising that it should reemerge precisely when questions of architecture and national identity were once again on the table, notably in 1930s Germany.[43]

Since the end of World War II and following the fall of the Berlin Wall, German art history has experienced moments of reckoning with its concern for its national style. For reasons I need not elaborate here (and obviously art history is just a symptomatic example of something much vaster), German art historians of the postwar period avoided the question of the Germanness of German art. As Hans Belting has pointed out, the overwhelming concern with national style up to the war years was redirected toward an international, Occidental culture.[44] In the postwar period, internationalism, previously so problematic, became, if not redeeming, then at least palatable.

We have come a long way from the nineteenth century, when art history urgently engaged in shaping national identity. As I hope to have shown, because the Jesuit style was internationalist in its essence, it came about as the antitype—the evil twin, if you will—of national styles. The Jesuit style can be seen, in other words, as the problematic but necessary supplement in the art historical polis. What may have been at stake in identifying a Jesuit style in the nineteenth century might be best appreciated by rephrasing the question, *"Im welchem Style sollen wir bauen?"* posed by Heinrich Hübsch. To the question, rephrased in the negative—*"Im welchem Style sollen wir* nicht *bauen?"*—one could easily have answered throughout the last two centuries: the Jesuit style.[45]

ENDNOTES

1. For fears of socialist uprising in Germany in the 1840s and 1860s, see Michael Hughes, *Nationalism and Society in Germany 1800–1945* (London: Edward Arnold, 1988), 95–96, 113, 138.

2. I discuss the authors and origins of the Jesuit style more extensively in my forthcoming book, *Propaganda and the Jesuit Baroque* (Berkeley: University of California Press, forthcoming), chap. 1. My account focuses on the nineteenth-century interlocutors on the subject, pushing the origins of the term back four decades earlier than had been known. A fairly comprehensive, though wildly biased and polemical, review of the literature on the Jesuit style (with examples from architectural history from the 1870s on, but focusing on the twentieth century) is found in Carlo Galassi Paluzzi, *La storia segreta dello stile dei gesuiti* (Rome: Francesco Mondini, 1951). A recent discussion of the Jesuit style is found in Gauvin Alexander Bailey, "'Le style jésuite n'existe pas': Jesuit Corporate Culture and the Visual Arts," in *The Jesuits: Cultures, Sciences, and the Arts, 1540–1773,* ed. John W. O'Malley, et al. (Toronto: University of Toronto Press, 1999), 38–89.

3. Micheline Ishay, *Internationalism and Its Betrayal* (Minneapolis: University of Minnesota Press, 1995), xvi.

4. The Enlightenment's version of secularized universalism was an intermediate step, superseded in the post-Napoleonic period by the assertion of what Ishay terms the particularistic rights of ethnically or historically defined nations (Craig Calhoun, foreword to *Internationalism and Its Betrayal,* by Micheline Ishay [Minneapolis: University of Minnesota Press, 1995], x.)

5. I have relied for what follows on Ishay, *Internationalism and Its Betrayal.*

6. The most important work on the question of Jesuit prototypes, viewed in comparative context, is Richard Bösel, "Typus und Tradition in der Baukultur gegenreformatorischen Orden," in *Römische Historische Mitteilungen* (1989), 31:239–53. See also the contributions by Luciano Patetta, "Le chiese della Compagnia di Gesù come tipo: complessità e sviluppo," in *Storia e tipologia. Cinque saggi sull'architettura del passato* (Milan: CLUP, 1989), 160–201; Sandro Benedetti, *Fuori dal classicismo. Sintetismo, Tipologia, Ragione nell'architettura del Cinquecento* (Rome: 1984), 67ff. See also my *Propaganda and the Jusuit Baroque,* chapter 5.

7. For observations on this phenomenon in Central Europe see Thomas DaCosta Kaufmann, "East and West: Jesuit Art and Artists in Central

Europe, and Central European Art in the Americas," in O'Malley et al., *The Jesuits*, 289–94.

8. For a list of translations and editions of Pozzo's treatise see Bernhard Kerber, *Andrea Pozzo* (Berlin: Walter de Gruyter, 1971), 267–70. For the Central and East European reception of Pozzo's treatise see Jerzy Kowalczyk, "La fortuna di Andrea Pozzo in Polonia. Altari e finte cupole," in *Andrea Pozzo*, ed. Alberta Battista (Trent: Luni, 1996), 440–51 (with previous bibliography); Pavel Preiss, "Pozzo e il pozzismo in Boemia," in *Andrea Pozzo*, 430–39; see also Levy, *Propaganda and the Jesuit Baroque*, chap. 5.

9. On the "Jesuitness of Jesuit Architecture," see Levy, *Propaganda and the Jesuit Baroque*, chap. 3.

10. *Allgemeine deutsche Real-Encyklopedie für die gebildeten Stände. Conversations-Lexikon*, 9th ed. (Leipzig, 1845), 7:657–58, s.v. "Jesuitenstyl." This is a selection from a longer text. Translation mine. This passage was incorrectly dated to 1843 in Bailey "'Le style,'" 74, n. 13. The date is important. This entry was preceded by other nominations of the term (by Burckhardt and others) in 1842, for which see Levy, *Propaganda and the Jesuit Baroque*, chap. 1.

11. The entry was, typically, unsigned. Burckhardt's authorship (known to specialists of Burckhardt's work but totally eclipsed by time and unknown to the considerable group of historians who have discussed the Jesuit style) is discussed, to my knowledge, only in the extensive study of Burckhardt's *Nachlass* by Werner Kaegi, *Jacob Burckhardt. Eine Biographie* (Basel: Benno Schwabe, 1950), 2:528ff. I intend to flesh out Burckhardt's views on this subject in the context of his political journalism and the equally complex situation of the Jesuits in Switzerland in a future study, *The Jesuit Style: Art History and Politics from Burckhardt to Hitler*.

12. My account of this cause-and-effect relationship is not entirely dissimilar from Galassi Paluzzi's. Where we differ is in my emphasis on Jesuit character providing the foundation of the Jesuit style. Galassi Paluzzi avoids the vexed question of character, pointing to (without mapping out) larger fields of political and social anti-Jesuitism, as if politics had no place in the serious matter of designating art historical styles. Paluzzi, *La storia segreta dello stile dei gesuiti*, especially 20–21.

13. See, most notably, Joseph Braun, *Spaniens alte Jesuitenkirchen. Ein Beitrag zur Geschichte der nachmittelalterlichen kirchlichen Architektur in Spanien* (Freiburg: Herder, 1913).

14. This view of the "Devil's Ditch" and the cathedral in Bamberg is typical of the domination of Gothic and vernacular architecture in this

book of views of German architecture and landscape views. In its omission of Jesuit churches entirely and the paucity of Italianate early modern examples generally, it makes an argument for a German style of architecture. Kurt Hielscher, *Deutschland. Baukunst und Landschaft* (Berlin: Atlantis, 1924), 136.

15. Kaufmann makes this point with reference to the contrast between the stone masonry of the Jesuit churches in Poland and the Orthodox churches, so often made of wood. Kaufmann, "East and West," 284–87.

16. There is a large literature on this subject. I have found the following particularly useful in mapping out the French and German milieus: Michael J. Lewis, *The Politics of the German Gothic Revival. August Reichensperger* (New York: MIT Press, 1993); and Barry Bergdoll, *Léon Vaudoyer, Historicism in the Age of Industry* (New York: MIT Press, 1994).

17. Heinrich Hübsch, *In What Style Should We Build?* (1828), in *In What Style Should We Build? The German Debate on Architectural Style*, Getty Texts and Documents series, trans. and introd. Wolfgang Hermann (Los Angeles: Getty Center for the History of Art and the Humanities, 1992), 63–101.

18. Of the growing literature on the subject I have been stimulated by Elie Kedourie, *Nationalism*, 4th ed. (1960; repr. Oxford: Blackwell, 1993); Eric Hobsbawm, *Nations and Nationalism Since 1780: Programme, Myth, Reality* (Cambridge, Mass.: Cambridge University Press, 1990); and the recent problematization of the latter in Adrian Hastings, *The Construction of Nationhood: Ethnicity, Religion and Nationalism* (Cambridge, Mass.: Cambridge University Press, 1997).

19. Theodor Griesinger, *The Jesuits, A Complete History of Their Open and Secret Proceedings from the Foundation of the Order to the Present Time*, trans. A. J. Scott, based on the 3rd German ed. (1866; repr. London: W. H. Allen, 1892), 673. Griesinger's polemical history provides an excellent introduction to the nineteenth-century German conflation of Jesuitism with Catholicism, and the political implications of that widespread conflation.

20. There are two excellent studies on French anti-Jesuitism. The school debates provide the focus of Geoffrey Cubitt, *The Jesuit Myth: Conspiracy Theory and Politics in Nineteenth-Century France* (Oxford: Oxford University Press, 1993). Michel Leroy, *Le mythe jésuite: De Béranger à Michelet* (Paris: Presses Universitaires de France, 1992), places greater emphasis on literary anti-Jesuitism. See also the synthetic account of French anti-Jesuitism by the historian this volume honors, John W. Padberg, S.J., "The Demonization of the Jesuits," presented at the Georgetown University Centennial Conference, February 1998, "The Dreyfus Case: Human Rights

vs. Prejudice, Intolerance and Demonization." The paper is currently available at: http:www.georgetown.edu/guieu/Pappadb.htm.

21. *Le Juif errant* appeared in *Le Constitutionnel en feuilleton*. For editions and responses to it, see De Backer-Sommervogel, vol. 11, no. 2029–42.

22. Jules Michelet and Edgar Quinet, *Des Jésuites* (Paris: Hachette, 1843). For editions, translations, and responses to the lectures see De Backer-Sommervogel, vol. 11, no. 2003–13.

23. For Vaudoyer's political sympathies see Bergdoll, *Léon Vaudoyer*, especially chap. 2.

24. "Le style de l'architecture de cette église est celui que les jésuites importèrent dans tous les pays de l'Europe où ils formèrent des établissements de leur ordre. Ce style ne brille ni par la simplicité ni par la correction, mais il est empreint d'une grande richesse, et ne laisse pas que de produire un certain effet." Léon Vaudoyer, "Études d'architecture en France, ou notions relatives à l'âge et au style des monuments élevés à différentes époques de notre histoire. Des Églises au dix-septième siècle," *Magasin Pittoresque* (April 1846), 107.

25. Jules Gailhabaud, *Ancient and Modern Architecture; consisting of views, plans, elevations, sections, and details of the most remarkable edifices in the world* (London: Firmin Didot, 1849), s.v. "Church of St. Gervasius and St. Protasius." The incomplete English translation of this work (the text on Italian architecture was missing in the copy I consulted) appears to have been published before the French edition, which appeared in 1850. For Jesuit architecture see also the French edition of Jules Gailhabaud, *Monuments anciens et modernes...*, vol. 4, *période moderne* (Paris: Firmin Didot, 1850), s.v. "Eglise de Jèsus, à Rome." For Vaudoyer's contribution to Gailhabaud see Bergdoll, *Léon Vaudoyer*, 167.

26. For what follows I have relied on the excellent synthetic essay by Adolf M. Birke, "German Catholics and the Quest for National Unity," in *Nation-Building in Central Europe*, ed. Hagen Schulze (New York: Berg, 1987), 51–63.

27. See for example the simultaneously anti-Protestant and anti-Catholic position during the period of the Kulturkampf (1872–87) of Paul (Bötticher) de Lagarde. Lagarde saw both the demise of universal faith and the failure of Protestantism as pointing to the need for a new version of Christianity "appropriate for the German character." See Fritz Stern, *The Politics of Cultural Despair: A Study in the Rise of the Germanic Ideology* (Berkeley: University of California Press, 1961), chap. 3, especially 47–48.

28. On the use of the Jesuits as a scapegoat in the national debates in Switzerland in the 1840s, for example, see John R. Hinde, *Jacob*

Burckhardt and the Crisis of Modernity (Montreal: McGill-Queens University Press, 2000), 94ff.

29. The Kulturkampf is described as a function of the "general German trajectory of nation-building," rather than an extension of the Enlightenment church-state struggle in Helmut Walser Smith, *German Nationalism and Religious Conflict: Culture, Ideology, Politics, 1870–1914* (Princeton, N.J.: Princeton University Press, 1995).

30. The "Los von Rom" (Free from Rome) movement, funded by the Protestant league of Imperial Germany to convert German Catholics in Austria to Protestantism aptly sums up this sentiment. See Smith, *German Nationalism and Religious Conflict,* chap. 7.

31. Cornelius Gurlitt, *Geschichte des Barockstiles, des Rococco und des Klassicismus,* 3 vols. (Stuttgart: Ebner & Seubert, 1887–1889).

32. Smith, *German Nationalism and Religious Conflict,* 50.

33. Gurlitt, *Geschichte des Barockstiles und des Rococco in Deutschland* (Stuttgart: Ebner & Seubert, 1889), 15. For a less sympathetic reading see Galassi Paluzzi's mockery of Gurlitt's alternative model for the Jesuit style as a "'papistica romanizzazione' of national styles." Galassi Paluzzi, *La storia segreta dello stile dei gesuiti,* 20–25; 32–33.

34. Gurlitt mentions several secular buildings, palaces in the Italian style, before he comes to the Jesuit churches. "Viel mehr wird man sehen, dass die Jesuiten nicht im 'Jesuitenstil' bauten oder besser, dass dieser Namen eine völlig andere Auslegung erhalten muss." Gurlitt, *Geschichte des Barockstiles und des Rococco in Deutschland,* 16.

35. Gurlitt, *Geschichte des Barockstiles und des Rococco in Deutschland,* chap. 3.

36. Riegl, for instance, argued: "Bedeutung dieses Baues: eine Jesuitenkirche in Rom. Die Jesuiten kämpfen für die geistliche Weltherrschaft des Papstes in Rom; das ist ja die gegenreformatorische Tendenz, deren Träger eben die Jesuiten sind. Am Zentralsitz dieser Weltmacht, wo auch der Zentralsitz ihrer eigenen Tätigkeit ist, errichten sie ein Gotteshaus. Es muss also 1. Die gegenreformatorische Empfindung darin zum reinsten Ausdruck gelanden; 2. Schon mit Rücksicht auf den unweigerlichen Gehorsam der Jesuitenniederlassungen gegenüber der römische Zentralleitung muss diese römische Jesuitenkirche ein Typus werden für die Jesuiten-Tochterkirchen in den übrigen Ländern, aber auch für den neukatholischen, gegenreformatorischen Kirchenbau überhaupt, da er auch von den Jesuiten geführt wird." Alois Riegl, *Die Entstehung der Barockkunst in Rom,* 2nd ed. (Vienna: Anton Schroll, 1908), 101. Galassi Paluzzi previously *(La storia segreta dello stile dei gesuiti,* 34–37) pointed out

the synthesis of Riegl's thesis, but in the form of a somewhat hysterical dissection of what he called the "syllogistic" logic of this passage.

37. Gurlitt's nationalist sympathies are apparent throughout the book. They were explicit in his support of Julius Langbehn. See Stern, *Politics of Cultural Despair,* chap. 7. On Gurlitt's career see also Udo Kultermann, *The History of Art History* (New York: Abaris, 1993), 136–37.

38. The remarks were made 21–22 July 1941. Adolf Hitler, *Hitler's Secret Conversations 1941–1944,* trans. Norman Cameron and R. H. Stevens (New York: Farrar Straus and Young, 1953), 5:8.

39. My thanks to Joseph Leo Koerner for wise counsel on this passage. See the introduction to Levy, *Propaganda and the Jesuit Baroque* for further contextualization of this remark, one which I intend to treat more fully in a future study, *The Jesuit Style.*

40. Heinrich Heine, *Religion and Philosophy in Germany,* trans. John Snodgrass (Boston: Beacon Press, 1959), especially 40–41. The essays were written in 1833–34 and first published in France. For the intersection of Heine's anti-Jesuitism and his art criticism see Margaret A. Rose, *Marx's Lost Aesthetic. Karl Marx and the Visual Arts* (Cambridge, Mass.: Cambridge University Press, 1984), 21–22.

41. Alfred Rosenberg, *Der Mythus des 20. Jahrhunderts* (Munich: Hoheneichen, 1930), 374–75.

42. Ilg's praise of Jesuit architecture in an essay of 1886 was quoted at length in Bernhard Duhr, *Jesuiten-Fabeln. Ein Beitrag zur Kulturgeschichte* (Freiburg im Breisgau: 1891), 683–85. My thanks to Joseph Imorde for putting Duhr's book in my hands and leading me to this important source. On Ilg see Friedrich Polleross, ed., *Fischer von Erlach und die Wiener Barocktradition* (Vienna: Boehlau, 1995), especially the essays by Polleross and Elisabeth Springer.

43. The question of national styles runs throughout German art history of the nineteenth and early twentieth centuries. For an overview see Hans Belting, *Identität im Zweifel. Ansichten der deutschen Kunst* (Cologne: Dumont, 1999). At times of war (or anticipation thereof) the issue became pressing. For a fascinating study of the development of Wölfflin's formalism as a response to (or rather, against) overtly nationalistic art history around World War I, see Martin Warnke, "On Heinrich Wölfflin," trans. David Levin, *Representations,* 27 (1989): 172–87. Wölfflin himself published a moving article in the *Neue Zuricher Zeitung* in 1936, arguing that national categories, while valid, are less important than art's capacity to transcend geographical divisions, to provide a locus for our common humanity. Heinrich Wölfflin, "Au sujet de 'l'art

national,'" in *Réflections sur l'histoire de l'art,* trans. Rainer Rochlitz (Paris: Flammarion, 1997), 170–72. The national socialists not only encouraged but insisted on nationalist thematics in all areas of cultural history. Symptomatic examples of such writing include A. E. Brinckmann, *Geist der Nationen. Italiener - Franzosen - Deutsche* (Hamburg: Hoffman und Campe, 1938). On German art history during the national socialist era see Heinrich Dilly, *Deutsche Kunsthistoriker 1933–1945* (Munich: Deutscher Kunstverlag, 1988).

44. Hans Belting, *The Germans and Their Art: A Troublesome Relationship,* trans. Scott Kleager (New Haven, Conn.: Yale University Press, 1998).

45. This paper is the revision of a lecture given at the Thirtieth International Congress of the History of Art (London, 2000). My thanks to Joseph Imorde, Michael Koortbojian, and Christina Corsiglia for reading that version of the paper. Research for this paper was funded by the Social Sciences and Humanities Research Council of Canada (2000) and the Canadian Centre for Architecture (1998). My thanks to the CCA library staff and to Alexandra Gerstein for her enthusiastic collaboration on my search for the origins of the Jesuit style.

PART III: STORY

The Council of Trent: Myths, Misunderstandings, and Misinformation

John W. O'Malley, S.J.

FOR EDUCATED PERSONS WITH AN INTEREST IN HISTORY, the word *Trent* rings a bell. Faint and muffled, however, is the sound. Wasn't Trent a church council? Against Luther? If those persons happen to be Roman Catholics, *Trent* might even clang like a summons to arms, for undoubtedly they hold one of two extreme views: that the council wrought all the bad things that Vatican Council II saved them from, or that it set forth all the good things Vatican II robbed them of. Few are those, including theologians, who move much deeper than these clichés. Yet even the clichés suggest that Trent—whatever it was—was important.

In 1975 Hubert Jedin, perhaps the most distinguished and prolific Catholic church historian of the twentieth century, published the fourth and final volume of his history of the Council of Trent, the first ever written with full access to the sources.[1] Anyone who has taken the trouble to read *Geschichte des Konzils von Trient* recognizes that its publication marked a great moment in ecclesiastical scholarship. Few, it seems, have bothered to do so. The first two volumes were translated into English in 1957 and 1961, shortly after their publication in the original German. They aroused interest to some extent because they appeared just as Vatican Council II was getting under way. Many people wanted to know what the relationship was between these two councils, especially if Vatican II was, as many said, "the end of the Counter-Reformation" just as Trent was its embodiment. But interest soon waned severely, as the old clichés reappeared despite Jedin's labors. The last two volumes have never been translated into English, and I know few English-language historians who have worked their way through them. Jedin's great work, as the little girl said about the book on snakes, tells people more about Trent than they could possibly want to know.

Except for Jedin's ongoing publications, few serious historical studies of Trent have appeared in any language since the 1960s.[2] Why? Scholars lost interest partly because Jedin did such a good job; he left few stones unturned. And interests shift. Lately interest in Catholicism in the sixteenth and seventeenth centuries has surged among scholars in France, Italy, and North America; but these scholars have bypassed Trent itself to concentrate on the period after the council.[3] Among other things, they are curious about how Trent was interpreted and implemented, which sometimes comes down to studying what crimes or good deeds were done in its name without necessarily reflecting what the council actually enacted.

It is now clear, for instance, that Charles Borromeo, archbishop of Milan (1564–82) and great implementer of Trent, in effect rewrote the decrees by giving them a specificity and sometimes a rigor they originally lacked, and by supplying what he thought the council ought to have done but had failed to do. The Papal Curia, in its tug-of-war with Borromeo and other bishops over who had the right to interpret and implement the council, moved along similar lines. These interpretations were foisted onto the council and became Trent.[4] In some ways, therefore, this new scholarship, for all its merits, has contributed to the tradition of ignorance and misunderstanding of the council itself. The Council of Trent fell victim to the law of unintended consequences and became "Trent."

In this essay I intend only to sketch the information essential for understanding the council, which I hope will dispel a few of the myths and misunderstandings that surround it. The essay is an altogether modest effort, yet it does explore the subject in greater depth than even specialized encyclopedias.[5] I offer it as a basic map of the council that suggests a few of the council's consequences. While the interpretation herein is surely my own, I am much indebted to the labor of other scholars, especially Jedin.

What It Was About

The Council of Trent opened on 13 December 1545. Many people had long before despaired of it ever happening. Two persons cooperated in bringing it into being: Pope Paul III (1534–49) and Emperor Charles V (1519–55).[6] They had overcome seemingly insuperable odds, including a mutual distrust that only two years later led to a final breach in their relationship and then to a forced adjournment of the council lasting until a new pope was elected. Yet Luther had posted his Ninety-five Theses in 1517. What obstacles had delayed the council for well over a generation?

The obstacles were many, but two were especially important: the vacillation of Pope Clement VII (1523–34), who feared that the council might depose him, and the obstructive tactics of King Francis I of France (1515–47), who feared that a council, if successful, would strengthen the political hand of his great rival, Charles V, by eliminating in Germany the threat of civil war created by the volatile and often violent religious situation.

What the delay meant, in any case, was that the Reformation had time to sink deep roots long before the council got under way. Did the delay mean that the breach could not be healed? Opinions differed. Charles V and his entourage hoped, for the sake of the peace of "the empire," that is, of Germany, that it could. The bishops who finally gathered at Trent in late 1545—practically all of them Italian—probably hoped that it could but thought it could not. This difference in assessment of the situation reflected an even more profound difference in priorities between the pope and the emperor.

Luther's challenge had been twofold. Its origin and center was an idea, an idea about how we are saved, namely, through justification by faith alone. This idea or doctrine soon led him to others: new definitions of the sacraments and an utter repudiation of the papacy, which he soon came to see as the Antichrist. Luther's second challenge was a practical one, a call for reform of various ecclesiastical and religious practices and especially of the lifestyle of the higher clergy. He first effectively hurled this challenge in 1520 in his famous "Appeal to the Ruling Class." This summons to action not only echoed grievances voiced by devout Christians for well over a century but also was directed pointedly against the popes and the papal curia, commonly seen as the principal offenders. The popular slogan rang out: "Reform Rome and you will reform the world."[7]

When Paul III and Charles V were finally able to accomplish the successful convocation of the council, they were agreed in a generic way that both of these challenges had to be answered. But that is where the agreement ended. The pope envisaged the council principally as a response to the doctrinal issues raised by Luther, issues that he and many others interpreted as just some old heresies in the new dress. They could, therefore, easily be dealt with. The Protestants were to be condemned, and with little more ado, the council could conclude its business. The condemnation would probably preclude any possibility of reconciliation with them, but Paul and many in his entourage thought that was a lost cause anyway. Orthodoxy would triumph, and in subsequent generations the wayward could be won back. The council needed to be much more circumspect about reform, however, which was an issue best handled by the pope, particularly where it involved the papacy and the papal curia.

Charles V had an agenda for the council almost diametrically opposed to Paul III's. He was not convinced that reconciliation with the Lutherans was impossible, and he therefore feared a condemnation of Luther's doctrine, believing it would seal the division irreparably, as well as lead to civil war in Germany. A practical man, he sincerely believed that the real problem was reform, and that the unreformed condition of the church had caused the Lutheran crisis. A reform of the church was therefore the precondition, at least, for resolving it.

The agenda for the council was thus set amidst a fundamental conflict of priorities over "the uprooting of heresies" and "the reform of the clergy and the Christian people," as the council itself came to describe these two goals. This double agenda persisted throughout the long history of the council, until well after the deaths of the two men who principally established it, and under these two headings all of its enactments can be gathered. In the early months of 1546, the bishops at Trent—only a few more than the meager thirty who opened the council—agreed that they would deal with both doctrine and reform alternately: first a decree on doctrine and then a decree on some aspect of reform.[8] The council proceeded according to this rhythm until it finally declared its business finished seventeen years later, in December of 1563.

"Doctrine and reform." Put in such terms, the agenda sounds global, without delimitation, as if comprehending every aspect of Catholic belief and life. No doubt, the agenda at Trent was ample, but it was much more restricted than those terms and subsequent myths imply. The council was far from being as all-encompassing as Vatican Council II tried to be. Under "doctrine," the council meant to treat only Protestant teachings that were seen to conflict with Catholic teaching. Thus Trent made no pronouncements about the Trinity, the Incarnation, and other Christian truths that Protestants accepted. In this regard Trent had Luther principally in mind, with only scant attention to Zwingli, the Anabaptists, and even Calvin. True, during the last period the council met, 1562–63, the threat of Calvinism in France was much on the council's mind, but the most important doctrinal decrees had already been formulated.

"Reform" had a similarly precise focus. For the bishops at Trent, "reform of the clergy and the Christian people"—or, as it was more commonly expressed, "the reform of the church"—meant essentially reform of three offices in the church: the papacy, the episcopacy, and the pastorate. This last office comprised, quite specifically, pastors of parishes, although it included a few others like certain chaplains who had the "care of the souls," in the strict canonical sense of the term. It included, therefore, members of the local "diocesan" clergy who were under the direct supervision of the bishop but *not* members of male religious orders like the Dominicans and Franciscans, whose superiors were not the local bishop.[9] In other words, the "church" that in this case was to be reformed was what today is sometimes called "the institutional church." Trent made some regulations concerning "regulars" (i.e., members of the religious orders) but principally clarified their relationship to bishops. The council dealt of course with the laity and directed its efforts to the "reform of the Christian people," but it did so almost exclusively through directives for pastors. "Reform" in Trent was much less comprehensive, you will note, than the *aggiornamento* of Vatican II.

The simplicity of the Tridentine doctrinal and reform agenda easily escapes students because the decrees and canons of the council are always published in chronological order, as they were formulated and ratified over the many years the council lasted. Those decrees and canons appear, therefore, as discrete units, with no connecting narrative, and can seem to be merely a jumble of edicts and pithy condemnations. The canons *de reformatione* in particular—about 150 of them scattered over various sections of the text—read like an endless scattershot of rules, regulations, and prohibitions devoid of plan and vision, framed in a language of canonical discipline that is darkly opaque today, even for well-educated readers. Nonetheless, Trent has, in both its doctrinal and disciplinary enactments, a remarkable and consistently maintained focus.

Trent on Doctrine

Despite their number and length, the doctrinal decrees deal substantially with only two issues: justification and the sacraments. Most of the bishops who assembled at Trent in 1545 had never read a word Luther wrote and knew only through hearsay what he supposedly had taught. Most of the theologians they called on to assist them knew little more, but among them were a few—like Girolamo Seripando, prior general of the Augustinian order—who were better informed.[10] Another such was Cardinal Reginald Pole, one of the three papal legates who presided over the council in that first, crucial period (1545–47).[11] Soon after the council got under way, therefore, the bishops realized that the justification issue was central to their task and that it would not be easy to resolve. Before addressing justification directly, however, they first had to address the closely related doctrine of original sin. The decree on original sin, though published in its own right, surely needs to be considered as a prelude to the decree on justification.[12] In the late spring of 1546 they set about constructing the latter decree, which took them seven months to complete.

Practically everybody who has studied the council without animus has assessed the decree of justification as its masterpiece.[13] It is surely one of the most considered, for every word was weighed and debated. Stung by Luther's criticism that Catholics were Pelagians who believed that "works" rather than grace saved them, the council insisted sedulously that justification was accomplished always and everywhere under the inspiration of grace; that the beginning, middle, and end of the process of justification was grace-inspired. One did not do what one could on one's own so that grace would be given. All movement toward grace was done under the impulse of grace. "Good works" were not good unto salvation unless they were grace-inspired. Thus, within the theological framework in which it formulated its decree, the council was resoundingly anti-Pelagian.

The council interpreted Luther, however, as denying any human part in justification, as altogether eliminating human responsibility—relying on "grace alone." Anti-Pelagian though the council was, it also taught that in some mysterious way, human beings played a role in their own justification. Indeed they somehow "cooperated" in it, though grace always held primacy. The clear though subtle and careful way the council enunciated this aspect of its teaching distinguished its position from what it understood Luther to propound.

The decree was solemnly approved on 13 January 1547. With that approval, many at the council thought they had accomplished their most difficult task and could bring the business to a rapid conclusion within a few months. It had already lasted too long. Among factors frustrating that hope was the protracted treatment the council found itself giving the sacraments. Luther had not only denied that there were seven but had also redefined the two that he saw as clearly taught in the New Testament: baptism and the Eucharist. The council decided to answer Luther point for point, sacrament for sacrament—a project begun in the first period (1545–47), continued in the second (1551–52), but not completed until the third (1562–63). For sheer quantity the sacraments comprise most of the "doctrine" of the Council of Trent.

In the opening weeks of the council, the bishops decided that, as far as possible, they would frame their teaching in the language of Scripture and the fathers of the church and would eschew the technical language developed by scholastic theologians of the Middle Ages. They were somewhat successful in observing this resolve in the decrees on original sin and justification but could not sustain it for the sacraments, principally because most of the teaching available on the sacraments, except to some extent on baptism and the Eucharist, had been developed by scholastics.

The scholastic framework of matter and form, of the four "causes," and of similar categories is the first distinguishing mark of the Tridentine doctrine on the sacraments. The second characteristic is its insistence on their sevenfold number, qualified by a further insistence that they were not equal in dignity or in necessity for the Christian life. Luther refused to accept the sevenfold number because it was not clear from the Scripture that each of the seven was instituted by Christ. The third, and quite special, characteristic of Trent's teaching is, consequently, not only an insistence that they were all instituted by Christ but that they have come down from him and the apostles to the present in an unbroken and undeviating tradition. No previous council had so repeatedly propounded such continuity and changelessness in the handing on of doctrine. This feature of Trent contributed to the Catholic penchant for emphasizing continuities among historical happenings and minimizing discontinuities.

Justification and the sacraments constitute the essence of Trent's doctrinal teaching. In dealing with those subjects, the council of course understood them with a certain amplitude, as necessarily including some of their implications and consequences. Under the rubric of justification, therefore, the council made statements about predestination, about the kind of certitude persons might have of their salvation, and similar matters. As mentioned, original sin received a separate decree, but—except for a brief statement on purgatory—this was done for no other doctrine. Furthermore, the council did not venture professedly into Christology, ecclesiology, pneumatology, or any similar doctrinal domain.

Nonetheless, Luther's interpretation of "Scripture alone" as the basis for all teaching meant that, even before the council began to address the doctrinal issues before it, it had to determine the basis on which it would argue them. What is "Scripture," that is, what books constitute the canon? Here the council decided to include the so-called deuterocanonical books, such as Judith and Wisdom, which Luther and other Protestants did not accept. What about "alone"? Although many medieval theologians, including Aquinas, had held a "Scripture alone" position, they could not interpret it rigidly because it was so difficult to find in Scripture confirmation of one of the articles of the Creed—Christ's "descent into hell"— or to find justification for certain practices of long standing that some Protestants would reject, particularly the practice of infant baptism. For that reason the council included with Scripture "apostolic traditions." Not just *any* traditions, but *apostolic* traditions, that is, those presumably few that were "handed on as it were from the apostles themselves at the inspiration of the Holy Spirit."[14]

The word, you will note, is in the plural—not *Tradition*, as some great flowing stream, but *traditions*, some quite particular teachings and practices that the council did not at this point specify. This very short and first decree of the council fired a salvo that, especially as time wore on, ever more fundamentally set the Catholic theological enterprise at odds with the Protestant.

Trent on Reform

Of the three offices in the church that needed reform, the papacy was first on just about everybody's list. During the council, reform of the papacy aroused some of the bitterest controversy because the large number of bishops who promoted it consistently felt themselves frustrated at every crucial turn by the maneuvers of the papal legates presiding over the sessions, who themselves sometimes felt frustrated by instructions from Rome. Over this issue the most serious crisis of the council occurred; for ten months beginning in September of 1562, the council ground to a standstill, and all sessions were suspended.[15] Only upon the appointment of a new legate, the masterful Giovanni Morone, who had recently been released from the papal prison, was the council able to renew its operation.[16] Except for a brief and perfunctory bit of sumptuary regulation for prelates that in passing mentioned the cardinals, it was agreed that the papacy would have complete control of its own reform.[17]

In the reform of the episcopacy, however, the council began cautiously. Nevertheless, by the third period, under Morone's leadership, it courageously passed a series of measures that aimed, as Jedin puts it, at transforming bishops from collectors of benefices into pastors of souls.[18] The bishops at the council found themselves unable to reform the papacy, but they could—despite the fear and resistance many of them felt—reform themselves. This meant reforming themselves where it hurt most—in their bank accounts. In that regard, the two most fundamental reforms the council instituted required bishops to reside in their dioceses and forbade them, under strict penalties, to hold and collect revenues from more than one bishopric at a time. These decrees were the foundation stones of the Tridentine reform. It is difficult for us to realize what a dramatic redefinition of episcopal lifestyle such decrees were perceived as entailing, and how deeply they were seen as cutting into the pocketbooks of many bishops. Indeed, it is amazing how much of the reform legislation of Trent deals with money. If there was a "moral miracle" at the Council of Trent, this was it!

The council also required bishops to hold regular synods with their clergy, to visit and oversee the parishes and other institutions of the diocese, to show greater stringency in admitting candidates to priestly ordination, to assure that confessors be properly qualified, and to promote teaching on Sundays and feast days, setting an example themselves. By early on defining preaching as the bishops' "chief task" *(praecipuum munus)*, the council provided its own impetus for the great flowering of preaching in Catholicism for the next century and a half.[19]

The council established a closer relationship between bishops and the parish clergy than was common earlier, even though the relationship was articulated in juridical and disciplinary terms. By its many canons concerning the parish, the council gave a new prominence to that institution, thereby promoting the idea that it was the site where pastoral activity properly took place. The pastor emerged with a clear profile of duties, traditional for the most part but articulated with new detail and enforced through new sanctions. Parallel to the bishop's obligation to reside in his diocese, the pastor's principal obligations included residing in his parish and not being pastor of more than one. The pastor's function consisted in properly administering the rites and sacraments of the church and in preaching on Sundays and holy days. The council made no mention of what we today would call social ministries.

In decreeing that every diocese should establish a seminary for the training of poor boys for the priesthood, the council made a break with the informal apprentice system widely operative up to that time, setting in motion a process of regularization that eventually was taken as normative and, for the diocesan clergy, finally eliminated all alternatives.[20] Although—as in its reform of bishops—the Tridentine program for the reform of the parish clergy was based largely on already existing legislation and tradition, it was nonetheless deep and far-reaching, particularly because of the stringent penalties it threatened for noncompliance.

The reform of the bishops and pastors had as its goal a more effective ministry. It accomplished this goal by codifying and enforcing the discipline proper to the pastoral functions of the bishops and diocesan clergy, and by this means dealt with the religious duties of the faithful. That is, the scope of the Tridentine reform of ministry seemed to assume that the only proper ministers were the bishops who were also the proper supervisors of all ministry in their dioceses and of the parish clergy who provided the "care of souls" for those under them. This purview excluded (except almost as a bothersome intrusion) the ministry of the members of mendicant orders like the Franciscans and the Dominicans. In mid-sixteenth-century Catholicism, not only did these friars *do* most of the preaching and hearing of confessions that took place, but they did so under the supervision of their own superiors, who operated out of large grants of independence from the papacy. At Trent the bishops passed measures that limited the pastoral prerogatives of the mendicants and that also tried to regulate various aspects of the life of members of all religious orders, but their efforts had to be modest because of the papal origin of the prerogatives of many of the orders and monasteries.[21]

These, then, are in the main the "disciplinary" decrees or "reform" decrees of the Council of Trent. These are the "pastoral" decrees of a council often not conceived of as pastoral. In time they had great impact on the way bishops and pastors functioned. They had, however, another great significance. They illustrated beyond a doubt how *episcopal* the reforms of the Council of Trent were. The council wanted not simply to reform the bishops but by so doing to strengthen their moral, their juridical, and their practical authority. Trent did not define the prerogatives of the papacy because, had it been able to do so, it would have in some measure tried to restrict them. This is another aspect of the Council of Trent that is little known or appreciated.

In its decrees and canons on reform the council set forth briefly its pastoral goals; it put teeth into them by the sanctions it threatened for noncompliance. "Discipline and Punish," as Michel Foucault's famous title has it, may seem like a leitmotif of the council. In trying to replace deeply imbedded attitudes and practices with others presumed to be pastorally more apposite, the council could hardly have proceeded otherwise. No realistic person thought exhortations would do the job, but in the long run such procedures reinforced "social disciplining" as an ecclesiastical style.[22]

What Else Is There? What's Not There?

A few of the enactments of Trent that specified the reaches of episcopal authority affected persons or institutions besides pastors and the faithful in their parishes. One of the best known was the decree insisting on the strict cloister of nuns, so that "no nun shall after her profession be permitted to go out of the monastery" except with episcopal approval. This decree applied only to the nuns in the strict sense of the word *(moniales*—in today's popular parlance, "contemplatives"), and did not apply to members of the Third Orders like Saint Catherine of Siena who, always depicted as wearing the Dominican habit, looks to us for all the world like a "nun." Nonetheless, although the decree reflected expectations of many devout Catholics of the day, including Teresa of Ávila, it effected great hardships—financial and psychological—on a number of women. More significant, it created obstacles for the freedom of women in the next century, especially in France, to engage in corporate ministries. Despite the obstacles, women emerged with strikingly new pastoral roles.[23]

The council issued the decrees on nuns and other matters pertaining to members of religious orders on 3 and 4 December 1563, just as it finally concluded its labors. That session of the council was an attempt to tie up loose ends with a grab bag of decrees that for the most part bore little relationship to one another, including a decree forbidding dueling and another that handed over to the Holy See the publication of a catechism, a revised missal and breviary, and an index of prohibited books.[24] In that session also appeared a decree commending the veneration of sacred relics and of sacred images.[25] This decree was obviously meant to counter Protestant attacks on such practices. It briefly specified that "all superstition . . . and lasciviousness" should be avoided in sacred images, thus warranting some later attempts by churchmen to censor all religious art. Promotion of the use of art in worship and piety was the substance of this decree that enunciated, reflected, and promoted a profound divide between Catholics and Protestants that was as much cultural as religious.

In that same session the council issued a decree confirming the existence of purgatory as known from "the sacred writings [Scripture] and the ancient tradition of the fathers taught in sacred councils." Here Trent basically and briefly reiterated the teaching of the Council of Florence, but with a lengthy caution about using purgatory as an occasion "for filthy lucre," an allusion made more explicit later in the decree that, on the very day the council ended, confirmed the validity of indulgences, the issue that had ignited the great religious conflagration a half century earlier.[26]

The council dealt in passing of course with other issues, but perhaps more striking are those that are absent. Surely one of the most ironical features of the Council of Trent is the absence of a decree on authority of the papacy. The council did not even reiterate—as it did for purgatory—the statement on papal primacy published at the Council of Florence.[27] Yet this was the one doctrine Protestants of every stripe, without exception, vociferously repudiated. All the prelates at Trent of course believed in the primacy—otherwise they would not have been present—but they very much disagreed among themselves on what practical prerogatives it entailed and especially on the relationship between the papacy and the episcopacy and even between the papacy and the council itself. True, in one of their last acts at the council they stated that nothing the council enacted was to be interpreted as compromising the authority of the Apostolic See, but they did not specify further.[28] They could not specify further without hopelessly tying up the council.

The attack of the Protestant Reformers on the papacy was just one piece of radical redefinition of the church as it had been understood in the late Middle Ages. In its intention to respond to all Protestant heresies, the council surely should have articulated its own redefinition. It did not and could not, however, for, despite the ecclesial reality that somehow bound the members of the council together, the bishops never could have articulated that bond in a way that would have dealt adequately with both the Protestants and the diversity of opinions among themselves. Trent issued no decree "On the Church."

Trent's focus on the practical matters of bishops and pastors accounts for two other omissions that, from our twenty-first-century perspective, are also striking. Few aspects of Catholicism, indeed, of Catholic "pastoral ministry" in the sixteenth century, are more characteristic and significant than the intense missionary activity that began with Portuguese and Spanish explorations and conquests in the late fifteenth century and continued with immense fervor and expenditure into the seventeenth. On this phenomenon Trent uttered not a word. It fell completely outside the council's purview.

Confraternities fared slightly better, for the council briefly mentioned that bishops had the right to conduct visitations and receive an annual account of their administration.[29] What is not even intimated by these casual mentions, however, is that in many places in Europe these institutions, and similar ones like the Third Orders of the mendicants, provided many—perhaps most—Catholics with their spiritual nourishment and were more important in their lives than the parish church. In them laymen and laywomen ministered to each other's needs, hired chaplains for strictly sacramental functions, and often organized the confraternities or Third Orders into centers for social assistance for the poor and needy.[30] Aside from whatever assistance the town or city supplied for these purposes, the confraternities in most urban centers were, at least in Latin cultures, the major organ of "social ministries." But again, Trent was interested in such institutions only insofar as they related to episcopal authority, and it conceived ministry narrowly as consisting essentially in administration of the sacraments and preaching of sermons in the parish church.

Reading the Bible in vernacular translations for spiritual nourishment was a devout practice among the literate in Catholic

Europe in the early sixteenth century, although it had been forbidden in some places, such as England, and was highly suspect in others. Luther's "Scripture alone" threw the issue into a hot glare. It was therefore expected that the council would pronounce on the matter, but it did not, not even in the decree on Scripture and traditions, where it would have logically fitted. In the session after the approval of that decree the council legislated the establishment of lectureships on Scripture for the education and edification of both clergy and laity, which allowed the inference that Bible reading should be promoted.[31]

Seventeen years later, however, just as the council concluded, it passed on to the pope for his consideration "ten rules" concerning prohibited books—"rules," not an "Index" as such, which would name specific authors and titles.[32] The fourth rule put severe restrictions on the practice of reading the Bible, providing that it could be allowed only with permission of the bishop or local inquisitor "to those who they know will derive from such reading . . . an increase of faith and piety." Although these "rules" do not constitute an official decree of the council, they nonetheless sent a powerful message and were one of the forces that, after the council, encouraged an official crusade against the reading of the Bible and in most Catholic cultures, effectively obliterated it. The radically diverging attitudes of Catholics and Protestants toward this practice became in time one of the most important lines of demarcation dividing them—more important even than the doctrine of justification by faith alone.

Finally, contrary to what often is said, Trent did not decree that the Mass must be celebrated in Latin. The council made two very brief, almost casual, statements on the matter. The first: "It has not been deemed advisable . . . that the mass be celebrated elsewhere *[passim]* in the vernacular tongue."[33] The second, which removes all doubt about the council's intent, occurs in the corresponding canon: It is forbidden to hold that "the mass ought to be celebrated in the vernacular tongue only" *[lingua tantum vulgari]*.[34] In other words, it is legitimate, despite what the heretics say, to celebrate the liturgy in Latin. This is a far cry from decreeing that it must be celebrated in that tongue and a far cry from forbidding the vernacular. Trent left the question open. Here we have an excellent illustration of how the council began to be misconstrued and manipulated almost before the ink was dry, and thus of how "Trent" began often to bear only a distorted relationship to what the council actually decreed and intended.

After the Council

The bishops at Trent realized that all their work would go for naught if it failed to receive papal approval. Though the council had been guided by a series of legates appointed by the popes, the city of Trent was a long way from Rome, and none of the three popes under whom the council met during its eighteen-year history had ever set foot as pope in the council chambers. Moreover, not everything that the council had determined could be presumed pleasing to the popes or to their entourages. Pius IV, pope when the council ended, refused to listen to those advisers who entreated him to delay approval of the decrees or to proceed selectively by omitting or correcting some of them. He forthwith decided to approve and promulgate the decrees in their entirety. This decision immediately put the council on almost unassailable ground within the Catholic context.

By this act Pius also implicitly put the papacy forward as the chief interpreter and implementer of the Trent decrees and initiated the battle over who should interpret and implement them. Three groups of rival claimants soon emerged. The first was the popes, who assumed that interpretation and implementation were their prerogatives, a claim to which Pope Sixtus V gave institutional grounding in 1588 by creating the Congregation of the Council, a bureau of the Roman Curia empowered to issue authoritative interpretations of Trent. The council itself had supported this claim by commending to the papacy the publication of an Index, catechism, missal, and breviary.[35]

The second claimants—best exemplified by St. Charles Borromeo as archbishop of Milan—placed emphasis on the leadership of the local churches and on the right and duty of bishops to adapt, regulate, and even expand upon what the council had decreed. This claim based itself solidly on the fundamental principle of church order promoted and insisted upon again and again by the council's decrees—the dignity and leadership role of the local bishop. Trent was, to say it again, a radically *episcopal* council.

In accordance with the provisions made by the council, Borromeo held a series of important synods with his clergy and with suffragan bishops, eventually publishing the results as the *Acta ecclessiae Mediolanensis,* the "decrees of the church of Milan." This volume, along with some of Borromeo's treatises on subjects like confession and ecclesiastical furnishings, became best-sellers among high churchmen and to some extent replaced the reform decrees of the council itself.[36] But Borromeo often found himself at odds with a papal curia that viewed these developments with distrust and sometimes tried to obstruct them.

The third claimants were the "Catholic princes," for whom Trent was too important to be left in the hands of the churchmen, especially in its regulations about benefices and bishops. King Phillip II almost immediately allowed the decrees to be promulgated in Spain and his other extensive dominions, but he made it clear that no important measures would be enacted without his knowledge and approbation. In France, where religious wars persisted until 1549, a widespread resistance to the council among both clergy and laity as well as other factors delayed official acceptance of Trent until 1615. The crown was by then strong enough to protect its traditional prerogatives in many ecclesiastical matters.

Bit by bit, however, the impact of "Trent," already at least a step removed from the actual decrees, became evident. The most notable effect, perhaps, was that within a century bishops were, for the most part, resident in their dioceses and taking their pastoral responsibilities more seriously than before.[37] They established seminaries and insisted on a new standard of deportment for the parish clergy. In other ways the council soon had a direct or indirect impact on almost every aspect of ecclesiastical life, although the pattern was very uneven.

By the seventeenth century Rome had for the most part established itself as the effective interpreter of the council and, in responding to various pressures of the era, more and more presented the council as a systematic, complete, and exhaustive response to every problem. From Rome itself, therefore, sprang the myth still prevalent today that "Trent" was comprehensive in its scope and exhaustively detailed in all its provisions. Closure became the watchword. As Giuseppe Alberigo said, "Under the aegis of the council, Catholic theology in the post-Tridentine era closed a great number of open questions, which at Trent were indeed recognized as such. The effect was to put a blight on theological pluralism and to promote a false identification of the certainties of faith with theological intransigence."[38] His observation applies broadly.

Endnotes

1. Hubert Jedin, *Geschichte des Konzils von Trient,* vol. 4 (Freiburg: Herder, 1949–75), hereafter "Jedin, *Trent.*" Only the first two volumes have been translated into English: *A History of the Council of Trent,* vol. 2, trans. Ernest Graf (London: Thomas Nelson and Sons, 1957–61). For a bibliography of Jedin's publications over his long career, most of which pertain in some way or other to Trent, see Robert Samulski, "Bibliographie Hubert Jedin 1926–1975," *Annali dell'Istituto storico italo-germanico in Trento,* 6 (1980): 287–359, and Giorgio Butterini, "Bibliografia Hubert Jedin 1976–1980," *Annali dell'Istituto storico italo-germanico in Trento,* 6 (1980): 360–67.

2. The collection of articles in *Concilium Tridentinum,* ed. Remigius Bäumer (Darmstadt: Wissenschaftliche Buchgesellschaft, 1979), consists almost exclusively of articles published in the 1950s and 1960s. A wonderful exception is Alain Tallon, *La France et le Concile de Trente, 1518–1563* (Rome: École Francaise de Rome, 1997).

3. See Paolo Prodi and Wolfgang Reinhard, eds., *Il Concilio di Trento e il moderno* (Bologna: Il Mulino, 1996) and Cesare Mozzarelli and Danilo Zardin, eds., *I tempi del Concilio: Religione, cultura e societa nell'Europa tridentina* (Rome: Bulzoni, 1997).

4. See Giuseppe Alberigo, "Du Councile de Trente au tridentinisme," *Irenikon,* 54 (1981): 192–210.

5. See Alberigo, "Trent, Council of," in *The Oxford Encyclopedia of the Reformation,* ed. Hans J. Hillerbrand (New York: Oxford University Press, 1996), 4:173–77; John W. O'Malley, "Trent, Council of," in *Encyclopedia of the Renaissance,* ed. Paul F. Grendler (New York: Charles Scribner's Sons, 1999), 6:169–71. Paradigmatic is the article by Jedin himself, "Trent, Council of," in *New Catholic Encyclopedia* (New York: McGraw-Hill, 1967), 14:271–78.

6. The first volume of Jedin's *Trent* covers the long negotiations required to effectively convoke the council, especially 446–544.

7. On the situation among the cardinals, see Barbara McClung Hallman, *Italian Cardinals, Reform, and the Church as Property, 1499–1563* (Berkeley: University of California Press, 1985).

8. See Jedin, *Trent,* 2:13–51.

9. See John W. O'Malley, "Priesthood, Ministry, and Religious Life: Some Historical and Historiographical Considerations," *Theological Studies,* 49 (1988): 223–57.

10. See Hubert Jedin, *Girolamo Seripando: Sein Leben und Denken im Geisteskampf des 16 Jahrhunderts*, 2 vols. (Wurzburg: Rita Verlag, 1937). In English as *Papal Legate at the Council of Trent: Cardinal Seripando*, trans. Frederic C. Eckhoff (St. Louis, Mo.: Herder, 1947).

11. See Dermot Fenlon, *Heresy and Obedience in Tridentine Italy: Cardinal Pole and the Counter Reformation* (Cambridge, Mass.: Cambridge University Press, 1972).

12. See Jedin, *Trent*, 2:125–65. For the decree itself, see Norman P. Tanner, ed., *Decrees of the Ecumenical Councils* (London: Sheed & Ward, 1990), 2:665–67.

13. Tanner, *Decrees*, 2:671–81. See Jedin, *Trent*, 2:166–96, 239–316. The decree has been much commented upon. See Heiko Oberman, "Das tridentinische Rechtfertigungsdekret im Lichte Spätmittelalterlicher Theologie," in Bäumer, *Concilium Tridentinum*, 301–40.

14. Tanner, *Decrees*, 2:663–65; Jedin, *Trent*, 2:52–98.

15. See Jedin, *Trent*, 4/1:237–70, and his *Crisis and Closure of the Council of Trent: A Retrospective View from the Second Vatican Council*, trans. N. D. Smith (London: Sheed and Ward, 1967).

16. See Jedin, *Trent*, 4/2:3–79, and his *Crisis*.

17. Tanner, *Decrees*, 2:744–53, 759–74. See Jedin, *Trent*, 4/2:50–79, 140–63, and Jedin and Alberigo, *Il tipo ideale di vescovo secondo la riforma cattolica* (Brescia: Morcelliana, 1985), especially 3–98.

18. Tanner, *Decrees*, 2:784–85.

19. Tanner, *Decrees*, 2:669.

20. Tanner, *Decrees*, 2:750–53.

21. Tanner, *Decrees*, 2:776–84.

22. On this complicated question, see John W. O'Malley, *Trent and All That: Renaming Catholicism in the Early Modern Era* (Cambridge, Mass.: Harvard University Press, 2000), especially 114–17, 130–40.

23. See Elizabeth Rapely, *The Dévotes: Women and Church in Seventeenth-Century France* (Montreal: McGill-Queen's University Press, 1990).

24. Tanner, *Decrees*, 2:774–99. See Jedin, *Trent*, 4/2:164–89.

25. Tanner, *Decrees*, 2:774–76.

26. Tanner, *Decrees*, 2:774, 796–97. For Florence on purgatory, see Tanner, *Decrees*, 1:527.

27. For Florence, see Tanner, *Decrees*, 1:528.

28. Tanner, *Decrees*, 2:796. Here is the full wording of canon 21: "Finally, the holy council declares that each and every matter that has been laid down in this council about reformation of conduct and ecclesiastical discipline, in whatever phrasing and form of words, both under Popes Paul II and Julius III of happy memory and under the blessed Pius IV, are so decreed that the authority of the Apostolic See is and is understood to be intact in all of them."

29. Tanner, *Decrees*, 2:740.

30. The literature on confraternities during this period has exploded in the last ten years. One of the early books responsible for turning historians' interest to the subject is Brian Pullan, *Rich and Poor in Renaissance Venice: The Social Institutions of a Catholic State to 1620* (Cambridge, Mass.: Harvard University Press, 1971). Developments in this field can now be followed in the serial *Confraternitas*.

31. Tanner, *Decrees*, 2:667–69. See Jedin, *Trent*, 2:99–124. See also John W. O'Malley, *The First Jesuits* (Cambridge, Mass.: Harvard University Press, 1993), 104–10.

32. This document can be found in English translation in *The Canons and Decrees of the Council of Trent*, ed. and trans. H. J. Schroeder (St. Louis, Mo.: B. Herder, 1941; reprint Rockford, Ill.: Tan Books and Publishers, 1978), 273–78.

33. Tanner, *Decrees*, 2:735.

34. Tanner, *Decrees*, 2:736, canon 9.

35. On the liturgical books, see Jedin, *Trent*, 4/2:238–41, and his "Das Konzil von Trient und die Reform der liturgischen Bucher," in the collection of his publications entitled *Kirche des Glaubens: Kirche der Geschichte* (Frieburg: Herder, 1966), 2:499–525.

36. See Jedin and Alberigo, *Il tipo ideale*, 99–189, and Franco Buzzi and Danilo Zardin, eds., *Carlo Borromeo e l'opera della "grande riforma": Cultura, religione e arti del governo nella Milano del pieno Cinquecento* (Milan: Credito Artigiano, 1997).

37. See Joseph Bergin, *The Making of the French Episcopate, 1589–1661* (New Haven, Conn.: Yale University Press, 1996).

38. Alberigo, "The Council of Trent," in *Catholicism in Early Modern History: A Guide to Research*, ed. John W. O'Malley (St. Louis, Mo.: Center for Reformation Research, 1988), 223.

Novices in the Early Society of Jesus: Antonio Valentino, S.J., and the Novitiate at Novellara, Italy

Peter J. Togni, S.J.

THE REALITY AND THE IDEAL

By 1547, THERE WAS ALREADY TALK IN ROME ABOUT THE inadequacy of keeping the novices in regular Jesuit communities with the professed members. In a letter written by Juan de Polanco under commission from St. Ignatius to Simão Rodrigues in Coimbra, Polanco stated that "the plan is to build or acquire a house here in Rome for those freshly entering who intend to join the Society but have not yet been tested or admitted and are not ready to be sent to studies." The letter went on to state that trusted and experienced members should be assigned to this community and that part of its purpose would be to truly test the candidates "for five or six months" so that "those unsuited for the Society will be dismissed from this house before they can enter our own."[1]

The reasons given for this move reveal a number of issues and tensions that existed in the professed house in Rome. One reason was financial, since scholastic houses could be endowed but professed houses could not. Another was "to get rid of the constant agitation of the members of the house," since there would be so much movement with new members arriving all the time. Other reasons included a better reputation for the professed house, since only formed and mature members would be living there. Thus they could devote themselves more to their ministries, not having to worry about those in the probationary period of their training. Similarly, a separate house of probation with more room would be able to accept more of the influx of new members, and so too, the colleges, not just the professed houses, would benefit since those sent to colleges would have been tested and found suitable for the Jesuit life. Whatever the good intentions and sound reasoning behind Polanco's letter, the first separated novitiate was the one in Messina on the island of Sicily, begun in 1550, only two years after the foundation of the Jesuit college there. A separate house of probation or novitiate in Rome was not established during Ignatius's lifetime, perhaps because he himself so enjoyed living and working with the new candidates for the Order. It was not until Francisco de Borja's generalate in October of 1566 (ten years after Ignatius's death) that Sant' Andrea al Quirinale was founded as a novitiate.[2]

Points made in Polanco's letter are mirrored in a number of similar problems that the professed house in Venice was experiencing in the years immediately preceding the foundation of the novitiate in Novellara—for it too doubled as a house of probation. A somewhat disordered life is described in a letter of 16 August 1569 from Francesco Adorno, the provincial, to Rome:

> Those who are novices are occupied with the work of the other coadjutors, when they go out to confess women or for other tasks. . . . The novices are kept busy accompanying them and doing other tasks that keep them from their exercises. All the services in the house, refectory, [room] for their own exercises, can be provided for them in the corridor above in the six rooms designated [for them] looking out towards the garden and the corridor. Instead they are mixed with all the others throughout the house, and not in a separated place . . .with two priests. Father [Beringucci] is more confessor than master of novices and desires greatly to be relieved of this office.[3]

Adorno adds that the novices can serve as companions for the coadjutors when they go on errands, such as confessing women, but they should not go out on ordinary tasks, nor should they be given jobs that impede their proper exercises and formation. Fifteen novices are currently in the six rooms he mentioned overlooking the garden, and the rector has placed some of the older novices in one of the rooms. Some separation could be effected, Adorno adds, if one of the staircases was designated only for the novice community, but then he repeats one of the basic problems, namely, that "the Master of Novices attends more to other tasks and has a coadjutor" to help with the novices. Moreover the novice master does not even give the novices penances in the refectory; this the minister does. It was only a short time after this letter that Adorno became involved in the first negotiation with Count Camillo Gonzaga's offer to establish a Jesuit presence in his seat at Novellara.

The annual letter written by the rector Antonio Micheli the following year helps to fill out the picture of the house in Venice. Thirty-seven Jesuits are in the house; eleven of these are priests, of whom two are novices. Three are coadjutor brothers, and the rest are novices. The twenty-five novices (including the two priests) would have provided a distinct tone to a house intended as a residence for professed and mature fathers. The quality of the novices is generally judged to be quite good. A few of them are even nobles "of good talent and judgment, and of not little expectation for the service of Christ our Lord, since some of them have spent many years in the study of law, others in philosophy, others rhetoric, and others in humanist and other literary studies." There would be even more novices, Micheli adds, if the house were larger,

> but for the present it is not possible to accept more because those that are here are very confined, taking up not only the normal rooms but even rooms used for other purposes such as the library, the tailor's room, the guest rooms, [and] some are even in the infirmary.[4]

The situation is presented as trying but not hopeless. Perhaps some of Adorno's recommendations from the previous year had been heeded.

Among the tasks undertaken by the novices, Micheli chose to add one of the mortifications already specified in the *Constitutions*, namely, the wearing of old clothing.[5] This exterior mortification was intended to bring about both a sense of humility and, as the clothes from one's previous life wore out, to serve as a sign of the ending of one's old life and the beginning of the new. Apparently, during the previous summer the novice master had managed to acquire a box of old worn clothes made of canvas and twill that he gave to the novices to wear for several days. To profit from even greater mortification, the novices said more rosaries, recited the seven penitential psalms, fasted, and engaged in other disciplines—"and some of them went to the Arsenal with these clothes to pick up firewood given as alms, and then helped the porters to load and unload [the wood] from the boats and bring it into the house." Many of the novices were also sent to the colleges—both in Venice and nearby Murano, where the Jesuits had recently taken on some new apostolic works—where they demonstrated great industry in teaching doctrine.

Two further letters present two slightly different pictures of the Venetian house of probation. Mario Scaduto reports that when Ribadeniera passed through the house as the General's visitor, he found good people but a disordered community "not run the same way as one did in Rome and as the general desires."[6] The novice master who spent more time doing other jobs than being novice master was Mario Beringucci (1536–1604), whom Ribadeniera judged as "without a good attitude and talent for this work."

> The Master of Novices is usually very busy in confession and in other things that keep him from caring for the novices. It would be good to keep an eye on him, so that he might attend more often to his office.
>
> Many times the novices are sent to colleges to study, once the first year of probation is over, without having taken their

vows to the Society. It would be convenient for the superior of this house and for the novice master to be advised about what their responsibilities are along these lines. I have advised the Provincial about the customary usage of the Society [with respect to the care of novices].

As long as there is a house of probation in Venice, charged with formation, it needs to be better accommodated, and better built, which could be done if the [professed] house were raised one floor and another corridor of rooms placed on top of the present one.[7]

Beringucci was eventually shipped off in 1571 with the Venetian fleet to serve as a chaplain in the campaign against the Turks at the battle of Lepanto. According to Scaduto, the one compensation for the house's somewhat chaotic state was Cesare Elmi, the rector for eighteen years who was "of great edification in the city and much loved."[8]

Another problem that the move to Novellara would hopefully solve was provision for a more ordered environment for the giving of the Spiritual Exercises to the novices and for the other exercises important for their spiritual development. Paramount, too, was having capable Jesuits in charge of the novices. Writing in his "Booklet of Consolation" to Jerónimo Domènech, the provincial in Sicily, and dated 20 July 1570, the often apoplectic Nicolo Bobadilla complained:

> Oh, how many have left the Society for the same reason! I have seen things that would have been enough to fill a large book on this same subject, since the Society of Jesus was a new religious order, and it did not have members experienced in government, they would overexert those who entered, and thus they could easily come and go from the house, especially when they did not have a noviceship of sufficient spiritual and corporal exercises, and thus—the superiors being inexperienced and the subjects, weak—it would take but a slight temptation to blow them away, as they say.[9]

Whether these words overstated the case or not, a similar problem relating to giving the Exercises was expressed in the report issued by Sebastião Morais (1535–88), visitor to the Lombard province, during his visit to the novitiate in Arona:

> The discipline of the house as far as the novices are concerned seems to me to be going well enough, and the latest Ordo issued by Provincial is followed, and the quality of the novices, for now is satisfactory, because I see that all are well disposed to receive every good [grace], and they are excited about our Institute and particularly about prayer.
>
> However, I find that some of Ours are not solid, as they give the Exercises to three or four in the same room and take recreation together even though they have already been warned. It also seems to me that the novices are being reared with softness in this, that they never go on pilgrimage except for two or three days . . . and never have to suffer or exercise themselves in humble jobs. . . . They never go to serve in hospitals, because there are none here, and I think this could be provided for by sending them to Milan sometimes, provided that the community at San Fidele would be notified, or to the college as the rules of the novice master state.
>
> I also find in the government of the novices that they are not always engaged in the exercises, as is the custom at Sant' Andrea [in Rome and] which seems necessary to me and that they go to recreation at villa together and nobody stays with them.[10]

Morais goes on to lay the blame on the rector and the minister, who are more concerned with their own "quiet and devotions and find little solace in observing many rules." Eventually in the orders he left behind, he included making sure the novices did experiments and that they did not sleep overnight at the villa.

These two letters provide a context of how the rules of the day and the actual practice differed. The rules were in place—they were officially decreed—but many customs from earlier days, when the procedures were more ad hoc or even haphazard, remained in practice. One need only consider some of the rules that Manuel Ruiz Jurado cites in the appendix of his book, *Origines del Noviciado en la Compañía de Jesus,* to see what the ideal comportment of the novitiate was. Moreover, in the *Regulae* volume of the Monumenta series, there are a number of rules that seek to create a certain style or manner of living proper among the novices. They were not to speak without necessity and only for edification; certainly laughter and "murmuring" were to be avoided. Nothing should be done that could not be made manifest to God, and the novices were to always imagine themselves before God. All the novices' actions were to lead to love of the other novices, and if anyone was to do something "of little edification," he should quickly ask for a penance from the novice master. Conversation should always be conducted in modesty, "trying to appear neither sad or grave, nor very happy and dissolute" *(travajando por no nos mostrar tristes y graves, ni muy alegres y disolutos).*[11] What these rules exhibit, good as they may be in themselves, is a certain tone of silence, sobriety, perhaps even somberness in the life of the novice. To get a sense that the rules themselves, while presenting a spiritual ideal, do not tell the entire story, one need only consider the issues raised in various novitiates where life seemed more "disorderly" than the rules imply.

These cases from various novitiates also serve to illumine how Antonio Valentino's own descriptions of life at Novellara did and did not follow the rules in practice. His own spiritual sensibilities show that he had great interest in the well-being of the novices but also in their proper instruction and guidance so that they could indeed be of service to the Society and to the church. However, the great stress on love and on the novices coming to love the Society and to love God always provided a foil to more severe interpretations of the rules.

Novices Who Entered the Novitiate at Novellara

There is no record of when Antonio Valentino left the Jesuit college in Siena and arrived at the professed house in Venice. Descriptions of the arrival of the novices at Novellara on 31 October 1571 list Valentino as already having been novice master in Venice.[12] Ribadeniera's account of his visit to Venice dated from the beginning of August 1569. Scaduto reports that Beringucci left for his sea adventure during Carnival of 1571.[13] His departure presumably provided the occasion for Valentino to assume the duties of novice master.

The largest source of information concerning the life of the novices comes from the catalogue entries and from the record that Valentino himself kept, much of it anecdotal. The catalogues provide a wide variety of information within a fairly tight boundary. László Lukács, S.J., explained the characteristics of Jesuit catalogues in an article dating from 1957:

> The very special and strongly centralized government of the Society of Jesus required that the superior general himself make decisions in the most important matters that concerned his subjects. It was thus necessary that he know them as intimately as possible. That is why it is not surprising to find in the 12 volumes of Ignatius's correspondence an abundance of information filling a considerable part of this correspondence. However much the founder of the Society already received through the official letters, the copious information of his sons, he nevertheless saw the necessity for a service of information even more regular. Especially the rapid increase in numbers of religious in the Society led him to issue an order to find a new system of keeping track. These new pieces of information would be the "catalogues." Even in the *Constitutions* the saint made mention of these catalogues of persons in two places [part VIII, chapter 1, number 9, notes N and P, and part IX, chapter

6, number 3]. According to his plan, these should contain not only the names of the persons belonging to the different houses in the Society, but at the same time minute information concerning the character of each religious.[14]

Beringucci had reported that the group of novices in Venice the previous year was quite well educated, and the same can be said about the group that arrived with Valentino in Novellara. The first community was composed of the following:

1. *Nicolo Spinola*, from Genoa, age 21, entered 10 March 1571

2. *Gio. Antonio Vezzani*, from Parma, age 17, a student, entered 6 November 1570

3. *Francesco Murtio*, from Nicosia, Cyprus, age 35, doctor of law and philosophy, also studied theology for four years, entered 29 August 1571

4. *Scipione Biaggi*, from Brescia, age 20, entered 30 October 1570

5. *Gio. Battista Graffoglietti*, from Milan, age 35, a priest, Abbot of San Giovanni, canon lawyer, entered 10 March 1571, and became Minister of the community

6. *Steffano Cibò*, from Genoa, age 19, entered 7 February [no year]

7. *Gasparo Pallavicino*, from Genoa, age 19, entered 1571

8. *Giulio Negroni*, from Genoa, age 18

9. *Cesare Doria*, from Genoa, age 19, arrived with Negroni, both having stayed a month already at the college in Parma [thus not entering the Society in Venice]

10. *Ciro Lusco*, from Vicenza, age 18 [date not clear, also spelled de Luschi]

11. *Guido Maria Tagliaferri*, from Parma, age 20

12. *Giovanni Castagneri,* from Turin, age 18

13. *Camillo Barbieri,* from Brescia, age 18

Several more names are indicated separately:

14. *Br. Giacomo Credia,* a Spaniard, a novice brother [about whom there is no more record]

15. *Fr. Melchior Brocca* (1534–90)[15]

16. *Br. Ludovico Bitio,* from Forlì, coadjutor brother (1510–1594)[16]

17. *Br. Giovanni Riva,* from Milan, coadjutor brother

18. *Br. Bartolomeo di Chierici,* from Ferrara, coadjutor brother and mason (1513–1605)

19. *Br. Gio. Battista da Rimini,* coadjutor brother

This list is taken from the Fondo Gesuitico at the Roman Archives, and the writer of the list ended it with the comment that the last five persons (i.e., from number fifteen [Melchior Brocca] to number nineteen [Br. Gio. Battista]) were known to him and were not novices.[17] They would have filled out the community, providing Valentino with a priest assistant and with coadjutors who could help deal with the newly constructed buildings.

One can learn a number of things from the list of the first novices. First, some of the new members carried family names of great nobility, for example, Spinola, Cibò, and Doria in Genoa. Second, the largest group were twenty years of age or younger, and these almost always came from cities where there were Jesuit colleges already in operation.[18] Third, a small but significant number also entered as priests or as people who had reached a remarkable degree of education. These novices, much like Murtio and Graffoglietti, were often in their mid-thirties. Further, the youngest members were more likely to be kept in the novitiate for more than one year, as was the case with Biaggi and Vezzani. Finally, not all of the novices in Venice left with Valentino's group. Twenty-five were listed in the professed house in Venice in March of 1570, and Valentino took with him thirteen, according to the Fondo Gesuitico list. Presumably, some of the original twenty-five would have moved on to vows and studies, while others might have left the Society altogether; nevertheless, in 1580 Beringucci reports that "thirteen or fourteen coadjutors and novices of the second year" are still at the house in Venice. The practice of dispensing novices from their second year in the novitiate in order to begin studies was common and continued for several more decades in spite of the legislation from the General's office. It also appears likely that a serious factor in the size of a novitiate community was its endowment, that is, how many people could be supported in a given house. Count Camillo Gonzaga had promised funding for twenty-five, but Adorno had suspected that twenty would be a better number, and that is basically the number in the first community at Novellara.

In some of his chronicles of the house, Valentino gave more detailed accounts of why certain members left or how they came to be Jesuits. Thus in the "memorie" of the novices who left, he wrote that on 30 October 1575 Francesco Murtio, the novice from Nicosia on Cyprus, left the Society to console his mother when his sister died, to which Valentino added that he was "hardheaded and of little talent" *(testa dura e di poco talento)*[19] and thereupon listed the belongings he took with him when he left.

Of more interest is the story of Spinola, the young noble Genovese whose call to the religious life contained a certain irony that was not lost on Valentino:

> Nicolo Spinola, of a most noble family and a very wealthy Gentleman of Genoa (son of Francesco Spinola), was greatly loved by his father, but very vain and pompous more than anyone else in Genoa, since he would often go about dressed so that he seemed to be a Nymph ["Ninfa"], he found every vice and would gamble ten thousand scudi at a time, taking more glory in losing than in winning. He would come to the church of our college in order to jeer at our preacher (Fr. Otello), telling his companions, "Let's go hear the spiritual buffoon for a

while." But finally the joke came back on him who, touched by the Spirit of God, converted in fact and entered into the Society (in the professed house in Venice, 20 March of 1571, and in about eight months came with us to this house of Novellara at the age of 21). He became the most humble servant, mortified, obedient, and devoted to all the others, much to the surprise of everyone, especially those who knew him previously. And if in the beginning he was excessive through indiscretion with meditations, spending many hours in them during the time for sleep, becoming thinner and thinner every day, when told of this by the master of novices, immediately would he apply himself and do all that he was asked. And the person who previously had been soft and slept ten to twelve hours in the secular world, became strong in suffering every adversity in religious life, so much that he grew fat in the suffering and the obedience with a spirit always joyful and with a similar expression upon his face, with an excellent conscience, and with a soul willing to endure much for the love of God. He was recently found worthy in the Lord and judged so by the Superior to go to India, and that is where he is now.

This young person that I had in the novitiate carried himself with such patience and obedience that he accepted everything willingly from those who governed him, and manifested great edification when he was away from the novitiate, sent to Reggio [Emila] to the house of Signora Leonora to get a change of air. Through his religious modesty and his spiritual joy and affability two from Reggio entered the Society. . . . This was the gain of Nicolo Spinola who with his example helped Alessandro of Correggio not only to become a religious but also to live and die as one.[20]

Valentino wrote these reminiscences of the house in 1579, approximately eight years after their arrival in Novellara. One of the letters from the General's office was dated 11 January 1576 and addressed to Spinola concerning his request to go to the missions in Asia:

For various occupations our Paternity has not responded to your letter of 28 October [1575], nevertheless he has not failed to consult on what you wrote concerning going to India, and it seems to him that for now you should not think about anything but maintaining your good desires. His Paternity desires for the rest that you attend cheerfully in God to doing that which obedience commands as you have done until now with God's grace. As for coming to Rome, it does not seem to our Paternity that you should interrupt your exercises, for when Divine guidance wishes it will give some light provided that we do not fail to consult his Paternity in these matters, and give over [to him] to see if it be to the greater glory of God.[21]

Since Spinola entered in 1571 at the age of twenty-one, he would have been about twenty-five, and presumably in studies, when he sent his request to Rome. By 1579, at the age of twenty-nine, his request appears to have been granted, according to Valentino's account.[22]

The catalogue records for the second year in Novellara, 1572, show an increase in the community to twenty-six.[23] The priest novice Graffoglietti, who entered from Milan in 1571, was no longer listed as a novice in 1572, but as minister and consultor for the community. Having entered as a priest one year earlier at the age of thirty-five and already a canon lawyer, there was no need to send him to studies. Whether he made his vows after only one year is not mentioned, but he is not listed as one of the novices. Two other priests are listed as members of the community: Mark Antonio Pagano, who was assistant novice master, consultor, and admonitor; and Giovanni Battista Costa, age forty, a priest novice from Genoa and a doctor in both civil and canon law *(dott. in utroque iure)*. Costa entered in October 1572. Of the coadjutor brothers, Giovanni di Ricca remained as the cook, and David Beretta arrived for his long term as the infirmarian and apothecary. Girolamo Paolo Dova was listed as the tailor. Four of those listed the previous year—di Chierici the mason, Bitio, Gio. Battista da Rimini, and the priest Melchior Brocca—are now gone, perhaps a sign of the constant mobility of the members of the order.

As with the previous year, there are two separate lists of the novices in the Jesuit archives. Both list fifteen novices in the class for the year (including Costa the priest novice),[24] but one also adds the names of four more novices who entered in January 1573 (the former list places them among those who entered in 1573 instead). The fuller catalogue listing (from ARSI Ven. 36) also notes the ages and origin of the novices. Again ten novices of the fifteen who entered in 1572 are twenty years of age or younger. The two oldest are the priest novice Costa, who was forty, and Francesco Centurione, who was thirty-six and brother of a bishop who made the Spiritual Exercises under Valentino at Novellara. Eight of the novices were from Genoa, three were from Milan, and the rest were from Forlì, Ferrara, Camerino, and Brescia, with one listed as "seems to be Portuguese but born in France" and another with no mention of where he was from.

This list also includes comments on the academic abilities of the novices. Eleven of the younger novices were judged to be talented *(ingegno),* and fourteen of them had Latin. Only one is listed with no educational background (Battista Gottuccio), and three are cited as having little Latin yet talented nonetheless. Thus the second year at Novellara again saw a group of people coming from an educated background, including some among the older novices with a great deal of education. Costa and Ludovico Chizzuola, age thirty-nine, were both doctors of civil and canon law; Antonio Guigno, twenty-four, had four years of philosophy; and Filippo Contarini, thirty-one, was noted as having good judgment and being diligent in studies *(buon guidicio e asseguitis li studij).*[25] The novices entered for the most part in the late summer and fall, and Valentino later noted in his Report on the Spiritual Practice at Novellara that he preferred to give the Exercises during the more temperate times of year. Only one novice, Celso Confalonieri, entered in February, and only one, Gio. Battista Passeto, entered as late as November, and this might have been due to a matter of health.[26] The novices from the previous year, 1571, are no longer listed in the catalogue and presumably were sent on to studies without their vows, as was the common practice at the time. This practice continued, of course, and resulted in admonitions from Rome, especially in the 1590s, concerning the two-year novitiate.[27]

Between 1573 and 1580, a total of 137 novices entered at Novellara, not including departures that were dropped from the list at some point. In five of those years, priests also entered, but never more than two in any year. The smallest novice class numbered ten in 1577, while the largest was twenty-eight in 1579. (Ascanio Marazzi from Parma, the long-term third novice master at Novellara and the one who took the novice community on its journeys to Padua and Piacenza was a novice under Valentino in 1579.[28]) Novices came from throughout northern Italy, but the cities with the largest number were those in which Jesuit colleges were established: Genoa, Milan, Brescia, Verona, Como, and Venice. Beginning in 1574 entrants were also recorded from cities in the local area—Correggio, Carpi, Ferrara, and Bologna—to be joined in a few years by candidates from Reggio Emilia, Modena, Mantua, Piacenza, Mirandola, Parma, and Padua. Some novices came from as far away as Nice, Piedmont, Florence, and Rome (one was even listed as English), but by and large the provenance was the regions surrounding the Po River. After 1578, with the splitting of the province, large numbers of novices from Genoa and Milan were sent to Arona, but they were promptly replaced by people from Emilia Romagna and the Veneto. The months in which the novices entered during these first ten years were most likely August and October, followed by June and February.

In the same history that relates the story of Nicolo Spinola, Valentino summarized the group of novices who had entered in the first eight years:

> As far as what is expected in the novices, in these eight years many good persons have come to the novitiate, such as Venetian gentlemen, and vicars of Genoa, Ferrara, and others of quality from Genoa and Brescia, and other places, who tried themselves in the house with mortifications and self-denial, and outside the house with teaching Christian doctrine in the cities nearby and in five or six other places and also in Reggio.[29]

Valentino completed his argument here with an interesting aside about why this instruction in doctrine was so important. He continued:

> [This instruction] was most necessary in these parts, almost like another India, because they were not even able to make the sign of the Cross, and some, instead of signing themselves with the Trinity, signed themselves with the quaternity, saying, "In the name of the Father, and of the Son, and of the 'Tiblino,' and of the Spirit," together with similar nonsense and errors.

In spite of this positive assessment, however, Valentino's letters reveal that things did not go any more smoothly with the novices than they did with buildings, which had been hastily and poorly constructed in the first place. For example, during the same time that Valentino was writing to the General about moving the novitiate to Reggio Emilia in 1574, he also told the story of two of the more promising novices, as evidenced at least from their previous background. One was the priest novice Costa, already mentioned, who had entered in 1572. He had left behind an important position as vicar in Genoa and was a doctor in civil and canon law. In a letter dated 11 April 1574, Valentino wrote to Rome to report on his good progress.[30] He was by nature "cool and distant" *(freddo e tardo)*, but virtuous, prudent, and most willing to submit to the novitiate mortifications and the novice master's rule. He left a good impression in the house *(buon odore)* and, as a priest novice, even served as Valentino's assistant or *sottomastro*. His time at Novellara lasted slightly less than two years—"nineteen or twenty months," according to Valentino. Of particular note, however, was Costa's desire to complete the full two years of novitiate. In most other cases it would seem the novices would leave after one year for their studies. In his history of the house and of some of the novices from 1579, Valentino again mentioned how Costa always insisted on being seated last *(nell'ultimo luoco)* and would often defer to others in order to increase his humility, something done with such gentleness that "the novices hardly noticed, but the Novice Master, who knew this art, noticed and noted everything."[31] Valentino's description of Costa's novitiate thus shows how someone from an important position in the church and somewhat distant could incorporate a true spirit of humility, which would make of him not only a good novice but a good Jesuit priest. The next example, though similar, has quite a different outcome.

Writing on the anniversary of the house's dedication, 1 November 1574, Valentino noted that eighteen of the novices had finished their year and been sent to various locales for studies.[32] Valentino added: "We are now 20, among whom is the vicar of Ferrara and a few others who give me great hope, and I await a few more so that we can arrive at 24 in number." (Little did he know how poorly was his hope placed in this vicar from Ferrara.)

Certainly not all the novices were so easy to deal with. Cosmo Puccio, who had been Cardinal d'Este's secretary before entering, occupied a number of Valentino's letters to Rome. The first notice of his arrival comes in a letter dated 26 November 1576, in which Valentino wrote that, after the turmoil over moving the novitiate and Camillo Gonzaga's illness earlier in 1576, he was especially "happy in the Lord with Father Francesco Flogni ... and Cosmo Puccio who was secretary to Cardinal d'Este, and who is of a good and vivacious nature, and was moved to take another road ... which gives me great hope."[33] This vivacious nature again occupied part of a letter dated 9 March 1577:

> Cosmo Puccio secretary of Cardinal d'Este gave me much to do with his great liveliness and with his disordinate desire for study which he brought with him from the beginning, and who clearly still has not been able to acquire indifference. Not even Fr. Provincial wanted to assign him to studies, as I indicated, and thought it best to let His Paternity know that it might be good to see how he does. Rather I indicated that either he resolves this indifference or he is not for the Society and with this he seemed ready to leave but with tears and pangs of conscience. God help him.[34]

Valentino was using language that seemed to express an unusual sense of exasperation, but later in the same letter he related how he had to confront Count Camillo about the unrest among his subjects. By 5 July 1577, Valentino reported to Rome that Francesco Flogni, the priest novice, had finished his first year with great humility, obedience, and devotion, and that he with eight other novices had been sent on to colleges. As for Puccio: "Three have been sent home, one for a notable illness of the body and the other two for even worse illnesses, for 'the wicked root of distorted intention,' among whom was Cosmo Puccio."[35]

In the *memoralia* of those who left the Society, Valentino put some more flesh on this issue: For Puccio, everyone else was his inferior; he extolled his nobility and abilities *(sufficienza)*, and his courtly friends; he transgressed the rules, saying they did not bind under pain of mortal sin; he was unstable in his vocation (to be sure!), and scandalized others by always threatening to write to Rome; his obduracy rendered him incapable of being a Jesuit, and in any case he had entered only for studies. Valentino ended his summary with a certain brevity: "He was not liked by anybody, because he upset the whole house."

There is only one extended catalogue reference from the 1580s that lists the community membership for the year 1581.[36] The novices that year numbered fourteen, one of whom—Giovanni (or Johannes) Verbier, of Flemish background—became Valentino's successor as rector and novice master for a brief period of time in the 1590s.[37] Also of interest is the scholastic/regent Giovanni Francesco Calvi, master of humanities, listed as working in the school that the novitiate community had accepted under pressure from Gonzaga in 1575, for which they had received a special permission from the General Everard Mercurian. By this time, Novellara had sufficient income to house a community of about twenty-five, up from twenty in its earliest years.

The next several years record a sharp increase in the number of novices: twenty-four in 1582, thirty-one in 1583, twenty-two in 1584, but only seventeen in 1585. Numbers for the rest of the decade, however, fluctuated between twelve in 1586 and 1589, fourteen in 1590, eighteen in 1587, and a high of twenty-three—among them two priests—in 1588. By 1589 the novitiate property had been significantly enlarged, ensuring it greater privacy.

With the 1590s and the last several years of Valentino's term as novice master and rector, there are a number of more complete references to be found in the triennial catalogues in ARSI Veneta 37. These entries also include references to the income of the community, which was steadily increasing. In 1590, for example, the regular annual income *(rendita)* is listed at 800 scudi, and the total income accounting for other sources, such as bequests, was 1,400 scudi.[38] Beretta continued his work in the apothecary, listed as *"aromatus"* in the Latin catalogue, and one scholastic, Fausto Vertimi, age twenty-six, carried on the charge of teaching in the school. The total number of novices was twenty-four in 1590, and the group included two from Flanders, four from Trent, and one from Novellara itself. In 1591 there were twelve novices, thirteen in 1592, ten in 1593, eighteen in 1594, and seventeen in 1595.[39] The next five years after Valentino's term fall in the same range, from ten in 1596 and 1598, to fifteen in 1597 and 1599, and nineteen novices in 1600. The case is similar in 1598 with eighteen novices.

The ages of the novices entering, which are given for the years 1590 and 1595, reflect the pattern already established in the 1570s: that the largest number of novices were twenty years of age or younger. Of the twenty-four listed for 1590, two were priests, and twelve were twenty or younger. Three were over thirty years of age, including one of the priests, and nine were between twenty-one and twenty-nine. For the year 1595—Verbier's first year as novice master—eleven novices were under twenty, the youngest being fourteen and a half years old. Five were between twenty and twenty-five, and one, a novice brother, was thirty-six. Moreover, these catalogues also show the novices coming from throughout the Veneto and Emilia-Romagna regions, again especially from cities where there were Jesuit colleges—Verona, Parma, Piacenza, Mantua, and Bergamo.

Of particular interest in the triennial catalogues of the 1590s, however, are the additional lists of novices in studies at various Jesuit schools in Bologna, Brescia, and Padua. Invariably, names that appear in Novellara one year are listed the next year as pursuing a course of studies, as novices, in the humanities or metaphysics. These lists provide the most detailed examples of the continuing common practice of novices leaving Novellara after one year's probation before a year of studies and vows. Valentino alluded to this fact in his Report on the Spiritual Practice at Novellara, and certainly the admonitions from Rome and the visitors also note this practice, but the catalogues give the actual names of some of the novices. The *Constitutions* stipulated that the novitiate was not to be a time of studies but a time of "growth in virtue and devotion." Nevertheless, they also allowed the superior to grant dispensations "for some particular individual to study other matters also."[40] What seems to have been the common practice in Novellara was to routinely grant this dispensation to most of the novices. Only certain cases record novices doing two years at the novitiate, such as the priest novice Costa, who insisted on it.

By 1595 the community list included an additional ten from France, who had been expelled over the plot on Henry IV's life. The catalogue also notes an increase in income from Camillo Gonzaga of ten scudi per person to support the French exiles.[41] Also of note in the catalogue of 1595 was the listing of two priests doing their third probation, or tertianship, before final profession. The house took on more of this task over the next decade, especially once the novice community had left for Padua. A list of their various tasks is provided with a note from Valentino—the rector and now also tertian instructor—on how well they did. This third probation followed the guidelines established by Ignatius in the General Examen for candidates to the Society,[42] and through it we can also get a sense of what the novices were doing during their time at Novellara, since the experiments for all of the probations had their source in the General Examen. For Exupirus Roger from France, the first experiment, the Spiritual Exercises, produced fruit. The second experiment was not done since there was no hospital, nor the third, the pilgrimage, since he had already experienced anonymous charity in his expulsion from France. For the menial and humbling tasks of the fourth experiment, he was judged not to have "abhorred his vices much," but in the garden he pursued "sufficient mortification." In the fifth experiment, he was judged good and zealous in teaching children catechism. The sixth he was dispensed from, since he had no knowledge of Italian and thus could not preach or hear confessions.

Octavio Beringucci, another Jesuit from Siena, also did his first experiment with spiritual fruit. He too was exempted from the second since there was no hospital, and from the third because he was already experiencing anonymous charity in the area. He was not diligent in the menial tasks of the house and did not do sufficient work in the garden. However, he did well in the fifth, instructing children, and also in the sixth, preaching, Masses, and confessions. In general, Beringucci was judged by Valentino to be somewhat lacking in self-contempt, fraternal charity, and simplicity of life—and his sense of humble obedience left much to be desired.

The income of the house reached 1,200 scudi in 1597, with another 500 from settling part of Camillo Gonzaga's will to help provide for the French exiles.[43] Finally, in the catalogue for 1600, with Ascanius Marazzi now rector and novice master, for the first time the novices were divided into two groups: one for the first year and one for the second. A separate list gives the names of those doing the third probation.[44]

Novice Departures and Deaths

The "memorial" of those who left during this time records twenty-three who left between the years 1575 and 1588.[45] (These, in turn, were not included on the novice list in ARSI Ven. 71, covering 1570 to 1642.) Ruiz Jurado listed among the reasons for dismissal at the house of probation in Rome ineptitude and laziness, sin, disobedience, and other defects, especially those of a physical or psychological nature.[46] To these one could also add pressure from the novice's family. Valentino's own descriptions from his "memorial," written thirty years after the period described by Ruiz Jurado, bear out most of these same difficulties.

Murtio the Cypriot from the first class, who left on the death of his sister—that is, for family matters—is the first one named.

Antonio Berzera had health problems but was "very inconstant in his vocation, one moment seeking to enter the Carthusians, the next seeking to go home." He left in 1576. Hipolito Guzzone, who was thirty-six, did not mind the mortification and the discipline, but only when he asked for it, not when it was asked of him. When his sister died he tried to bypass Valentino's authority by going to the Provincial. He was greatly distressed at his dismissal and wrote a penitent letter to the community. One of the novices, Francesco Maffei, was given to complaining, saying that he would do better in the secular world. Valentino judged him as stubborn or disobedient *(testa dura)*. In December of 1585 Georgio Masi from Trent was sent from Modena for spiritual help *(per aiuto spiri.)*, for he was suffering from temptations in his vocation. He was sent to Mantua in May of 1586, where his temptation was victorious over his religious vocation. He asked for dismissal there and was so resolute that he accepted no arguments to the contrary *(risoluto et essendo incapace d'ogni ragione)*. Gianpietro Arrigone was a coadjutor novice who kept to himself, rarely sought anyone's company, but left because he did not care for contemplative life.

Annibal Ruggieri, who left on 8 June 1588, enjoyed his own little devotions *(divotionelli)* and left the novitiate property several times on his own. When he was sent to Venice under obedience, he "capriciously" went to Loreto instead. Valentino wrote of him: "When things did not go the way he wanted, and that was often, he would ask to leave." Another novice, Antonio Calzaetto, was very melancholy, but a good person. He stayed to see if things would go better, and when they did not, he left. With the case of Biagio de Grassi from Genoa, who left on 31 October 1575, Valentino exhibited a truly discerning charity. He was of little academic ability and not suited to being a coadjutor brother, since he was small and with little strength. He had come from the orphanage-hospitals of Genoa, being of uncertain parentage *("per incertis parentibus natus,"* Valentino added in Latin). He was sent away with one and a half *scudi d'oro* and other necessities, presumably since there was no real family to receive him. Ottavio Mazzuola from Brescia had some health problems, but his real problem seems to have been homesickness. Valentino described it as "perhaps an inordinate love of his mother." Apparently he departed with a certain amount of edification for everybody. The minister of the house accompanied him as far as Parma, and he was sent on his way with two *scudi d'oro* and three reals.

Some of the novices exhibited little desire to live by sharing with the community, and certainly a union with one's companions was as important a virtue to acquire as union with God.[47] Giovanni Antonio Vezzano had left once before in Genoa and was sent to Novellara to help him confirm his vocation. But in one year he did not improve. Valentino described him as "greedy, deceitful, a vagabond, curious, and very detached" *(goloso, bugiardo, vagabondo, curioso, et molto astreto).* These words almost seem to describe the opposite of what a good novice should be. He was caught with two good pieces of bread on him once, and he refused to say where he got them. Another time he was found in the basement taking pears, and in the garden he would take grapes. Many other items were also found hidden in his room. Valentino judged him to be *"incurabili,"* and he was sent to Parma with two of his cohorts, Maffei (who was mentioned above) and Christoforo del Conte, who also was found with books and writings in his room that he had taken from the library without permission. He, together with Maffei, tended toward complaining, and he was sent on his way with the belongings he had brought with himself, a *scudo d'oro*, and a letter of recommendation to the bishop of Cremona. It may be hard to discern if Vezzano's taking of food was the result of his natural appetite and if del Conte's books merely exhibited youthful curiosity; nevertheless Valentino judged them not to be good material for the trials of a Jesuit's life. Given how lenient he was with their departures, it would seem that he thought they still might do something with their lives.

Dorotheo Bonardi exhibited more serious symptoms of a psychological nature. Valentino wrote that he was

> stupid, and almost insensate, even to demonstrating signs of madness and the doctor feared the worse, one moment laughing, the next crying, without any reason and responding at times with the same answer [as he just was asked], if he was asked:

"Did you go to Mass?" He would answer, "Did you go to Mass?". . . [he gave] excellent edification, most observant with all that concerned obedience. I kept it quiet about sending him to Verona with a servant of the "sacromosa," dressed in secular clothing, and thus he went peacefully.[48]

Most of the rest of the list included novices who were dismissed for illnesses that rendered them unfit for the Society, for wanting only to engage in studies, or for not wanting to work very hard. One novice accepted as a coadjutor brother was tempted to study and to the priesthood *(dir messa)*. The provincial was never happy about accepting him, but he had been accepted by the superior and the community in Parma. Finally, one other novice, Francesco Irlandi, was too vivacious for the Jesuit life, exhibiting what Valentino took to be signs of frenzy. As much as one can sense Valentino's experience with the spiritual life through his writings on the Exercises, one can also feel that he had seen much of what human nature had to offer in these cases of departures. A few of the dismissals seem to have tried his patience, and Puccio and Vezzano seem to incur the harshest language from Valentino. On the whole, though, his response seemed wise and charitable, especially when it came to giving those departing funds for their journey.

Separately, Valentino also listed four novices who died at Novellara: Nicolo Cocco, who had been a novice for six months, died on 25 September 1574 and was buried in the novitiate church. Valentino wrote of him to Rome:

I arrived in time to give the holy oils to a novice of six months, who was at the point of death from dysentery. It seemed good for God our Lord to call him to glory because he gave himself so quickly to the way of perfection, that I believe he had acquired in six months, that which another could only acquire in a life's worth of work. He was very humble, chaste, obedient, and sealed by every virtue. He made all marvel. With his irreprehensible conversation, suitable not only for novices but for priests, he passed finally with much peace to a better life on the 25th of September.[49]

That same year Bartolomeo Gorla, a novice of eight months, died. On 2 August 1583 Lelio Nichesoli died after eight months. In 1584, Pietro Bondinaro died, and on 10 October 1586, Pietro Busselim, a coadjutor novice, died and was also buried in the church.

On the occasion of the death of Nichesoli, Valentino wrote his longest letter to Rome, comprising three full pages of text with further testimony from thirty-one members of the community.[50] Practically everything that could be said about an edifying death was included in the letter. Mention was made of humble resignation and of a serenity as the last hours were approaching. His physical difficulties reached the point where his extremities were cold, and he could not swallow. Valentino makes two references to Ignatius in this letter. First he alluded to the statement that one leaves the care of the body to the doctor and the infirmarian, and that of the soul to God and holy obedience. Secondly, the morning after his death Valentino had the community recite the Lord's Prayer, "slowly as Fr. Ignatius teaches in the Exercises." As death approached, Nichesoli was quoted as seeing angels all around him. Of particular note is the mention that when he received the last rites and viaticum, Valentino allowed him to pronounce his vows of religion, dispensing him, the letter states, from the prescribed two years before vows, so that he could take them after only ten months. His passing was described as so serene that hardly a tear could be shed. Valentino ended his letter by noting that he had passed from this house to the one of eternity, from the cell to heaven *(dalla Cella al Cielo)*.

Of the testimonies left by other members of the community, eleven remain in the Roman archives, one by a priest and the others by fellow novices. They are primarily statements about Nichesoli's goodness of character rather than the moment of his death. They speak of his energy in teaching Christian doctrine, of his humility and patience and obedience, and of a holy resignation in death. These remaining documents form a curious testimony, given that his was not the only death and that most of Valentino's stories are about how novices came to the novitiate, not about the ways in which they left. Without a doubt Valentino found the episode deeply moving, but it would seem reasonable that he might also be culling testimony should a devotion grow and lead to a cause for canonization. In this way Novellara could have its own saint.

Accounts of novices' departures and deaths, like concern about their health when the novitiate first opened in its less-than-adequate buildings, give evidence that Valentino's care for his charges was not just in theory. In his Report on the Spiritual Practice his language certainly shows his concern in general about how the novices could grow in humility, obedience, and the other virtues that would make them good followers of Ignatius and the early companions. The tone he uses to describe those who left, especially the care he showed to some, and the anxiety evident in the cases of those who died provide further evidence of how important these young novices were to him.

Novice Experiments and Daily Order

A certain number of questions remain about the Novellara novitiate and the novices' tasks, and to find answers to them one needs to comb through most of Valentino's writings for references and examples. For example, Nigel Griffin has noted that the Society of Jesus during this period tended to attract "the lower nobility and the professional classes."[51] Catalogue lists and the memorials of Valentino certainly seem to bear this out, but not to the point of systematically excluding others of modest backgrounds. Valentino's writings often seem to give the impression that much good can be expected from those of the higher classes who chose to leave secular life for the life of religion. In addition to his descriptions of the promise of a Costa or a Spinola, Valentino also described Filippo Contarini as a "Venetian gentleman, who was held in great expectation of ascending to grand honors and had already received lavishly of earthly goods," but who was also capable of finding in humility and obedience a vehicle to love the lowly, even to the point of serving his sister when she came for a visit.[52]

For all his humility he was still described by Valentino as "prudent, expert and cultured," traits he would not lose as a Jesuit, but use to different ends.

If anything, education and the promise of learning were more prized. The older vocations often possessed high levels of education, and many, if not most, of the young candidates were described as *"ingegno."* That still did not mean that Valentino would shun someone of simple educational background. In 1575, he sent to the General a letter carried by a young candidate named Jeronimo, who had "a certain impediment that he would report orally" to the General. Valentino was quite impressed by the youth's spiritual devotion, having seen him receive the sacraments regularly "for three or four years" and knowing how well he worked with the children of the orphanage. Jeronimo's goal was not to receive much in the way of education, but to serve in the Indies as a coadjutor brother, and for this reason Valentino recommended him to the General, in spite of his impediment, with all "charity and prudence" and in spite of the fact that the provincial was reluctant to accept him.[53]

Thomas Cohen in his article "Why Jesuits Joined: 1540–1600" noted that it is difficult to ascertain how many of the candidates came from the Jesuit schools, but given the age of entrance of most of the candidates, which would put them at an average age of nineteen, he places the proportion of Jesuit alumni as "certainly high."[54] Evidence from the records of Novellara is that most of the younger novices came from cities that had Jesuit colleges in operation and that many of them had facility in Latin. They had certainly received schooling, and they came from places where Jesuit education was available. The desire for education, however, was not the only criteria for new Jesuits, and some of Valentino's most serious difficulties, such as the case of Cosmo Puccio, involved those who only sought studies and were not willing to take on the spiritual program of the novitiate.

Cohen interprets part of this spiritual program in terms of obedience. He writes, "One reason the Company of Jesus could at once be very active in the world and yet feel protected from menaces to salvation was that it adhered to a very strict cult of obedience."[55]

Among the virtues cited by Valentino was the readiness to do what one was told to do, and the opposing vice cited in those who left was the inability to submit one's own judgment to that of the superior (the often cited *"testa dura"*), that is, complaining about decisions and taking matters into one's own hands. However, Cohen misses an important nuance when he cites obedience as the key virtue for producing a sense of stability for new Jesuit recruits, and this nuance comes very close to the heart of Ignatius and what was going on in Novellara. Valentino knew the rules and the *Constitutions* of the order very well. They were recorded extensively in his handbook, including the entirety of Ignatius's letter on obedience to the Jesuits in Portugal, but Ignatius himself, much less Valentino, did not always follow the rules slavishly. Here again is the case of a superior—who himself knew the rules yet did not always follow them—seeking to instill the importance of obedience in his novices and judging them for their willingness to grow in this virtue. What needs to be understood is the further principle of Ignatius that decisions could be taken by the superior on the scene depending on the situation, trusting in his good judgment and, more importantly, in his "discrete charity."

One need only look at the listing of house customs and reports from official visitors to find the areas that needed remedy. According to the rules no novices were to leave the novitiate house without being well tested, an allusion to the full novitiate term. The rector at Novellara was not to absent himself from the community for more than two days without specific permission of the provincial. Should an occasion arise that required more than two days absence, he was to send another priest, so as "not to leave the novices for long without his presence."[56] One can imagine that incidents such as Borromeo's retreat on horseback and the calls from various other members of the nobility who would accept no one else but Valentino took him away regularly throughout his term as novice master. Again, the judgment of the superior was a key component in deciding where the greater glory of God and service to the church would be.

Consistently throughout this period the requirement of the novices to stay in the novitiate for two full years was dispensed.

The customary practice was that the novices entered sometime in the fall and then were sent to studies by the provincial at the end of the first year. Already in 1569, a note was made concerning the novices in Venice remaining for the full biennial term.[57] In 1593, there was still strong insistence that the novices in Novellara complete the two years before going to studies.[58] Moreover, the General Congregations—especially decrees 12, 13, and 63 of General Congregation V—strongly insisted on this point, though the practice continued throughout the 1590s of granting dispensations from the second year, and it was only in the catalogue for 1600 that two years of novice classes were listed for the first time.[59]

In a similar vein, the growing pattern of situating novitiates in separated country settings was changed abruptly in 1603, again as a reaction to the particular difficulties with the Gonzaga regent Countess Vittoria Capua. After they left Novellara in 1603, the novitiate moved to Padua, far away from its isolated and ideal environment, yet a place where the novices would not suffer from hunger. What could have been reasons that accounted for a practice that consistently departed from the rules that everybody knew and acknowledged? Part of the answer is practical, and part lies in the tradition that had existed from the earliest days of the Society. Those who were within living memory of the manner in which new members, including themselves, were accepted knew that the practice could vary without ill effect, provided that other important criteria were met. Valentino himself took his vows the same month he arrived in Rome in 1557, but only after six months in Padua doing what would have been the first probation. Economics were also a factor. Many candidates presented themselves, but the houses of formation had incomes that could only allow for so many mouths to feed. The ideal of a separated novitiate—such as Sant' Andrea, Novellara, or Arona—was not something to be given up lightly, but circumstances could make leaving a better decision. Similarly, moving one group of novices to studies a year early, though not the ideal, would allow more novices into the subsequent group.

What did the novitiate accomplish? It allowed the novice master to ascertain if the given novice was fit and could grow in those virtues that would make of him a good religious and a good Jesuit. It also allowed the novice to see if this life were truly God's call. The accounts of departures show that at times the situations reflected more of Valentino's assessment; at other times it was the novice who saw that this life was not what he wanted. The first probation and the experiments of the second were the key components that allowed this process to work.

Over the course of the century, the first probation changed from what Valentino had experienced and what the *Constitutions* described. Granero has already traced the pattern during the 1540s of the three-month probation doubling to six, followed by two years before vows. Basically this meant that the six key experiments became part of the second probation and helped to fill up the time in novitiate before studies. It must be remembered that Ignatius himself in the Society's legislation allowed for novices to study once they had completed the proper training through spiritual guidance and mortification. But the first probation did not disappear. Valentino noted in his Report on the Spiritual Practice that he would use the first probation "to get to know the novices' spirit and intention, giving them the papal bulls and the usual Examen, examining them as required by the Institute and the Rules."[60] What the narrative evidence provides are the examples of how he followed this practice. In the case of Giovanni Barone, a young Venetian who entered in the year 1574, Valentino wrote that he experienced a very circuitous route to Novellara.[61] Upon arrival, Valentino put Barone in the first probation, during which he met with the novice master a few times to see how the Spirit was guiding him. Valentino presented him with the Institute and the documents of the Society. In Barone's case Valentino found him remarkably imperturbable in terms of sorrow for his past life. When he questioned him further, he learned that Barone had once consulted a member of a religious order about why he never got upset; the religious responded by telling Barone that serenity came from always accepting what God sent and never going contrary to it.

Certainly, some sense of a break with one's previous life was part of the key to progressing into and through the novitiate. The issue of wearing one's original clothes in the novitiate was part of this matter. In some vivid accounts Valentino relates other difficulties novices had with entering religious life. In one case it was the local bishop who tried to keep someone from the Jesuits. The Brescian noble Ludovico Chizzuola, who entered in 1573 at the age of thirty-nine, was tempted by his bishop with a benefice worth "several hundred scudi a year" in order to get him to stay in Brescia. His father responded to the bishop's attempt to involve him in the complicity by saying that he had always tried to let his children decide for themselves about their lives. Ludovico himself told the bishop that he wanted nothing more than to be "a poor priest." When the bishop presented him with the prospect of marrying a young woman "of great wealth and noble birth," Chizzoula firmly decided that his call was to the Society of Jesus.

The next two involved difficulties with members of the family. Gasparo Pallavicino had great disagreements with his parents, "especially his mother," over his vocation. A friend and benefactor of the Jesuits in Venice was enlisted by Gasparo's parents to visit him in Novellara and deliver to him a letter, hoping to convince him to leave. The young novice immediately took the letter and his troubles to Valentino, asking for protection from these attempts by his parents.

On Wednesday of Holy Week, 30 March 1580, the father of a young novice who had entered a month earlier came to retrieve his child. The parents had already failed in an attempt to get their son to travel to a nearby city where they could take hold of him, so this time the father, after pleading with Valentino in vain, tried to enlist the support of Camillo Gonzaga. Eventually, Valentino, under pressure from Gonzaga, allowed the father and son to meet. Upon seeing his son's resolution to remain, the father exclaimed that "this son [was] harder than a stone, and that he had never seen someone so obstinate." The story ended happily, for the novice's resolution eventually turned his father around. He served him at table several times, and seeing how happy his son was, the father eventually made a general confession and received communion with the entire Jesuit community on Easter Sunday.

The cornerstone of the novitiate was the Spiritual Exercises, and Valentino made use of them in a variety of ways. His experience with them gave him a keen sense of what could happen to those who went through them. He did not use them to fashion young novices into a certain pattern or way of thinking, for his experience told him that the Exercises could serve a variety of purposes given the specific situation. If a novice was having difficulties in his vocation, Valentino would give him some of the Exercises to see if the novice could come to clarity. If a young person was thinking about religious life—such as Jeronimo in Novellara or Luigi Gonzaga in Mantua—Valentino would give him the Exercises to help him deepen his sense of commitment. His knowledge of the method of the Exercises was such that he could even create his own Exercises to give to the novices to help them develop a love for the Society that they were joining. So important were the Exercises that many of the meditations in his handbook, given throughout the course of the year, were modeled on the method of the Exercises, such as colloquies with Christ on the cross, or with the Blessed Mother. Even more important, many of Valentino's points were guided by the strong use of the imagination, by using all of the senses in true Ignatian contemplation to deepen one's prayer and ultimately one's relationship with God.

Moreover, the Exercises were in no way to be secretively reserved to the Jesuits only, for he gave them to many men and women in the region, and some, such as Carlo Borromeo, made frequent use of them. Valentino tended to record in his histories the doings of the nobility, but on occasion, as with Signora Leonora in Reggio, there are glimpses of the ministry as it was carried on among a wider population. What Valentino saw in the Exercises was how they could combine in the exercitants' prayer a sense of self-abnegation with a positive regard for the ways in which the Lord was at work. Reform of one's life often followed, but also a certain zeal or enthusiasm to be of service.

As for the other experiments listed in the *General Examen*, there is ample record that the novices did not spend all of their time on the novitiate property. The growing concern in the Society and in the Tridentine church for separated novitiates was certainly important in the establishment of the novitiate at Novellara, and it was a model, almost like Sant' Andrea itself, in its long tenure in that locale. But the novices were kept busy in the teaching of Christian doctrine to the people of the area, and not just to the children. Valentino noted that this ministry of the novices was so effective that everyone reacted "with such fervor that they attended the conferences as if they were novices, and nothing else could be heard in the streets or in the fields than the songs they had learned in their classes, especially among the young in place of more secular songs."[62] Also of note was the way in which children "would instruct their parents in doctrine at home, since they being older were ashamed to learn it in church." When Francesco Centurione entered the novitiate, after having made his first probation in Corsica, he was sent to a church six miles distant from Novellara,

> . . . to teach doctrine, and he would often have the contadini recite the Lord's Prayer. He was sharply rebuked by the curate, who told him, "I thought they would have a preacher and a priest to send me, and instead they sent me a novice with a round hat who can't say anything but the Pater Noster." At which the good novice humbly got down and asked for pardon, if he had erred, begging his Reverence to tell him how to improve and mend his ways. And he responded, "I did not say you erred, but that you did not know how to say anything except the Pater Noster, and that they sent me novices here who can't say anything else." Once the curate learned that this Centurione was the brother of the Bishop whose fame was still noted in these parts, he became very ashamed and asked him for pardon. Once Count Camillo learned what happened he gave the curate a good rebuff and he himself would accompany the novices to various churches, giving authority to their work.[63]

On several occasions, Valentino recorded sending the novices on pilgrimage to Loreto. He would have the novices go in groups usually, and the distance itself was no more than fifty or sixty miles.[64] If there was some particular issue about a given novice's vocation to be resolved, Valentino notes that he would send a novice to Loreto by himself, sometimes also to Rome for resolution of the issue.[65] There was certainly plenty of opportunity to be engaged in the lowly tasks of the house and the garden, especially as the size of the property grew. Many of the comments about humility among the novices usually involved how eagerly they took to these tasks. There was no mention of the novices doing any work in the hospitals, though it would be possible that they did spend time helping the infirmarian, their health being a regular preoccupation of Valentino's letters to Rome. As in Arona, there was no hospital in the town, and although the novices did move around quite a bit for their experiments in doctrine, there is no mention of their working in hospitals in the neighboring cities of Reggio, Parma, or Modena.

The novice priests were certainly engaged in the sacramental work of the novitiate church, and often they would be given additional responsibilities in the community, such as minister or even assistant novice master. Experiments that were deemed suitable seemed to have been quite tailored to the person and the needs of the house. It is also of interest that the community had a scholastic to teach in the town grammar school and that the novices, priests or not, were never mentioned in the histories as working in that school. Even with the example of the two tertians from the late 1590s one can see that the experiments of the General Examen, as much as they were tailored to an urban ministry and an urban novitiate, were not forgotten and were indeed considered the norm by which spiritual progress of novice or tertian could be ascertained. Nevertheless, they were not slavishly followed, but used or not as circumstances warranted. The rules of the order were clearly understood, but the practice allowed for a certain discretion by the appropriate superiors, even to the point of Valentino allowing Nichesoli to pronounce his vows on his deathbed while only in his first year of novitiate. Other novices died, but it was the judgment of the novice master and rector that in this case the novice was ready to take his vows.

It is much more difficult to discern the daily schedule of the novices from Valentino's writings, but here Ruiz Jurado is correct in supposing that the order was regularly followed. Valentino's handbook notes all of the proper rules for the novices that had been mandated by Rome, but it does not speak about daily orders. The daily orders promulgated by the first General Congregations were known, but the archival records at Novellara and Modena only give brief hints that these orders were followed as they were written. For example, Valentino mentions that Bishop Centurione and his companion participated in the classes on doctrine and in the repetitions that followed, which were conducted in pairs. This practice was part of the daily order established by Juan de la Plaza in the Jesuit novitiate in Córdoba, and it was part of the daily order implemented for the entire Society's novitiates in the first General Congregation.[66] The documents also mention evening recreation, which was also part of de la Plaza's order. Valentino made note of a room, a *"cantina,"* that was part of the poorly constructed early building, but that was eventually sealed off against the elements sufficiently so that the novices could do their writing in common. This practice again followed de la Plaza's order of the day, though, in fact, such a practice of novices studying together was probably not that different from the order of the day found in novitiates of other religious orders. One can presume that trips of six miles or so to teach doctrine would alter the order of the day for some of the novices, since the journeys themselves would take a large part of the day. There is no sense, however, of how these experiments outside of the house affected the daily order, even though Valentino gave high praise to the good work the novices did. The order of the day was not of sufficient note to be mentioned in any of the writings, and only in the anecdotal evidence can confirmation of certain aspects of it be found. One can presume that in this particular matter the decrees of the Congregations were basically followed, with exceptions made based upon the circumstances at hand.

For the most part, novices entered in groups during the fall, with a few exceptions noted, for example, when five novices entered in January of 1573. The first probation and perhaps some of the Exercises were given on something of an individual basis, but Valentino himself noted in his 1581 Report on the Spiritual Practice at Novellara that he did not give the Exercises individually throughout the year but preferred to give them to a group at the beginning of the noviceship. From that point the novices entered into the mainstream of the community life and followed the regular schedule of the rest of the novices. That they stayed in the house more in the earlier part of their novitiate and ventured out more on experiments in the later months seems plausible, but there is no evidence to that effect. That they were engaged in active ministry in the area is certain, as is the fact that they would be sent on pilgrimage, usually to Loreto, if Valentino thought that experiment was warranted.

The economics of the house did have a decided influence in a number of areas. For one, it limited the number of novices who could be accepted, and it was probably the main reason for the practice of a one-year novitiate with a dispensation to begin studies in the second year. Economics also led to the establishment of multiple novitiates within a province. Arona and Novellara functioned at the same time in Lombardy for several years, partly because of the foundations established by the Gonzagas and the Borromeos. Records also show novices in Genoa, Bologna, Padua, and Venice. In most cases these were novices of the second year pursuing their studies. In other cases the probation and the experiments were done in an urban setting, as they had been in the first generation, and after this first probation the novices were sent to Novellara for the second probation. Mention is made of novices coming from cities such as Ferrara or Parma with their probation already completed.[67] The ability to accept more candidates for the Society this way probably was a factor in its general acceptance as a practice.

Moreover, the early Society's custom of allowing superiors and provincials to make decisions on the spot without consulting Rome also continued to be exercised. In some cases, it was thought wise for novices to leave one novitiate and go to another. On certain occasions Rome would send a novice to Novellara in the hopes that that would clarify issues in the novice's vocation. In other instances, Valentino would send a candidate to Rome for the same reasons. Similarly, in the memorial of the novices who left, Valentino records the case of a novice sent from Genoa to Novellara to help him in his vocation.[68]

The other economic factor of note was dependence on the largesse, or lack thereof, of the local nobility. Their wealth vastly surpassed that of everyone else, and it was only with time that the novitiate in Novellara developed some financial independence. Francesco Adorno was quite accurate when he noted the problems of dealing with the local nobility. Moreover, the fact that Valentino's tenure as rector ended the same year as Camillo Gonzaga's death would imply that he remained in office for twenty-six years not just because he was a good novice master, which he was, but also because the count was very happy to have him as rector. Valentino knew both how to confront the count and how to console him. He was called upon to do so on numerous occasions. These qualities probably would not have made him as good a provincial as Adorno was—with his accurate and forth-right judgment, his constant movement around northern Italy, and his ability to make hard decisions—but Valentino's own qualities did make him a good seer of hearts and souls, and a good companion on the journey from this life to the next.

The *Constitutions* of the Society of Jesus followed in the long tradition of the rules of earlier religious orders. The novice master was to be one who could be trusted, who could instruct by word and example in the way of religious life, and who could help to discern the matters of the human heart as it encountered God. Antonio Valentino, with his understanding of the strengths and weaknesses of human beings, had learned this lesson well and carried it out with great grace at Novellara.

Endnotes

Commonly used abbreviations:

Archivum Romanum Societatis Iesu = ARSI

Archivo Communale di Novellara = ACN

Archivo dello Stato di Modena = ASM

Fondo Gesuiti Sopressi = Fondo GS

Institutum Historicum Societatis Iesu = IHSI

Archivum Historicum Societatis Iesu = AHSI

Monumenta Historica Societatis Iesu = MHSI

1. *Monumenta Ignatiana* (Rome: MHSI, 1903), 1:603–06, letter #204. Translation here by M. Palmer, S.J.

2. Manual Ruiz Jurado, S.J., *Origenes del Noviciado en la Compañia de Jesus* (Rome: PUG, 1980), 191–92, and Mario Scaduto, S.J., *L'Opera di Francesco Borgia* (Rome: Edizioni "La Civiltà Cattolica," 1992), 197–98.

3. ARSI Ital. 137, 198r.

4. ARSI Ital. 138, 73r.

5. *The Constitutions of the Society of Jesus,* trans. and commentary George Ganss, S.J. (St. Louis, Mo.: Institute of Jesuit Sources, 1984), [19]. (Hereafter cited as Ganss.)

6. Scaduto, *L'Opera,* 94.

7. ARSI Ven. 93, 40r.

8. Scaduto, *L'Opera,* 94.

9. Mario Scaduto, S.J. "Il Libretto Consolatorio di Bobadilla," in *AHSI* 43 (1974): 99.

10. ARSI Med. 74, 74r.

11. Ruiz Jurado, *Origenes del Noviciado en la Compañia de Jesus,* 151–53. See also MHSI *Regulae,* 141–43.

12. ARSI Fondo Gesuitico 1477/16, Novellara thecla #106, and ASM Fondo GS XXV, 14r.

13. Scaduto, *L'Opera,* 94.

14. László Lukács, S.J., "Le Catalogue-Modèle du Père Lainez (1545)," in *AHSI* 26 (1957): 57.

15. The years in parentheses for Brocca, Bitio, and di Chierici are taken from Scaduto, *Catalogo dei Gesuiti d'Italia: 1540–1565* (Rome: IHSI, 1968), 150.

16. Scaduto lists his first name as Filippo.

17. ARSI Fondo Gesuitico 1477/16, Novellara thecla #106. The same list is also found in ASM Fondo GS XXV, 14r.

18. For example, the college in Parma dated from 1564; Genoa, from 1554; Turin, from 1566; Brescia, from 1567. (See Scaduto, *L'Opera*, 279–346, on the Jesuit colleges in the Lombard province.)

19. ASM Fondo GS XLIII, 2r.

20. ASM Fondo GS XXV, 38r–38v.

21. ARSI Ven. 1, 131r.

22. A namesake, Carlo Spinola, also went to the Indies in 1594, was martyred in Japan in 1622, and was beatified in 1867. It should also be noted that the term "Indies" was often used at this time in reference to all of Asia.

23. ARSI Ven. 36, 35r.

24. ARSI Ven. 71, 2r.

25. ARSI Ven. 36, 35r, and ARSI Ven. 71, 2r.

26. A note also added that Passeto was sent home for a while for a problem *(una praga)* on his face (ARSI Ven. 36, 35r).

27. ASM Fondo GS, Novellara, Libri economici #41, 10r.

28. ASM Fondo GS XX, 48r. Marazzi served a total of thirty years as novice master in Novellara in two different terms. He died in 1640 at the age of eighty.

29. ASM Fondo GS XXV, 37r.

30. ARSI Ital. 144, 149r.

31. ASM Fondo GS XXV, 39r.

32. ARSI Ital. 145, 200r.

33. ARSI Ital. 152, 309r.

34. ARSI Ital. 153, 196r.

35. ARSI Ital. 154, 176r.

36. ARSI Ven. 115: *Fund. Dom. Prob. Nov.,* 371r.

37. ASM Fondo GS XX, 48r. Verbier was novice master from 1595 to 1598.

38. ARSI Ven. 37, 26r and 55r.

39. ARSI Ven. 71, 2r ff.

40. Ganss, 166, [290].

41. ARSI Ven. 37, 176r.

42. "In the case of scholastics, when their studies have been finished, in addition to the time of probation required to become an approved scholastic, before one of them makes profession or is admitted as a formed coadjutor, another year must be spent in passing through various probations, especially those mentioned above [64] if he did not make them previously, and through some of them even if he did make them, for the greater glory of God," from the *General Examen* in Ganss, [71].

43. ARSI Ven. 37, 176r.

44. ARSI Ven. 37, 260r. Presumably, the insistence on two years in the novitiate itself was finally taking hold.

45. ASM Fondo GS XLIII, 190r, 192r, and 173r.

46. Ruiz Jurado, *Origenes del Noviciado en la Compañia de Jesus,* 96–99.

47. Ibid., 109.

48. ASM Fondo GS XLIII, 192r.

49. ARSI Ital. 145, 200r.

50. ARSI Ital. 157, 82r–84r.

51. Nigel Griffin, *"Virtue versus Letters": The Society of Jesus (1550–1580) and the Export of an Idea* (Florence: European University Institute, 1961), 9.

52. ASM Fondo GS XXV, 39r.

53. ARSI Ital. 148, 274r.

54. Thomas Cohen, "Why Jesuits Joined: 1540–1600," in *Canadian Historical Papers* (1974), 251.

55. Ibid., 238.

56. ARSI Ven. 93, 91v.

57. ARSI Ven. 94, 17r.

58. ASM Fondo GS, Novellara, Libri economici #41, 10r.

59. ARSI Ven. 37, 260r (see appendix 7, for the year 1600).

60. M. Palmer, S.J., *On Giving the Spiritual Exercises* (St. Louis, Mo.: Institute of Jesuit Sources, 1996), 78.

61. ASM Fondo GS XXV, 39r: He could not find a horse to take him once he got to Mantua, so a kindly Jew gave him passage on a canal barge, prompting Valentino to write that "Out of this [occurrence] Divine Providence worked through the means of a Jew bringing a Christian to the religious life."

62. ASM Fondo GS XXV, 37v.

63. Ibid.

64. ARSI Ven. 105, 63r–63v. Mention here is made of pilgrimages to Loreto and to the Madonna degli Angeli.

65. ARSI Ven. 4, 119v. Mention is made of a pilgrimage to Loreto used to help a novice discern his vocation, whereupon the novice will be sent to Rome.

66. Ruiz Jurado, *Origenes del Noviciado en la Compañia de Jesus*, 178–81.

67. ARSI Ital. 155, 43r.

68. ASM Fondo GS XLIII, 192r.

The Jesuits and the Santa Casa di Loreto: Orazio Torsellini's *Lauretanae historiae libri quinque*

Paul V. Murphy

THROUGHOUT THE RENAISSANCE AND THE REFORMATION, one of the most popular pilgrimage routes in Latin Christianity led the pious to the Santa Casa di Loreto, the Holy House of Loreto, in the March of Ancona. According to a fifteenth-century tradition of the shrine, this was the house of Nazareth that the Virgin Mary occupied at the time of the Annunciation. This house became particularly noteworthy, according to tradition, because of its purported removal from Nazareth by angels from heaven as a consequence of the fall of Palestine to the forces of Islam. Angels were said to have flown the house first to Dalmatia in 1294; they returned a few months later to move it to the March of Ancona. This tradition can be seen as part of a broader *translatio sacri* of the Late Middle Ages and Renaissance when Latin Christians carried to the West relics that could no longer be visited after the Islamic victory. Whatever the origins of this house, the increasing difficulty of completing a pilgrimage to Jerusalem in the fifteenth century made a visit to the shrine of Loreto an important substitute for visiting shrines in the Holy Land.

In the sixteenth century the House of Loreto achieved notoriety among Protestants, who cited it as a typical example of what they considered Catholic superstition. A pilgrimage to Loreto ranked with all of the customs surrounding veneration of the saints and relics that they wished to eliminate. Many Catholics too became sensitive to what they considered the more incredible and disreputable elements of late medieval piety. They too called for a purified religious practice that focused on an inward, heartfelt devotion. The preferences of the so-called *spirituali* of sixteenth-century Italy and Erasmus's Philosophia Christi were just two examples of this Catholic response to what came to be deemed religious excess.

The cult of the Santa Casa di Loreto is noteworthy in this period because it does not seem to have been especially singled out for criticism even by those Catholics who sought reform. Erasmus, for example, composed a liturgy in honor of Our Lady of Loreto.[1] Cardinal Gasparo Contarini, one of the leaders of the *spirituali*, held the post of cardinal-protector of the shrine.[2] The distinguished lyric poet Battista Mantuanus composed a lengthy poem in honor of the house and the pilgrims to it while he was the leader of the Carmelite community at Loreto.[3] The Roman noblewoman and poet Vittoria Colonna went on pilgrimage to the house more than once after she came under the influence of Bernardino Ochino.[4] Even as realistic and politically minded a cardinal as Ercole Gonzaga of Mantua, whose life shows little other interest in personal piety or spiritual growth, went on pilgrimage to Loreto on at least two occasions.[5] Even figures who were most willing to concede to the Protestants the need to clean house on some issues of piety seem not to have questioned the authenticity or spiritual value of the shrine of Loreto.

Jesuits of that time were no exception to the general acceptance of the validity of the traditions surrounding the house. Ignatius of Loyola himself seems not to have questioned in any way the historicity of the shrine's relocation, and several of his first companions visited Loreto in 1537 while on their way to Rome.[6] Early Jesuits in general seem to have been quite devoted to this shrine, and their interests intensified in subsequent generations.[7] Possibilities for pastoral work at the shrine soon became apparent to the Jesuits, and they opened a school there—the Illyrian College.

It was not education, however, that attracted the Jesuits to Loreto. Rather, it was the opportunity to work with the large numbers of pilgrims to the Santa Casa. Jesuits became the official confessors at the shrine, and by 1575 an estimated 60,000 penitents annually availed themselves of these confessors.[8] Obviously, business was brisk. In 1575 Jesuit Gaspar de Loarte responded to this market by publishing a manual on how to make a good pilgrimage and singled out Loreto in particular.[9]

The most extensive example of the Jesuit view of the shrine of Loreto, however, comes from the pen of Orazio Torsellini, S.J. (1544–99).[10] He spent twenty-two years as a professor of classical literature at the Jesuit Roman College and also served as director of the Roman Seminary and rector of the Jesuit college in Florence. Most of his published works reflect his interest in literature. He expressed his views on rhetoric in *De Particulis Latinae Orationes,* published in Rome in 1596 by Luigi Zannetti. His apostolic interests and gifts as a rhetorician found expression in an early biography of the Jesuit missionary Francis Xavier, published in 1593.[11] In 1598 he published his most ambitious work, *Historiarum ab origine mundi usque ad annum 1598.*

Torsellini's association with the shrine of Loreto dates at least from 1584 when he became rector of the Jesuit college there. Based on his experience he published his *Lauretanae historiae libri quinque* in 1597. In this work he tried to give a historical account of the shrine, including a recounting of the tradition of its angelic translation. He also described subsequent pious practices and accounts of miracles there. Torsellini emphasized the role of the popes in particular as patrons and sponsors of the shrine and underscored their devotion to it. This history was soon translated into Italian, Spanish, German, English, French, Flemish, Czech, and Hungarian. Torsellini's attitude toward the Marian shrine of Loreto reflects late-Renaissance views on European expansion, Latin culture, early modern Catholic piety, and a new emphasis on the church's missionary activity. The Santa Casa di Loreto, unusual as it was, served him in all of these areas.

Torsellini reinforced traditional Catholic devotion to the Virgin, but with emphases that reflect the interests of the world of early modern Catholicism. Compared to other foci of Catholic piety during this age, the Marian shrine at Loreto has a more universal context. It is not merely a shrine dedicated to a Virgin who protects the local population in a particular way, but a shrine to a Virgin with global significance.[12] This context accords with the tendency in post-Tridentine Catholicism to replace local cults with more universal ones.[13] Torsellini presents his history of this devotion and its peculiar nature as the inverse of shrines tied to a particular setting. Loreto is holy, in his eyes, not because of the place itself, but because of the house that has been placed there. It is not the geographical site that is holy. This is a cult for faith on the move and will be particularly useful to the Jesuit Torsellini as he draws the outline for a practical Marian devotion in an age of European expansion.

Evidence of this attention appears not only in the body of Torsellini's text but also in his dedicatory letter to Cardinal Pietro Aldobrandini (1571–1621) that serves as a prologue. Here Torsellini distinguishes the House of Loreto from other Marian shrines because of its universality. Other shrines are those of a particular people or nation, attached to a particular location or site. Loreto is, as he terms it, the "common refuge of all people and nations."[14] The shrine is the focus of pilgrims from many parts of the world.[15] The papal states thus become a focus of piety that replaces the Holy Land after the expansion of Turkish power in the Near East and southeastern Europe.

Loreto, moreover, becomes the culmination of a pilgrimage route that has the pope, the universal pastor, for its "impresario," to borrow a term from Peter Brown.[16] Torsellini organizes his history by pontificate and is careful to include material on papal patronage. For example, he states that Pius II (1458–64) was cured of an ailment at Loreto while on his way to Ancona to meet the Crusader army he hoped would confront the Turks. This cure, Torsellini asserts, was important in the spread of the cult of Loreto because until that time many well-known preachers, including Saint Antonino of Florence, were unaware of the shrine.[17]

The role of Julius II (1503–13) is of particular significance in the growth of the devotion to Our Lady of Loreto. The shrine was in the northern regions of the papal states, territories over which the pope was seeking to reassert his control. Julius II officially promulgated the tradition of the translation in his bull *In sublimia* in 1507, that is, at the time of Julius's recovery of Bologna, Perugia, and the Romagna. He further highlighted the importance of the shrine by means of architectural and artistic projects. Designs that the architect Donato Bramante carried out for Julius at Loreto reflect the pope's desire to restore the imperial splendor of Rome and extend it to the papal states. These designs included fortification and embellishment of the church and the adjacent Palazzo Apostolico, which made the complex "at once sanctuary, fortress, hospice, and dwelling."[18] It has been suggested that the emphasis laid on Loreto by Julius and Bramante's colonnaded courtyard before the basilica of Loreto recall the pope's interest in restoring the image of the Emperor Julius Caesar, whose forum in Rome included a temple dedicated to *Venus Genetrix*.[19] Bramante was not the only prominent artist to work at the shrine. Others who worked at Loreto included Melozzo da Forlì, Luca Signorelli, Giuliano da Sangallo, Andrea Sansovino, and Antonio da Sangallo the Younger.[20] Quite obviously, Loreto was not a remote shrine of marginal significance. It played a central role in the plans of Julius II and other sixteenth-century popes. While Torsellini does not limit his account of Julius's interests in the shrine to the opportunity to score ideological and propaganda points, he nevertheless credits much of Julius's interest in the shrine to his efforts to recover the Romagna. He even claims that Our Lady of Loreto saved him from a canon shot that "overthrew the consistory, but left the pope unharmed."[21]

Papal patronage increased further under Pope Leo X (1513–21), who made the basilica at Loreto a collegiate church and granted pilgrims to the house of Loreto all the combined indulgences available at all of the station churches in Rome.[22] He also commanded that the only September fair in that region would be the one in Loreto. Thus the town became, in Torsellini's description, an "international" market where Italians, Dalmatians,

Germans, Flemings, Greeks, Armenians, Jews, and Turks ("lately expelled out of Spain") did business together. Orthodox and Latin Christians, he says, prayed together at the shrine.[23] In this Torsellini did not exaggerate, for during the period from the late-fifteenth to the mid-sixteenth century nearby Ancona thrived as a major international port.[24]

Torsellini's account of papal involvement from the time of Pius II serves to present the popes as both leaders of the religious cult of Our Lady of Loreto, with all of its international significance, and organizers of a Christian counterattack on the Turks. The possibility of rolling back the Turks had, according to Torsellini's description, offered the first opportunity for a European expansion that continued into his own day. Attention to the role of the popes was not misplaced because without their patronage the shrine could never have experienced the popularity it enjoyed. Indeed, prior to 1500 little attention was paid to Loreto, a situation that had changed dramatically by Torsellini's day.

Torsellini also used the theme of universality as an opportunity for expressing his views on Latin culture. His appreciation of Latin provided him with a rationale for the language in which he wrote the work. It is a restatement of the cultural norms of fifteenth-century Italian humanism. Torsellini chose to write the work in Latin rather than Tuscan because he viewed it as more universal. As he put it, "The Roman tongue may extend further than in times past the Roman Empire did." This humanist appreciation for Latin as a vehicle for cultural and religious beliefs is reminiscent in particular of the views of Lorenzo Valla who asserted in his *Elegantiae linguae latinae*, "There is the Roman Empire where the Roman language rules" ("Romanum imperium ibi esse, ubi Romana lingua dominatur").[25] The universality that was once the goal of the Romanization of culture, however, takes on a religious significance in terms of Torsellini's appraisal of Loreto. Moreover, Torsellini transforms Valla's appreciation of the role of the Roman Curia and the pope as potential agents for the expansion of Latin culture. Torsellini makes the pontiffs into agents for spreading the renewed Catholicism of the sixteenth century. His use of Latin is linked directly, therefore, to the spiritual conquests of the generations just before and after his own birth. He speaks specifically of the spread of Christianity beyond the borders of Europe and of his book being carried "over most remote nations."[26] Here again we see two facets of Torsellini's career. He was a veteran teacher of Latin in Jesuit colleges and authored at least two texts for use by students in such schools. Further, as noted above, he authored an early biography of that paradigmatic Jesuit missionary, Francis Xavier. Thus, we see combined here a humanist rhetorical model for the use of Latin and an early example of the use of Mary as a universal patroness of the missions. The cult, if not the house, of Loreto would continue to move.

Torsellini was, however, not only a promoter of papal patronage and a late-Renaissance rhetorician. He was also a pastor of souls much like other early Jesuits. The shrine of Loreto became, in his hands, an instrument for Jesuit pastoral work. The Santa Casa was, first and foremost, a physical structure. It could serve therefore not only as the culmination of a pilgrimage route but also as the focus for meditation on the life of the Virgin and Christ after one had arrived there. The opportunity to appreciate the holy places in this vicarious manner had a particular appeal for a Jesuit such as Torsellini. Early in the career of Ignatius Loyola, the soldier-turned-pilgrim attempted to go to and stay in the Holy Land; he actually did reach the Middle East and visited a number of shrines there in 1523.

In *The Autobiography of St. Ignatius Loyola,* which he dictated to a fellow Jesuit many years later, Ignatius spoke of his intention "to remain in Jerusalem, continuously visiting the holy places, and in addition to this devotion, he also planned to help souls."[27] Ignatius detailed a visit he made to Mount Olivet, where he examined very closely the footprints, which according to pious tradition, were those left by Christ at his ascension into heaven. Ignatius was so intent on noting precisely how the footprints were positioned that he returned to the shrine and even bribed a custodian to gain entry. Soon the Basque pilgrim wore out his welcome with the Franciscan protectors of the Christian holy places and was forced to leave.[28] Later in life, Ignatius, along with that small band of friends who became the Society of Jesus, bound himself by a vow to go to Jerusalem. Only if they were not able to reach the holy places were the first Jesuits to place themselves at the disposal of the pope. Thus, in the early history of the Jesuits the shrines of the Holy Land played a very prominent role.

The anecdote about the footprints on Mount Olivet in the early career of Ignatius also calls to mind the importance he paid in *The Spiritual Exercises* to the need to be physically and psychologically attentive to one's spiritual experience. He urged the person undertaking the Spiritual Exercises to employ, among other techniques of prayer, what he termed "application of the senses" in meditation. This technique was especially important in the Second Week of the Spiritual Exercises, when Ignatius asked the exercitant to contemplate the life of Christ. Near the beginning of that section of the *Exercises* he encouraged the individual to apply the senses to meditations on the Incarnation and the nativity of Christ. In short, in meditating upon the Incarnation one might try to fully imagine with the "five senses of the imagination" the event when the angel is said to have appeared to Mary in her home in Nazareth and announced that she would bear the Messiah. As Ignatius put it, "to touch with the touch, as for instance, to embrace and kiss places where such persons put their feet and sit, always seeing to my drawing profit from it."[29] This application of the senses was intended to immerse the individual as fully as possible into the events of Christ's life.

Related to this exercise is the method of prayer that Ignatius termed "composition of place" and described in the First Week of the Exercises. This activity was intended to use the imagination to place oneself in the scenes of the Gospel as they took place: "The composition will be to see with the sight of the imagination the corporeal place where the thing is found which I want to contemplate."[30]

Herein lies the particular spiritual value of Loreto for Torsellini. As a Jesuit he sought to model himself on the example of Ignatius. The *Autobiography* in many ways serves to provide that model for all later Jesuits. The importance of the trip to Jerusalem narrated therein and the attention to the shrines of Christ's life enhanced reflection on the person of Christ. The Spiritual Exercises had the same goal. Torsellini, unlike most other Jesuits, was able to spend a significant part of his life in the presence of what he considered at least one of those shrines where Ignatius himself had sought to remain. This presence allowed him to fulfill, even as Ignatius had not, the vow to go to the holy places. Moreover, by living at the shrine of the Santa Casa, Torsellini was able to employ the physical structure itself to focus the prayer of penitents, retreatants, and those who heard Jesuit preaching. In directing the prayer of pilgrims he could ask them to imagine just how the Annunciation happened as they prayed within the structure that was claimed to be the site of the event itself.

Torsellini demonstrates his attentiveness to imagining things just as they would have taken place in a curious story that he includes in his history about the exorcism of a woman beset by seven devils. The woman was brought into the Santa Casa itself, where an exorcism took place. In a short time six of the devils fled. The seventh was about to make his escape when the exorcists decided to hold him up in order to interrogate him. In particular they asked him to say exactly where the angel Gabriel had stood when he entered the room and where the Virgin sat. The devil willingly gave the information and then exited.[31] This story added colorful detail for the pilgrim visiting the shrine. Moreover, Torsellini and others using the Spiritual Exercises as the basis for their pastoral work could now use the exorcism account as a mechanism for focusing the attention of an individual on events surrounding the Incarnation. Loreto provided a concrete opportunity for "composition of place" and the "application of the senses." The house offered the pious the opportunity to do what all reformers had been asking. In this unusual site pilgrims could focus, in a particularly concrete manner, on the life of Christ and the Virgin while enhancing their own interior lives.

Loreto is both a point of arrival and a point of departure. It is a point of arrival in that, according to pious tradition, one of the Holy Places had been transferred to the March of Ancona, thus shifting the spiritual center of gravity from the Holy Land to Italy. It also serves as a point of departure because it represents religious and cultural expansion well beyond the boundaries of the Italian peninsula. As Torsellini's confreres in the Society of Jesus established missions in Latin America or Asia, they carried with them this universal Madonna of Loreto. Establishment of numerous towns named for and shrines dedicated to Loreto attests to an ongoing translation of the cult of the Holy House to many areas of European expansion in the early modern period. The Madonna of Loreto could assist with interior journeys as well, however. The shrine of Loreto served to further the purposes of the Spiritual Exercises and Jesuit pastoral work by encouraging interior spiritual growth. In the end, as unusual as the traditions of the Santa Casa were, this effort at inculcating a more fervent spirituality based upon the life of Christ and practical devotional activity was not far removed from the efforts of Erasmus and other humanist reformers of the generations that preceded Torsellini.

Endnotes

1. Erasmus of Rotterdam, *Opera Omnia,* vol. 5-1, ed. L. E. Halkin (Amsterdam: North Holland, 1977), 5-1:87–109.

2. See Gasparo Contarini to Ercole Gonzaga, 4 November 1539, Edmondo Solmi, "Lettere inedite del cardinale Gasparo Contarini nel carteggio del cardinale Ercole Gonzaga (1535–36)," *Nuovo archivio veneto,* nuova serie, 4 (1904): 245–74. See also 259.

3. Battista Mantuanus, *Opera omni a* . . . (Bologna: B. Hectoris, 1502).

4. Letter of Agostino Gonzaga to Isabella d'Este, 12 March 1535. Quoted in Alessandro Luzio, "Vittoria Colonna." *Rivista Storica Mantovana,* 1 (1885): 1–52, cf. 26. Agostino Gonzaga mentioned that Vittoria Colonna was now given to the spirit and listens to the preaching of Bernardino Ochino. He wrote that she intended to go to Loreto and then upon her return into the "regno" to sequester herself in a monastery erected by a Signora Longa. Colonna apparently made at least one other pilgrimage to Loreto in the summer of 1542. It is mentioned in a letter of Nino Sernini to Ercole Gonzaga, 23 August 1542, cited by Luzio, 38, n. 2.

5. Letter of Ercole Gonzaga to Isabella D'Este, 17 March 1524. Archivio di Stato, Mantova, B. 1150, f. 287r.

6. James Brodrick, *The Origin of the Jesuits* (Chicago: Loyola University Press, 1986), 56.

7. On the early Jesuits see John W. O'Malley, S.J., *The First Jesuits* (Cambridge, Mass.: Harvard University Press, 1993), 271. See also Peter Togni, S.J., "Antonio Valentino, S.J. and the Jesuit Novitiate at Novellara. A Case Study of the Second Generation of the Society of Jesus" (Ph.D. diss., Berkeley, Graduate Theological Union, 1996), 238–39. Togni notes that the novice master at Novellara sent groups of novices on pilgrimage to Loreto to test their vocations.

8. Marta Pieroni Francini, "Itinerari della Pietà negli ani della contrariforma. Pelegrini romani sulla strada di Loreto," *Studi romani,* (1987): 296–320. Statistic on penitents found on 299.

9. Gaspar de Loarte, *Trattato delle sante peregrinazioni* . . . (Venice: Domenico and Giovanni Battista Guerra, 1575; also published at Rome: G. Degli Angeli, 1575). On this work see O'Malley, *First Jesuits,* 271.

10. On Torsellini see Carlos Sommervogel, S.J., *Bibliothèque de la Compagnie de Jésus* (Paris: A. Picard, 1890–1932), 8:138–56; and Uwe Neddermeyer, "Das katholische Geschichtslehrbuch des 17. Jahrhunderts:

Orazio Torsellinis Epitome historiarum," *Historisches Jahrbuch* 108 (1988): 469–83.

11. Orazio Torsellini, *De Vita Francisci Xaverii qui primus e Societate Iesu in India et Iaponia Evangelium invexit* (Rome: Gabiana, 1593).

12. On this universal role of Mary see William A. Christian Jr., *Local Religion in Sixteenth-Century Spain* (Princeton, N.J.: Princeton University Press, 1981), 21.

13. See R. Po-Chia Hsia, *The World of Catholic Renewal 1540–1770* (Cambridge, Mass.: Cambridge University Press, 1998), 56.

14. Orazio Torsellini, *Lauretanae historiae libri quinque* (Rome: Zanetti, 1597), hereafter *History*. I have been able to consult the translation of the work by Thomas Price, *The History of the B. Virgin of Loreto* (St. Omer: 1608), my own pagination for dedicatory letter, 3.

15. Bernard Hamilton also notes this fact in "The Ottomans, the Humanists, and the Holy House of Loreto," in *Renaissance and Modern Studies*, 31 (1987): 1–19.

16. See Peter Brown, *The Cult of the Saints. Its Rise and Function in Latin Antiquity* (Chicago: University of Chicago Press, 1981), 10.

17. Torsellini, *History*, 116.

18. Arnaldo Bruschi, *Bramante* (London: Thames and Hudson, 1973), 118–119. See also Torsellini, *History*, 159–60.

19. See Charles L. Stinger, *The Renaissance in Rome* (Bloomington, Ind.: Indiana University Press, 1985), 269–70.

20. Stinger, *Renaissance in Rome*, 42.

21. Torsellini, *History*, 161.

22. Ibid., 172–73.

23. Ibid., 175–76.

24. On the local economy see Peter Earle, "The Commercial Revolution of Ancona, 1479–1551," *Economic History Review*, 22 (1969): 28–44.

25. See John D'Amico on the role of Valla in Roman Humanism in *Renaissance Humanism in Papal Rome* (Baltimore, Md.: Johns Hopkins, 1983), 118–19.

26. Torsellini, *History*, 4.

27. Ignatius of Loyola, *The Autobiography of St. Ignatius of Loyola, with Related Documents*, trans Joseph F. O'Callaghan, S.J. (New York: Harper Torchbooks, 1974), 49.

28. Ibid., 50–51.

29. Ignatius of Loyola, *The Spiritual Exercises of St. Ignatius. A Literal Translation and a Contemporary Reading,* trans. Elder Mullen, S.J. (St. Louis, Mo.: Institute of Jesuit Sources, 1978), [125].

30. Ibid., [47].

31. Torsellini, *History,* 147–49.

Peter Canisius: Jesuit Urban Strategist

Thomas M. Lucas, S.J.

ON 5 AUGUST 1596, PETER CANISIUS MOUNTED THE PULPIT for the last time. The occasion was a solemn one: the dedication of a splendid new college in Fribourg. Such an event was hardly a novelty for the seventy-five-year-old teacher and preacher; in fifty years of service, he had personally founded or contributed to the establishment of eighteen colleges in Germany, Austria, Hungary, and Poland, and another twenty missions, residences, and novitiates throughout northern Europe. When the seventeenth century began a few years later, the student populations of the colleges he founded at Cologne, Vienna, Munich, Mainz, Dillingen, Würzburg, Ingolstadt, Innsbruck, and Fribourg averaged nine hundred each.[1] The religious map of the Empire had been dramatically altered by the efforts of the more than one thousand German-speaking Jesuit companions who had joined his company.

Canisius's final sermon that August day was delivered in a whisper and contained none of the triumphalist rhetoric one might expect on such a grand occasion. Rather, Canisius took up the theme closest to his heart, the theme that had animated his half a century of service. He spoke of what Jesuits are made for, the *ratio, modus vivendi, finisquae institutae Societatis Iesu:* "to teach the young, to preach to the people, to absolve sinners in the confessional, to help the sick, to comfort the suffering, to strengthen the dying, to bring back those lost in heresy to the way of truth."[2]

Those simple words describe Peter Canisius's apostolic life; moreover, they summarize concisely the *consueta ministeria* exercised by the Society of Jesus as it expanded into cities around the world during its first half-century of existence.

Until 1538, the image of Jerusalem and the idea of traditional missionary work among the infidels formed and informed the minds and hearts of Ignatius and his first companions. They vowed to go to Jerusalem and work in literal imitation of Jesus, as his missionary companions. Thanks to the interference of geopolitical reality that impeded their travels and to their keen attention to the social realities surrounding them, Ignatius and his companions moved to Rome instead. Their goal of the historical Jerusalem was transposed into work in the contemporary City of Man, wherever the pope might send them. The Jerusalem metaphor no longer encapsulated or constrained their mission; rather it expanded to embrace the cities of the globe.[3]

The realities of the world that Ignatius had encountered in his wide travels and that the companions met each day in their diverse urban pastoral works made new demands, prompting a new form of religious life to evolve out of their missionary commitment. Their oblation to the pope and their readiness to go anywhere to undertake any mission given to them by the Holy See was nothing less than a "vow of mobility" that effectively removed the Society from the tradition of the monks and the "order-centric" obedience of the mendicants.[4]

An early document, the "Constituciones circa missiones" (1544–45), testifies to the radical unrootedness of the first Jesuits:

> Coming from diverse countries and provinces and not knowing which regions to go to or to stay in, among the faithful or unbelievers, we made this promise or vow that His Holiness might distribute or send us for the greater glory of God our Lord, in accordance with our promise and intention to travel through the world, and if we did not find the desired spiritual fruit in one city or the other, to pass on to another and yet another, and so on and so forth, going about through cities and

other particular places for the greater glory of God our Lord and the greater spiritual profit of souls.[5]

In practice, this vow makes the Jesuit a cosmopolitan being, a citizen of every city in the world. Ignatius could well have been describing Canisius when he defined the Jesuit as one who was to live "always with one foot raised, ready to hasten from one place to another, in conformity with our vocation and our Institute."[6] Canisius's thousands of kilometers of journeying throughout Europe reflect Jerome Nadal's famous dictum: "There are missions, which are for the whole world, which is our house. Wherever there is need or greater utility for our missions, there is our house."[7]

Articulation of that mission and the schematizing of the Society's conceptual framework were tasks the first companions entrusted to Ignatius in 1539, even as some were beginning to disperse on papal missions of preaching and teaching in Italy, and others were preparing to sail for Portuguese India or set off toward Spain or Germany. Three months of deliberation among the companions had laid down the general parameters for the Institute. They would have a general superior, elected for life. They would vow special obedience to the pope "as regards the missions." They would teach the rudiments of the faith "to children and everyone else" for forty days a year. Recruits to their company would make the Spiritual Exercises, go on pilgrimage, and "serve the poor in hospitals or elsewhere" for a total of three months.[8]

Drafting the Society's foundational documents, and in particular its *Constitutions,* occurred over the space of almost twenty years. In order to understand the evolution and novelty of the Jesuit urban vision articulated in these documents, two strands of questions, two interwoven issues, must be examined in some detail. Those issues are, first, how the Society defined its mission in the world and, second, how changing apostolic demands (particularly the opening of schools) determined the locations where that fundamental mission would be carried out.

Ignatius had learned in his extensive travels throughout Europe that the Renaissance city was a complicated overlapping mosaic of social, linguistic, and ethnic groups—it is helpful to recall that only about a quarter of the population of Rome was native Roman.[9] Each urban constituency, moreover, had particular pastoral needs and its own voice and dialect, whether linguistic or social. In order to converse with them, Jesuits had to develop a highly articulate and extensive ministerial vocabulary, one that could successfully engage and communicate with the pope or local prince one minute and the prostitutes who lived around the corner the next.

The first principle and foundation of Ignatius's Spiritual Exercises is preeminently practical: use what you need, do what you need to do—and, conversely, do not use what you do not need, and do not do what you do not need to do—in order to serve God and save souls. This principle, summarized in the rhyming Latin *tantum quantum,* is a basic descriptor of how the Jesuit is to relate to the created world.

Of course, that principle requires a careful calculus—in Jesuit-speak, "discernment"— of what assists the work at hand and what impedes it. This Ignatian discernment is a dialectic between practical experience and spiritual goods: practical experience always measured reflectively and prayerfully against the goal of the greater good and the service of God and neighbor.

Practical apostolic discernment led the first companions to eliminate a number of the most hallowed elements of religious life from their own new Institute: there were to be no distinctive habits, no fixed penances, and no mandatory choir. The reasons for dispensing with the obligation of choir and for mandating simplicity in liturgical celebrations are particularly relevant for they are grounded in the exigencies of the apostolate. Priests were obliged to recite the divine office, but "not in choir lest they be diverted from the works of charity to which we have fully dedicated ourselves." Moreover, simplicity of liturgical services is mandated "since according to the nature of our vocation, besides the other necessary duties, we must frequently be engaged a great part of the day and even of the night in comforting the sick both in body and in spirit."[10] Eminently practical in its layout, this new model of ministry put demands of active service before requirements of tradition.

While early Jesuits agreed upon the general goal of working "for the good of souls," the specification of the Society's ministries underwent an evolution that can be seen in a comparison of the texts of *The Formula of the Institute*, the Society's equivalent to the Rule of monastic orders. Based on the deliberations of 1539, the *Formula* underwent two distinct redactions: the 1539 *Quinque Capitola* presented to Paul III and the expanded version found in the 1550 bull of confirmation *Exposit debitum*.

The first version of the *Formula* describes who the Jesuit is: "He is a member of a Society founded chiefly for this purpose":

> To strive especially for the progress of souls in Christian life and doctrine and for the propagation of the faith by the ministry of the word, by Spiritual Exercises, by works of charity, and expressly by the education of children and unlettered persons in Christianity and the spiritual consolation of Christ's faithful through hearing confessions.[11]

Additions and changes found in the 1550 version of the *Formula (Exposcit)* are shown in italics; deletions appear in brackets:

> To strive especially for the *defense* and propagation of the faith and for the progress of souls in Christian life and doctrine, by means of public preaching, *lectures, and any other ministration whatsoever of the word of God, and further by means of the* Spiritual Exercises, [and expressly] the education of children and unlettered persons in Christianity, and the spiritual consolation of Christ's faithful through hearing confessions and *administering the other sacraments.*
>
> *Moreover, he should show himself ready to reconcile the estranged, compassionately assist and serve those in prisons or hospitals, and indeed to perform any other works of charity, according to what will seem expedient for the glory of God and the common good.*[12]

The second version of the *Formula* clearly shows development from the 1539 draft. *Exposcit* of 1550 includes lectures and the administration of other sacraments and requires a readiness on the part of the applicant to engage in any work of charity that "will seem expedient for the glory of God and the common good." The "defense" of the faith seems to have been added to the 1550 text in direct reference to the Order's increased work in combating the Protestant Reformation in northern Europe, since such work was certainly not an explicit priority when the order was founded.[13]

The Society's vision and aims, as they emerge from these texts, are profoundly apostolic and evangelical: the Jesuit, in virtue of his vowed obedience to the Holy See and his superiors, in fulfilling his mission, is required to be *ready* to undertake a wide variety of different ministries, ministries whose exact scope would evolve as existential circumstances changed. Moreover, insistence on the ministries of the word—preaching, lecturing, teaching, and spiritual conversation, with the confessional holding pride of place—point to an understanding of the priesthood that is more prophetic than cultic. Even the corporal works of mercy, excellent in themselves, were seen as secondary to this fundamental work of communication and conversation: the Jesuit is "to show himself ready" to perform those corporal works, but the imperative weight rests on "whatsoever ministry of the Word of God."[14]

For the early Jesuits, a privileged form of this ministry of the Word was the spiritual conversation, a sympathetic and patient colloquy with unbelievers and heretics. Ignatius laid down the guidelines for Laínez and Salmerón before they went to Trent in 1546. He instructed them to engage in ordinary pastoral ministries of visiting the sick and teaching catechism, but advised them to be positive and respectful in their style of conversation:

> I should be slow to speak, and should do so only after reflection and in a friendly spirit, particularly when a decision is given . . . profit by listening quietly to learn the frame of mind, feelings, and intentions of the speakers, so that I might be the better able to answer in my turn or keep silent. . . . I should not touch upon

matters that are in controversy . . . but simply exhort the people to live a good life and practice the devotions of the church. I should move them to acquire a knowledge of their own hearts and a greater knowledge and love of their creator and lord, appealing to the intellect.[15]

Near the end of his long career of dialogue with Protestants, Canisius reechoed these same sentiments in a long chapter entitled "De officio nostrorum ad coversandum cum proximis ubique locorum" addressed to Superior General Claudio Acquaviva:

> It is assuredly wrong to meet non-Catholics in a temper of asperity, or to treat them with discourtesy, for this is nothing else than the reverse of Christ's example, inasmuch as it is to break the bruised reed and quench the smoking flax. . . . They ought always be instructed in a spirit of meekness, to the end that by wholehearted charity and good will we may win them over to us *in domino*.[16]

The first Jesuits were committed to training their own recruits and to teaching catechism to children and the unlettered. Discerned utility and external pressure, however, rather than a deliberate, strategic decision, occasioned their move into the classroom. While the earliest documents were openly opposed to such undertakings, Jesuits sometimes held in-house courses and review sessions for their own seminarians or scholastics, employing the *modus parisiensis*.[17]

As early as 1543, though, Jesuits began teaching a variety of subjects at a seminary for local boys at Goa, and the Order assumed responsibility for the institution in 1548. At about the same time, the imperial court and the Catholic bishops of Germany put great pressure on the Jesuits to provide professors for theology faculties decimated by Reformation defections.

In November 1545, at Francisco Borja's insistence, non-Jesuit students were admitted to the Society's seminary in Gandia and received instruction alongside scholastics. At Borja's request, Paul III chartered the school as a university.[18]

Civic need and appeals of friends led to the establishment of the first Jesuit school designed specifically for lay students. In 1548, the magistrates of the city of Messina joined forces with the Viceroy Don Juan de Vega and his wife Doña Leonora Osorio, who had actively supported the Roman charitable works of the Society before their transfer to Sicily. They appealed directly to Ignatius to provide teachers of theology, the arts, grammar, rhetoric, and ethics. Ignatius sent ten of his most promising men from eight nations, including Nadal, Peter Canisius, André des Freux, and Cornelius Wischaven, to begin the enterprise in the spring of 1548.

Canisius's stay in Messina was, however, a short one. In 1549 Ignatius bowed to pressures from the empire and reluctantly sent Canisius, together with two of the first companions—theologians Claude Jay and Alfonso Salmerón—to lecture at the University of Ingolstadt.[19] In short order, Canisius was named dean, rector, and vice chancellor of the faltering university. Similar pressures led to Canisius's foundations of Jesuit colleges in the Palatine cities of Vienna, Prague, Augsburg, and Innsbruck, and induced him to accept Cardinal Truchsess's University of Dillingen for the Society in 1563.

In a circular letter to the Society, Polanco outlined the advantages of colleges for the Society, the students, and the local community. Teaching provided the order's recruits with pedagogical skills useful for preaching and organizational skills useful for pastoral ministries. The schools provided solid learning and moral training, and promoted vocations to the Society. The town was served because parents were relieved of financial burdens of education; local people were helped by the Jesuits' preaching and sacramental ministries; parents were influenced by children's progress in virtue; Jesuits encouraged and helped in the establishment of hospitals and charitable institutions; and students matured to fill important posts for the common good, becoming, among other things, pastors, civic officials, and administrators of justice.[20]

Colleges provided the Society with solid platforms for its pluriform social ministries and raised the Society's profile within the cities where colleges were founded. Firmly grounded in the humanistic traditions of the Renaissance, the Jesuits believed in the moral power of education for the good of the city *ad aedificandum et reformandum*. "If we see to the education of youth in letters and morality, then great help for the republic will follow, for good priests, good senators, and good citizens of every class come from these efforts."[21]

Indeed, education itself was understood as a work of charity in the fullest sense. "We accept for classes and literary studies everybody, poor and rich, free of charge and for charity's sake, without accepting any remuneration," Ignatius wrote in a circular letter to the Society. He insisted that there be "no distinction between rich and poor students."[22] Canisius was certainly inspired by this insistence when he established in Vienna and Prague residences both for noble and poor students. Admission was based on intellectual ability alone; students from all classes studied together. The Jesuits' network of free schools for boys of all classes has been called Europe's first systematic attempt to provide education to a substantial portion of the urban population.[23]

In a very brief span of years, the colleges became indispensable apostolic centers for the Jesuits. Not only did Jesuits teach in the schools, but they used the college facilities—especially the church, which was considered an integral part of any college complex—as centers for preaching, counseling, and other pastoral ministries. Time and again Canisius argued eloquently for provision of a church unencumbered by parochial or choir obligations for the Society's ministries. While negotiating for the College at Innsbruck in 1555, he wrote:

> I would ask that a church not be forgotten when the boundaries of the college are determined. It is not possible for us to do without one. . . . for it would be intolerable if our Fathers had always to be sought out, approached in somebody else's church, especially when they were wanted for priestly duties. This too is part of our institute, to devote as much care to the people in church as to the students in school, since it is our conviction that what priests do for the edification of souls, not only by lecturing but by instructing the simple, administering the sacraments, and healing with divine assistance every species of

spiritual disease, is the most acceptable sacrifice in the eyes of God. Such services, however, are not conveniently rendered except in a church of one's own, which can afford great comfort to devout souls when easily accessible.[24]

Writing to Prince Albert's counselors at Prague, Canisius was even more direct:

We are not hunting after a magnificent temple. All we ask for is a place of spiritual consolation for ourselves and our students, a place where unmolested we can pray for our illustrious Patron, for your excellencies, and for the whole country, and where both ailing and strong [Jesuits] may say their Mass without inconvenience.[25]

Much to Canisius's dismay, magnificent temples were often provided or built *ex novo* for the Society.[26]

Very early in the order's history, the question arose about *where* the Society's colleges and churches should be erected. It is treated in one of the earliest and most important sections of the Society's *Constitutions,* the seventh chapter entitled "The distribution of the incorporated members in Christ's vineyard and their relation there with their fellowmen."[27] Its fifty-one constitutions and explanatory declarations [603–54 in the standard text numbering[28]] lay out with precision and clarity answers to the crucial definitive questions—the who, what, when, where, and why—of the Jesuit mission.

Detailed and practical considerations—about *who* is to send and be sent, *what* is to be done, *when* works should be modified or abandoned, and *where* the Jesuits should focus their energies—are organized around two simple, typically Ignatian concepts: the greater glory and service of God, and the more universal good.[29] Together, they form a single foundational criterion:

To proceed more successfully in this sending of subjects to one place or another, one should keep the greater service of God and the more universal good before his eyes as the norm to hold oneself on the right course.... *The more universal the good is, the more it is divine.* [622 a, d (italics mine)]

Ignatius drew up guidelines for discerning what "the greater service of God and the more universal good" meant at any given moment or in a situation where a choice had to be made among several valid options. The methodology Ignatius proposed was the same one that he laid out for making an election or choice of a way of life "in a time of tranquillity" in the Spiritual Exercises.

When applied to the question of the choice and management of undertakings, this methodology is eminently practical and thoroughly unromantic. It proposes a careful weighing of a large number of factors: apostolic needs; levels of commitment appropriate to meet those needs; physical factors of manpower, location, and available resources; and a balancing of chances for success against personal and corporate dangers.

The most notable linguistic feature of part 7 is the unremitting *ostinato* of comparative adjectives and adverbs. The underlying criterion of the *greater* service of God and the *more* universal good grounds all choices in what the modern social sciences call "the multiplier effect." All decisions—about whom to send, where they are to work, what they are to do, what norms they are to follow—are subordinated to the unrelenting demand of the *magis*, the greater service, the more universal good. At the same time, Ignatius acknowledged that any one existential situation can and usually does differ from the next, so the norms he proposed function *ceteris paribus*, "when other considerations are equal." Given that other considerations are rarely equal, that liberating qualifier left superiors room to diverge from past decisions in any given situation.

Part 7 [622, 623] proposes an interlocking series of criteria for judging apostolic importance of works and choosing a place to work. The norms are shot through with sturdy realism that always aims at maximizing impact. Work that will last is to be chosen over transitory hit-and-run ministry. Work that impacts large numbers of people is generally to be chosen over work that is focused on individuals—unless, of course, the individuals in question are in positions of great influence and can make the effects spread more widely.[30] "Great nations such as the Indies, important cities, and universities which are generally attended by numerous persons who by being aided themselves can become laborers for the help of others"[623e] are deemed ideal target locations.

What emerges from these norms is a clear-cut preferential option for urban settings for Jesuit works in the developed world. The multiplier effect clearly mandates the choice of "important cities, and great universities, which are being attended by numerous persons who by being aided themselves can become laborers for the help of others." Cities and major universities, located perforce in an urban setting,[31] are the chosen arenas for the multiform ministries sketched out in the *Formula* and fleshed out in the programs of the *Constitutions*. The urban setting provided the greatest diversity of possibility "where the greater fruit will probably be reaped through the means that the Society uses" [622 a, b]. The city afforded a critical mass of population and wealth; apostolic needs and opportunities; possibilities for spiritual, social, and pastoral ministries; public preaching and private conversations; the long-range social impact of work with those who have power to effect systemic change; and the promise of reforming a world by educating its youth.

At the end of a long list of exhortations on "our way of proceeding" that Ignatius sent out with those founding new colleges and residences, there is some solid advice:

> Take special care that you obtain a good and sufficiently large site, or one that can be enlarged with time, large enough for house and church, and if possible, not too far removed from the conversation of the city; and having bought that, it will be a good beginning for all that follows.[32]

No one followed this good advice as assiduously as Ignatius himself, who six weeks after the Society's first approval in 1540 obtained the run-down but superbly located church of Santa Maria della Strada in Rome. This site, located at a crossroads on the Via Papalis next to Paul III's favorite Palazzo San Marco, was one long block from the Campidoglio, in the midst of an urban redevelopment zone bordered by the Jewish ghetto and the bordello district. Its well-placed pulpit became the archetype for Jesuit ministerial foundations.

Although the *Constitutions* were not promulgated until 1558—two years after Ignatius's death and almost a decade after Canisius's great years of building in Vienna, Prague, Munich, and Ingolstadt—it is utterly clear that Peter Canisius was of one mind with Ignatius on the issues surrounding the Society's urban mission. Moreover, he shared Ignatius's shrewd and hardheaded skills as a negotiator. Methodical yet diplomatic, he routinely got the Society what property it needed, where it was needed.

In 1552 the Emperor Ferdinand "borrowed" Canisius from Ingolstadt to found an imperial college in Vienna. Canisius had to navigate a potential minefield when Ferdinand tried to force the Dominicans out of their nearly empty monastery not far from the university. Canisius convinced the court to pay rent for the Jesuits to the Preachers, began looking around, and found—between his work as cathedral and court preacher, catechism writer, and prison chaplain—an even more centrally located Carmelite monastery in the very center of town. Canisius carefully negotiated a fair settlement with the Carmelites, lest a forced eviction "give the religious a cause for great indignation . . . and causing an evil smelling reputation to spread about Germany concerning us."[33] Once negotiations were completed and the "beautiful church with its great influx of people" was released from its choir obligations, the Jesuits moved in and established a boarding school for lay students as well. The tide of public opinion decidedly turned in the Society's favor when the fathers, scholastics, and their students were recognized for providing exquisite care for plague victims and sustenance for injured soldiers returning from the Turkish war.

Looking toward Bohemia, Canisius had to sidestep a gracious offer from the bishop of Laibach, who offered the Society an abandoned monastery in the Silesian hinterlands for a new college. Canisius replied:

> It did not seem advisable for our Society to settle in retired and thinly populated places, such as where some monastic lands are wont to be, and that it would be more conducive to the glory of God and the edification of our neighbor if the college were established in the chief city of some province where a more abundant harvest of souls for the love of Jesus Christ Crucified might be anticipated. The letter was shown to the King, and his Majesty, in consequence, decided that the college should be established in Prague, out of the revenues of the aforesaid lonely and unprotected monastery. . . . Truly we can hope for the greatest edification and most abundant help for souls, once Ours are established in Prague, which is the capital and chief metropolis of Bohemia, and from which issued the first roots of Germany's heresies.[34]

Bolstered by Canisius's preaching in the Prague cathedral, much hard negotiating ensued, and the final result was spectacular: the Society was granted the nearly deserted Dominican priory at the strategic Charles Bridge, in the heart of a city

> just like Rome, very noble and densely populated. . . . The location is pleasing to us, at the very center of the city and convenient for the students, and has sufficient space for classrooms and school facilities, for meeting rooms and a residence and a good plot of garden as well.[35]

Mutatis mutandis, similar stories could be related about the foundations at Munich, Ingolstadt, Würzburg, Mainz, and Innsbruck. Each city was an intellectual and social crossroads. In all these places the Society was granted sparsely populated monastic properties, and Canisius was required to engage in delicate negotiations with the Jesuit headquarters in Rome and the superiors general of the other congregations. In each case, Canisius argued for fair treatment and just recompense of the displaced religious.

More important than the actual physical sites occupied within the urban fabric was the choice of which important cities and important universities should be served by the Society. When looking for a strategically located headquarters for his peripatetic ministry as provincial, Canisius chose the belvedere of Germany, the imperial city of Augsburg: *"Arcem excellentem, ex totam contemplarit Germaniam et iuvare facile possimus domino cooperante."*[36] There he served with great effect for seven turbulent years as preacher in the cathedral—a position he had held at Cologne, Vienna, Prague, and Würzburg—and was renowned for his simple works of charity among the poor, the imprisoned, and the unlettered. His great success in the pulpit and his unrelenting criticism of the corruption of the local clergy raised the jealousy of the cathedral chapter, which tried to deprive him and his fellow Jesuits of faculties to perform their various sacramental ministries. This painful situation led to Canisius's most eloquent defenses of the Jesuit *consueta ministeria* of preaching, teaching, and sacramental ministry.[37]

After his retirement as provincial in 1570, Canisius concentrated his energies on writing and preaching in the university towns of Dillengen and Innsbruck, where he served for five years as court preacher to the archduke. Indeed, preaching was the one constant throughout his long and eventful life—week after week, year after year, sermon after sermon, lesson after lesson, in high pulpits of cathedrals, in the market squares of Ingolstadt and Fribourg, in the rural reaches of Bohemia and Bavaria. His steadfast if unspectacular devotion to his beloved ministry of the Word left behind 12,000 pages of sermon notes and countless changed hearts. In his last years at Fribourg his preaching often turned to Marian themes as he supported the growing sodality movement with sermons, catechetical lessons, and exhortations to service of the poor.[38]

Canisius understood, internalized, and incarnated the early Society's commitment to the complex urban realities of his time. He crisscrossed Europe, living in great cities and serving diverse populations in Germany, Holland, Belgium, Italy, Sicily, Poland, Switzerland, and the Austrian Empire, all the while physically and metaphorically building up Jesuit institutions. In pulpit and in prison cells, in the confessional and in the royal court, in the university *aula* and in street-corner catechesis of the simple and unlettered, he embodied a new model of integrated urban ministry that flowed from the Ignatian vision of the greater glory of God and the greater service of souls: "to teach the young, to preach to the people, to absolve sinners in the confessional, to help the sick, to comfort the suffering, to strengthen the dying, to bring back those lost in heresy to the way of truth."[39] Canisius, Jesuit humanist and urban strategist, knew that the human heart needs to be addressed and challenged where it dwells, in the City of Man as it strives toward the City of God.

Endnotes

1. John W. O'Malley, *The First Jesuits* (Cambridge, Mass.: Harvard University Press, 1993), 276; James Brodrick, *Saint Peter Canisius* (Chicago: Loyola University Press, 1962), 766–67. Brodrick's biography is the only serious work on Canisius available in English. This present monograph originally appeared in *Petrus Canisius, Humanist und Europäer*, ed. Rainer Berndt (Berlin: Akademie Verlag, 2000), a collection of essays from a 1997 conference held in Frankfurt to celebrate the 400th anniversary of Canisius's death.

2. *Beati Petri Canisii Societatis Jesu Epistulae et Acta*, ed. Otto Braunsberger (Freiburg: Herder, 1896–1923), 8:881 (hereafter Canisius, *Epistulae et Acta*).

3. For a good discussion of this metaphorical shift, see P. de Leturia, "Jerusalén y Roma en los designos de San Ignacio de Loyola," *Estudios Ignacianos* 1 (1957): 181–200. Cf. John C. Olin, "The Idea of Pilgrimage in the Experience of Ignatius Loyola," *Church History*, 48 (1979): 387–97. For a more complete development of the central urban thesis of this monograph and extensive bibliography, see Thomas M. Lucas, *Landmarking: City, Church, and Jesuit Urban Strategy* (Chicago: Loyola Press, 1997), especially chaps. 6, 7, 8.

4. "The vow of stability is what made the man the monk, in other words, the promise to live his entire life in the monastery, where he would seek his own sanctification. The Jesuits' Fourth Vow was in essence a vow of mobility, that is, a commitment to travel anywhere in the world, for the 'help of souls.' . . . The Fourth Vow was thus one of the best indications of how the new order wanted to break with the monastic tradition. The vow assumed, moreover, that the pope had the broad vision required for the most effective deployment in the 'vineyard of the Lord,' which by definition extended throughout the world. The implicit model . . . was Jesus sending his disciples—the 'vicar of Christ' (the vicar of Jesus) sending the Jesuits." O'Malley, *First Jesuits*, 299; cf. O'Malley's very important study, "To Travel to Any Part of the World: Gerónimo Nadal and the Jesuit Vocation," *Studies in the Spirituality of the Jesuits*, 16 (March 1984): 2.

5. "Constituciones circa missiones," in *Constitutiones et Regulae Societatis Iesu*, 4 vols. (Rome: Monumenta Historica Societatis Iesu [MHSI], 1934–48), 1:159–64; excerpt on 160 (hereafter *ConstMHSI)*. The "Constituciones circa missiones" served as the sketch for the seventh chapter of the *Constitutions of the Society of Jesus* and is one of the oldest and most important texts on the missions of the Society.

6. *Sancti Ignatii de Loyola epistolae et instructiones,* 12 vols. (Madrid: MHSI, 1903–11), 2:581 (hereafter *EpistIgn).*

7. *Epistolae et monumenta P. Hieronymi Nadal,* 5 vols. (Madrid: MHSI, 1898–1962), 5:469–70. Cf. M. Scaduto, "La strada e i primi Gesuiti," *Archivum Historicum Societatis Iesu,* 40 (1971): 323–90. Nadal extensively used this paradoxical image of the journey, mission, and pilgrimage as the "ideal house" and "most peaceful house" of the Society. O'Malley has laid out and explicated a number of these texts in "To Travel to Any Part of the World."

8. "Conclusiones septem sociorum," in *ConstMHSI,* 1:9–14. See André Ravier, *Ignatius Loyola and the Founding of the Society of Jesus,* trans. Maura Daly, Joan Daly, and Carson Daly (San Francisco: Ignatius Press, 1987), 89–94.

9. Peter Partner, *Renaissance Rome* (Berkeley, Calif.: University of California Press, 1976), 76. Interpretation of the census figures for 1526–27 (the only detailed census of the sixteenth century) allow for estimates of approximately 25 percent Romans, 55 percent non-Roman Italians, and 20 percent non-Italians.

10. Antonio M. de Aldama, *The Formula of the Institute: Notes for a Commentary,* trans. Ignacio Echániz (St. Louis, Mo.: Institute of Jesuit Sources, 1990), 18. For the difficulties that these exceptions to common practice caused, see Ravier, *Founding,* 107–116; Aldama, *Formula,* 28–33.

11. Aldama, *Formula,* 1, 3.

12. Ibid., 2, 4.

13. See O'Malley, *First Jesuits,* chap. 7 and Aldama, *Formula,* 40–45 for the impact on the order of the Jesuits' apostolic work among the Protestants.

14. Aldama, *Formula,* 42.

15. *EpistIgn,* 1:386.

16. Canisius, *Epistulae et Acta,* 8:131.

17. For a detailed study of the Parisian methodology and its implications, see O'Malley, *First Jesuits,* 215–25; Ricardo Garcia-Villoslada, *San Ignacio de Loyola: Nueva Biografia* (Madrid: BAC, 1986), 890–92.

18. Cf. Juan de Polanco, *Vita Ignatii Loiolae et rerum Societatis Iesu Historia seu Chronicon,* 4 vols. (Madrid: MHSI, 1894–98) 1:249 (hereafter: Polanco, *Chronicon).*

19. For Goa, see García-Villoslada, *Nueva Biografía*, 880–81. For Ingolstadt, see Brodrick, *Canisius*, chap. 4.

20. *EpistIgn*, 4:4–7, paraphrased in O'Malley, *First Jesuits*, 212.

21. Polanco, *Chronicon*, 5:535; cf. *Chronicon*, 2:19, 651.

22. *EpistIgn*, 4:10; *EpistIgn*, 12:310.

23. Paul Grendler, *Schooling in Renaissance Italy: Literacy in Learning, 1300–1600* (Baltimore, Md.: Johns Hopkins University Press, 1989), 365.

24. Canisius, *Epistulae et Acta*, 1:570–72.

25. Ibid., 577–78.

26. See Canisius, *Epistulae et Acta*, 8:386, for his negative reaction to the construction to St. Michael's Church, Munich.

27. For a very detailed analysis of this text, its history, and solid bibliography, see Antonio M. de Aldama, *The Constitutions of the Society of Jesus: Part VII Missioning*, trans. Ignacio Echániz (Anand, India: Gujarat Sahitya Prakash and Rome: Centrum Ignatianum Spiritualitatis, 1990). The text of part 7 is an amplification of Ignatius's "Constituciones circa missiones" of 1544–1545, found in *MHSJConst*, 1:159–64.

28. All English translations of the *Constitutions* are from *Constitutions of the Society of Jesus*, trans. George Ganss (St. Louis, Mo.: Institute of Jesuit Sources, 1970). For simplicity, references are given directly in the text using the standard text numbering in square brackets.

29. In the 51 paragraphs, the idea of the universal (or more universal) good appears at least 8 times [613, 615, 618, 622a, 622d, 623e, 626, 650], "more universal benefits" 4 times [618, 623a, 623f, 624]. The "greater glory" and/or "greater service of God" is the most characteristic phrase of the document: it appears in 18 places [twice in 603, twice in 605, 608, 609, thrice in 618, 622a, 623a, 623g, twice in 624k, 634, 645, 647, and 650]. The comparative adjective "greater" *(mejor)* appears another 25 times in the chapter in the following contexts: aid to souls [605], devotion [610, 622b], spiritual fruit [615, 622b], facility [618], security and safety [618, 619], need [622a, 631], indebtedness [622c], perfection [twice in 623b], confidence [624a], bodily labors [624b], spiritual dangers [624c], edification [625c, 645], importance of those to whom the Society is sent [626, 638], and care proportionate to the nature of the work [629].

30. Canisius's acceptance of Cardinal Truchsess's poorly endowed University of St. Jerome in Dillingen is an interesting case where the importance of maintaining the benefactor's goodwill outweighed the obvious limitations of locale and inadequate financing. See Brodrick,

Canisius, 569. Brodrick's dry British take on the situation is apropos: "From the natural point of view, it was certainly a very precarious investment, like buying, out of simple kindness, somebody's grand piano, without anywhere to store it or anybody to play on it. The town of Dillingen was barely on the map, a bit of a place that led nowhere and was famous for nothing."

31. Polanco identified the importance of urban and university ministry for attracting recruits to the Society: "Living in large and well-traveled locations—After universities, we ought to prefer for this goal [promoting vocations] large centers where there is great transit of able people, and among many cities there are some in particular, such as Rome and Venice in Italy, Valladolid, Toledo, Sevilla, and the Court in Spain, etc." *Polanci Complementa* (Madrid, MHSI, 1916–17), 1:726.

32. *EpistIgn,* 3:548.

33. Canisius, *Epistulae et Acta,* 1:446–47.

34. Ibid., 1:495–99 for full text.

35. Ibid., 1:547–48; cf Brodrick, *Canisius,* 259. Mention of securing a garden points to one of Canisius's nonnegotiable demands: that each urban college have a generous garden space. From his first negotiations for a residence in Cologne in 1545 throughout his career, he was adamant on this provision. Consult the index entry *hortus* in the eight volumes of *Epistulae et Acta* for many examples. Canisius even preached on the garden's spiritual value; cf. *Epistulae et Acta,* 8:603–06.

36. Canisius, *Epistulae et Acta,* 2:397.

37. The second half of Canisius, *Epistulae et Acta,* 4, and Brodrick, *Canisius,* chap. 14, detail in depth Canisius's struggles with the decadent chapter of Augsburg. Not even a papal brief dated 30 September 1564 "sealed under the ring of the fisherman" by Pius IV was sufficient to diffuse the local clergy's opposition to Canisius's successful ministry. *Epistulae et Acta,* 4:905–06. For an account of similar crises that Ignatius faced see Lucas, *Landmarking,* 151–53.

38. Cf. Brodrick, *Canisius,* chap. 18.

39. Canisius, *Epistulae et Acta,* 8:881.

Jesuit Book Production in the Netherlands 1601–1650

Paul Begheyn, S.J.

JESUITS AND THEIR APPRECIATION OF "THE BOOK"

IN 1640, JEAN BOLLAND (WHOSE NAME IS IMMORTALIZED in the Bollandists, the internationally renowned group of scholars) and other Flemish-Belgian Jesuits produced the magnificent and controversial *Imago primi saeculi Societatis Iesu* (Portrait of the First Century of the Society of Jesus), published by the famous Antwerp printer Christoffel Plantijn. In this book they marked the first centenary of their Order. They focused especially on the Flemish-Belgian province, part of which is the present kingdom of The Netherlands. In one chapter, the writers enumerated twelve important activities in which Jesuits were involved, comparing them with the twelve labors of Hercules. The twelfth was writing and publishing: "Even if we wanted to, we can not hide how involved our province is in this enterprise because the evidence is clear and well-known worldwide."[1] They then reviewed the literary contributions of important authors. The productivity of the Provincia Flandro-Belgica is indeed remarkable as is demonstrated by an analysis of two bibliographies published in 1643, the *Bibliotheca scriptorum Societatis Iesu* by Philippe Alegambe (1592–1652), a Jesuit from Brussels, and the *Bibliotheca Belgica* by Valerius Andreas (1588–1655), a professor at Louvain.

The Situation in the Northern Netherlands

In 1585, the provinces north of the great rivers declared their independence from Spain and formed the Dutch Republic. Rome described this area as the Dutch Mission. As opposed to their confreres in the Southern Netherlands, Jesuits in the Northern Netherlands were active as missionaries and usually lived on their own or in small communities with two or more Jesuits. Their opportunities to write and publish were rare. Only in Jesuit colleges in North Brabant and Limburg—two provinces still controlled by, or should we say, still loyal to the Spanish king—were Jesuits able to write.

Between 1601 and 1650 the number of Jesuits on the Dutch Mission increased from two to ninety. They were active in sixty-three mission stations and four colleges, some of which were short-lived. Remarkably nearly 140 volumes by Jesuits were published in the first half of the seventeenth century.[2]

Publications by the Four Jesuit Colleges

Between 1601 and 1650 there were four Jesuit colleges in the present-day Kingdom of The Netherlands: Maastricht, Den Bosch, Roermond, and Breda. The role that education played in the Society's apostolic activities is well known. Education was the basis for the Society's social influence and, at the same time, the spearhead of its activities. Although two of the four colleges operated only for a short period and the lives of the other two were temporarily interrupted, more than a quarter of the Jesuit publications during this period were edited by, and for the benefit of, these four institutions.

The oldest college was founded in Maastricht in 1575 and, despite two interruptions (1578–83 and 1639–73), survived until the suppression of the Society in 1773. It was the third largest in the province with approximately seven hundred students during the Twelve-Year Truce (1609–21). Because there was no printer active in Maastricht between 1608 and 1634, Jesuits employed Jan Ouwercx and Leonaert Streel at Liège.[3] Three volumes were published in Maastricht: two polemical works and a catechism [108, 109, 138].[4] Because there are no extant copies, and we know of their publication only from references, there is some doubt that they were actually printed.

The second Jesuit college opened in 's Hertogenbosch in 1610; it lasted nineteen years.[5] Paul Scheffer (1577–1620), a Jesuit connected to the college, was related to a family of printers—his father Jan (II) and his brothers Anthonie and Jan (III) Scheffer were active printers in the city.[6] The three printed thirteen volumes for the college. In fact, their works were the first books published for the Jesuits in The Netherlands in the seventeenth century. They printed three editions of a catechism written by Lodewijk Makeblijde (1565–1630), who was active in Delft [1, 8, 27]; three editions of an explanation of the Mass by Johannes van Gouda (1571–1630), a native of Utrecht [2, 12, 14]; a report on China by Nicolas Trigault (1577–1628), who had just returned from that country [5]; two editions for the Marian Congregations [7, 15]; a commentary on the readings for Sundays and feast days and a catechism, both by Peter Canisius (1521–97) from Nijmegen [9, 10]; a posthumous polemical work by Jan David (1546–1613) [11]; and a "Mirror of Penitence," by an unidentified Jesuit [41].

Another local printer, Jan van Turnhout, published a polemical work [3] by Joannes de Roy and two books written in 1614 and 1615 by students of the college on the occasion of the death of Bishop Gisbert Masius and the installation of his successor, Nicolaes Zoesius [4, 6]. Six years after the college's demise, Jan (III) Scheffer published a Dutch translation of the *Imitation of Christ* [77], based on the edition by Heribert Rosweyde (1569–1629) from Utrecht, one of the founders of the Bollandists.

Roermond was deemed appropriate as the site for the third Jesuit college in The Netherlands. Founded in 1611 it endured until the suppression in 1773. Between 1611 and 1650 it averaged three hundred students. A local printer, Caspar du Pree, published eleven works for the Jesuits between 1645 and 1650. Nine were pamphlets written by the indefatigable Jesuit Jodok Kedd (1597–1657) from Emmerich. His polemical works, written in several languages, had considerable influence and were responsible for the return of many to the Catholic Church [93, 102, 103, 106, 107, 112, 113, 117, 135]. The other three items were Lodewijk Makeblijde's catechism, a work published earlier for the Jesuits in Den Bosch [94], and a Dutch translation of *De Bello Belgico,* a history of the United Provinces' struggle for independence from Spain between 1555 and 1590. This history was written by the Italian Jesuit Famiano Strada (1572–1649) at the request of Alexander Farnese, Duke of Parma [115]. The final book was an adaptation of *The Imitation of Christ* in chronograms [133] by Anton van der Stock.

Plays for the Roermond college were published in Liège by Jan Ouwercx and Leonaert Streel, also employed by the Maastricht Jesuits, and by the Antwerp printer Heyndrick Aertssens.[7] Louvain publisher Joannes Christoph Flavius printed the first work produced by the college in 1613: *Ruremunda illustrata,* a Latin ode on the city of Roermond, written by students under the direction of Father Otto van Zijl (1588–1656).

The college at Breda opened in 1625 and closed in 1637. During its brief life it was responsible for only one book, a play [29], published in 1626 by Jacob Seldenslach, forefather of a well-known Breda family of printers. Ten years after the college closed, the city printer Jan van Waesberge published a pamphlet by the prolific, previously cited Jodok Kedd [110].

Publications in Amsterdam

Twelve Catholic booksellers were active in Amsterdam in the first half of the seventeenth century.[8] We shall focus on eight of the twelve because of their association with Jesuits who, after occasional appearances in sixteenth-century Amsterdam, became permanent fixtures after 1606.

Special consideration must be given to Franciscus van den Enden (1602–74), a native of Antwerp. A Jesuit from 1619 to 1633, he pursued an unsuccessful career as a bookseller in Amsterdam from 1644 to 1652. Later he was the rector of a Latin school. In this capacity he had significant influence on the Jewish philosopher Baruch Spinoza (1632–77). It is not known whether van den Enden had any professional contact with Jesuits after his departure.[9]

There was contact, however, between the Society and the aristocratic Amsterdam Hartoghvelt family, who were active as printers for three generations. In 1612, the youngest, Hendrik Barentsz Hartoghvelt (1586–1663), married Ghiertrut Jacobs from another Catholic family involved in publishing, the Paets. Her father, Jacob Pietersz Paets (c. 1555–1612), her brothers Claes (c. 1582–1620) and Pieter (c. 1587–c. 1657), and her nephew, Pieter's son Jacob (1626–73), were printers and publishers. Two sons from the third marriage of Hendrik Barentsz Hartoghvelt became Jesuits: Ignatius (1628–58)[10] in 1644 and his brother Barent (1629–81) four years later; two daughters, Alida and Maria, served as *klopjes* with the Jesuits at their station at the Verwersgracht. *Klopjes*, or "spiritual virgins," were unmarried or widowed Catholic women who devoted themselves to a sober, religious life in the world and applied themselves to all kinds of good works.

Nine volumes by Jesuits, each one beautifully illustrated by Christoffel van Sichem II (1577–1658),[11] were published by Pieter Jacobsz Paets. He published Heribert Rosweyde's edition of *The Imitation of Christ* in Dutch [31], a life of Our Lady [35], and two different editions of the lives of the Desert Fathers [88, 121]. He also published a meditation on the Our Father [49] by the recently deceased Charles Scribani (1561–1629) and two posthumous editions [92, 116] of a Dutch translation of the popular emblem book *Pia desideria* by Herman Hugo (1588–1629). Meditations on the life of Jesus by the Spanish Jesuit Luis de la Puente (1554–1624) [30, 34] were so popular that they were reprinted.

In 1648 (the year he was admitted into the Amsterdam guild of booksellers), Joachim van Metelen published the second volume of *De bello Belgico* on the Dutch Revolt by the Italian Jesuit Famiano Strada [124].

But the ten volumes published by Catholic printers in Amsterdam are insignificant when compared with the eighty-two volumes published by non-Catholics. The famous Willem Jansz Blaeu (1571–1638) and his son Joan Blaeu (1596–1673) lead the list with fifty-six and twelve titles respectively. On the title page, however, they always hide behind the names of the Cologne editors Cornelis van Egmond, Bernardus Gualteri, and Jodocus Kalcoven, whose brothers, Matthäus and Adam, were members of the Society of Jesus.[12]

By birth a Mennonite, Willem Jansz Blaeu had his children baptized in the Remonstrant church. Nonetheless he published books written by Socinians as well as Catholics. Averse to all ecclesiastical discord, he adopted an attitude that, when it came to business, treated religion as a personal matter. That his behavior was a persistent thorn in the side of the Reformed Church Council is obvious from the complaints filed with the Amsterdam city council in 1626–27.[13] They complained about "a large missal with new illustrations and other papist volumes like the office of the Blessed Virgin and works by Bellarmine," all printed by Blaeu. They were especially concerned about "the fame of the papists abroad because these kind of books could be printed in Amsterdam." Blaeu did not pay the slightest attention to their complaints. In fact, in 1631, he employed the German classics scholar and Catholic convert Bartholdus Nihusius[14] to supervise his Catholic publications. Blaeu's list of publications for 1633 contained a large number of Catholic books, among them works by Jesuit authors Robert Bellarmine and Jeremias Drexel.[15] His tolerance had repercussions. In a letter written on 14 October 1638 to Hugo de Groot, a week before Blaeu's death, the Dutch scholar Gerardus Joannes Vossius explained that he preferred that Blaeu not publish his works because of the large profits the publisher made from his Catholic books:

> This man, more concerned with his own success than that of others, yearns more for money than honour; his sole aim is profit. He claims that nothing is more profitable than his geographical maps. But he could have added the Massbooks etc., which he prints in such a way, that they carry the name of the Cologne printer on the title page.[16]

Publication of Catholic works did not stop, however, with the death of Willem Jansz Blaeu; his son Joan continued the custom.

Thirty-four of the fifty-six Jesuit books published by Willem Jansz Blaeu were from the pen of Jeremias Drexel (1581–1631) [13, 19–21, 32, 33, 39, 40, 42–48, 51–59, 66–74, 76], generally considered one of the most prolific spiritual authors of the century.[17] According to his publisher Cornelius Leysser, 158,700 copies of his books were published in Munich between 1620 and 1639, and a further 12,000 in the period 1639–42. Leysser also claimed that clandestine editions of Drexel's works appeared at Antwerp, Douai, Pont-à-Mousson, Amsterdam, and Leiden before 1639.[18]

Robert Bellarmine (1542–1621), who possibly enjoyed special renown in The Netherlands because he had taught theology in Louvain for six years (1570–76), was also popular. Blaeu published eleven of his works [22–26, 61–65, 79]; five editions of the Bollandist Heribert Rosweyde's Latin version of *The Imitation of Christ* [16, 28, 36, 75, 80]; and five Latin editions of the works of Saint Augustine [37, 38, 50, 78, 81], edited by Henri de Sommal (1534–1619) from Dinant.

Blaeu's final Jesuit publication was a revision of a popular treatise on magnetism [86] by the inventor and scholar Athanasius Kircher (1601–80). The first impression of 1641 was a limited edition, and according to the author, there were no available copies north of the Alps, except for the few sent to princes and another fifty copies to someone in Holland, whose name is not mentioned.[19] Thus Blaeu's edition, under the false imprint of Jodocus Kalcoven in Cologne, clearly filled a need.[20]

Only twelve Jesuit books were published under the direction of Joan Blaeu. He did continue the publishing policy of his father with works by Jeremias Drexel [90, 91] and editions of Saint Augustine by Henri Wangnereck (1549–1617) and Henri de Sommal [105, 114]. He also opted for other bestsellers: poetry by the German Jakob Balde (1604–68) [99, 101] and several editions of Famiano Strada's work on the Eighty Years' War [123, 126, 134]. Moreover he published a theological treatise by the Spanish Jesuit Juan Martínez de Ripalda (1594–1648) against the Louvain theologian Michael Baius and his followers [119]. Together with his colleague Lowijs Elzevier, Blaeu was a benefactor of the library of the Jesuit college in Brussels.[21]

Lowijs (III) Elzevier published three editions of the poetry by Jakob Balde [89, 98, 100]; each listed Jodocus Kalcoven of Cologne as the printer. Johannes Janssonius and Nicolaes van Ravesteyn printed respectively three [95, 122, 125] and two [104, 129] editions of Strada's work. In 1650, Tymon Houthaak published a work by Georg Scherer on the legendary Pope Joan [132]. There was apparently a curious fascination with her in 1650, because other books on her also appeared on the Dutch market. In 1649, the *Opkomste der Nederlandsche Beroerten* [130], in which Augustijn van Teylingen (1587–1669) traced the origin of the division of The Netherlands, was published. In 1624, Broer Jansz published the second edition of *The Natural and Moral History of the West Indies* [17] by the Spanish Jesuit José de Acosta (1540–1600) in a Dutch translation by Jan Huygen van Linschoten. In the same year a Dutch translation [18] of Edmund Campion's (1539–81) *Ten Reasons* issued from the press of Marten Jansz Brandt. Finally an unidentified Amsterdam printer published an apologetical work [85] by the Portuguese Jesuit Francisco Freire (†1644) and three anti–Reformed Church pamphlets [111, 136, 137] by Jodok Kedd.

Publications in Leiden and Rotterdam

The Elzeviers in Leiden published five works by foreign Jesuits. The first was a description of China by Nicolas Trigault and others [82] in 1639. In the same year two other works appeared; both were in part printed in Arabic. They were lives of Jesus and St. Peter, written by the Spanish missionary Jerónimo Xavier (1549–1617), a great-nephew of Saint Francis Xavier, to win over the Great Mogul of India to Christianity [83, 84]. Six years later Elzevier published a work on the miracles of Christ [97] by the French Jesuit François Vavasseur (1605–81) and a French translation of Strada's *De bello Belgico* [96]. A Latin edition of the second [87] had been printed by Jacob Marcus. In 1650, an unknown Leiden printer published a funeral oration on the poet Caspar Kinschot [131] by the Delft Jesuit Isaac van der Mye (1602–56), neighbor of the painter Johannes Vermeer.[22]

Only two Jesuit works from a Rotterdam press are known: Heribert Rosweyde's edition of *The Imitation of Christ*, published by Isaac van Waesberghe in 1633 [60], and a book of moral instructions for Dutch youth [120] by the previously mentioned Isaac van der Mye, published by Thomas Cel-Born.

Concluding Observations

The editors of the *Bibliotheca Catholica Neerlandica Impressa*[23] have collected titles of all Catholic spiritual books published in Netherlandish dioceses between 1500 and 1727. An analysis of this valuable bibliographical aid demonstrates that Jesuits were responsible for more than a third (34.3 percent) of the volumes published during the first half of the seventeenth century (2,037 out of 5,943). The numbers fluctuate: in 1601, only eighteen volumes were published; in 1625, fifty-four, the largest number produced in any one year. In 1614, Jesuits were responsible for only 19.2 percent of Catholic publications; in 1648, Jesuits contributed 48 percent of Catholic writings. Although such data must be treated with caution, the facts nevertheless clearly reveal the important role played by the Jesuits in the production of Catholic books throughout The Netherlands.

Restricting our consideration to the territory that comprises the present kingdom of The Netherlands, 138 books were published under Jesuit auspices during the first half of the seventeenth century. Aside from four anonymous works, thirty-one Jesuits either wrote or edited these books (seventeen titles). Fourteen were members of the Flemish-Belgian Province. The five most popular Jesuit authors were Jeremias Drexel (thirty-six), Jodok Kedd (sixteen), Famiano Strada (twelve), Robert Bellarmine (eleven), and Heribert Rosweyde (eleven), the only member of the Flemish-Belgian Province among the five.

The range of Jesuit publications was impressive. Although there was a strong emphasis on spirituality with a special interest in emblem books, books on practical theology, catechetics, homiletics, and exegesis appeared alongside works of poetry, drama, and history.[24] Of these publications eighty-eight were in Latin, forty-six in Dutch, and four in French.

One final question should be addressed: Who commissioned these books? Obviously those produced for the four Jesuit colleges were made at the request of the local Jesuits. It is more difficult, however, to ascertain who initiated the others because so little data is extant. In 1647, Petrus Laurentius wrote from Amsterdam to another Jesuit, Johan de Boeye in the Southern Netherlands, that three crates of books printed in Amsterdam were on their way to Bruges.[25] In December of the same year, Bartholdus Nihusius, assistant to the Amsterdam printer Blaeu, said that "he now was printing a book by Father Martínez de Ripalda against Baius and his followers. This was done at the request of the Jesuits for whom he wanted to do a favor."[26]

It would be premature to draw broad conclusions regarding Jesuit book production in The Netherlands during the first half of the seventeenth century. Nonetheless this research does show that

Jesuits made a much larger contribution to book production than one would have expected from a religious group that functioned under such restraints. Another surprise is Jesuit association with non-Catholic printers and publishers. Such involvement, on the one hand, may be evidence of a more tolerant attitude toward Catholics in general and Jesuits in particular than was encouraged by political authorities. On the other hand, it may simply show that the anticipated success of certain publications by Jesuit authors, especially in scientific and spiritual areas, was so economically attractive that other considerations paled in comparison.[27]

Appendix

Catalog of Publications by Jesuits in the Northern Netherlands, 1601–1650

Locations of copies verified (not *all* known copies are mentioned):

CC Museum Catharijneconvent, Utrecht

KB Koninklijke Bibliotheek, The Hague

KUB Katholieke Universiteit Brabant, Tilburg

KUN Katholieke Universiteit, Nijmegen

RG Ruusbroecgenootschap, Antwerp

RUL Rijksuniversiteit Limburg, Maastricht

UBA Universiteitsbibliotheek, Amsterdam

UBL Universiteitsbibliotheek, Leiden

UBU Universiteitsbibliotheek, Utrecht

000 no copy known

1. [Makeblijde, Lodewijk], *Catechismus voor de jonckeyt van 's Hertogenbossche,* Den Bosch, Jan Scheffer, 1611 (000).

2. [Gouda, Johannes van], *Corte uutlegginghe der Missen,* Den Bosch, Jan Scheffer, 1612 (KUB).

3. Roy, Joannes de [Christianus Philomasius], *Cort onderwijs voor Gerardo Livio,* Den Bosch, Jan van Turnhout, 1613 (KUB).

4. *In obitum Gisberti Masii Episcopi Silvae-ducensis funebria,* Den Bosch, Jan van Turnhout junior, 1614 (KUB).

5. [Trigault, Nicolas], *Waerachtich verhael van Syna,* Den Bosch, Anthonie Scheffer, 1615 (KB).

6. *Nicolao Zoesio quinto Sylvaeducensium episcopo gratulatur,* Den Bosch, Jan van Turnhout junior, 1615 (000).

7. *Alphabetum sodalitatis B. Virginis,* Den Bosch, Anthonie Scheffer, 1616 (KUB).

8. [Makeblijde, Lodewijk], *Catechismus voor de ionckheyt van t'Shertogenbossche,* Den Bosch, Anthonie Scheffer, 1618 (KUB).

9. Canisius, Petrus, *Epistolae et evangelia dominicis festisque diebus,* Den Bosch, Anthonie Scheffer, 1619 (KUB).

10. Canisius, Petrus, *Institutiones christianae pietatis,* Den Bosch, Anthonie Scheffer, 1619 (UBL).

11. David, Jan, *De schildwachte,* Den Bosch, Jan Scheffer, 1619 (000).

12. [Gouda, Johannes van], *Corte uutlegginghe der Missen,* Den Bosch, Jan Scheffer, 1620 (UBA).

13. Drexel, Jeremias, *Zodiacus christianus,* Keulen, Cornelis van Egmond [= Amsterdam, Willem Jansz. Blaeu], 1622 (Augsburg SB).

14. [Gouda, Johannes van], *Corte uutlegginghe der missen,* Den Bosch, Jan Scheffer, 1622 (000).

15. [Pretere, Willem de ?], *Hantboexken der sodaliteyt,* Den Bosch, Jan Jansz. Scheffer, 1622 (KUB).

16. Rosweyde, Heribert (ed.), *Thomae a Kempis De imitatione Christi,* Keulen, Cornelis van Egmond [= Amsterdam, Willem Jansz. Blaeu], 1622 (RUL).

17. Acosta, José de, *Historie naturael ende morael van de Westersche Indien,* Amsterdam, Broer Jansz., 1624 (UBA).

17a. Acosta, José de, *Historie naturael ende morael van de Westersche Indien,* Amsterdam, Hendrick Laurensz., 1624 (UBA).

18. Campion, Edmund, *Thien redenen,* Amsterdam, Marten Jansz. Brandt, 1624 (RUL, UBU, KUB).

19. Drexel, Jeremias, *Horologium auxiliaris tutelaris angeli,* Keulen, Cornelis van Egmond [= Amsterdam, Willem Jansz. Blaeu], 1624 (Paderborn).

20. Drexel, Jeremias, *Zodiacus christianus,* Keulen, Cornelis van Egmond [= Amsterdam, Willem Jansz. Blaeu], 1624 (000).

21. Drexel, Jeremias, *Zodiacus christianus,* Keulen, Cornelis van Egmond [= Amsterdam, Willem Jansz. Blaeu], 1625 (Berlin SB).

22. Bellarmino, Roberto, *De aeterna felicitate sanctorum,* Keulen, Cornelis van Egmond [= Amsterdam, Willem Jansz. Blaeu], 1626 (RUL).

23. Bellarmino, Roberto, *De arte bene moriendi,* Keulen, Cornelis van Egmond [= Amsterdam, Willem Jansz. Blaeu], 1626 (KUN).

24. Bellarmino, Roberto, *De ascensione mentis in Deum,* Keulen, Cornelis van Egmond [= Amsterdam, Willem Jansz. Blaeu], 1626 (KUN).

25. Bellarmino, Roberto, *De gemitu columbae,* Keulen, Cornelis van Egmond [= Amsterdam, Willem Jansz. Blaeu], 1626 (KUN).

26. Bellarmino, Roberto, *De septem verbis a Christo in cruce prolatis,* Keulen, Cornelis van Egmond [= Amsterdam, Willem Jansz. Blaeu], 1626 (KUN).

27. [Makeblijde, Lodewijk], *Catechismus voor de jonckheyt van 's Hertogenbossche,* Den Bosch, Jan Scheffer, 1626 (KB).

28. Rosweyde, Heribert (ed.), *Thomae a Kempis De imitatione Christi,* Keulen, Cornelis van Egmond [= Amsterdam, Willem Jansz. Blaeu], 1626 (UBA).

29. *Réprésentation: Scylarius, Roy de la Scytie,* Breda, Jacob Seldenslach, 1626 (000).

30. Puente, Luis de la, *Der zielen lust-hof,* Leuven, Isbrandt Jacobsz. Voor Pieter Jacobsz. Paets [Amsterdam], 1628 (000).

31. Rosweyde, Heribert (ed.), *De navolginge Christi. Door Thomas Hamerken van Kempen,* Leuven, Jan Maes, Voor P.J.P. [= Pieter Jacobsz. Paets, Amsterdam], 1628 (KUN).

32. Drexel, Jeremias, *Heliotropium,* Keulen, [Cornelis van Egmond ?] [= Amsterdam, Willem Jansz. Blaeu], 1629 (Berlin SB).

33. Drexel, Jeremias, *Recta intentio omnium humanarum actionum amussis,* Keulen, Cornelis van Egmond [= Amsterdam, Willem Jansz. Blaeu], 1629 (Paris BN).

34. Puente, Luis de la, *Der zielen lust-hof,* Leuven, Isbrandt Jacobsz. Voor Pieter Jacobsz. Paets [Amsterdam], 1629 (UBA).

35. Rosweyde, Heribert, *Het leven vande moeder Godts,* Leuven, Franchoys Fabri. Voor Pieter Jacobsz. Paets [Amsterdam], 1629 (KUB).

36. Rosweyde, Heribert (ed.), *Thomae a Kempis de imitatione Christi,* Keulen, Cornelis van Egmond [= Amsterdam, Willem Jansz. Blaeu], 1629 (RG).

37. Sommal, Henri de (ed.), *Aurelii Augustini Libri XIII confessionum,* Keulen, Cornelis van Egmond & Cie [= Amsterdam, Willem Jansz. Blaeu], 1629 (RUL).

38. Sommal, Henri de (ed.), *Aurelii Augustini meditationes, soliloquia et manuale,* Keulen, Cornelis van Egmond & Cie [= Amsterdam, Willem Jansz. Blaeu], 1629 (RG).

39. Drexel, Jeremias, *Aeternitatis prodromus mortis nuntius,* Keulen, Cornelis van Egmond & Cie [= Amsterdam, Willem Jansz. Blaeu], 1630 (RUL).

40. Drexel, Jeremias, *Heliotropium,* Keulen, Cornelis van Egmond & Cie [= Amsterdam, Willem Jansz. Blaeu], 1630 (KUN).

41. P. G., *Een spiegel van poenitentie ende godvruchtigheyt,* Den Bosch, Jan Jansz. Scheffer, 1630 (KUB).

42. Drexel, Jeremias, *De aeternitate considerationes,* Keulen, Cornelis van Egmond & Cie [= Amsterdam, Willem Jansz. Blaeu], 1631 (KUN).

43. Drexel, Jeremias, *Horologium auxiliaris tutelaris angeli,* Keulen, Cornelis van Egmond [= Amsterdam, Willem Jansz. Blaeu], 1631 (KUN).

44. Drexel, Jeremias, *Infernus damnatorum carcer et rogus,* Keulen, Bernardus Gualteri [= Amsterdam, Willem Jansz. Blaeu], 1631 (Cologne UB).

45. Drexel, Jeremias, *Nicetas,* Keulen, Cornelis van Egmond [= Amsterdam, Willem Jansz. Blaeu], 1631 (KB, KUN).

46. Drexel, Jeremias, *Orbis Phaethon,* Keulen, Cornelis van Egmond [= Amsterdam, Willem Jansz. Blaeu], 1631 (KUN).

47. Drexel, Jeremias, *Recta intentio omnium humanarum actionum amussis,* Keulen, Cornelis van Egmond [= Amsterdam, Willem Jansz. Blaeu], 1631 (KB, KUN).

48. Drexel, Jeremias, *Trismegistus christianus caelitum corporis,* Keulen, Cornelis van Egmond [= Amsterdam, Willem Jansz. Blaeu], 1631 (RUL).

49. Scribani, Carolus, *Ghebedt onses Heeren,* Amsterdam, Pieter Jacobsz. Paets, 1631 (RUL).

50. Sommal, Henri de (ed.), *Aurelii Augustini meditationes, soliloquia et manuale,* Keulen, Cornelis van Egmond & Cie [= Amsterdam, Willem Jansz. Blaeu], 1631 (UBA).

51. Drexel, Jeremias, *Gymnasium patientiae,* Keulen, Cornelis van Egmond [= Amsterdam, Willem Jansz. Blaeu], 1632 (KB).

52. Drexel, Jeremias, *Infernus damnatorum carcer et rogus,* Keulen, Bernardus Gualteri [= Amsterdam, Willem Jansz. Blaeu], 1632 (RG).

53. Drexel, Jeremias, *Tribunal Christi,* Keulen, [Cornelis van Egmond ?] [= Amsterdam, Willem Jansz. Blaeu], 1632 (000).

54. Drexel, Jeremias, *Zodiacus christianus,* Keulen, Cornelis van Egmond [= Amsterdam, Willem Jansz. Blaeu], 1632 (KUN).

55. Drexel, Jeremias, *De aeternitate considerationes,* Keulen, Cornelis van Egmond [= Amsterdam, Willem Jansz. Blaeu], 1633 (000).

56. Drexel, Jeremias, *Aeternitatis prodromus mortis nuntius,* Keulen, Cornelis van Egmond & Cie [= Amsterdam, Willem Jansz. Blaeu], 1633 (KUN).

57. Drexel, Jeremias, *L'avantcoureur de l'eternite,* Keulen, Cornelis van Egmond [= Amsterdam, Willem Jansz. Blaeu], 1633 (RUL).

58. Drexel, Jeremias, *Infernus damnatorum carcer et rogus,* Keulen, Bernardus Gualteri [= Amsterdam, Willem Jansz. Blaeu], 1633 (UBU).

59. Drexel, Jeremias, *Zodiacus christianus,* Keulen, Cornelis van Egmond [= Amsterdam, Willem Jansz. Blaeu], 1633 (000).

60. [Rosweyde, Heribert (ed.)], *Navolginge Christi. Door Thomas de Kempis,* Rotterdam, Isaac van Waesberghe, 1633 (000).

61. Bellarmino, Roberto, *De aeterna felicitate sanctorum,* Keulen, Cornelis van Egmond [= Amsterdam, Willem Jansz. Blaeu], 1634 (KUN).

62. Bellarmino, Roberto, *De arte bene moriendi,* Keulen, Cornelis van Egmond [= Amsterdam, Willem Jansz. Blaeu], 1634 (RUL).

63. Bellarmino, Roberto, *De ascensione mentis in Deum,* Keulen, Cornelis van Egmond [= Amsterdam, Willem Jansz. Blaeu], 1634 (KUB).

64. Bellarmino, Roberto, *De gemitu columbae,* Keulen, Cornelis van Egmond [= Amsterdam, Willem Jansz. Blaeu], 1634 (RG).

65. Bellarmino, Roberto, *De septem verbis a Christi [!] in cruce prolatis,* Keulen, Cornelis van Egmond [= Amsterdam, Willem Jansz. Blaeu], 1634 (RUL).

66. Drexel, Jeremias, *De aeternitate considerationes,* Keulen, Cornelis van Egmond & Cie [= Amsterdam, Willem Jansz. Blaeu], 1634 (KUN).

67. Drexel, Jeremias, *Gymnasium patientiae,* Keulen, Cornelis van Egmond [= Amsterdam, Willem Jansz. Blaeu], 1634 (KB, KUN).

68. Drexel, Jeremias, *Heliotropium,* Keulen, Cornelis van Egmond & Cie [= Amsterdam, Willem Jansz. Blaeu], 1634 (KUN).

69. Drexel, Jeremias, *Horologium auxiliaris tutelaris angeli,* Keulen, Cornelis van Egmond [= Amsterdam, Willem Jansz. Blaeu], 1634 (UBA).

70. Drexel, Jeremias, *Nicetas, ou bien l'incontinence vaincue,* Keulen, Cornelis van Egmond [= Amsterdam, Willem Jansz. Blaeu], 1634 (000).

71. Drexel, Jeremias, *Orbis Phaethon,* Keulen, Cornelis van Egmond [= Amsterdam, Willem Jansz. Blaeu], 1634 (KB,RG).

72. Drexel, Jeremias, *Recta intentio omnium humanarum actionum amussis,*

Keulen, Cornelis van Egmond [= Amsterdam, Willem Jansz. Blaeu], 1634 (KUN, RG).

73. Drexel, Jeremias, *Trismegistus christianus caelitum corporis,* Keulen, Cornelis van Egmond [= Amsterdam, Willem Jansz. Blaeu], 1634 (RG, UBA).

74. Drexel, Jeremias, *Zodiacus christianus,* Keulen, Cornelis van Egmond [= Amsterdam, Willem Jansz. Blaeu], 1634 (KUN).

75. Rosweyde, Heribert (ed.), *Thomas a Kempis, De imitatione Christi,* Keulen, Cornelis van Egmond [= Amsterdam, Willem Jansz. Blaeu], 1634 (000).

76. Drexel, Jeremias, *Tribunal Christi,* Keulen, Cornelis van Egmond & Cie [= Amsterdam, Willem Jansz. Blaeu], 1635 (KB, KUN).

77. Rosweyde, Heribert (ed.), *De naervolginghe Christi van Thomas a Kempis,* Den Bosch, Jan Jansz. Scheffer, 1635 (RUL).

78. Sommal, Henri de (ed.), *Aurelii Augustini Libri XIII confessionum,* Keulen, Cornelis van Egmond & Cie [= Amsterdam, Willem Jansz. Blaeu], 1637 (KB).

79. Bellarmino, Roberto, *De gemitu columbae,* Keulen, Cornelis van Egmond [= Amsterdam, Willem Jansz. Blaeu], 1638 (RUL).

80. Rosweyde, Heribert (ed.), *De Imitatione Christi,* Keulen, Cornelis van Egmond [= Amsterdam, Willem Jansz. Blaeu], 1638 (000).

81. Sommal, Henri de (ed.), *Aurelii Augustini Meditationes, soliloquia et manuale,* Keulen, Cornelis van Egmond [= Amsterdam, Willem Jansz. Blaeu], 1639 (UBA).

82. [Trigault, Nicolas; Góis, Bento de; Paulus, Marcus], *Regni chinensis descriptio,* Leiden, Ex officina Elzeviriana [= Bonaventura & Abraham Elzevier], 1639 (KB).

83. Xavier, Jerónimo, *Historia Christi persice conscripta,* Leiden, ex officina Elseviriana [= Bonaventura & Abraham Elzevier], 1639 (UBA).

84. Xavier, Jerónimo, *Historia S. Petri persice conscripta,* Leiden, ex officina Elseviriana [= Bonaventura & Abraham Elzevier], 1639 (UBA).

85. Freire, Francisco, *Apologia veritatis,* Amsterdam, [uitgever onbekend], 1642 (000).

86. Kircher, Athanasius, *Magnes sive de arte magnetica,* Keulen, Jodocus Kalcoven [= Amsterdam, Willem Jansz. Blaeu], 1643 (UBA).

87. Strada, Famiano, *De bello Belgico decas prima,* Leiden, Jacobus Marcus, 1643 (UBA).

88. Gorcum, Jan van and Rosweyde, Heribert, *'t Bosch der eremyten ende eremitinnen,* [Amsterdam], Pieter Jacobsz. Paets, 1644 (CC, UBA).

89. Balde, Jakob, *Lyricorum libri IV, et Epodon liber unus,* Keulen, Jodocus Kalcoven [= Amsterdam, Lowijs Elzevier], 1645 (UBA).

90. Drexel, Jeremias, *Aeternitatis prodromus mortis nuntius,* Keulen, Cornelis van Egmond & Cie [= Amsterdam, Joan Blaeu], 1645 (KUN).

91. Drexel, Jeremias, *Horologium auxiliaris tutelaris angeli,* Keulen, Cornelis van Egmond [= Amsterdam, Joan Blaeu], 1645 (KUN).

92. Hugo, Herman, *Goddelycke wenschen,* [Amsterdam], Pieter Jacobsz. Paets, 1645 (UBA).

93. Kedd, Jodok, *Examen des fondamens vande gereformeerde religie,* Roermond, Caspar du Pree, 1645 (RUL).

94. [Makeblijde, Lodewijk], *Catechismus,* Roermond, Caspar du Pree, 1645 (000).

95. Strada, Famiano, *De bello Belgico decas prima,* Leiden, Jacobus Marcus [= Amsterdam, Johannes Janssonius], 1645 (KB).

96. Strada, Famiano, *Histoire de la guerre de Flandre [deel I],* [Leiden, Bonaventura & Abraham Elzevier], 1645 (UBA).

97. Vavasseur, François, *Theurgicon,* Paris, Pierre le Petit [= Leiden, Bonaventura & Abraham Elzevier], 1645 (UBU).

98. Balde, Jakob, *Lyricorum libri IV, et Epodon liber unus,* Keulen, Jodocus Kalcoven [= Amsterdam, Lowijs Elzevier], 1646 (UBA).

99. Balde, Jakob, *Lyricorum libri IV, et Epodon liber unus,* Keulen, Joannes Busaeus [= Amsterdam, Joan Blaeu], 1646 (000).

100. Balde, Jakob, *Sylvae Lyricae,* Keulen, Jodocus Kalcoven [= Amsterdam, Lowijs Elzevier], 1646 (UBA).

101. Balde, Jakob, *Sylvarum libri IX,* Keulen, Joannes Busaeus [= Amsterdam, Joan Blaeu], 1646 (000).

102. Kedd, Jodok, *Statera veritatis dat is goudtwaegh der waerheyt,* Roermond, Caspar du Pree, 1646 (RUL).

103. Kedd, Jodok, *Verrekycker,* Roermond, Caspar du Pree, 1646 (RUL).

104. Strada, Famiano, *De thien eerste boecken der Nederlandsche oorloge,* Amsterdam, Nicolaes van Ravesteyn, 1646 (UBA).

105. Wangnereck, Henri (ed.), *Aurelii Augustini Confessionum libri X*, Keulen, Jodocus Kalcoven & Cie [= Amsterdam, Joan Blaeu], 1646 (RUL).

106. Kedd, Jodok, *Statera veritatis Dat is goutwaegh der waerheyt,* Roermond, Caspar du Pree, 1647 (000).

107. Kedd, Jodok, *Deductio articulorum fidei,* Roermond, Caspar du Pree, 1647 (000).

108. Kedd, Jodok, *Deductio articulorum fidei [in het Nederlands],* Maastricht, [Ezechiel Boucher?], [ca. 1647] (000).

109. Kedd, Jodok, *[Examen van thien propositien ofte voorstellingen],* [Maastricht, Ezechiel Boucher?, 1647] (000).

110. Kedd, Jodok, *Examen van thien propositien ofte voorstellingen,* Breda, Jan van Waesberge, 1647 (UBA).

111. Kedd, Jodok, *Gheloofsspieghel,* Amsterdam, [editor unknown], 1647 (000).

112. Kedd, Jodok, *Geloofs-spiegel,* Roermond, Caspar du Pree, 1647 (KB).

113. Kedd, Jodok, *Verclaringe van het Roomsch-catholyck geloof,* Roermond, Caspar du Pree, 1647 (RUL).

114. Sommal, Henri de (ed.), *Aurelii Augustini Libri XIII confessionum,* Keulen, Cornelis van Egmond & Cie [= Amsterdam, Joan Blaeu], 1647 (UBA).

115. Strada, Famiano, *Nederlantsche oorloge,* Roermond, Caspar du Pree, 1647 (Copenhagen KB).

116. Hugo, Herman, *Goddelycke wenschen,* [Amsterdam], [Pieter Jacobsz. Paets], [1648] (KUN).

117. Kedd, Jodok, *Predikanten wildesanck,* Roermond, Caspar du Pree, [1648] (000).

118. Kedd, Jodok, *Acht bedenckingen,* [place and editor unknown], 1648 (000).

119. Martinez de Ripalda, Juan, *Adversus articulos damnatos libri duo,* Keulen, Cornelis van Egmond & Cie [= Amsterdam, Joan Blaeu], 1648 (RUL).

120. Mye, Isaac van der, *Musa paraenetica ad juventutem Belgicam,* Rotterdam, Thomas Dircksz. Cel-Born, 1648 (000).

121. Gorcum, Jan van and Rosweyde, Heribert, *'t Bosch der eremyten ende eremitinnen,* [Amsterdam], Pieter Jacobsz. Paets, 1648 (KUN).

122. Strada, Famiano, *De bello belgico decas prima,* [Amsterdam, Johannes Janssonius?], 1648 (UBA).

123. Strada, Famiano, *De bello belgico decas prima,* [Amsterdam, Joan Blaeu], 1648 (UBL).

124. Strada, Famiano, *De bello Belgico decas secunda,* [Amsterdam, Joachim van Metelen], 1648 (RUL).

125. Strada, Famiano, *De bello belgico decas secunda,* [Amsterdam, Joannes Janssonius], 1648 (UBA).

126. Strada, Famiano, *De bello belgico decas secunda,* [Amsterdam, Joan Blaeu], 1648 (000).

127. Sommal, Henri de (ed.), *Aurelii Augustini Libri XIII confessionum,* Keulen, Cornelis van Egmond & Cie [= Amsterdam, Joan Blaeu], 1649 (RG).

128. Sommal, Henri de (ed.), *Aurelii Augustini meditationes, soliloquia et manuale,* Keulen, Cornelis van Egmond & Cie [= Amsterdam, Joan Blaeu], 1649 (RG).

129. Strada, Famiano, *Het tweede deel der Nederlandsche oorlogen,* Amsterdam, Nicolaes van Ravesteyn, 1649 (KB).

130. Teylingen, Augustijn van, *Opkomste der Nederlandsche Beroerten,* Keulen / Amsterdam, Willem Jacobsz., 1649 (KUN, UBU).

131. Mye, Isaac van der, *Idyllium, de morte Casparis Kinschoti,* Leiden, [editor unknown], 1650 (000).

132. Scherer, Georg, *Grondelyck onderzoek [over] een Paus die een kind ghebaard heeft,* Keulen, Johan Brakel [= Amsterdam, Tymon Houthaak], 1650 (UBA).

133. Stock, Anton van der, *De spiritali imitatione Christi,* Roermond, Caspar du Pree, 1650 (000).

134. Strada, Famiano, *De bello belgico decas secunda,* [Amsterdam, Joan Blaeu], 1650 (UBL).

134a. Balde, Jacob, *Werck meer werck en noch meer wercks voor een mispriester,* Amsterdam, Paulus Matthijsz., c. 1650 (UBL).

135. Kedd, Jodok, *Den gereformeerden duymen-drayer,* Roermond, [Caspar du Pree?], [year unknown] (000).

136. Kedd, Jodok, *Den gereformeerden duymen-drayer,* Amsterdam, [editor and year unknown] (000).

137. Kedd, Jodok, *Deckmantel der gereformeerde religie,* Amsterdam, [editor and year unknown] (000).

138. Villegas, Jacques de, *Kleynen catechismus,* Maastricht, [editor and year unknown] (000).

Endnotes

This paper was presented at the conference The Jesuits: Cultures, Sciences, and the Arts 1540–1773, held in 1997 at Boston College in Chestnut Hill, Massachussetts. An earlier Dutch version, "Uitgaven van jezuïeten in de Noordelijke Nederlanden 1601–1650," was published in *De Zeventiende Eeuw* 13 (1997): 293–308.

1. See *Afbeeldinghe van d'eerste eeuwe der Societeyt Iesu* (Antwerp: 1640), 558, 588–90.

2. See appendix.

3. See Carlos Sommervogel, *Bibliothèque de la Compagnie de Jésus*, 9 vols. (Brussels-Paris: 1890–1900), 5:291–93, 9:627; L. van den Boogerd, *Het jezuïetendrama in de Nederlanden* (Groningen: 1961), 226.

4. Numbers in square brackets refer to the appendix to this article, "Short Title Catalog of Publications by Jesuits in the Northern Netherlands, 1601–1650," 314–23.

5. See G. J. W. Steijns, *Inventaris van het archief van het jezuïetencollege (1609–1629) te 's-Hertogenbosch*, 2nd ed. ('s-Hertogenbosch: 1980).

6. See C. J. A. van den Oord, *Twee eeuwen Bosch' boekbedrijf 1450–1650* (Tilburg: 1984).

7. Sommervogel, 7:329–30; van den Boogerd, 227.

8. See Lienke Leuven, *De boekhandel te Amsterdam door katholieken gedreven tijdens de Republiek* (Epe: 1951).

9. See O. Proietti, "Le 'Philedonius' de Franciscus van den Enden et la formation rhétorico-littéraire de Spinoza (1656–58)," *Cahiers Spinoza* 6 (1991): 9–82.

10. On Ignatius Hartoghvelt, S.J., who died as a missionary in Siam and on his letters to his father and others, see Jerome Heyndrickx, ed., *Philippe Couplet, S.J. (1623–1693): The Man Who Brought China to Europe* (Nettetal: 1990), 30–32, 89–95.

11. See Helmut Lehmann-Haupt, "Christoffel van Sichem: A Family of Dutch Seventeenth Century Woodcut Artists," *Gutenberg-Jahrbuch* (1975): 274–306; K. G. Boon, *Hollstein's Dutch and Flemish Etchings, Engravings and Woodcuts ca. 1450–1700* (Amsterdam: 1983), 27:39–56.

12. Judocus Kalcoven to Athanasius Kircher, S.J., Cologne 17 March 1649 [?], Rome, Archivio Pontificia Universitas Gregoriana [APUG], Athanasius Kircher Miscellanea Epistolarum, 3, inv. 557, ff. 436r-v.

13. See I. H. van Eeghen, "De Acta Sanctorum en het drukken van katholieke boeken te Antwerpen en Amsterdam in de 17e eeuw," *De Gulden Passer* 31 (1953): 51–52.

14. A letter by Athanasius Kircher to Bartholdus Nihusius, from Rome, dated 6 March 1655, was recently offered for sale by Bernard Quaritch Ltd. See his catalog 1226, *The Society of Jesus 1548–1773* (London: 1996), no. 114.

15. See Cornelis Koeman, "Willem Blaeu's Catalogus Librorum of 1633: Analysis of the Cartographic Books," *Quaerendo* 3 (1973): 129–40; the text of the catalog on 134–40, and also in J. Keuning and Marijke Donkersloot-De Vrij, *Willem Jansz Blaeu. A Biography and History of His Work as a Cartographer and Publisher* (Amsterdam: 1973), 122–28.

16. Gerardus Joannes Vossius to Hugo de Groot in Paris, Amsterdam 14 October 1638, published in Paulus Colomesius, ed., *Gerardi Joannis Vossii et clarorum virorum ad eum epistolae* (London: 1690) 1:327.

17. See Gerhard Dünnhaupt, *Bibliographisches Handbuch der Barockliteratur* (Stuttgart: 1980–81).

18. See his foreword to Drexel's posthumously published work, *Noe, der Archen Bawmeister, und des Sündfluß Schiff Herr* (Munich: 1639). I have not found any clandestine Leiden editions of Drexel.

19. Athanasius Kircher, S.J., to an unknown person, Rome, n.d., Rome, APUG, Athanasius Kircher Miscellanea Epistolarum, 7, inv. 561, f. 79. J. Fletcher, "Athanasius Kircher and the Distribution of His Books," The Library V/23 (1969), 108–17, erroneously identifies this unknown person as Jesuit Jacobus Viva, who lived in Ingolstadt and Loreto.

20. Joan Blaeu to Athanasius Kircher, S.J., Amsterdam 29 March 1641, Rome, APUG, Athanasius Kircher Miscellanea Epistolarum, 3, inv. 557, f. 393.

21. See J. Andriessen, *De jezuïeten en het samenhorigheidsbesef der Nederlanden 1585–1648* (Antwerp: 1957), 300.

22. See Paul Begheyn, "Johannes Vermeer en de jezuïeten," *Streven* 63 (1996): 220–27.

23. *Bibliotheca Catholica Neerlandica Impressa 1500–1727* (Hagae Comitis: 1954).

24. See Karel Porteman, *Emblematic Exhibitions at the Brussels Jesuit College (1630–85)* (Brussels: 1996), 10–23.

25. See Andriessen, *De jezuïeten*, 300.

26. Bartholdus Nihusius to Athanasius Kircher, S.J., Amsterdam 16 December 1647, Rome, APUG, Athanasius Kircher Miscellanea Epistolarum, 3, inv. 557, f. 227r.

27. I would like to thank Thomas McCoog, S.J., for his help with the English version of this text.

Sparrows on the Rooftop: "How We Live Where We Live" in Elizabethan England

Thomas M. McCoog, S.J.

I

DURING THE DELIBERATIONS PRECEEDING APPROVAL OF a Jesuit mission, Father General Everard Mercurian worried that conditions in England would prevent Jesuits from living according to the standards of the Society's Institute.[1] Such apprehension was symptomatic of his generalate. As colleges proliferated, as vocations steadily climbed, as Pope Gregory XIII (one of the greatest benefactors in the Society's history) involved Jesuits in diplomatic and political matters, and as spiritual writers extolled the beauty of a quasi-Carthusian contemplative life, Mercurian worried lest the Society divert from its original Ignatian inspiration. He was a cautious general with a more narrow understanding of "our way of proceeding" than his successor Claudio Acquaviva.

The Third General Congregation (1573) commissioned Mercurian and his assistants to examine and, if necessary, amend the *Summarium Constitutionum* and the general rules.[2] The first edition of *Regulae Societatis Iesu* (Rome, 1580) appeared in the last year of his generalate. The fourth rule of the *Summarium Constitutionum* reminded Jesuits: "In other respects, for sound reasons and with attention always paid to the greater service of God, in regard to what is exterior the manner of living is ordinary."[3] Almost simultaneously, the ordinary manner of Jesuit living was being regularized to such an extent that a uniform, distinctive style of Jesuit life evolved. Each province added its own adaptations, but in general, customs and practices became universal. Historians have recently made us aware of the role that colleges played in the regularization (or, perhaps, "monasterization") of Jesuit religious life.[4]

All Jesuits, even those on journeys, were expected to adhere to these standards. We know from the common rules that traveling Jesuits should stay in the Society's colleges and residences whenever possible.[5] But what type of life would they find in these residences? What did Jesuits do at home in the sixteenth century? What was their daily order?[6] Alas, no one has investigated this aspect of Jesuit history, and so the routine and daily order of the early Jesuits remain relatively unknown to us. But we do know many of the ideals from documents such as Mercurian's instructions to Robert Parsons, Edmund Campion, and Ralph Emerson.[7]

Mercurian exhorted the Jesuits to "observe exactly the Society's mode of life so far as the conditions allow where they are stationed." He knew, however, that conditions (i.e., the penal legislation against Catholics) would not only hamper their ministry but prevent public disclosure of their identity. The Acts of Supremacy and of Uniformity, the first two acts passed after Elizabeth's accession to the English throne in 1558 (1 Eliz. c. 1, c. 2), established her as the "Supreme Governor" of the Church in England and prescribed the modified second Edwardian *Book of Common Prayer*. Recognition of any foreign religious authority could be punished by loss of office, property, and, for the third offence, life. No other liturgical service besides that of the *Prayer Book* was permitted; clerics who attempted to use other services could be deprived of office and imprisoned; and failure to attend the established services resulted in fines. Elizabeth's second Parliament in 1563 made the laws even stricter (5 Eliz. c. 1). On 25 February 1570, Pope Pius V excommunicated Elizabeth in his bull *Regnans in Excelsis.* Elizabeth's third Parliament (April and May of 1571) retaliated: anyone claiming that Elizabeth was either a heretic or a schismatic, and not the legitimate monarch, was guilty of high treason (13 Eliz. c. 1). Reconciliation with Rome and recognition of papal authority was forbidden (13 Eliz. c. 2), and anyone seeking absolution from a papal representative, or anyone granting absolution, was guilty of high treason (13 Eliz. c. 3). Enforcement of these laws varied as local authorities lacked either the will or the means. Few were executed. In the calendar of martyrs, the first Catholics to die were executed in 1570. Between 4 January 1570 and 3 February 1578, seven laymen and priests were executed.[8] In 1580 Catholics anticipated greater liberty—if not general tolerance—after the marriage of Queen Elizabeth and Francis Valois, Duke of Alençon, then under discussion. Perhaps as a foretaste of improvement, persecution diminished. Whereas three were executed for religious reasons between November of 1577 and February of 1578, there was a hiatus until July of 1581, by which time negotiations for the marriage had broken down.

In these conditions "discreet charity"—or in the terminology of the instructions, "a right intention and a combination of distrust in themselves with a firm confidence in God to whom alone they can look for grace and light"—was essential. Ideally Jesuits were mortified men who examined and evaluated all practices, procedures, and proposals in light of the Society's goals. The foremost historian of the Society's Institute, Antonio M. de Aldama, S.J., argues that adaptability was the fruit of "discreet charity." And this is what Mercurian demanded of his missioners "armed with two weapons especially: firstly, with virtue and piety out of the ordinary; and, secondly, with prudence." In England, prudence meant "knowing with whom, when, in what way and with what subjects they should deal."[9]

English conditions prevented the missioners from living in community. Nonetheless, Mercurian counseled them "to visit one another as often as possible" for advice, consolation, and mutual support "as has been our custom." Jesuits lived outside community and disguised their religious and sacerdotal identity on the mission, but there were no guidelines, no *regulae*, for this manner of life. Thus, in addition to the English penal laws, Jesuits were exposed to dangers and temptations not encountered by their brethren throughout the world. They embarked on a religious life with few, if any, precedents.

Food, dress, and finances especially concerned Mercurian. According to the common rules, Jesuits needed their superior's permission to dine outside their community.[10] In England, the missioners should "usually have their meals in private" and avoid "convivial gatherings." Whether Jesuits dined alone or with the laity, temperance in food and drink was necessary lest they offend and disedify guests. Ordinarily Jesuits should not possess "clothes of the sort customary in the Society" unless they could be stored safely and securely. Even then Jesuits should wear this attire "for the purpose of holding services, hearing confessions, and carrying out other duties of this kind." In public, Jesuits, out of necessity, dressed as laymen. But necessity must not provide an excuse for extravagance. Secular clothing "ought to be of a modest and sober kind, and to give no appearance of levity and vanity." In 1588, Father General Claudio Acquaviva forbade Joseph Creswell and William Holt "to be seen anywhere in the Society's dress" as they journeyed toward England.[11]

"Poverty, as the strong wall of the religious life, should be loved and preserved in its integrity as far as this is possible with God's grace."[12] Loyola's exhortation was included in the *Summarium Constitutionum*. In the name of poverty, a Jesuit's food, drink, clothing, and style of life should reflect that of the poor. To experience such poverty, a Jesuit should be prepared to beg when necessary or commanded.[13] The *regulae* further stipulated that no Jesuit was to carry any money on him nor to deposit money with another.[14] To prevent arousing "even the slightest suspicion of avarice and greed," Jesuits in England were neither to seek nor to accept alms unless their need was dire. Even then they should only accept alms from a few "loyal and tried men." In light of the experiences of the first missioners some instructions were revised. In 1586 Acquaviva lifted restrictions on begging in instructions to Robert Southwell and Henry Garnet: "Leave is given them to receive and distribute money in England as shall seem expedient in the Lord, and also any money which they may receive from penitents, by way of restitution, to be spent on the poor or on works of piety, provided there is doubt to whom it is owing."[15]

II

Fearful of reenforced surveillance at English ports due to rumors of an Hispano-Papal invasion, Robert Parsons and Edmund Campion donned disguises for easier entry into their homeland. Assuming "the person and countenance of a captain and a soldier that returned from Flanders to England," Parsons crossed from Calais to Dover on 11 June 1580. He wore a "suit of a general's apparel . . . which was of buff laid with gold lace with hat and feather suited to the same wherewith."[16] Campion—attired as an Irish jewelry salesman—and Emerson followed on the 24th.

A few days after Parsons's departure, Campion wrote to Mercurian about the former's disguise. Dressed as a soldier, Parsons was "so well made up and showed such a choleric disposition that he would have eyes, indeed, who could discern beneath that costume, face, and gait the goodness and modesty that lay in hiding." As he and Emerson awaited word from Parsons at the Jesuit college in St. Omers, they acquired their own disguises. Campion, however, worried about the expense:

> What do you think all this will cost? Especially since things are not available as once they were. As we wish to disguise ourselves, and imitate the vain fashions of life around us, many trifles which we think altogether silly had to be bought for us. The money for the journey, these clothes, and four horses which we have to buy on the spot in England, will account for our funds. These must come from the same kind of providence whereby loaves were multiplied in the wilderness.[17]

But, as Campion noted, shortage of funds was the least of their problems!

In Southwark, Parsons searched for lodgings, but "none would receive him."[18] After some deliberation and prayer, he decided to visit the secret Jesuit Thomas Pounde in the Marshalsea prison. According to Parsons's later unfinished biography of Campion, Pounde and the other Catholic prisoners knew of the Jesuit mission and of their imminent arrival. Parsons spent the day in prison, where he dined with Pounde and other Catholics. Pounde introduced Parsons to a Catholic visitor, Edward Brooksby, who conducted the Jesuit "to a Catholic house in the city, where he lodged and found other priests and other gentlemen." Most important for the Jesuits' ministry, Parsons found at this unnamed house George Gilbert, whom he had reconciled to Roman Catholicism a few years earlier. After his return to England, Gilbert had organized a group of Catholic laymen to receive arriving clergy and to escort them throughout the countryside. He had rented this large house in Chancery Lane from the chief pursuivant. Through bribes, he acquired the protection of Dr. Adam Squire, son-in-law of John Aylmer, bishop of London.[19] Until the arrival of Jesuits, "when times grew to be much more exasperated," Catholics had easy access to the house, where they could find daily Mass.[20] Almost immediately Parsons departed for neighboring shires at the request of "certain principal Cath. gentlemen" with Henry Orton as escort.[21]

Parsons left instructions for Campion and arranged that Thomas James should meet him and Emerson on their arrival. On the morning of 26 June, James conducted the two Jesuits to the house in Chancery Lane. On 29 June, Feast of Saints Peter and Paul, Campion preached on Peter's confession of faith in the great hall of a house near Smithfield rented by Thomas, Lord Paget, from Henry, Lord Norris. Word of Campion's arrival rapidly spread through London. Employing spies and informers, the Privy Council sought his apprehension. But Campion, "being advertized of this intention by some principal persons of the court," prudently retired to "particular and secret friends' houses," where he discreetly met with and exhorted Catholics.[22] Later in his biography, Parsons commented that upon his return to London in early July, he found Campion "in a certain poor man's house in Southwark near the Thames where men might repair without great show of suspicion both by land and water."[23] Whether Parsons resided with him is not known. Sometime in early July, George Gilbert provided Campion and Parsons with "two suits of apparel apiece convenient to travel the country in, and to each of them two very good horses for them and for their men and besides delivered to each one threescore pounds in money" with a promise to provide more as needed. He provided for all their material needs "so they could preach the Gospel freely according to their profession."[24] In early or mid-July, the spy Charles Sledd, familiar with different English Catholics from his time in Rome, followed Henry Orton from his lodgings in Smithfield to the house where the Jesuits were staying, but abandoned his surveillance before Orton arrived.[25] This was their first escape after their arrival in England.

Following the so-called Synod of Southwark (a meeting between the two Jesuits and a number of secular clergy at a house near St. Mary Overies, Southwark), Campion and Parsons withdrew separately to Hoxton, a village near London. Gilbert was Parsons's escort; Gervase Pierrepoint, Campion's.[26] In Hoxton they stayed "in the house of a certain gentleman who at that time was no Catholic though his wife were."[27] There is some disagreement about the identity of the host. Richard Simpson, Campion's first modern biographer, thought he was Sir William Catesby, whose wife was the Catholic Anne Throckmorton.[28] Francis Edwards, S.J., believed him to be Sir Thomas Tresham, married to Muriel Throckmorton.[29] A third possibility was a Mr. Gardiner of Hoxton, described by Parsons as "the first man gayned from heresy in this sommer."[30] As they prepared to embark on missionary tours of the counties, Thomas Pounde, having in some unexplained way obtained temporary release from the Marshalsea, arrived with news of a vicious whispering campaign started by the government: false rumors were circulating that the Jesuits arrived in England "for rebellion and matter of State." The Catholic prisoners in the Marshalsea met to discuss these reports. Believing that the campaign would intensify during the Jesuits' absence from London, the prisoners sent Pounde to recommend that each Jesuit write a brief statement "declaring the true causes of our coming, and what we meant, desired, or pretended." Said statements would be entrusted to a friend for release after a Jesuit's capture, to defend and justify his ministry in the face of anticipated governmental lies.[31] Consequently Campion composed his famous "Brag" and Parsons his less notorious "Confession" before their departures.[32] Parsons toured the shires of Northampton, Derby, Worcester, Gloucester, and Hereford,[33] but there is some disagreement about Campion's itinerary. According to Father Hicks, Campion operated closer to London and traveled through Berkshire, Oxford, and Northampton,[34] but Henry More, the first historian of the English province, claimed that Parsons "as the man responsible for directing the whole mission . . . stayed closer to London" while Campion journeyed to the remoter districts in the north.[35] A later comment in Parsons's unfinished biography of Campion substantiates More's claim: Campion reaped a great harvest in the country "farther off from great towns where the infection of ministers beareth most rule."[36] Although occasionally the Jesuits seem to have stayed at inns,[37] generally they resided with Catholic families:

> We entered for the most part as acquaintance or kinsfolk of some person that lived within the house, and when that failed us as passengers or friends of some gentleman that accompanied us, and after ordinary salutations we had our lodging by procurement of the Catholics within the house, in some part retired from the rest, where putting ourselves in priest's apparel and furniture which ever we carried with us we had view and secret conference with the Catholics that were there, or such of them as might conveniently come whom we ever caused to be ready for that night late to prepare themselves to the Sacrament of Confession, and the next morning very early we had Mass and the B. Sacrament ready for such as . . . would communicate and after that an exhortation and then we made ourselves ready to depart again.[38]

Regardless of the length of the visit (not all visits lasted only one night), the same procedure was followed, and according to

Parsons, their reception was overwhelming. Persons traveled long distances to converse with the Jesuits; benefactors consistently pressed on them clothes, horses, and "all other equipment" in abundance;[39] secular priests cooperated, or "rather I should say they obey us in all things with the greatest goodwill."[40]

Parsons returned to London in early October to find renewed persecution and increased vigilance because of the commotion caused by the release of Campion's "Brag." Quickly judging that London was too dangerous for Campion, Parsons advised him to delay his return. Campion traveled to the house of William Griffith near Uxbridge to await Parsons.[41] After their meeting, Parsons remained in the London area to oversee the mission's business, the erection of a printing press, and the publication of a few books. Campion departed for Lancashire "both for that it was more distant from London and more generally affected to the Cath. religion, and for that there was more hope to find commodity of books for him to write or answer the heretics, if perhaps they should provoke him as it was supposed they would shortly."[42] Campion departed circa 16 November and remained in the north until Pentecost of 1581.

Parsons resided in London, but we do not know the exact site. He admitted to Alfonso Agazzari that "though I have many places in London where I can stay, yet in none of them do I remain beyond two days, owing to the extremely careful searches that have been made to capture me." To elude pursuivants, Parsons worked in different places from early morning until late at night. After morning Mass and sermon, he worked on "solving cases of conscience which occur, directing other priests to suitable places and occupations, in reconciling schismatics to the Church, in writing letters to those who are tempted in the course of this persecution, in trying to arrange temporal aid for the support of those who are in prison and in want."[43] A few months later he could have added to his list another occupation: writing and publishing books. In late November, Parsons set up a printing press in Greenstreet near Barking, east of London, in a house owned by the Brooksby family of Leicestershire. The following month his first book appeared under the pseudonym John Howlet: *A brief discours contayning certayne reasons why catholiques refuuse to go to Church* (Doway [vere London], 1580).[44] Soon thereafter the press was dismantled because Parsons feared discovery. Once the press was reassembled early in 1581 at the home of Francis Browne, brother of Anthony Browne, Viscount Montague,[45] two other works were published: *A brief censure uppon two bookes written in answere to M. Edmonde Campions offer of disputation* (Doway [vere London], 1581] and *A discoverie of I. Nichols Minister, misreported a Iesuite, latelye recanted in the Tower of London* (n.p., n.d. [London, 1581]). During the same eight months, Parsons was nearly captured three times. The third attempt occurred in late April of 1581. Parsons had rented a commodious room in the inner part of the house of a Protestant. Being situated at the riverbank within the city, it served for the secret nightly meetings of priests. There too Parsons stored books, vestments, etc. This spot was eventually betrayed by a bookseller who had formerly bound books there. Two days earlier, Parsons had departed for the countryside. Consequently the pursuivants found nothing but bronze crosses, medals, Agnus Dei, books, unimportant papers, and some clothing that Campion had left behind at this departure.[46]

Historians have reconstructed much of Campion's northern itinerary from details revealed in his confessions, but his whereabouts between his departure from Uxbridge in mid-November until Christmas remain unknown. Because he mentioned them in his confessions without precise dates, Campion may have stayed at the homes of William, Lord Vaux, Sir Thomas Tresham, and Sir William Catesby in Northamptonshire and Warwickshire during this period.[47] From Christmas 1580 until 10 January, he resided with the Pierrepoints at Holme Pierrepoint, Nottinghamshire, the home of his guide Gervase. Between the 12th and the 16th, he passed through West Hallam, Morley, Longford in Derbyshire, and Throwley Hall in Staffordshire to either Hassop or Nether Hurst, Derbyshire, before crossing into Yorkshire. His hosts were the Pierrepoints, Powtrells, Longfords, Fuljameses, and Eyres.[48] In Yorkshire his guide was a certain Tempest. Between mid-January and mid-Lent (circa 26 February, the third Sunday of Lent), Campion visited the Rookbys of Yeafford, the Vavasours in York, the Bulmers, the Babthorpes of Osgodby, the Grimstons, the

Hawkeworths, and Cleesbys. Tempest transferred Campion to a third guide, a Mr. Smyth, who escorted him to Mount St. John, the home of his brother-in-law William Harrington. There Campion remained for a longer period to work on his manuscript.[49] Mr. Price—a Yorkshireman and a former pupil—and his wife conducted Campion into Lancashire where he stayed with the Talbots, Worthingtons, Southworths, Heskeths, Houghtons, Westbys, Rigmaidens, and Mrs. Allen, widow of William Allen's brother. According to William Cecil, Campion spent most of the tour at the Talbots and Southworths, but Simpson claimed (without citing his source) that, according to Parsons, Campion spent longer periods at Mrs. Allen's and at the Worthingtons' residence, "where he was fully occupied in preaching to the crowds that pressed to have conference with him."[50] According to Campion's confessions, the Lancashire tour extended from Easter (26 March) until Whitsun (14 May). Once Parsons had received Campion's manuscript and Thomas Fitzherbert had verified all Campion's citations in different London libraries (sometime in early June), Parsons summoned Campion to London to see the volume through the press.[51] On his way to London and during his stay in the London area, Campion resided with a Mr. Price (or Ap-rice) of Huntingdon; William Griffith of Uxbridge; Edwin East of Bledlow, Buckinghamshire; the Stonors; the Yates of Lyford Grange; the Dormers of Wyng, Buckinghamshire; the Widow Pollard; the Bellamys in Uxenden Hall; a Mrs. Brideman in Westminster; a Mr. Barnes in Tothill Street; and Lady Babington's houses in Twyford, Buckinghamshire (where he spent the anniversary of his arrival in England); and in White Friars.[52] Printed on the secret press assembled at Stonor Park, Berkshire, *Rationes decem* appeared in time to be distributed surreptitiously in the University Church of St. Mary in Oxford on 27 June 1581. Less than a month later, on 17 July, Campion was captured at Lyford Grange. Tortured, interrogated, debated, and tried, he was executed on 1 December 1581. During Campion's imprisonment in the Tower of London, Parsons hid first in Henley at the home of Francis Browne, and later in Michelgrove, Sussex, home of William Shelley.[53]

After Campion's and Parsons's separation in November of 1580, any lingering possibility of a marriage between Elizabeth and Anjou ended when Robert Dudley, Earl of Leicester, succeeded in splitting the coalition supporting the match. The government now gave vent to anti-Catholic hysteria fanned by Protestant preachers warning their congregations of the dire consequences of the projected match and by the high-profile antics of Campion and Parsons. A royal proclamation on 10 January 1581, "Ordering Return of Seminarians, Arrest of Jesuits," charged members of the Society with fomenting rebellion and disturbing the kingdom:

> Her majesty being further given to understand that there are divers of her subjects that have been trained up in the said colleges and seminaries beyond the seas, whereof some of them carry the name of Jesuits under the color of a holy name to deceive and abuse the simpler sort, and are lately repaired into this realm by special direction from the pope and his delegates, with intent not only to corrupt and pervert her good and loving subjects in matter of conscience and religion, but also to draw them from the loyalty and duty of obedience and to provoke them, so much as shall lie in them, to attempt somewhat to the disturbance of the present quiet that through the goodness of Almighty God and her majesty's provident government this realm hath these many years enjoyed.[54]

At the opening of a new Parliament in the same month, Sir Walter Mildmay warned the members:

> To confirm them [Catholics] herein, and to increase their numbers, you see how the Pope hath and doth comfort their hollow hearts with absolutions, dispensations, reconciliations, and other such things of Rome. You see how lately he hath sent hither a sort of hypocrites, naming themselves Jesuits, a rabble of vagrant friars newly sprung up and coming through the world to trouble the Church of God; whose principal errand is, by creeping into the houses and familiarities of men of

behaviour and reputation, not only to corrupt the realm with false doctrine, but also, under that pretence, to stir sedition.[55]

Despite Mercurian's careful definition of the purpose and nature of the Jesuit mission in his instructions, official proclamations, sermons, and speeches accused Jesuits of entering the kingdom to "corrupt" true religion and to "disturb" the government. The very first law passed by this Parliament—"Act to Retain the Queen's Majesty's Subjects in Their Due Allegiance" (23 Eliz. c. 1)—dealt with this new threat. Convicted Catholic recusants could pay fines of £20 for the first month, £40 for the second, £100 for the third, and imprisonment at the monarch's pleasure with confiscation of all estates and goods for the fourth. Anyone convicted of withdrawing English subjects from their natural loyalty to their monarch and converting them to the Church of Rome would be guilty of high treason. Anyone reconciled to the Roman Church would suffer the same penalty. Catholics risked financial and personal ruin for their adherence to the old religion.

The second wave of Jesuits, William Holt and Jasper Heywood, landed near Newcastle in June of 1581 under the protection of Henry Percy, Earl of Northumberland.[56] After a night at an inn, they traveled to London to meet Parsons at the Bellamy house in Harrow. After brief visits to family and friends, Holt and Heywood met again in Staffordshire before separating for their work. Both apparently worked in the north of England. By the end of December of 1581, Holt was in Scotland as Parsons's representative to meet with Scottish Catholics. Holt returned to London in February of 1582 to inform Bernardino de Mendoza, Spanish ambassador, of the details of the meeting. He returned almost immediately to Scotland, where he resided with the Setons.

Heywood returned to London in October of 1581 with alms collected from northern nobility and gentry for imprisoned Catholics. Apparently Heywood's public display of wealth and grandeur protected him from discovery: "He rode much in coach accompanied with many and in costly apparel."[57] From noblemen (or their sons) with whom Heywood had been raised at the English court (e.g.,

Anthony Browne, Viscount Montague; William, Lord Vaux; Thomas, Lord Paget; John, Lord Lumley; Henry, Lord Morley; Philip, Lord Wharton; and Henry Stanley, Earl of Derby) the Jesuit had cash and promissory notes totalling £1,300 annually. Using his contacts, epecially the extensive Percy entourage, Heywood supplemented the work done by the Parsons and Vaux family with another network of safe houses. A royal proclamation on 1 April 1582 threatened everything. Fearing the "great mischiefs" that might follow from the presence of Jesuits and seminary priests in the kingdom, the queen notified her subjects

> that if any of them or any other within her highness' dominions . . . should receive, maintain, succor, or relieve any Jesuit, seminary men, massing priests, or other like persons . . . or should not discover the receiving or harboring of the same persons . . . then they should be reputed as maintainers and abettors of such rebellious and seditious persons, and receive for the same their contempt such severe punishment as by the laws of the realm and her majesty's princely authority might be inflicted upon them.[58]

Nonetheless Heywood, to the best of our knowledge, experienced no problems. In late 1582 he recruited twenty candidates from Oxford and Cambridge for English seminaries abroad; in August of 1583 fifty more followed. By early 1583 he had established contact with Philip Howard, Earl of Arundel. Despite such success, Parsons and William Allen decided that Heywood was "a good man, but not altogether suitable for work connected with the English mission" because "he does not walk in step with Fr. Parsons, nor according to the same rules as ourselves."[59] Summoned to France to confer with Parsons in Rouen in late 1583, Heywood was captured, arrested, sent to London, and committed to the Clink prison on 9 December 1583.

William Weston, with Ralph Emerson as his escort and the layman Henry Hubert (or Hubbard), landed on the Norfolk coast between Yarmouth and Lowestoft on 10 September 1584. On 26 September Emerson was committed to the Poultry prison in

London because a search revealed Catholic books in his possession. Without Emerson, Weston had no guide and no escort. Parsons, however, had given him certain tokens of friendship to present to Catherine Bellamy of Uxenden in an emergency. Weston traveled the nine or ten miles to speak with her. Initially she protested that she neither recognized the tokens presented nor understood a word Weston said, nor had ever set eyes on Parsons. Twice more Weston was rebuffed. Finally, through Hubert and his wife, then residing in a larger recusant household to give birth, Weston gained admission into the closed network of Catholic families.[60]

The assassination of William (the Silent) of Orange, Prince of Nassau, on 10 July 1584 shocked Protestant Europe. Fearful that English Catholic conspirators with papal and Spanish backing would make comparable attempts on Queen Elizabeth, Parliament convened in November of 1584. Its first act—"An Act for the provision to be made for the surety of the Queen's most royal person" (27 Eliz. c. 1)—excluded from the English throne any claimant found guilty of involvement in a plot or conspiracy against Elizabeth if she died a violent, unnatural death. The second—"An Act against Jesuits, seminary priests and such other like disobedient persons" (27 Eliz. c. 2)—attacked the most likely fomentors of conspiracies. Henceforth one's identity as a Jesuit or a seminary priest was ipso facto sufficient for a charge of treason because they rejected the queen's spiritual authority and engaged in plots against her. Anyone contributing to the support of a priest in England or a student at a foreign seminary could be found guilty of praemunire.[61] Anyone in England who knowingly assisted a Jesuit or a seminary priest could be convicted as a felon, suffer death, and forfeit everything to the crown. The new law increased the risks for the Catholic gentry. Weston wondered how the legislation would affect the mission:

> As far as I was concerned, I thought it would be well to retire by myself to some place where I could judge from my own observation the way things were likely to go. I would be able then to see how Catholics thought and felt: whether they would

retain their old loyalty to the faith, search out priests, ask them to their houses and maintain them; or whether they would keep them at a distance and agree to be abandoned by them in a time of such peril. Far better, I thought, that they should invite or summon me to them, than that I should thrust myself on them and have them risk their lives and property for my sake.[62]

In April of 1585, some clergy and laymen conferred at the home of Mr. Wyford in Hoxton to find an alternative. Among those present were Weston, Lord Vaux, Sir Thomas Tresham, and Sir William Catesby.[63] The host and the three nobles pledged one hundred marks annually to a common fund to support the priests. A national appeal to other Catholics increased the fund. Henry Vaux was named the fund's administrator. With this money the clergy could fend for themselves and promised to avoid the residences of Catholics, at least those represented at the conference, unless invited to do so. Presumably later Jesuits working on the mission, such as Henry Garnet and John Gerard, drew on this fund (or its equivalent) to pay for houses they rented to prevent putting their hosts at risk.[64]

In early July of 1586, Henry Garnet and Robert Southwell arrived in England. They dined with Weston at an inn in London where they were staying on the 13th. The three spent the night at Weston's accommodation, probably a house, placed at his disposal by Mrs. Francis Browne, in Hog Lane on the boundaries of Bishopsgate and Shoreditch. The following morning they left for eight days of prayer and discussion at the home of Richard Bold—a recent Weston convert and a former favorite of Robert Dudley, Earl of Leicester—at Harlesford near Marlow. Weston revealed to them "the names of Catholic houses where they might go and make their residence, and arranged for reliable guides to take them there." Circa 23 July at the end of the meeting, Garnet was conducted either to Lord Vaux's residence at Harrowden, Northamptonshire, or to his daughter's, Mrs. Brooksby's, at Shoby, Leicestershire. Around this time Eleanor Brooksby moved to the manor house at Great Ashby near Northamptonshire's border with

Warwickshire. Here her brother Henry died, apparently with Garnet at his bedside, on 19 November 1587. Southwell had returned to Lord Vaux's residence at Hackney a day earlier. On 3 August Weston was arrested outside Bishopsgate.[65]

From the Tower of London, Weston watched as men personally known to him and accused of involvement in the Babington Plot,

> Catholics, tied hand and foot, were ferried along the river, up and down between the Tower of London and the tribunals.... It was easy to notice when these men were taken along the river in boats, for you could pick them out by the uniforms and weapons of the soldiers, and you could see the vast hustling mob of spectators and the countless people who took off in light boats and followed them the entire reach of the river.[66]

Southwell lamented the treatment of Catholics and castigated "the men who set on foot that wicked and ill-fated conspiracy, which did to the Catholic cause so great mischief, that even our enemies, had they had the choice, could never have chosen aught more mischievous to us or more to their mind."[67] In the same letter, Southwell explained that he was in extreme danger twice as pursuivants searched the house for him, but without success. Sometime in late 1587 (probably after the raid on the house in early November), Southwell left Hackney and moved into either Arundel House or a house in Spitalfields as chaplain to Anne Dacre Howard, Countess of Arundel and wife of the imprisoned Philip.[68] Generally Garnet moved through the counties maintaining and expanding the circuit of missions as Southwell remained in London to receive secular clergy, many of whom he knew from Rome. Occasionally Garnet traveled to London for business, and Southwell at times escaped to the country for a break.

William Holt and Joseph Creswell received instructions to proceed to England on 24 February 1588. Neither completed the journey. After the failure of the Armada, Holt remained in Belgium as a chaplain in the Spanish forces, and Creswell was back in Rome by 26 August 1589. John Gerard and Edward Oldcorne departed for England in September of 1588, barely a month after their admission into the Society. In December they landed in East Anglia. Garnet welcomed their appearance in London despite qualms about their lack of proper formation:

> Although their arrival is of the greatest pleasure for us, we fear that it may not be a safe one, and because they are novices, we hardly think that they can be treated by us with that care which is necessary for novices. We hope that, having become perfect in such a short period of time, they know and can live immediately the ways of the Society and thus sustain the Society's esteem.[69]

Because danger was greater during festivities, the four Jesuits dispersed just before Christmas. Gerard traveled to Grimston about six miles northeast of King's Lynn. Through his host, Edward Yelverton, the Jesuit met many East Anglian gentry. He dressed as a "gentleman of moderate means . . . [because it] was thus that I used to go about before I became a Jesuit and I was therefore more at ease in these clothes than I would have been if I had assumed a role that was strange and unfamiliar to me."[70] In the summer of 1589 Gerard moved to Lawshall, about six miles southeast of Bury Saint Edmunds, to direct its owner Henry Drury through the Spiritual Exercises of St. Ignatius Loyola. There he was more easily able "to live the life of a Jesuit, even in the external details of dress and arrangement of time."[71] Under Gerard's guidance Lawshall became a spiritual center. Among Catholics who made the Exercises were future Jesuits Thomas and John Wiseman, Thomas Everard, and the apostate secular priest Anthony Rouse.

Oldcorne remained in London with Garnet until early spring of 1589 when the two departed for Warwickshire and Worcestershire. Garnet introduced Oldcorne to the different mission stations in that area. Oldcorne remained at Baddesley Clinton until his conversion of Dorothy Habington resulted in his transfer to Hindlip House, Worcestershire, in 1590.[72] John Curry and Richard

Holtby augmented Jesuit numbers with their arrival in the spring of 1589.[73] Both had worked in England as secular priests before returning to the continent to enter the Society. Now as Jesuits they returned to the regions they knew best: Holtby worked in the north with John Trollope's residence in Thorneley in the diocese of Durham as his base;[74] Curry returned to the southwest to Chideock Castle, Dorset, the home of his patron Sir John Arundel, his most likely base.

An undated document, *Instructiones quaedam pro hominibus Societatis viventibus in Anglia his temporibus,* composed sometime before the death of Queen Elizabeth in 1603 and possibly upon the mission's elevation into a prefecture in 1598, repeated or developed many of the themes in the original instructions to Campion and Parsons.[75] The unknown author argued that Jesuits should ordinarily reside with nobles *(cum nobilibus)* both "because greater profit may follow and because nobles have the power to protect the fathers." Another practical reason for preferring the nobility was the size of their households, which could accommodate two Jesuits, who could thus support and encourage each other. As we have seen, the Jesuits in England did live *"cum nobilibus"* but rarely in twos, perhaps because of the risks and dangers.

During the final years of the 1580s Garnet rented at least one house in London, a small cottage in Finsbury Fields, which he acquired by midsummer of 1588. It remained his refuge until he abandoned it in 1591 after it had been discovered and raided. As he explained to Acquaviva, "Many of the citizens of London own small gardens beyond the city walls, and a number of them have built in these gardens, cottages to which they resort from time to time to enjoy the cleaner air." Garnet's cottage had three rooms: a kitchen and dining room on the ground floor with a chapel/bedroom above. Because it was believed that no one actually resided there, conversations were conducted in hushed tones and food was cooked at night. Garnet went there to write letters and to confer with clergy and laity.[76] Such sites were not as comfortable as Garnet's other residences, but they reduced risks to laity threatened with severe punishments for harboring and aiding clergy, and granted freedom to the clergy themselves.

III

At the end of the Society's first decade in England, six Jesuits ministered to Catholics: Henry Garnet, Robert Southwell, Edward Oldcorne, John Gerard, John Curry, and Richard Holtby.[77] Of the six, Garnet, Southwell, and Oldcorne were eventually executed; Gerard spent years in different prisons, escaped from the Tower of London, and left England in May of 1606 during the hysteria following the Gunpowder Plot; Curry died in England in 1596; and Holtby survived on the mission until 1640. They and their predecessors established a missionary style that would affect Jesuit life in England for many generations.

Unfortunately we know very little about day-to-day operations within the clandestine Catholic community before the arrival of the seminary priests and the Jesuits. We know that Catholic priests ordained during the reign of Elizabeth's sister Mary Tudor (1553–58) or according to the Catholic rite under her father, Henry VIII, continued to minister to Catholics throughout Elizabeth's reign, but we remain relatively ignorant of their number, their organization, and their ministry.[78] But Professor Patrick McGrath and Mrs. Joy Rowe concluded that there was enough movement that "a number of Catholic families got into the habit of looking after the priests in the form of fixed residences or short stay visits, and on this foundation much more elaborate systems could be built when the seminary priests arrived in large numbers."[79] Presumably George Gilbert and his association built on these foundations. Parsons found these laymen already organized upon his arrival in London, but interestingly, he did not get in touch with them immediately upon arrival, opting instead to search for accommodation in Southwark. Through these laymen, Parsons gained access into Catholic households. These men (or others like them) escorted Campion and Parsons on their itineraries throughout the counties to houses ready to provide them with hospitality and to allow them to officiate at Mass and celebrate the sacraments. Some hosts were relatives of English exiles, friends of Jesuits, or former students. Had they been part of the Catholic network prior to the arrival of Campion and Parsons, or did they become involved as a result of their friendship with one or the other?

William, Lord Vaux, survived without any major problems in Elizabeth's England until the arrival of Campion. Godfrey Anstruther, O.P., refers to this period of peace as "the calm before the storm"—a storm that "broke at Harrowden, with a crash that was heard all over Europe, when Edmund Campion returned to England, a Jesuit."[80] Parsons encountered Lord Vaux's son-in-law Edward Brooksby by chance in Pounde's cell in the Marshalsea prison. Brooksby accompanied Parsons to Gilbert's safe house and, presumably, introduced him to other members of the Vaux family. But the real link between this family and the Jesuit mission was Henry Vaux, Campion's former student, who threw himself totally into the Society's mission out of fondness for his former tutor. Many of the households visited by Campion and Parsons were owned by members of the Vaux family or by families to whom they were related through marriage (e.g., Treshams, Beaumonts, Catesbys). With their support the Jesuits constructed a missionary circuit in the Thames valley either *ex nihilo* or on the foundations laid by their clerical predecessors. Through excursions into the midlands and the north, they sought to create something similar there. Subsequent Jesuits established networks in Essex (Gerard), Warwickshire and Worcestershire (Garnet and Oldcorne), Durham (Holtby), and the southwest (Curry). Persecutions, arrests, executions, and apostacies demonstrated that no network was totally secure; all required careful maintenance.

Gilbert fled to the continent in the spring of 1581. Sometime in 1583, he wrote *"Il modo come si può procedere con tutti sorti di persone per convertirle e ridurle a miglior vita secondo l'ordine e modo che tennero il padre Roberto Personio e Padre Edmondo Campiano"*—presumably to explain to someone in Rome the organization and methods of the Jesuit missioners.[81] Gilbert stressed the importance of a "zealous, loyal, discreet," reputable lay gentleman with a wide circle of relations and friends, familiar with the local geography and able to underwrite the priest's expenses as a companion. Priests should seek these qualities "so as to be able with his aid to appear and mix freely everywhere, both in public and in private, dressed as a gentleman and with various kinds of get-up and disguises so as to be better able to have intercourse with people without arousing suspicion." Priests should be stationed in different parts of the country. Each should "stay at the house of some gentleman or other, as though he were a relation, friend or steward, or in some office of dignity but little work." From this base the priest would exercise pastoral responsibility for the district or a certain number of neighboring families. Periodically he should change places with another priest. Although Gilbert does not explicitly state it, his comments suggest two types of missionary life: besides priests stationed in a country house, others would move from place to place without lingering too long at any one place.

On 17 January 1609 the future Jesuit Thomas Fitzherbert and Lady Manners, sister of Roger Manners, Earl of Rutland, presented information on the organization of the Jesuit mission to Pope Paul V. The document, entitled *Oedipus Schedularum*, related the opinions of different Jesuit "parishes" on the feasibility of establishing a bishopric in England. The report named seven Jesuits with the church *(ecclesia)* to which they ministered. One illustration is sufficient. Robert Jones, referred to under the cipher "A.B.," cared for Henry Somerset, Baron Herbert, son and heir of Edward Somerset, Earl of Worcester; Edward Morgan, head of a staunchly Catholic family related through marriage to the Somersets; and other unnamed Catholics.[82] Since there were forty-seven Jesuits in England and Wales at that time, the seven mentioned in the report are but a fraction. Can we deduce that the forty Jesuits omitted from the report had no geographical church? A few years later, Robert Jones, superior of the mission, lamented that "no small number of them [Jesuits in England and Wales], however, suffer from want of fixed residences and appliances for their work: hence they have no regular workshops, which were much desired, but they labour up and down through various localities with good results, like missioners from place to place."[83] Jones may have preferred more Jesuits with stable residences and pastoral responsibilities, but that was beyond his control.

The first historian of the English province, Henry More, drafted his classic exposition of Jesuit life, *Modus vivendi hominum Societatis*, in 1616.[84] By then Jesuits on the mission could be found living in one of three different ways, each with distinct advantages and disadvantages. The first led a very private life "in the upper stories or attics of the house; as remote as possible from the observation of domestics and visitors." Movement within the house was restricted; travel outside the house, either for works of charity or reasons of health, took place during the night. The priest lived and dined alone. Indeed, with the exception of the daily Mass and periods for the sacraments and counseling, he was always alone. His only contact with other members of the Society was a visit from his religious superior.

The second style was one of almost constant movement. Each priest usually had at least one house on his circuit where he could remain for a few days to minister to Catholics in the area, but he usually moved about on foot or horseback. Through disguises and aliases they managed to deceive authorities. Such Jesuits had frequent contact with Catholics, other Jesuits, and their religious superior, but they consistently risked exposure and capture.

Certain Catholic households—either because of the prestige and influence of the family or because of their amiable relations with their non-Catholic neighbors—were "superior, as it were, to the action of the laws." Jesuits living in such establishments lived cautiously, but not in fear. They moved freely but discreetly, working with the family and other Catholics in the neighborhood. According to More, "though they were formerly numerous enough," fewer Jesuits lived this way in the early seventeenth century. Presumably increased fear of persecution as a result of the Gunpowder Plot resulted in the loss of freedom and mobility for Jesuit missionaries. Many Jesuits in households were now forced to live the first type: now they "sit like sparrows upon the house top," awaiting the glory of God.

More's second and third types correspond to the styles described by Gilbert and Jones. Fear, as More suggests, transformed the third into the first. But Jesuits suffering these restrictions were few. There were more Jesuits without a stable residence than there were housebound. Only the establishment of Jesuit houses, despite the risks involved, would provide unconditional stable accommodation.

McGrath and Rowe remarked that the work of Gilbert and Pounde has "received considerable attention because of their close association with the Jesuits and because a good deal of material about them has been preserved," but there were others about whom we know little.[85] Were there other associations or simply isolated individuals? Were other clergy maintaining current networks and developing new ones, or were the Jesuits unique? Henry Garnet may have exaggerated in order to emphasize the Society's importance, but he twice lamented the absence of an adequate system for reception and distribution of newly arrived clergy. Indeed, he was not sure that more should be sent until the problem had been corrected.[86] If there was a system independent of that forged by the Society, there is no evidence.

IV

Nearly twenty years ago Dr. Christopher Haigh ignited a controversy in English Catholic studies with his Copernican suggestion that we invert the question about the preservation of Catholicism in post-Reformation England. He suggested that Jesuits and seminary priests, instead of being the heroes in Catholicism's continuation, were actually responsible for its reduction to minority status.[87] Haigh stressed the prevalence and popularity of Catholic sentiment on the eve of the Elizabethan Reformation. Upon their arrival in England, the seminary priests and the Jesuits "inherited, if not a safe seat, at least a strong minority vote in need of careful constituency nursing." Moreover, Haigh recommended that we measure their success "by their ability to maintain party allegiance."[88] Therefore, instead of seeking explanations for the preservation of Catholicism in the face of Protestantism and persecution, historians must explicate the reasons for Catholicism's waning. A major reason, according to Haigh, was clerical concentration on the south and east of England instead of on the far north and Wales, where Catholic sentiment remained strong. Why did the clergy select the south and east? Haigh's anwer was: "Another reason [besides the magnetic attraction of London] for the geographical concentration of priestly effort was the tendency, pronounced from the earliest stages of the mission, to devote most attention to the substantial gentry, who were most numerous in the prosperous counties of the South and might attend part of the year in London."[89] At least for the Society of Jesus, a preferential option for the gentry was a strategic decision.

On 24 September 1549 Ignatius Loyola counseled the Jesuits sent to Germany to maintain good relations with these social elites:

> You must try to be on good terms with those in government positions and be kindly disposed toward them. It will help to this if the Duke [William IV of Bavaria] and the members of his household who *have a wider influence* confess to Ours, and insofar as their duties permit, make the Spiritual Exercises. You should win over the doctors of the university [Ingolstadt] and other persons of authority by your humility, modesty and obliging services.[90] (Italics mine.)

In 1552 Ignatius expressed the same sentiment in his general instructions to missionaries:

> With regard to the neighbor, we must be careful with whom we deal. They should be persons from whom we can expect greater fruit, since they [the missionaries] cannot deal with all. They should be such as are in greater need and those in high position who exert such influence because of their learning or their possessions . . . and, generally speaking, all those who if helped will be better able to help others for God's glory.[91]

The *Constitutions* explained this approach thus:

> The more universal the good is, the more it is divine. Therefore preference ought to be given to those persons and places which through their own improvement, become a cause which can spread the good accomplished to many others who are under their guidance or take guidance from them.
>
> For that reason, the spiritual aid which is given to important and public persons ought to be regarded as more important, since it is a more universal good.[92]

The Society concentrated on the moral, intellectual, and spiritual formation of the classes who ruled society so that they, in turn, would affect a renovation of society.

Jesuit preoccupation with social elites, according to Haigh, resulted in the decline of Catholicism in England. If Jesuits and the other missionaries had carefully cultivated their Catholic constituency instead of closeting themselves in comfortable country retreats, Catholicism would not have waned. From the foundation of the mission, the Jesuits pursued a "strategy for disaster, for it dictated a concentration upon the least promising areas [of England] and a neglect of the majority of Catholics."[93] Indeed, Dr. Haigh suggested that Jesuits might have been even safer in "peasant households" because the government viewed isolated Catholic manor houses with increasing suspicion.[94]

To echo Professor McGrath in his rejoinder, "the mission was in some respects a failure" because it failed to convert England.[95] In England practical necessity supported Jesuit preferences. Gentry families who welcomed and escorted Campion and Parsons provided the missionaries not just with clothing and money but with a relatively secure residence to which Catholics could resort without attracting attention. Could the "peasant households" recommended by Dr. Haigh provide a room large enough to serve as a chapel to accommodate the crowds that came to hear Campion preach? Could Catholics flock to "peasant households" without arousing suspicions as they could to the more grand houses often with furnished chapels and claims to extraparochial status? Moreover, as English Jesuits later explained to Father General Muzio Vitelleschi in the seventeenth century, the residences were often isolated, under titled protection, and secure. In the 1620s English Jesuits often used the expression "sanctuary" but not in the canonical sense; by it they meant that no armed men could enter without the express order of the king with the exception of the king himself, his councillors, and his heralds.[96]

Through Gilbert and his association, the first Jesuits established a network of recusant households that opened their doors to the missionaries in their travels and to other Catholics for the services. The network was small and, apparently, based on personal relations and contacts (e.g., Gilbert's friendship with Parsons and Campion's relations with the Vaux family). But clandestine Catholic ceremonies would not be permanent; perhaps naively, many Catholics, including supporters of the original Jesuit mission, believed that some type of tolerance would follow Elizabeth's marriage to Anjou.[97] As new penal legislation supplanted fading hopes of tolerance, Campion, Parsons, and their successors sought to expand the network into areas not frequented by Catholic clergy. William Holt and Jasper Heywood were sent to the north of England. Because new legislation threatened aiders and abettors with penalties most severe, such expansion was slow. We have noted Weston's difficulties as doors closed in his face after the arrest of Emerson. Isolation and quasisanctuarial status collapsed as an increasingly effective spy network revealed the location, not of religious dissidents, but of disloyal traitors. Fewer households were willing to risk losing everything. Professor McGrath rightly observed that

> in the 1580s the conflict with Spain made Catholicism seem a religion for traitors in an England which was increasingly conscious of its nationalism and proud of a queen who was "mere English." The penal laws against Catholics became more and more severe, and the government's resources for dealing with Catholics reached a new level of sophistication in intelligence and propaganda. This is not to belittle the considerable achievement of Catholics in England before 1580 but they were batting on a much easier wicket than those who came later.[98]

Perhaps the *Oedipus Schedularum* (a shadow ecclesiastical structure of "parishes" comprised of mission stations in different households chosen for reasons of security) portrayed the model envisioned by Jesuits after the collapse of the marital negotiations. But ideals must have given way to reality. As long as Jesuits depended on the gentry for hospitality, their apostolic zeal, out of necessity, was tempered by the fears of their hosts. More and more gentry hosts were hesitant about their resident clergy ministering in a quasipublic way. Dr. Haigh grants that household chaplaincies with parochial responsibilities were Henry Garnet's "theory" and the "practice of energetic priests such as Edward Oldcorne," but then concluded that "the gentry household may have been envisaged as a base, but it soon became a chaplaincy and, in the minds of many priests, a benefice."[99] But Haigh also contended that exhaustion and fear were not the motives that resulted in the "domestication of the mission."[100] No, the clergy "fostered a brand of piety which created a demand for domestic chaplains, and the pattern of intense family religiosity . . . was followed, not always with success, in manor houses across the country."[101] That the priests residing with families fostered a godly household should not be a surprise to anyone, but Dr. Haigh did not explicate the spirituality that would have permeated such a household. Was it as introspective and quasipietistic as he suggested? Was it an attempt by clergy "to recreate their student experience" by sharing "the intense spirituality of an institutional spiritual life?"[102] Or was the spirituality itself directed at the conquest of fears and anxieties, the cultivation of resolution, and the primary importance of Christian allegiance? Parsons wrote *The first booke of the Christian exercise, appertayning to resolution* (n.p. [Rouen], 1582), commonly known as *The Christian Directory*, to help English Catholics ground their desire to serve God so firmly that they would resist any temptation to conform to the established church. Rooted in Ignatian spirituality, the manual stressed a Christian's firm resolution to serve God and the necessary perseverance. Robert Southwell's *A short rule of good life* (n.p, n.d. [London?, 1596–97]), written for the Countess of Arundel, argued similarly. Perhaps the

Jesuits intended, not to withdraw to manor houses, but to guide their hosts to a more sophisticated spiritual life.

According to Haigh, Catholic religious authorities either encouraged or failed to prevent Catholicism's withdrawal into the manor house and the Catholic minority's tranformation into "a seigneurially structured minority."[103] But Haigh fails to appreciate Jesuit attempts to avoid the suffocating embrace of the gentry. Indubitably individual Jesuits served as domestic chaplains, perhaps attempting to direct their hosts to the desired spirituality, but the Society did not wish them to remain "like sparrows on the rooftop" in a lonely garret. To maintain the freedom required to minister to a Catholic population beyond the household, Jesuits established their own houses from the 1590s.[104] If, as a consequence of the "domestication," English Catholicism "became more and more seigneurial,"[105] Haigh should credit the Elizabethan government for an effective countermaneuver.

V

Twelve years ago, John Padberg's "How We Live Where We Live" chronicled changes in the Jesuit style of life.[106] Since the 1960s, "our way of residing" has changed from common life through commune to condominium. As one has come to expect from the works of Father Padberg, he flavors his insights with anecdotes and humor. Father Padberg recounts the final days of the "long, black line" and the adjustments required for a new style of Jesuit life. The Elizabethan Jesuits were at the beginning of that line. As the Society designed the infrastructure of community life, Jesuits in England encountered dangers and problems unforeseen. In this essay I have focused on one aspect, residence, with its repercussions on questions of Jesuit attire and poverty. As Roman soutanes infiltrated northern Europe, English Jesuit dress "of necessity must be secular and, for the most part, in the style of noblemen."[107] English

Jesuit behavior was falling outside the definitions of the Society's "way of proceeding," so much so that continental brethren often questioned whether they were members of the same religious order. Instructions may have exhorted them to avoid all appearances of avarice, all signs of levity and vanity, and to follow the Society's Institute as much as they could, but there was little initial accountability because few observed whether individual Jesuits lived these instructions. The temptation to spin personal comfort and self-indulgence as apostolic necessity must have been great. Cultural conditions dictated that sixteenth-century English Jesuits adopt a style of life more secular than that of their continental brethren. That they did so with "prudence" and "discreet charity" may provide norms for Jesuit adaptation today.

Endnotes

1. For these discussions see Thomas M. McCoog, S.J., *The Society of Jesus in Ireland, Scotland, and England 1541–1588: "Our Way of Proceeding?"* (Leiden: E. J. Brill, 1996), 129–41.

2. John W. Padberg, S.J., Martin D. O'Keefe, S.J., John L. McCarthy, S.J., eds., *For Matters of Greater Moment: The First Thirty Jesuit General Congregations* (St. Louis, Mo.: Institute of Jesuit Sources, 1994), 144, decree 27.

3. I have used the translation of the relevant section from *The Constitutions of the Society of Jesus*, trans. George E. Ganss, S.J. (St. Louis, Mo.: Institute of Jesuit Sources, 1970), 80. For the Latin original see *Regulae Societatis Iesu* (Rome: Monumenta Historica Societatis Iesu, 1948), 2. (Hereafter *Regulae*.)

4. John W. O'Malley, S.J., comments that "The tension between the continuing insistence on the necessity of mobility and the long-term commitment required by the schools would remain throughout Jesuit history." *The First Jesuits* (Cambridge, Mass.: Harvard University Press, 1993), 239. See also 335–45 for background on the *Regulae*.

5. *Regulae*, 24.

6. We know little about the evolution of a daily order in the early history of the Society. In June 1566, Jerome Nadal introduced into the Jesuit residence of Augsburg "the regular daily routine common to Jesuit colleges," i.e., grace at meals; reading at table; regular times for prayer and meals; no women may enter the community; no non-Jesuit may reside in a Jesuit community; and no Jesuit may leave the community without a companion. See William V. Bangert, S.J., *Jerome Nadal, S.J. (1507–1580): Tracking the First Generation of Jesuits*, ed. Thomas M. McCoog, S.J. (Chicago: Loyola University Press, 1992), 319.

7. The instructions were published with an English translation in Leo Hicks, S.J., *Letters and Memorials of Father Robert Persons, S.J.* (London: Catholic Record Society, 1942), 316–21. (Catholic Record Society cited hereafter as CRS.)

8. Stephen and Elizabeth Usherwood, *We Die for the Old Religion: The Story of the 85 Martyrs of England and Wales Beatified 22 November 1987* (London: Sheed and Ward, 1987), 97–99.

9. *The Constitutions of the Society of Jesus: An Introductory Commentary on the Constitutions* (St. Louis, Mo.: Institute of Jesuit Sources, 1989), 15.

10. *Regulae,* 19.

11. The instructions can be found in Hicks, *Letters and Memorials,* 363.

12. *Constitutions* (1970), 251.

13. *Regulae,* 7–8.

14. Ibid., 18.

15. These instructions can be found in Hicks, *Letters and Memorials,* 356.

16. Robert Parsons, "Of the Life and Martyrdom of Father Edmond Campian [sic]," *Letters and Notices* 12 (1878): 16.

17. Campion to Mercurian, (St. Omers) 20 June 1580 in Henry More, *The Elizabethan Jesuits,* ed. and trans. Francis Edwards, S.J. (London: Phillimore, 1981), 77–79.

18. Parsons, "Edmond Campian," 18.

19. Squire was master of Balliol College, Oxford, during Parsons's tenure as bursar. Squire sided with Christopher Bagshaw in his dispute with Parsons regarding, among other things, financial irregularities (Francis Edwards, S.J., *Robert Persons: The Biography of an Elizabethan Jesuit, 1546–1610* [St. Louis, Mo.: Institute of Jesuit Sources, 1996], 5–8). No one, to my knowledge, has pointed out the irony that Parsons and his confederates had secured the protection of Parsons's old adversary through bribes.

20. Robert Parsons, S.J., "The First Entrance of the Fathers into England," ed. John H. Pollen, S.J., in *Miscellanea II* (London: CRS, 1906), 2:201.

21. Parsons, "Edmond Campian," 21. Orton is identified as Parsons's companion on 32.

22. Ibid., 22.

23. Ibid., 27–28.

24. Ibid., 28.

25. Ibid., 32–33. Shortly thereafter fortune turned against Orton. On his way to the meeting, he and Robert Johnson were apprehended through Sledd and committed to the Poultry Counter prison on 12 July 1580 (John H. Pollen, S.J., ed., "Official Lists of Prisoners for Religion from 1562 to 1580," in *Miscellenea I* [London: CRS, 1903], 1:67).

26. At least Simpson claimed that Pierrepoint was Campion's companion (*Edmund Campion: A Biography,* new edition [London: John Hodges,

1896], 224). Leo Hicks thought he was Charles Basset *(Letters and Memorials,* xxii).

27. Parsons, "Edmond Campian," 45.

28. Simpson, *Edmund Campion,* 224.

29. Edwards, *Robert Persons,* 36.

30. "Father Persons' Autobiography," ed. John H. Pollen, S.J., in *Miscellanea II* (London: CRS, 1906), 2:27.

31. Parsons, "Edmond Campian," 46.

32. Parsons's "Confession" can be found in Hicks, *Letters and Memorials,* 35–41. Campion's "Brag" has been reprinted often, e.g. Evelyn Waugh, *Edmund Campion* (London: Longmans, 1935), 219–23.

33. "Father Persons' Autobiography," 27.

34. Hicks, *Letters and Memorials,* xxiii. Godfrey Anstruther, O.P., cites some evidence for this interpretation, but many of the dates specified in the charges were before the Hoxton meeting or could be interpreted as stops on Campion's northern journey. See *Vaux of Harrowden: A Recusant Family* (Newport, Monmouth: R.H. Johns Limited, 1953), 135.

35. More, *Elizabethan Jesuits,* 86–87.

36. Parsons, "Edmond Campian," 57.

37. Parsons wrote to Alfonso Agazzari that he had arranged to stay in inns before Campion's arrival (5 August 1580 in Hicks, *Letters and Memorials,* 44).

38. Parsons, "Edmond Campian," 51–52. Campion reported the same procedure: "I ride over some part of the country where I am now nearly every day. The harvest, indeed, is great. While on horseback, I think out my short addresses, which I polish upon arriving at a house. Then if any come to me I talk with them or hear their confessions. In the morning, after Mass, I give a talk. Their ears strain eagerly for what is said. The Sacraments they receive very frequently. In administering them, we are helped here and there by priests whom we find everywhere. In this way we meet the people's needs, and the work of the district becomes more manageable for us" (Campion to Mercurian, England, November 1580, Archivum Romanum Societatis Iesu [= ARSI], Fondo Gesuitico 651/612, translated in More, *Elizabethan Jesuits,* 89).

39. Campion confessed "my dress is very simple, but I change it often; likewise our names" (Campion to Mercurian, England, November 1580, ARSI, Fondo Gesuitico 651/612, translated in More, *Elizabethan Jesuits,* 89).

40. Parsons to Agazzari, London 17 November 1580 in Hicks, *Letters and Memorials*, 59.

41. Parsons, "Edmond Campian," 62; "Father Parsons' Autobiography," 29; Simpson, *Edmond Campion*, 251. Parsons's letter to Antonio Possevino is dated "hurredly London 20 October 1580" (ARSI, Fondo Gesuitico, 651/640, published in Thomas M. McCoog, S.J., "Robert Parsons and Claudio Acquaviva: Correspondence," *Archivum Historicum Societatis Iesu [= AHSI]*, 68 [1999]: 87).

42. Parsons, "Edmond Campian," 62.

43. Parsons to Agazzari, London 17 November 1580 in Hicks, *Letters and Memorials*, 61.

44. On the date of its publication see Hicks, *Letters and Memorials*, xxxii, n. 49.

45. According to Anstruther he had a house in Southwark in the parish of St. Savior's (*Vaux of Harrowden*, 141). On page 142, Anstruther cites notes written by the infamous pursuivant Richard Topcliffe that mention Browne's house at St. Mary Overy's. Did Browne have two houses in Southwark, or is this the same house?

46. Parsons to Acquaviva, London 16 June 1581, ARSI, Fondo Gesuitico 651/640, published in McCoog, "Parsons and Acquaviva," 91.

47. Because the original confessions signed by Campion are not extant, some historians (e.g., Richard Simpson) claim that they were forgeries. John Hungerford Pollen, S.J., however, believes they are authentic. See "Blessed Edmund Campion's Confessions," *The Month* 134 (1919): 258–61.

48. See Michael Hodgetts, "Campion in Staffordshire and Derbyshire 1581," *Midland Catholic History* 7 (2000): 52–54.

49. The exact length is unknown. Campion admitted that he arrived on Tuesday of the third week of Lent (28 February) and remained twelve days. Later he said that he spent Easter there. See his confessions, British Library, Lansdowne MSS 30, no. 78.

50. Simpson, *Edmond Campion*, 266.

51. "Father Persons' Autobiography," 29. We do not know the precise date of Campion's return. We know from Parsons's letter to Acquaviva from London on 16 June 1581 (ARSI, Fondo Gesuitico 651/640 [published in McCoog, "Parsons and Acquaviva," 89]) that he had received Father General's letter of 27 March on 3 June: "With what sentiments we read this letter, I can not tell you! (Providentially we were gathered together at

that time. I had called my father [Campion] from distant parts; I had not seen him for eight whole months.) I will say only: we read it; reread it; a third and a fourth time we read it; we showed it to our friends; we were exultant, delighted. May God thank you for so great a consolation."

52. See his confessions and Simpson, *Edmond Campion,* 283, 305–06.

53. Parsons, "Autobiography," 30.

54. Paul L. Hughes and James F. Larkin, C.S.V., eds., *Tudor Royal Proclamations,* 3 vols. (New Haven, Conn.: Yale University Press, 1964–69), 2:483.

55. Quoted in J. E. Neale, *Elizabeth I and Her Parliaments,* 2 vols. (London: Jonathan Cape, 1953–57), 1:383–84.

56. For more information on Heywood, his background and mission, see Dennis Flynn's articles "The English Mission of Jasper Heywood, S.J.," *AHSI* 54 (1985): 45–76; "'Out of Step': Six Supplementary Notes on Jasper Heywood," in *The Reckoned Expense: Edmund Campion and the Early English Jesuits. Essays in Celebration of the First Centenary of Campion Hall, Oxford (1896–1996),* ed. Thomas M. McCoog, S.J. (Woodbridge: Boydell and Brewer, 1996), 179–92; and "Jasper Heywood and the German Usury Controversy," forthcoming.

57. John H. Pollen, S.J., "The Notebook of John Southcote, D.D., 1628–36," in *Miscellanea I* (London: CRS, 1905), 1:112.

58. Hughes and Larkin, *Tudor Royal Proclamations,* 2:489.

59. The first part of the quotation comes from Allen's letter to Acquaviva, Reims 4 April 1585, in Penelope Renold, ed., *Letters of William Allen and Richard Barret 1572–1598* (London: CRS, 1967), 58:148; the second, Allen to Acquaviva, Reims 8 March 1585, ibid., 142.

60. See Philip Caraman, S.J., ed., *William Weston: The Autobiography of an Elizabethan* (London: Longmans Green, 1955), 1–9.

61. *Praemunire* is the title of a series of acts in late medieval England (the first was passed in 1353) designed to protect rights claimed by the English church against papal encroachment. Recognition of papal authority could result in fines, imprisonment, and execution.

62. Caraman, *William Weston,* 22–23.

63. James Price, a gentleman servant of the Earl of Northumberland, may have been present. See Flynn, "'Out of Step,'" 189, n. 35.

64. McCoog, *Society of Jesus,* 172; Anstruther, *Vaux of Harrowden,* 159; Caraman, *William Weston,* 28, n. 3; Patrick McGrath and Joy Rowe, "The

Elizabethan Priests: Their Harbourers and Helpers," *Recusant History* 19 (1989): 211–15.

65. Caraman, *William Weston,* 69–79, especially 78, n. 16; Anstruther, *Vaux of Harrowden,* 169–71, 181.

66. Caraman, *William Weston,* 83.

67. Southwell to Acquaviva, 21 December 1586, in John H. Pollen, S.J., ed., *Unpublished Documents Relating to the English Martyrs 1584–1603* (London: CRS, 1908), 5:314.

68. McCoog, *Society of Jesus,* 237, 274.

69. Garnet to Acquaviva (early 1589), ARSI, Fondo Gesuitico 651/624.

70. Philip Caraman, S.J., ed., *John Gerard: The Autobiography of an Elizabethan,* 2nd ed. (London: Longmans, 1956), 17–18.

71. Caraman, *John Gerard,* 24.

72. According to Gerard, "On his first arrival in England, he [Oldcorne] stayed with the Superior, as he had no home of his own to go to" (Caraman, *John Gerard,* 44). Most likely that home was Baddesley Clinton. According to Michael Hodgetts, Oldcorne remained there until 1590 after his conversion of Dorothy Habington (*Secret Hiding Holes* [Dublin: Veritas Publications, 1989], 71).

73. We can date their arrival from a cryptic comment about "four veterans" and "two recruits" in Garnet's letter to Acquaviva on 1 May 1589 (ARSI, Fondo Gesuitico 651/624). See Philip Caraman, S.J., *Henry Garnet (1555–1606) and the Gunpowder Plot* (London: Longmans, 1964), 96–97.

74. See "Father Richard Holtby on Persecution in the North," in *The Troubles of Our Catholic Forefathers Related by Themselves,* 3 vols., ed. John Morris, S.J. (London: 1872–77), 3:113–14.

75. ARSI Rom. 156/II, ff. 165r–168v.

76. Garnet to Acquaviva, London 17 March 1593, Archivum Britannicum Societatis Iesu (= ABSI), London, Stonyhurst MSS, Anglia I, 73. I have used the translation in Caraman, *Henry Garnet,* 68. See also 122, 126.

77. I do not include Jesuits such as Thomas Pounde and Weston in prison.

78. For what we do know see Patrick McGrath and Joy Rowe, "The Marian Priests under Elizabeth I," *Recusant History* 17 (1984): 103–20.

79. McGrath and Rowe, "Elizabethan Priests," 211.

80. Anstruther, *Vaux of Harrowden*, 108.

81. Two copies of this document exist: ABSI, Stonyhurst MSS, Coll P, ff. 330–37, and ARSI Rom. 156/II, ff. 172r–176v. The document (with an English translation) was published in Hicks, *Letters and Memorials*, 321–40.

82. ARSI, Anglia 36/II, f. 268r.

83. Robertus Hilarius (vere Jones) to Claudio Acquaviva, London 3 November 1613, ABSI, Stonyhurst MSS Anglia IV, 45 (translated in Henry Foley, S.J., *Records of the English Province of the Society of Jesus*, 7 vols. [Roehampton: Manresa Press, 1877–84], 4:385).

84. ABSI, Stonyhurst MSS Anglia IV, 45 (translated in Foley, *Records*, 2:3–6).

85. McGrath and Rowe, "Elizabethan Priests," 228.

86. Garnet to Acquaviva, [early 1589], ARSI, Fondo Gesuitico 651/624; same to same, 12 September 1589, ABSI, Stonyhurst MSS Anglia I, 41.

87. Haigh's "From Monopoly to Minority: Catholicism in Early Modern England" (*Transactions of the Royal Historical Society*, 5th series, 31 [1981]: 129–147) and "The Continuity of Catholicism in the English Reformation" (*Past and Present* 93 [1981]: 37–69) appeared around the same time. Patrick McGrath rebutted Haigh in "Elizabethan Catholicism: a Reconsideration," *Journal of Ecclesiastical History* 35 (1984): 414–28. Haigh's reply was "Revisionism, the Reformation and the History of English Catholicism," *Journal of Ecclesiastical History* 36 (1985): 394–405, with a short reply from Dr. McGrath immediately following (405–06).

88. Haigh, "From Monopoly to Minority," 132.

89. Ibid., 136.

90. *Letters of St. Ignatius of Loyola*, ed. William J. Young, S.J. (Chicago: Loyola University Press, 1959), 213.

91. Ibid., 268.

92. *Constitutions* (1970), [622d, e], 275.

93. Haigh, "From Monopoly to Minority," 139.

94. Ibid., 136.

95. McGrath, "Elizabethan Catholicism," 422.

96. See Thomas M. McCoog, S.J., "The Creation of the First Jesuit Communities in England," *The Heythrop Journal* 28 (1987): 47–48.

97. See Thomas M. McCoog, S.J., "The English Jesuit Mission and the French Match," *Catholic Historical Review,* forthcoming.

98. McGrath, "Elizabethan Catholicism," 422.

99. Haigh, "From Monopoly to Minority," 141, 142.

100. Ibid., 141.

101. Ibid., 138.

102. Ibid.

103. Ibid., 147.

104. See McCoog, *Society of Jesus,* 274–75; " The Creation of the First Jesuit Communities," 44–45.

105. Haigh, "From Monopoly to Minority," 145.

106. *Studies in the Spirituality of Jesuits* 20/2 (1988): 1–38.

107. ARSI Rom. 156/II, ff. 165r–168v.

"Habits of Industry": Jesuits and Nineteenth-Century Native American Education

Gerald L. McKevitt, S.J.

FEW NAMES ARE MORE FREQUENTLY IDENTIFIED WITH Catholic schooling in the United States than the Jesuits. As historian Edward J. Power has written, "The most persuasive European influence on American Catholic higher education was Jesuit." The spirit of the order's *Ratio studiorum* permeated pedagogy in the nation's Catholic colleges, and the curriculum of Georgetown was a nationwide model until the first decade of the twentieth century. The Society of Jesus exercised a dominant influence not only on higher education, Philip Gleason argues, but also on Catholic high schools through its promotion of the combined secondary-collegiate program of studies.[1]

One aspect of the order's educational activity that has been overlooked by scholars, however, is its teaching of Native Americans. During the nineteenth and early twentieth centuries, Jesuits, like several other Catholic religious congregations, made a concerted effort not only to evangelize the native peoples of the Far West but also to hasten their assimilation into Euroamerican culture through education. The Society operated schools in Kansas for boys and girls of the Osage and Potawatami tribes until the 1870s, when the natives removed to Indian Territory in Oklahoma. In the Dakotas, Jesuits worked among various Sioux bands, establishing schools on the Rosebud and Pine Ridge Reservations.[2] Farther to the west, the order founded an even more extensive educational network in its Rocky Mountain Mission, which is the focus of this case study.

Founded in 1841 by Pierre Jean de Smet, the mission embraced the modern states of Montana, Washington, Oregon, and Idaho; by 1873, its network of churches, farms, and boarding schools claimed nearly 107,000 Native American converts.[3] By 1896, the mission reported an enrollment of a thousand Indian students in fifteen schools.[4]

A hallmark of the Jesuit schools in the Pacific Northwest was their location in the heart of Indian country. In this, they differed from many boarding schools of the era, which were deliberately situated off-reservation in order to hasten the assimilation of Native American young people to white culture. Another characteristic of Jesuit institutions in their heyday was their reliance on federal funds, a consequence of the cooperation between church and state that characterized the administration of U.S. Indian affairs in the 1880s and 1890s. Governmental support enabled the schools to achieve success, but it also had far-reaching consequences for both church and state. By attracting public funds, Catholics eventually provoked a backlash that not only ended government support but also produced a reinterpretation of the first amendment of the U.S. Constitution.[5]

From Preaching to Teaching

Education of Native Americans emerged gradually as a correlative to the order's missionary activity. Unlike Protestant missionaries, for whom church and school marched hand in hand, Catholics initially focused on the religious conversion of the aboriginal population. "Our aim," said Joseph Joset, an early Jesuit missionary, "has been to make Christians of the Indians." Thus religious training took priority over all other forms of instruction. "When I arrived in the

Fig. 1. Industrial School for Native American boys, St. Ignatius Mission, Montana, 1889. Students and their instructors hold instruments used in the various trades and crafts taught at the school, including blacksmithing, carpentry, gardening, photography, and harness making *(courtesy of Jesuit Oregon Province Archives, St. Ignatius Mission Collection)*

Mountains in 1844," recalled Joset, "there was never a question of teaching school—nothing but catechism, catechism endlessly."[6] Eschewing instruction in academic subjects the mastery of which was not judged essential for membership in the church, the priests instead concentrated on introducing the people to Christian prayer and to the basic tenets of Catholic theology.

Jesuits were less inclined than Protestant counterparts to fuse the goals of civilization and Christianity. However, they did endeavor, in the words of spokesman Lorenzo Palladino, to promote "habits of industry and useful toil" among their Native American converts. Believing that economic stability and subsistence were the foundation of a worthy human existence, they offered instruction in various skills—carpentry, animal husbandry, and especially farming—that would guarantee their converts a more reliable food supply than was provided by nomadic hunting. This instruction was effected by preaching the gospel, a missionary wrote, but also by "the preaching of *example*," which "we did from the start.... Our little garden and every year increasing farm was an object lesson to them."[7]

Many missions also inaugurated modest boarding schools for boys whose parents wished them to learn useful skills. "From the beginning of this mission," wrote Camillo Imoda, missionary to the Blackfoot, we "have been keeping Indian children in our house, boarding, clothing, and teaching them at our own expense."[8] The same arrangement occurred at other missions. "Our students do a little bit of everything," wrote Giuseppe Giorda at St. Ignatius, "wash dishes in the kitchen, prepare the refectory, split and carry wood, clean the rooms, etc. They do carpentry work and like it; they work in the fields when the seasons allow, and some are learning to drive the oxen."[9] Describing the early training program for the Coeur d'Alenes, Joset noted that it deliberately eschewed formal academic schooling.

It was thought more advisable to train them to habits of industry, to love of labor. Therefore, a farm was started where everyone could be employed. A small number of boys from eight to twelve were boarded and employed in all the works of farming and building. All were assiduously taught the principles of Christian religion.[10]

"Experience proved the plan to be correct," Joset concluded. When the boys grew up and left school, "they started small farms and, of course, received encouragement; others, witnessing how they had always plenty of food, imitated them.... Now all are farming more or less according to their means. By selling grain, they are able to purchase their necessaries."[11]

In some places the missionaries taught reading and writing, although on an informal and irregular basis. The Jesuit school at the Blackfoot agency in Montana was typical of the fledgling institutions. It had "but one teacher and about a dozen pupils," a missionary writes, "mostly children of employees, because the Indians are nearly always away hunting. And it is only when they come to get their annuities that the teacher is able to muster a larger number for a few days."[12] Lack of funds and personnel prevented attempting anything more ambitious. Writing from Lapwai Agency among the Nez Percé in Idaho in 1874, Giuseppe Cataldo writes, "I have now more than fifty pupils in my Sunday school,

Fig. 2. Blackfoot Indian students and faculty assembled for a late-nineteenth-century photograph at Holy Family Mission, Montana *(courtesy of Jesuit Oregon Province Archives, Northwest Albums Collection)*

of whom about 20 receive some literary instruction from me whenever I have leisure to do so, namely, whenever I am here." But thus far the missionaries had not been able to organize "a school properly speaking for want of means."[13]

The first step toward more organized instruction occurred in 1863 on Montana's Flathead Reservation. According to the treaty that created the agency, the U.S. government agreed to send teachers, a blacksmith, a carpenter, and other helpers to the confederated tribes of Flatheads, Pend d'Oreilles, and Kootenais. Responsibility for the project was offered to the Jesuits of nearby St. Ignatius Mission. In 1864, the Jesuits and the Sisters of Charity of Providence opened a day school for boys and girls that promptly expanded into a boarding school the next year.[14] Similar programs offering practical training and basic instruction followed in quick succession elsewhere. In 1874, a school for Blackfoot children opened at St. Peter's Mission, Montana. In 1878, Jesuits opened a boys' school at Sacred Heart Mission, near DeSmet, Idaho, and at St. Francis Regis Mission in Washington, where Sisters of Providence already operated a school for girls. By 1879, the Rocky Mountain Mission operated thirteen schools throughout the Northwest.

Several factors prompted the Jesuits' shift from an almost exclusive focus on catechetical and sacramental ministry to formal teaching. Chief among these was the rapid inundation of Indian country by white farmers and miners, whom Joset denounced as "Protestant and mostly adorers of the god of the dollar and in general full of hatred for the poor Indians."[15] The gradual advance of the railroad across the Pacific Northwest brought still more settlers. Recognizing the impossibility of the tribes remaining aloof from the alien culture that increasingly surrounded them, Jesuits recommended industrial schools as an antidote to annihilation. The goal of these institutions, writes Palladino, was "to enable the Indian to make a living and become self-supporting."[16] Missionary Pietro Prando doubted the Blackfoot could survive without schooling, especially without practical training in the trades:

> The Blackfeet are sunk in want and misery, and, in my opinion, they will have trouble in getting through this winter without dying of hunger. Furthermore, I am persuaded that the mission among them will not succeed, if we confine ourselves solely to spiritual ministrations. These poor people need beyond all to be trained and encouraged to agricultural labors: they themselves now admit the necessity of this, and are anxious to receive instruction.[17]

Fig. 3. Native American girls of Montana and their Ursuline teachers demonstrate domestic skills mastered in boarding school: drawing, leatherwork, sewing, needlepoint, knitting, and music *(courtesy of Jesuit Oregon Province Archives)*

Some tribal leaders began to seek schools for their people. In 1873, Chief Seltice of the Coeur d'Alenes petitioned President Grant for missionary teachers. "Our good morals come from our Christian teaching," he writes, "and therefore, we wish to stick to that teaching and have our children educated according to it. First of all, we want schools and Catholic schools for boys and girls separate [sic]."

"The Indians begin to be aware of the benefit of schools," observes Jesuit Giuseppe Cataldo in 1878, "and are very anxious to have their children instructed," especially the Kalispels and Pend d'Oreilles. The native rationale for education was summarized in 1884 by Painted Red, a Blackfoot chief influenced by the Jesuits. Addressing a conference of Kootenais gathered at St. Ignatius Mission in 1884, he declared:

> Whites ... have hunted us from all of the land, and now all we have left is a strip of land here and there. The white man even

wants the little we have left and they surround us from every part and lead us to our ruin. In the midst of all this the Blackrobe [Jesuit] comes and shouts out to us: 'My sons, cultivate the land, put up fences, learn the white man's language, teach your children how to read and write so that they can face the white man and be able to keep their lands.' I have seen that this is true, that this is the only way to save our land.[18]

Grant's Peace Policy

The new emphasis on schools was accompanied by a crucial transition in the federal government's Indian policy. Reformers, arguing that the rapid disappearance of tribal lands meant that the Native Americans could no longer follow their traditional nomadic life, began to advocate a new approach that would prepare them for coexistence with whites. Thus it was that the government became dedicated to the principle of total assimilation of natives into the mainstream of American society by means of education. The question then became: Who best to run the schools? The answer was: Those who manifested the greatest interest in the Native American's welfare—the Christian churches. Beginning in 1869, during the Grant administration, the government started making contracts with religious denominations not only to maintain schools for natives and to teach them farming and trades but also to administer reservations themselves. Thus began the Peace Policy, which one scholar has characterized as "the most extensive and prolonged attempt in United States history at cooperation between the churches and the federal government."[19]

Despite the Catholic Church's long engagement in Indian affairs, the Peace Policy began primarily as a Protestant program. Catholics, excluded from membership on the Board of Indian Commissioners, were barred from ministering to Native Americans on many reservations where they had been active for decades. Expecting that their previous missionary labor would earn them assignment to thirty-eight agencies, they received only seven from the all-Protestant board. Methodists, who had done little missionary work, got fourteen, Quakers ten, Presbyterians nine, with the remainder going to other Protestant groups. Although the Jesuits were eventually given authority at the Flathead Reservation, other tribes with many Catholic members—for example, Nez Percé, Yakima, and Blackfoot—fell under the Protestant mantle. With the stroke of a pen, some 80,000 Catholic Native Americans in the Pacific Northwest were assigned to the religious care of Protestant denominations.[20]

Exclusion of Catholics from participation in the Peace Policy had far-reaching consequences. Because Protestants now controlled most Indian reservations, it was they who received the bulk of the federal monies appropriated for educating tribal children in the so-called contract schools. But the Protestant bias of the Peace Policy spurred Catholics into action. Denied seats on the Board of Indian Commissioners and turned away from Indian agencies that they felt were rightfully theirs, Catholic leaders began aggressively promoting their own interests. A key step in that reorganization was the founding of the Bureau of Catholic Indian Missions (BCIM) in Washington, D.C. in 1879. Created to centralize the church's missionary work and to lobby on its behalf with the federal government, the bureau launched a resurgence of Catholic activity. The organization raised money from private sources in support of Indian education, its chief benefactors being Katharine Drexel and her two sisters, daughters of the wealthy Philadelphia financier Francis Drexel.

BCIM fought for federal funding for schools. The bureau's greatest achievement was in persuading Congress and the Indian Office to enable Catholic Indian schools to participate in the contract-school system, whereby the government annually issued per capita allotments for training native children. As a result, Catholic missionaries, who had been more or less reluctant bystanders during earlier years, emerged in the 1880s as major participants in the federal educational program. Federal aid to boarding schools assisted by the BCIM grew from $54,000 in 1883 to $394,533 six years later. By 1886, there were fifty institutions for

Native Americans in the United States supported jointly by the government and by religious societies. Thirty-eight of them, with a total of 2,068 pupils, were under Catholic control, and only twelve, with a total of 500 students, were run by Protestants. Alarmed at "Roman aggressiveness" in procuring federal support for their schools, Protestant leaders warned fellow Americans of the Catholic Church's "growing power with the government in Washington."[21]

The contract-school system opened a new world of educational possibility for the Rocky Mountain Mission and the tribes affiliated with it. Encouraged by the prospect of outside support, Giuseppe Cataldo, superior of the mission, envisioned in 1878 the founding of schools in every mission operated by Jesuits in the Northwest. Schools soon experienced unprecedented enrollments. The influx of federal funds helped inaugurate what historian Robert I. Burns has called an era of "autumnal achievement" in the Rocky Mountain Mission. "Missions extended from the Yakimas, Umatillas, and Nez Percés over to the Cheyennes, Assiniboines, and Crows," writes Burns. "Schools and churches became large modern buildings." In 1890, in Montana alone there were over 7,000 Catholic Indians out of a federal census count of 10,000. By 1895, the Rocky Mountain Mission operated eighteen federally subsidized schools for 1,318 Native Americans. Over a third of all the 3,613 native children enrolled in Catholic mission schools in the country attended Jesuit establishments in the Pacific Northwest. Even today, according to historian Andrew F. Rolle, still-flourishing churches on many reservations represent "the tangible results of a far-flung missionary system rivaling the Spanish California mission chain of adobe and brick." While public funding was not the sole cause of that expansion, it played a significant role in the enterprise.[22]

The transformative power of federal dollars was exemplified by the mushroom growth of the school at St. Ignatius Mission. Described in 1874 by a government inspector as "an extensive establishment [with] a large church, large school house, mills, residences, barns, gardens," the mission had three hundred to four hundred acres under cultivation "with large herds of horses and cattle and farming implements of all kinds."[23] The number of students enrolled in the mission's two schools, however, was small. Although it boasted a boarding institution for girls, run by the Sisters of Charity of Providence, and a small day school, the mission lacked a dormitory and could therefore school only five or six boys.[24] Two years later, St. Ignatius received its first federal contract. Congress allotted $108 a year for each of its forty pupils, an appropriation that was increased in 1884 to school seventy-five students and later 150.[25]

More significant help arrived in 1885 when BCIM director John Mullan informed the Jesuits that Congress had recently voted a special appropriation of $2,000 "to found and to organize at St. Ignatius a first class industrial and *mechanical* boarding school" (italics mine). The establishment envisioned by Mullan would "not only rival Carlisle" (a model non-Catholic industrial school in Pennsylvania—see below) but would convince Congress that this type of institution could be successfully established "right in the very heart of the Indian country."

> We want St. Ignatius in the future to be a model mechanical and industrial boarding school to which Congress and the U.S. Indian Department may be able to point as a type and a pattern to be followed by all other Indian schools in the states and territories.

If St. Ignatius succeeded, Mullan argued, we "can point Congress to it next year as a visible voucher to aid our efforts at doing the same thing at Coeur d'Alene." Students would be taught to work in leather, wood, and iron "in workshops to be specially constructed and . . . fully supplied with all the necessary tools, materials, supplies to such ends, and with a first class mechanic in charge." Eager to implement the long-dreamed-of project as soon as possible, Jesuit superior Lorenzo Palladino, reported, "What was an airy nothing is now being shaped into objective reality."[26]

The experiment did not disappoint its investors. By 1890, Congress had increased the St. Ignatius contract to $150 per year for each of the three hundred boys and girls. According to a glowing report published in the Catholic journal *Sacred Heart Messenger*, the Indian Office's call to "save the papoose" was being carried out at St. Ignatius Mission, and the nation's "Indian problem" was fast nearing solution. In addition to nearly 250 older students, the mission housed fifty-four additional children, whose ages ranged from two to seven years, in a kindergarten run by the Ursuline nuns. "Away from the wigwam and from Indian customs," the journal predicted, these children, the majority of them orphans, would grow up as "real and true, little Americans."[27]

Without Reservation

The Jesuits, like their contemporaries in the U.S. Indian Office, favored boarding schools rather than day schools for Native American children. "It is the experience of the department," Secretary of the Interior Carl Schurz informed Congress in 1879, "that mere day schools, however well conducted, do not withdraw the children sufficiently from the influence, habits, and traditions of their home life, and produce for this reason but a . . . limited effect." Jesuit Giuseppe Cataldo was equally disdainful of day schools, dismissing them as "mere humbug." Such establishments were "of little use for Indian children as it is difficult to get them to attend," Palladino added, "and those that are prevailed upon to attend, generally attend but very irregularly." Among tribes still dedicated to hunting, "most of the day scholars are obliged to go with their parents on the semiannual buffalo hunt, and consequently much time is lost, to say the least." For such youngsters "even mere attendance is practically impossible," the Jesuit concluded. "How can the Indian go to school and live, or live and go to school, as long as his daily living depends upon that which he may catch day by day?"[28]

Residential schools, by contrast, offered many advantages. According to Jesuit superior Leopold Van Gorp, boarders "constantly under the eye of the teacher" and isolated from their home environment were more easily and more swiftly acculturated.

"These children are severed away from their lodges and brought to school," added missionary Pietro Paulo Prando,

> where they will lose the tracts of Indian mythology and foolish traditions that the old women are telling to their children during the old nights of winter, and in the mountain breeze in summer, filling up their brains with wild imaginations and stories. So the very fact of having the children out of their lodges is a great step towards civilization and religion.

The boarding school, wrote Palladino, "becomes necessarily and in the fullest possible way, the substitute for the home and the parent."[29]

Although Jesuits shared with the Indian Office a belief in the superiority of boarding schools, they disagreed with policymakers about where they should be located. After Richard Henry Pratt's founding of the Carlisle Indian School in Pennsylvania in 1879, the government favored removing students to locations as "remote from reservations" as possible in order that they be liberated from the negative influences of tribal life. They "would thus be free from the great pull-down of the camp," wrote Indian Commissioner Morgan, and "able to mingle with the civilized people that surround them." Thus Carlisle, which stood as a model for over two dozen industrial boarding schools in the United States, was designed, in the words of historian Robert A. Trennert, "to transform the Indians by placing them in direct contact with American society" in places where they "could be shorn of their cultural heritage." By the turn of the century, nearly 18,000 of the 21,568 Native American students attending school were in boarding institutions, and fully a third of the boarders lived in off-reservation locales.[30]

Jesuits opposed the Carlisle model. Instead, they advocated educating native children in Indian country in places close enough to satisfy parents, yet sufficiently detached to provide a break from the home environment. "To wrest the children from the parents and carry them thousands of miles away to train them . . . is a process as unnatural as it is cruel," wrote Palladino, and it will inevitably "alienate them from their own blood and country." Schools planted on reservations, by contrast, entailed "no unbearable separation" of children and parents since families "can see their children daily, at church, in the class-room, at play, at work, in the shop, or in the field." Boarding schools situated in the student's homeland had other advantages. Besides being more economical, such institutions were better able to adapt their training, whether in farming or stock raising, to the peculiarities of the local environment. They also brought "civilization and the uncivilized face to face" by providing "an example and incentive, not to the children only but to the whole tribe." St. Ignatius Mission, argued superior Leopold Van Gorp, "affords a clear proof of this."

> Here the grown-up Indians—men and women—can be seen striving to follow as best they can the examples of industrious civilized life daily set before them. . . . Their dairies, their meadows, their fields, their kitchen gardens, their little strawberry patches and orchards, are all so many and unquestionable proofs of what we state, since many of the old people were never given any direct instruction in all such matters. Their practical knowledge about many of these points was acquired by them simply from what they saw others do.[31]

The placement of schools near native communities enabled older boys to assist parents with farm chores at crucial times during the year. In 1886, Palladino, head of the school at St. Ignatius, wrote to Charles Lusk of the BCIM for clearance to release students from the classroom for this purpose.

> In the spring when the seedling season begins and in summer during the harvest, I have permitted some of the larger pupils, when their old people, either by age, weak health, or inexperience, would happen to be unable to do the work by themselves, to go and help them put in a little crop and gather it in. And thus some of the pupils would be out of school for three, four, five and even six weeks, between spring and fall,

teaching and helping their old people. I cannot believe it to be against the intention of the Government to allow this.[32]

Indian Resistance

Despite the Jesuits' enthusiasm for boarding-school education, Native Americans themselves were not of one mind regarding its benefits. As a result, Catholic educators, like their Protestant counterparts, often struggled to recruit students. Some tribes, eager that their children learn skills that would enable them to survive in a rapidly changing world, petitioned the missionaries to open institutions, but other Indians opposed the idea. "One of the great difficulties to be contended with in the boys' school," wrote an agent on the Flathead Reservation, "is the fact that the parents are not willing to leave their sons long enough under instruction to give them a proper training. For the sake of the assistance they can give in herding stock or working about home, the boys are taken from school . . . when they attain a certain age." "Though the Indians like the priest," wrote Prando, missionary to the Crows, "when there is question of giving their children to school, they cannot resolve themselves to part from them."[33]

Students themselves often resisted attending school. "It is no little sacrifice for the Indian child to be deprived for an entire year of his pony and saddle," a priest observed. And "to tear the child away from his parent is like inflicting a deep wound in the Indian's heart. . . . This will explain the stubborn opposition incessantly met with by the Government in its endeavor to force its education on the Indians."[34] Another Jesuit summarized: "This love for a roaming, lazy life, makes it at all times hard to get a boy or girl of ordinary school age to resign himself or herself to the confinement of a boarding school."[35]

Coeducation elicited a mixed response from Native American parents. "We want our boys educated," declared Arlee, chief of the

Flatheads in 1876, "but not our girls." Missionaries insisted on training both males and females, however, arguing that schooling would enable young people to find partners of similar background, tastes, and training when they were ready to marry. "You must educate both sexes in order that the one shall support the other," Palladino said, and "in order that they may go out into battle against barbarism hand in hand."[36] While in school, however, students were strictly separated by gender, a practice that sometimes took extreme forms. A French Christian brother who taught at one of the Jesuit schools for boys recorded his amazement at steps taken by his Ursuline coworkers to circumvent males. The nuns prepared meals for the boys but laid the food out on the tables before the pupils entered the dining room in order to avoid contact with them. "Once I took my boys on a walk up the canyon, unaware that the nuns had the girls there," another brother recalled. "Our coming was not expected and it created quite a panic among the nuns supervising. Sisters and girls turned around, faced to the cliff, while we filed along."[37]

Students, accustomed to the casual fraternization of camp life, also found segregation of the sexes curious. "The girls and boys couldn't play together," Blackfoot students recalled, and "you were not allowed to look at the boys." "When you went to church you were separated, the boys on one side, the girls on the other side. You could not mingle with each other or sit together." Such regulations also offended U.S. Indian Commissioner Morgan, who in 1892 decried separation of boys and girls in "these monastic schools" as "a serious defect." Despite pressure from the Indian Office to integrate the sexes, the Jesuits and Ursulines held their ground. The classrooms of St. Labre Mission School in Montana, for example, were not merged until 1922, a reform that, according to an Ursuline teacher, placed the Cheyenne girls at a disadvantage. "After the boys joined them in the classroom," she claimed, "they would not recite aloud even once during the nine months I taught them."[38]

Faculty

Industrial boarding schools required a heavy investment in personnel. The number of priests engaged in classroom work at a given mission was never large. Although they taught some academic subjects, most priests devoted the bulk of their time to sacramental ministry—which often necessitated frequent absences from the school in order to visit distant parts of the reservation—and to administration. Jesuit brothers exercised the most consistent and frequent influence over male students. These men, many of whom had labored as artisans, farmers, and tradesmen before entering religious life, were well suited to the needs of the industrial schools. It was the brothers' task, reported BCIM inspector John Mullan, to teach the boys the details and mysteries of steam machinery; to instruct them how to plow the ground, plant the seed, and reap their own harvest. They should also be taught, Mullen added, how to repair their own harness and wagons, clean and harness their own teams, use and repair their own wagons and tools, and prepare food for and feed their own stock.[39]

During times of recreation, the brothers joined students in field games and other outdoor sports. So essential was their contribution to the successful operation of an industrial boarding school that superiors continually lamented they never had enough of them. "A good brother . . . would be the resurrection of our mission," wrote the superior of St. Mary's Mission in Washington. "Much more could be done here if we had one."[40]

Lacking Jesuit manpower, most of the larger industrial schools hired lay teachers. One hundred and forty students enrolled at St. Xavier's Mission in Montana were instructed by a staff of three priests, eight sisters, and seven lay teachers. Cataldo reported in 1889 that, in addition to other personnel at the school in DeSmet, Idaho, "we have now a carpenter, a shoemaker, a blacksmith, a painter, three farmers, all hired hands." Laypersons constituted the majority of the staff at St. Paul's Mission. "All the discipline and teaching," observed superior Damiani, "has to be left in the hands of laypersons."[41]

Women religious who ran the orphanages, kindergartens, and girls' schools at the various missions played an even more central role. The free services provided by them gave Catholic Indian schools an advantage over understaffed Protestant institutions. By 1890, the number of Jesuits involved in educational and missionary work in the Rocky Mountain Mission totaled only thirty-eight men—eighteen priests, twelve brothers, and eight scholastics. The number of religious women assisting them—fourteen Sisters of Providence and sixty Ursuline nuns—was much greater.[42] Their presence testified to the growing reliance of the American Catholic Church on congregations of religious women not only to sustain Indian missions but also to staff the nation's network of parochial schools mandated by the Council of Baltimore.

If a residential school is to enjoy "any good repute among Indians," wrote Giuseppe Giorda in 1874, it must be run by sisters. The same assertion was made by Camillo Imoda in 1880 when he laid plans for the expansion of the Jesuit day school at St. Peter's Mission. "To make it a success," he wrote, "it should be a boarding school directed by four sisters."[43] In 1864, Sisters of Charity of Providence opened a day school for girls at St. Ignatius Mission that rapidly evolved into a residential institution. A similar establishment thrived at St. Regis Mission, where the sisters preceded the Jesuits by five years, and still another at DeSmet, Idaho, where a high school and commercial course for girls was largely supported by a dairy and vegetable garden. Ursuline nuns, popularly known in the Northwest as "Lady Black Robes," operated schools among the Assiniboines, Crows, Gros Ventres, Blackfoot, and the confederated tribes on the Flathead Reservation. In order to provide a dependable source of teachers for the girls' school at St. Mary's Mission on the Colville Reservation, Jesuit Stephen de Rouge founded his own community of religious, the Lady Missionaries of St. Mary's Mission.[44]

The Art of Craft

The primary purpose of the schools was industrial training. "These Indians want their children trained well, not only in reading and writing," a missionary in Idaho wrote, "but in different trades as carpenters, blacksmiths, harness makers, etc."[45] "What our children will do after leaving school is impossible to say," an official at St. Xavier's Mission, Montana, noted. But it was hoped that "the training they receive in the trades and in farming will enable them, when they have obtained the proper age, to earn their livelihood in these vocations."[46]

To this end, the mission schools, like those run by the government and by Protestant churches, created a two-tier program that offered both academic and industrial instruction. If a student remained in school for a sufficient length of time, he or she received the rough equivalent of an eighth-grade education. "A plain, common, English education, spelling, reading and writing, with the rudiments of arithmetic," said Lorenzo Palladino, "will be for the Indian at large book-learning enough for all purposes of his civilized life and social intercourse." Seeking primarily "to enable the Indian to make a living and become self-supporting," the typical school's course of study centered on "necessary industries and such, principally, as lie in the line of husbandry, farming, stock-raising and the like, since these are, of all others, the most suited to his actual needs."[47]

This curriculum reflected the educational policy of the federal government. "While proper attention is paid to book learning and to the moral and religious training of the pupils," an Indian Office official wrote approvingly of the program at St. Ignatius, "especial attention is paid to teaching them industrial pursuits." Agent Peter Ronan summarized:

> In addition to the usual branches taught in school—reading, writing, arithmetic, grammar, music, and geography—the girls are taught housekeeping, such as washing, ironing, sewing, dairy work, cooking, and general household duties. In the boys'

school the pupils are taught blacksmithing, carpentering, work in saw and grist mills, running shingle-machines, farming work, gardening, teaming, and all general farming work, tailoring, shoemaking, saddlery and harness, painting, and all work incident to the institution. The art of printing is also taught in a neat little printing office, where dictionaries of the Kalispel language, the Gospels, and innumerable pamphlets and circulars have been neatly printed.[48]

Classroom instruction was basic. Younger students studied elementary subjects such as reading, geography, history, penmanship, and arithmetic. Drawing on European practice, Jesuit teachers relied on melody to aid in the memorization of multiplication tables as they had once employed tunes to teach the catechism. "They sing their tables every day," a missionary reported, "from twice one to twelve times twelve." Older students, in addition to the usual secondary school subjects, received instruction in vocal and instrumental music and even stenography. It is not our aim "to make stenographers of our Indian boys," a Jesuit wrote, but since "this study is becoming so universal, we thought it well to give them some knowledge of it, which consists in their ability of writing from dictation."[49]

The girls' school at DeSmet was run by Sisters of Providence from Montreal, who instructed their pupils "in all the requirements of household duties." Thus, besides regular classroom subjects, they were taught "cutting and fitting plain and fancy needlework." "The girls do all the repairing on the boys' clothing," a teacher reported, in addition to making clothes for themselves, and they learn "cookery, laundry, needlework, dairy work, fancy work, and general housewifery. Painting and drawing and those branches common in convent schools are also taught here." Each girl maintained her own garden plot, Sister M. Amedee recorded, and "owing to the number of stock in our dairy farm, each pupil has the advantage of learning how to make butter" and how to perform "all such work as concerns the dairy."[50]

Mastery of English received top priority, although native proficiency varied from reservation to reservation. Many students arrived at school knowing only their native tongue. According to one estimate, by 1880 approximately one-fourth of the Flathead could read and write the language. As late as 1909, a missionary at the Holy Family School for the Blackfoot reported that about half "of our new students do not yet understand English at all."[51] When a government delegation led by Secretary of the Interior Carl Schurz inspected St. Ignatius Mission in 1883, the visitors were surprised to discover that students were instructed in both English and Flathead—a workable option since many teachers were bilingual. A missionary at St. Xavier Mission reported that English was used in the classroom, for the most part, but "we limit ourselves to encouraging" the youngest children "with little rewards, or prizes, to express themselves in English, if they can."[52]

The Jesuits resisted entirely abandoning the use of native languages, a feature that distinguished their schools from those run by other groups. Even after the federal government increased pressure to give all instruction in English, they continued to teach religion and prayers in the students' own tongue. At DeSmet Mission, catechism instruction was given to the boys in English, Kalispel, and Nez Percé on Sundays prior to their weekly *missa cantata* in Latin. Nonetheless, apart from religious instruction, reliance on native tongues gradually diminished as federal guidelines increasingly determined curricula. In 1880, the Indian Bureau threatened a cessation of government funding to schools that failed to offer English instruction in all subjects. "A mastery of idiomatic English is particularly essential," declared Commissioner Morgan, for teachers charged with "breaking up the use of Indian dialects and the substitution therefore of the English language."[53]

Although easier to command than to enforce, the federal mandate posed a challenge to teachers who labored under the same linguistic handicap as their students. English was not the first language of the European-born schoolmasters. This shortcoming did not escape the notice of government inspectors. The boys' school at St. Ignatius Mission was of "greatest interest," Carl Schurz remarked in 1883, but the English spoken by two Jesuit instructors from Italy was "frightfully fractured." As a result, the teachers had contaminated the speech of their pupils. "All the boys read well," Schurz noted, "although with a strange singsong, I might say Italian, intonation." After an inspector from the Indian Office complained that "Fathers Bandini and Crimont speak very broken English," BCIM director J. A. Stephan admonished the missionaries "that all employees shall be able to speak the English language fluently."[54]

There were, however, limits to the churchmen's willingness to accommodate government demands. After an agent at the Coville Reservation complained that Brother D'Agostino was "not sufficiently versed in English to constitute him an efficient teacher," the director of the BCIM rallied to his defense with the argument that teaching boys to become industrious farmers or mechanics did not require language mastery. "A dumb man can give it as well and as usefully as the best talker."[55] Nonetheless, the Jesuits remained sensitive to their linguistic handicap. "Without English, we are perfectly useless in this country," Giuseppe Cataldo observed. "We old timers make even Indian kids laugh when we misuse English." The arrival at St. Ignatius Mission of a fresh recruit, a scholastic from France, caused even Italian-born Jerome D'Aste to raise his eyebrows: "He can scarcely talk English," the priest wrote, and yet "he comes to be prefect of the boys."[56]

Catholics and Citizens

As the government's emphasis on English mastery made clear, the missionary schools were responsible for transforming their Native American charges into good citizens. They also sought to make them good Catholics by teaching them catechism, the sacraments, and the liturgical life of the church. For pedagogical purposes, Jesuit schools had always employed holidays and staged festive celebrations, thus highlighting the meaning of a church festival or the values exemplified by the life of a saint. In their Indian missions, the great feast days of the liturgical year were celebrated with great pomp by the entire tribal community, which traveled to the mission from the four corners of the reservation.

Students joined in the grand processions that accompanied the celebration of Good Friday, Holy Thursday, Easter Sunday, Corpus Christi, Christmas, and Rogation Days. May, the month of the Blessed Virgin Mary, with its practical involvement and solemn processions, appealed to students and parents alike. At St. Ignatius Mission, May was inaugurated with an elaborate ceremony involving the entire tribe. "The children of the schools and the Indians betook themselves processionally with the banners of their respective sodalities to the church," recorded a missionary, "where a special altar with flowers has been erected in honor of the Blessed Virgin Mary, for the opening of the month of Mary." Students collected "spiritual blossoms," acts of virtue inscribed on small slips of paper, which they performed during the month in honor of the saint. Devotion to the Sacred Heart of Jesus was imparted to Cheyenne students by "granting a half-holiday on the first Friday [of every month] to convince the boys that it was a great day of the month."[57] The celebration at Sacred Heart Mission in DeSmet, Idaho, typified observance of the event. At midday the student body processed toward the church, stopping en route as a member of the sodality "read the flowers of virtues performed by the sodalists during the month" and sodality officers "read three beautiful discourses." The dramatic highlight of the ceremony was a ceremonial burning of the flowers and special letters, each containing a petition to the saint, while the Jesuit director of the sodality delivered a sermon.[58] In addition to elaborate liturgical ceremonies, Christmas was marked by the decoration of a Christmas tree, an appearance by Santa Claus, and presentation of gifts to the students.

Just as religious feast days advanced the Indians' spiritual assimilation, civic holidays—celebrated by governmental mandate—furthered their cultural and political integration. "Special attention is paid in government schools to the inculcation of patriotism," wrote Indian Commissioner Thomas J. Morgan. "The Indian pupils are taught they are Americans, that the government is their friend, that the flag is their flag, that the one great duty resting on them is loyalty to the government." On February 8, contract schools were obliged to observe Indian Citizenship Day, or Franchise Day, a holiday created especially for Indian schools to commemorate the enactment of the 1887 Dawes Act, which had mandated the end of the reservation system. This celebration encouraged Indians, writes historian David Wallace Adams, "to join the white man's march of progress" by embracing the values of private property and citizenship.[59] Thanksgiving was marked at St. Ignatius Mission by a "first class dinner in the refectory with the traditional turkeys," and with elaborate entertainment. Washington's Birthday prompted the printing of special programs proclaiming the day's events—the performances of plays, declamations; singing in boys school, girls school, and kindergarten. As at all civic and religious celebrations, a missionary noted, "the boys' band plays a few national airs during recreation."[60]

Missionaries encouraged academic achievement in their pupils through techniques that blended Jesuit and Native American customs. Superior performance and good behavior were fostered by emulation, competition, and the bestowal of awards—the same system employed by Jesuits in their colleges worldwide. These devices assumed greater importance in the training of Native American youngsters, however, because, as one priest explained, their tender years and culture rendered them "doubly children." "They need these things essentially," and "they must be kept interested all the time."[61]

The traditional Jesuit system of "monthly places," whereby grades and class standings were publicly announced at the end of every month, served to reward both academic performance and good conduct. Students at St. Ignatius receiving a grade of "very good" in at least one branch of studies and also in diligence were sent to the superior to receive special congratulations and the award of a "premium." As a means of engaging the local community in the educational process, tribal leaders as well as teachers evaluated students at semester's end. Thus Philip Turnell recorded that students at DeSmet Mission were formally interviewed in 1883 by a board of examiners composed of the faculty; Seltice, the head chief; and "a large number of the most prominent members of the tribe."

Student recreation integrated features drawn from both native and white worlds. The boys of DeSmet played the American game of baseball, but they also engaged in traditional sport. "A few apples are put up as a prize for the winners at marksmanship," a missionary reported. "Here they rush for the bows and arrows to gain the apple suspended by a string seventy-five feet distant. Without waiting for a command, a shower of arrows reach the object so accurately that at times no vestige of the apple remains."[62]

The closing exercises of the year often occurred on July 31, the Feast of St. Ignatius. The program included the traditional Jesuit end-of-the-year repertoire centering on student performance—recitations, songs, dialogues, speeches, skits, and musical interludes rendered by the boys' band. Commencement provided an occasion for promoting the school to the assembled tribal chiefs, parents, and dignitaries from the native and white communities. It also publically recognized superior student accomplishment. "Our boys had a nice entertainment," a missionary wrote at the conclusion of an annual exhibition at St. Ignatius Mission, "and premiums were given to them who distinguished themselves." Prizes awarded for superior performance were calculated to please students—bridles, whips, and spurs on some occasions; spoons, knives, and belts at other times.[63]

Notwithstanding the teachers' efforts to keep pupils content, many students reacted negatively to the boarding-school experience. Although parents might smile on education, youngsters were often less inclined to accept the confinement and pressure to conform that schooling demanded. Thus, in Jesuit schools, as in those run by Protestants and by the government, student discontent manifested itself in homesickness, withdrawal, fear, and rebellion. The unhappiness recorded by a former boarder at St. Paul's Mission typified the experience of many students during their first weeks at school. "I was not a very good mixer and sort of kept out of everybody's way," she recalled. "I did work well [but] was very secretive [and] kept much to myself, absolutely dominated by fear and loneliness." In his autobiographical novel, *The Surrounded*,

D'Arcy McNickle described returning to St. Ignatius Mission, where he had attended school as a boy:

> These visits to the church awakened old images that lay in the beginning of life. They were disturbing, half fearful.... One lived in the perpetual tyranny of the life-everlasting.... It was inexplicable, the dread which had been instilled into the mind of the child never quite disappeared from the mind of the grown man.[64]

Resistance to assimilation took many forms. In 1896, a fifteen-year-old boy, after nine days at school, torched the boys' dormitory, an offense for which he was jailed, tried, and convicted.[65] Obliged for the first time in their lives to mix with members of other tribes, some students experienced depression while others behaved aggressively toward classmates.

The most common sign of discontent was desertion, a phenomenon of student life at all Native American boarding schools. The location of missionary schools on reservations, while offering many advantages, enabled unhappy students to slip away with relative ease. "The Indian camps are quite near our convent," recorded a nun at St. Labre's, and "hence it is with difficulty that we keep our Indian children." The construction of a tribal dance house in the neighborhood of the school the following year increased the temptation to flee. The villagers "are making a constant use of it," a priest noted, "and as long as our larger children are hearing the drum, it is hard to prevent them from running away."[66] The practice of permitting students to return home for summer vacation also presented a disciplinary challenge when classes resumed in the fall. After a summer "in the woods," as one sister put it, "the freedom from control of two months is evident in their conduct. This obliged us to take the upper hand. A good part of the disciplinary work must be recommenced.... Their response to correction is not good."[67]

Native American evaluations of the boarding-school experience varied. Some were grateful for the time spent in school, reporting later "they were the happiest days of my life." "They took care of the children," one graduate recalled. "You had three good meals a day and a clean place to sleep." According to a Blackfoot chronicler, students who attended the schools of St. Peter's, Holy Family, and St. Ignatius Missions "provided the Blackfeet with intelligent leadership for this time period," which was "a great asset," particularly considering the level of Indian education at the time. The schools at St. Ignatius Mission contributed not a little to the high literacy rate among the Flathead. According to a report from the reservation agent in 1900, about one thousand natives out of a total reservation population of 1,621 were able to speak English. Some students appreciated the physical security that the schools provided, as during the disastrous winter of 1883–84, when hundreds of Blackfoot died of starvation. "The few children that managed to escape this catastrophe were students either at St. Peter's Mission or at St. Ignatius." However, the large number of students who ran away from school testified powerfully to the resentment that many felt toward the restrictions that were forced upon them by the assimilation process.[68]

End of an Era

The apex of achievement of the boarding schools occurred during the last two decades of the nineteenth century. Despite native resistance to aspects of the educational enterprise, enrollments reached their highest point during that period, prompting many white observers to heap praise on the institutions. In 1888, government inspector E. D. Bannister reported to the secretary of the interior that St. Ignatius Mission ran "the best equipped and the most intelligently conducted school in the Indian services.... The buildings are all spacious and commodious, including the printing office, tailor, shoe, tinsmith, harness, carpenter, and blacksmith shops, and all are in perfect sanitary condition." His tribute to Leopold Van Gorp, superior of the mission, was unstinting. The Jesuit's "culture and education" and his "remarkable administrative abilities, ... coupled with his thorough knowledge of the Indian character, make him the peer of any man engaged in educational work in the Indian services."[69]

The industrial schools' success, however, eventually became the cause of their undoing. Rapid expansion of the network of Catholic boarding institutions unleashed a backlash that finally ended government support of church-run schools. As historians Robert H. Keller Jr. and Francis Paul Prucha have demonstrated, aggressive promotion of their schools by Catholics, coupled with growing support for public education, eventually brought the contract system to a close. In the 1880s, when Catholics began receiving two-thirds of the government funds, Keller writes, it became apparent to many Protestants, who had enthusiastically supported church-state cooperation during the earlier years, that they "had to rethink their constitutional principles." The rise of the anti-Catholic American Protective Association intensified the interreligious conflict, transforming it into a national political issue. With the appointment of Thomas J. Morgan as commissioner of Indian Affairs in 1889, the battle over Indian schools began in earnest. No admirer of the Catholic Church, which he publicly attacked as "an alien transplant from the Tiber" that was "recruiting her ranks by myriads from the slums of Europe," Morgan condemned the church for its "Jesuitical cunning" in promoting its own schools and for being "un-American, unpatriotic, and a menace to our liberties." Under his direction the funding of church-operated schools for Native Americans was curtailed and by 1900 finally terminated.[70]

Although Catholic missionaries, led by the Bureau of Catholic Indian Missions, reacted by turning to private charities for support, the Jesuit educational network in the Northwest had been dealt a severe blow by the withdrawal of governmental assistance. Some institutions were closed; others, including the famous industrial school at St. Ignatius, Montana, never fully recovered. Whatever the future might hold for the schools, a Jesuit wrote in 1901, "for the finances of these schools we now depend entirely on Divine Providence."[71] In the years that followed, public schools increasingly replaced religious institutions as the educators of Native American children.

From a Jesuit viewpoint, the experiment in church-state cooperation in Native American education had been a mixed blessing. Federal funding had enabled the missionaries to school native children on a scale that would have been inconceivable in an earlier generation. The impressive educational advances made by many tribes was in large part attributable to the combined efforts of the Rocky Mountain Mission and the U.S. Indian Office. But accomplishment came at a price. "Our schools alienate the hearts of the Indians," reported Mission Superior George de la Motte in 1901.[72] The extensive herds of cattle, horses, and sheep—and the vast acreage developed by the missionaries to support their large educational establishments—provoked criticism not only from white farmers but also from Native Americans. After the removal of federal funds, the priests relied more than ever on farm income to sustain the schools, thus increasing disapproval by their Indian congregations. "The Flatheads of St. Ignatius Mission are becoming antagonistic toward us," Jesuits complained, "because our efforts appear focused only on making money."[73] For their part, the missionaries regretted that their time was consumed by administrative tasks and that running schools and farms left them no time for pastoral ministry to the tribes.

Thus some Jesuits welcomed the collapse of federal funding. "I see the hand of the Lord" in the withdrawal of government aid, missionary Giuseppe Damiani declared in letters to the Jesuit Father General. "We have deviated not a little from the example" set by the first Jesuit missionaries in caring primarily for the Indians' spiritual welfare. "It used to be that all of our attention centered on the conversion of the Indians, but now, it seems to me, that we are trying to do nothing but open schools for Indian boys and girls." The establishments had grown so large and so numerous, he observed disapprovingly, that "all the discipline and teaching has to be left in the hands of laypersons." Damiani questioned the effectiveness of the boarding schools. Education is "a good and beautiful thing for young people," the priest concluded, but among some tribes it "amounts for nothing because upon leaving they live just as their Indian parents do."[74] More than one missionary observed that many Native American students abandoned Christianity as soon as they left school.

With the end of the contract-school system, the future of the schools of the Rocky Mountain Mission became increasingly problematic. By 1907, the situation was so precarious that the Jesuit leadership assembled at St. Ignatius Mission for a special meeting to reexamine their commitment to Native American schooling. Having learned that BCIM could no longer be depended upon for financial help, the missionaries asked themselves if they should continue their educational ministry. After much soul-searching, they unanimously concluded that "the closing of the schools would mean the closing and ruin of the Indian missions." They then proposed a series of pedagogical and curricular reforms to "make our schools more efficient, attractive, and interesting." The costly program of industrial training, although still favored by a few of the missionaries, was discontinued. In order to balance accounts, the priests decided to admit more tuition-paying white students to their schools "so long as their parents consent to their being treated no better than our Indian pupils." They also determined to ask Native American parents to shoulder more of the cost of educating their offspring, especially to pay for their children's clothing, an expense hitherto covered by the schools. In hopes of making their institutions self-supporting, the Jesuits committed themselves to "improve the farms connected to the schools and thereby diminish the amount needed for the running of the schools."[75]

Despite these innovations, Mission Superior George de la Motte conceded two years later: "Our Indian missions are not flourishing." Schools were unable to cope with the increasing poverty and social disintegration suffered by the tribes due to reduction of their lands by rapacious whites and the U.S. government. The destruction of the reservation system and tribal organization by federal legislation, the ongoing financial crises of the schools, and a host of other challenges meant that the missions of the Northwest, like their antecedents in the eastern United States, were "destined to come to an end before much longer." Within twenty years, "we will no longer have Indian missions," de la Motte darkly predicted. "They will have become American parishes where everything will be done in English."[76]

The Jesuit's prophecy proved erroneous. Despite continual setbacks, including the loss of several schools to fire, the missionaries remained among the tribes, and they continued to run schools, although on a much more modest scale than before. But the institutions never again occupied the role they played in their nineteenth-century heyday, when church and state conspired to assimilate the Native Americans through the unique experiment known as the contract-school system. "Our present conditions are not quite as brilliant" as they once were, summarized a missionary at DeSmet Mission in 1912. Classrooms that had once been filled with students now housed a mere handful: "To date we have only about one dozen pupils."[77] The golden age of Jesuit schooling of Native Americans in the Northwest had ended. Although Indian education remained an activity of the Society of Jesus, the order's apostolate to the tribes increasingly focused on pastoral work, thus inaugurating another chapter in the long history of Jesuit ministry to native peoples of the American West.

Endnotes

1. Edward J. Power, *A History of Catholic Higher Education in the United States* (Milwaukee, Wis.: Bruce Publishing, 1958), 55, 77; Philip Gleason, "American Catholic Higher Education: A Historical Perspective," in *The Shape of Catholic Higher Education*, ed. Robert Hassenger (Chicago: University of Chicago, 1967), 33–34.

2. See Ross Alexander Enochs, *The Jesuit Mission to the Lakota Sioux: Pastoral Theology and Ministry, 1886–1945* (Kansas City, Mo.: Sheed & Ward, 1996).

3. Maria Ilma Raufer, *Black Robes and Indians on the Last Frontier: A Story of Heroism* (Milwaukee, Wis.: Bruce Publishing, 1966), 122.

4. "Mission des Montagnes Rocheuses de la Compagnie de Jesus, Anné 1897–98," Provincial Papers, Box 6, Oregon Province Archives of the Society of Jesus, Foley Center, Gonzaga University, Spokane, Washington (hereafter JOPA).

5. For a thorough study of this shift, see Robert H. Keller Jr., *American Protestantism and United States Indian Policy, 1869–82* (Lincoln, Neb.: University of Nebraska Press, 1883).

6. Joseph Joset (Spokane) to Ruellan, 13 February 13 1883, Ruellan Papers, JOPA; Joseph Joset (Spokane Bridge, Wash.) to Charles Ewing, 19 July 1876, Bureau of Catholic Indian Missions Records, 9/1, Marquette University Archives, Marquette University, Milwaukee, Wisconsin (hereafter BCIM).

7. Lorenzo B. Palladino, *Indian and White in the Northwest, A History of Catholicity in Montana* (Baltimore: John Murphy, 1894), 93; F. Digmann (Rosebud Agency, S. Dakota) to William H. Ketcham, 12 November 1902, BCIM 43/2.

8. Camillo Imoda (St. Peter's Mission, Mont.) to J. B. A. Brouillet, 21 June 1880, BCIM 11/4.

9. Guiseppe Giorda (St. Ignatius Mission) to G. B. Baroni, 28 January 1879, Turin Province Archives of the Society of Jesus, Turin, Italy (hereafter ATPSJ).

10. Joset (Spokane) to Charles Ewing, 19 July 1876, BCIM 9/1.

11. Joset (Spokane) to Charles Ewing, 19 July 1876, BCIM 9/1; Joseph Joset, "Old Mission Church," Joset Papers, JOPA.

12. Imoda (St. Peter's Mission, Mont.) to Brouillet, 5 January 1878, BCIM 11/4.

13. Giuseppe Cataldo (Lapwai) to Charles Ewing, 30 November 1875, BCIM 9/1.

14. John Fahey, *The Flathead Indians* (Norman, Okla.: University of Oklahoma Press, 1974), 119–120; Edmund Robinson, "History of St. Ignatius Mission," *Mission Valley News*, 1 July, 1976, St. Ignatius Collection, Centennial Album, JOPA.

15. Joset (Spokane) to Ruellan, 13 February 1883, Ruellan Papers, JOPA.

16. Palladino, *Indian and White*, 94.

17. Pietro Prando (St. Peter's Mission) to Giuseppe Cataldo, 28 July 1881, in *Woodstock Letters* 12 (1883): 37.

18. Joset (Spokane) to Charles Ewing, 19 July 1876, BCIM 9/1; Andrew Seltice, Petition to President of U.S., 28 July 1873, correspondence, BCIM; Giuseppe Cataldo (Fort Show, Mont.) to J. B. A. Brouillet, 3 June 1878, BCIM 12/1; Painted Red quoted in Robert Bigart and Clarence Woodcock, "St. Ignatius Mission, Montana: Reports from Two Jesuits Missionaries, 1885 and 1900–1901," *Arizona and the West* 23 (summer 1981): 156–57.

19. Keller, *American Protestantism and United States Indian Policy*, 2.

20. Francis Paul Prucha, *The Churches and the Indian Schools, 1888–1912* (Lincoln, Neb.: University of Nebraska, 1979), 1–2; Peter J. Rahill, *Catholic Indian Missions and Grant's Peace Policy, 1870–1884* (Washington, D.C.: Catholic University of America Press, 1953), 60.

21. Prucha, *Churches and Indian Schools*, 3–4, 6–8.

22. Robert Ignatius Burns, *Jesuits and the Indian Wars of the North-West* (New Haven, Conn.: Yale University Press, 1966), 56; Caruana (Colville Mission, Wash.) to R. Freddi, Italian Assistant, 9 April 1895, Mont. Sax. 1003-V-22, Roman Archives of the Society of Jesus (Archivum Romanum Societatis Iesu), Rome, Italy (hereafter ARSI); *Bureau of Catholic Indian Missions, 1874–1895* (Washington, D.C., 1895), 20–25, BCIM; Andrew F. Rolle, *The Immigrant Upraised: Italian Adventurers and Colonists in an Expanding America* (Norman, Okla.: University of Oklahoma Press, 1968), 197.

23. J. D. Bevier (Flathead Agency) to E. P. Smith, 14 July 1874, BCIM.

24. Lorenzo Palladino (St. Ignatius Mission) to J. B. A. Brouillet, 29 October 1873, BCIM.

25. Palladino, *Indian and White*, 242–43.

26. John Mullan (Washington, D.C.) to Lorenzo Palladino and Van Gorp, 11 April 1885; Lorenzo Palladino (St. Ignatius Mission) to John Mullan, 23 April 1885, BCIM 15/7.

27. *Report of the Commissioner of Indian Affairs for 1889,* 228; Markham, "St. Ignatius Mission," *Sacred Heart Messenger* (July 1892): 521–22, JOPA.

28. Carl Schurz quoted in David Wallace Adams, *Education for Extinction: American Indians and the Boarding School Experience, 1875–1928* (Lawrence, Kans.: University of Kansas Press, 1995), 30; Giuseppe Cataldo (Lewiston) to J. B. A. Brouillet, 13 January 1878, BCIM 12/1; Palladino, *Indian and White*, 94–95.

29. Leopold Van Gorp (St. Ignatius) to Charles Ewing, 13 November 1873, BCIM; Pietro Prando, "St. Xavier's Mission," 1887, Prando Papers, JOPA; Palladino, *Indian and White*, 103.

30. Thomas J. Morgan, "The Education of American Indians," *Proceedings of the Seventh Annual Meeting of the Lake Mohonk Conference of Friends of the Indian, 1889,* 22; Robert A. Trennert Jr., *The Phoenix Indian School: Forced Assimilation in Arizona, 1891–1935* (Norman, Okla.: University of Oklahoma, 1988), 7–8; Adams, *Education for Extinction*, 58–59.

31. Palladino, *Indian and White*, 83, 96–100, 147; Van Gorp (St. Ignatius) to Charles Ewing, 13 November 1873, BCIM.

32. Lorenzo Palladino (St. Ignatius Mission) to Charles Lusk, 3 July 1886, BCIM 17/9.

33. The agent's report is contained in *Report of the Commissioner of Indian Affairs for 1889,* 228; Prando, "St. Xavier's Mission," 1887, Prando Papers, JOPA.

34. "The Holy Family Mission School in the Blackfoot Reservation," Holy Family Mission Collection, n.d., JOPA.

35. Peter Ronan, "Report of the U.S. Indian Agent to the Hon. Commissioner of Indian Affairs [extract]," 1890, BCIM 27/8.

36. Andrew Seltice, Petition to President of the U.S., July 28, 1873, Correspondence, BCIM; Palladino, *Indian and White*, 151.

37. Celestin Tregret, *Seven Years Among the Western Indians,* (n.p., n.d.), 108–09, 118, JOPA.

38. Student recollections are found in Jackie Parsons, *Educational Movement of the Blackfeet Indians, 1840–1979* (Browning, Mont.: Blackfeet Heritage Program, Browning Public Schools, 1980), 9–10; T. J. Morgan

(Washington, D.C.) to J. Rebmann, 22 March 1892, St. Ignatius Mission Collection, outgoing correspondence, JOPA; Sr. M. Imela Hanratty, "I Remember (Recollections of St. Labre's Mission, Ashland, Montana, 1922)," St. Labre's Mission Collection, JOPA.

39. John Mullan (Washington, D.C.) to Bureau of Catholic Indian Missions, 2 December 1886, St. Regis Mission Collection, JOPA.

40. Stephen DeRouge, *Account of St. Mary's Mission, Omak, Washington* n.d., St. Mary's Mission Collection, JOPA.

41. P. Bandini (St. Francis Xavier Mission) to J. A. Stephan, 20 May 1890, BCIM 27/7; Giuseppe Cataldo (DeSmet, Ida.) to Father Willard, 24 April 1889, BCIM 23/1; Giuseppe Damiani (St. Paul's, Mont.) to Anderledy, 7 February 1891, Mont. Sax. 1003-IV-23, ARSI.

42. Palladino, *Indian and White*, 234–35.

43. Giuseppe Giorda (Attanam, W.T.) to Charles Ewing, 13 May 1874, BCIM; C. Imoda (St. Peter's Mission) to Brouillet, 5 January 1878, BCIM 11/4.

44. Note of unidentified Jesuit, on reverse of photograph #50 (Ursuline nuns and kindergarten students), St. Ignatius Mission Collection, photographs, JOPA.

45. P. Tosi (DeSmet Mission) to Brouillet, 5 December 1883, BCIM 9/1.

46. "A Few Facts concerning St. Xavier's Mission," c. 1895, BCIM 33/56.

47. Palladino, *Indian and White*, 93–94.

48. E. D. Bannister (Helena) to secretary of the interior, 22 October 1888, BCIM 21/19; Ronan's account is found in *Report of the Commissioner of Indian Affairs for 1886*, 180.

49. "DeSmet Indian School, DeSmet, Idaho," report, c. 1895, BCIM 33/48.

50. Ibid.; *Fruit of Her Hands; Sketches from the History of the Institute of Providence during the First Century of Its Existence, 1843–1943* (Montreal: 1943), JOPA; Sr. M. Amedee (DeSmet) to J. A. Stephan, 12 May 1890, BCIM 26/4.

51. It was estimated that by 1880, about fifty-five reservation Flatheads out of a population of roughly two hundred could read and write English. See Fahey, *The Flathead Indians*, 183, 224; *Bureau of Catholic Indian Missions School Report*, Holy Family Mission, Montana, 1909, BCIM.

52. The classroom use of both English and Flathead at St. Ignatius Mission, as observed by the Schurz delegation, is reported in a clipping

from *Allgemeinen Zeitung* (Munich, Germany), 1883 (number 287), copy and translation in St. Ignatian Mission Collection, JOPA; P. Bandini (St. Francis Xavier Mission) to J. A. Stephan, 20 March 1888, BCIM 21/19.

53. "DeSmet Diary, 1878–1939," JOPA; Thomas J. Morgan, "The Education of American Indians," *Proceedings of the Seventh Annual Meeting of the Lake Mohonk Conference of Friends of the Indian, 1889,* 27; Adams, *Education for Extinction,* 140; Jon Reyhner, ed., *Teaching American Indian Students* (Norman, Okla.: University of Oklahoma Press, 1992), 199.

54. Clipping from *Allgemeinen Zeitung* (Munich, Germany), 1883 (number 287), translation in St. Ignatian Mission Collection, JOPA; J. A. Stephan to Leopold Van Gorp, 13 February 1891, BCIM 30/10.

55. J. A. Simms (Colville Agency) to J. B. A. Brouillet, 16 November 1879, BCIM 12/4; J. B. A. Brouillet (Washington, D.C.) to J. A. Simms, 13 December 1879, BCIM 12/4.

56. Giuseppe Cataldo (DeSmet, Id.) to Fortunato Giudice, 3 January 1888 and 23 May 1888, ATPSJ; Jerome D'Aste, "Diary, 1903–04," entry for 7 September 1903, JOPA.

57. Tregret, *Seven Years,* 71, JOPA.

58. "House Diary, St. Ignatius Mission, 1895–1901," entry for 30 April 1898, JOPA; "Minute Book of the B.V.M. Sodality, 1884–1910," entries for 1884, Sacred Heart Mission Collection, JOPA.

59. *Report of the Commissioner of Indian Affairs for 1891,* 69; Adams, *Education for Extinction,* 196–99.

60. "House Diary, St. Ignatius Mission, 1895–1901," entries for 25 November 1897, and 22 February 1898, JOPA.

61. George de la Motte (St. Xavier) to Luis Martín, 19 January 1901, Mont. Sax. 1003-III-3, ARSI.

62. "Notes," St. Ignatius Mission, 1902, St. Ignatius Mission Collection, JOPA; Philip Turnell (DeSmet) to J. B. A. Brouillet, 21 December 1883, BCIM 9/1; "DeSmet Indian School, DeSmet, Idaho," report, c. 1895, BCIM 33/48.

63. "House Diary," St. Ignatius Mission, 1901–1902, entry for 22 June 1902, JOPA.

64. Student's recollections found in "Notes on Sister Josephine," n.p., n.d., Ursuline Collection, JOPA; D'Arcy McNickle, *The Surrounded* (Albuquerque, N.Mex.: University of New Mexico Press, 1978), 99–100, 106.

65. Fahey, *Flathead Indians,* 266.

66. Sr. St. Ignatius (St. Labre's) to J. A. Stephans, 8 January 1888, BCIM, 2 1/22; Van der Velden (St. Labre's) to Bureau of Catholic Indian Missions, 31 December 1889, BCIM 24/8.

67. Sr. St. Ignatius (St. Labre's) to J. A. Stephans, 8 January 1888, BCIM; "Chronicles of Convent of Mary Immaculate, DeSmet," JOPA.

68. See interviews with Mary Ground, Mary Little Bull, George Bremer, and James Little Dog in Parsons, *Educational Movement of Blackfeet,* 6–11. The report of the Flathead agent is quoted in Bigart and Woodcock, "St. Ignatius Mission," *Arizona and the West* 23 (autumn 1981): 272, n. 73.

69. E. D. Bannister (Helena) to secretary of the interior, 22 October 1888, BCIM 21/19.

70. Keller, *American Protestantism and U.S. Indian Policy,* 208–09. Morgan is quoted in Paul Prucha, *American Indian Policy in Crisis: Christian Reformers and the Indian, 1865–1900* (Norman, Okla.: University of Oklahoma Press, 1976), 305–09, 317–19.

71. Augustine Dimier (St. Ignatius Mission) to Father Provincial, April 1901, quoted in Bigart and Woodcock, "St. Ignatius Mission" *Arizona and the West,* 23 (autumn 1981): 277. See also Gerald McKevitt, S.J., "'The Jump That Saved the Rocky Mountain Mission': Jesuit Recruitment and the Pacific Northwest," *Pacific Historical Review* 55 (August 1986): 450.

72. George de la Motte (St. Xavier Mission) to Luís Martín, 19 January 1901, Mont. Sax. 1003-III-3, ARSI. Jesuits especially complained about superior Leopold Van Gorp of St. Ignatius Mission, e.g., L. Taelman (St. Ignatius Mission) to Luís Martín, 12 January 1906, Mont. Sax. 1003-VI-53, ARSI.

73. Pietro Prando (Holy Family Mission) to Luís Martín, 4 November 1897, Mont. Sax. 1003-V-49.

74. Giuseppe Damiani (St. Peter's Mission) to Anderledy, 14 January 1890, Mont. Sax. 1003-IV-18, ARSI; Giuseppe Damiani (St. Paul's, Mont.) to Anderledy, 7 February 1891, Mont. Sax. 1003-IV-23, ARSI.

75. "Minutes of the Consultation . . . St. Ignatius Mission, 9 and 10 Jan. 1907," St. Ignatius Collection, OPA; George de la Motte (Spokane) to W. H. Ketchum, 23 January 1907, BCIM 57/33.

76. George de la Motte (St. Francis Mission, Wash.) to Franz Wernz, 3 May 1909, Calif. 1005-I-10, ARSI.

77. John Post, "DeSmet Mission and School," report, 25 September 1912, BCIM 80/7.

The Just Development of Mind and Heart: Jesuit Education at the Turn of the Century in Milwaukee, Wisconsin

Michael W. Maher, S.J.

A NYONE WHO HAS TAKEN A SON OR A DAUGHTER TO college, brought a car to the repair shop, or stayed at a hotel has seen something called a "mission statement," whether it was in a brightly colored brochure, in a dusty frame over the cash register, or engraved on a plaque surrounded by potted palms. The mission statement attempts to convey to the consumer the goals of the institution as well as the means to fulfill them. Creating mission statements, statements of purpose, or codification of goals has become very popular in recent years, if not de rigueur. Few in academia have escaped participating in a committee to create or rewrite a mission statement for a department, a college, or an entire academic institution.

The current emphasis on mission statements may lead some to believe that they are something new, but successful institutions have actually been using them to good advantage for centuries. From the very beginning, the Society of Jesus clarified its identity for its present and future members, as well as for non-Jesuits, by creating a mission statement in its foundation document *The Formula of the Institute*.[1] The *Formula* was first composed in 1539 and, after several additions and changes, formally approved in 1550. It directed each Jesuit "to strive especially for the defense and propagation of the faith and for the progress of souls in Christian life and doctrine."[2] This direction remains the goal, "the mission," of the Society of Jesus today. How this goal has been fulfilled in individual circumstances is revealed in the lives of Jesuit saints, scholars, and martyrs, but also by thousands of Jesuits who served church and community in such humble tasks as correcting Latin quizzes on half sheets of paper.

The purpose of this essay is to explore one specific episode from the vast expanse of Jesuit history, one concrete example of how the Jesuits fulfilled their fundamental mission of advancing souls in "the progress of . . . Christian life and doctrine." This essay will examine a mission statement created one hundred years ago at Marquette College—the institution that became Marquette University—in Milwaukee, Wisconsin, and the means used to implement what the statement expressed. This essay does not purport to speak definitively on the ends or purpose of a "Jesuit education" and the best means to achieve them, but rather to contribute to the ongoing conversation among church hierarchy, laity, and the Society of Jesus about the purpose of Jesuit education and the possible means used to attain its stated goals.

The Mission Statement of 1901

In the *Formula of the Institute*, Ignatius of Loyola briefly identified the goal of the Society of Jesus, and then spent the remainder of the document explaining how this goal was to be implemented. This pattern of identifying the goal of the endeavor, then setting out the means to fulfill it was characteristic of documents composed by Ignatius. *The Spiritual Exercises* and the *Constitutions* also begin with clear statements of purpose followed by a presentation of the best means to achieve the goal proposed. The Jesuit fathers who ran Marquette College followed the same pattern in their 1900–01 catalog:

> Marquette College is under the sole and exclusive control of the Members of the Society of Jesus. As educators they aim to secure the gradual and just development of mind and heart. They recognize moral training as an essential element of education, and spare no efforts to form their young charges to habits of virtue, while offering them every facility and aid to the highest mental culture. It is their ambition to form men of deep thought, solid principles, virtuous habits, and sound religious convictions, without which they deem education little better than worthless.[3]

From this mission statement we can identify five topics that provide a framework for examining how Jesuits advanced their goal of the just development of mind and heart: (1) The Society of Jesus and its selection of education as one of its primary works, (2) the content of the courses within this education, (3) the proper order of these courses in relation to each other, (4) the overriding sense of direction based on religious values, and (5) the specific environment in which this education took place.

(1) The Society of Jesus and the Ministry of Education

When the Society of Jesus was officially formed in 1540, it did not envision itself as directing a vast network of schools. During the first years of the Society's existence, Jesuits identified and worked in projects of a more one-on-one nature. Individual Jesuits taught catechism in the streets, established refuges for prostitutes, and served the church by responding to particular needs as defined by popes or heads of state. But the Society of Jesus did not come to put ever greater emphasis on education by accident. Soon after the founding of the order, Jesuit leaders quickly recognized the importance of sound academic formation for its new members. Ignatius, well aware of problems caused by ignorant clergy, made sure that Jesuits in training received an education that went well beyond the standards for ordination at the time. At first, Jesuit academic formation was undertaken in houses located near major universities in such cities as Paris, Louvain, Padua, Coimbra, Alcalá, and Valencia.[4] These houses not only provided room and board but also included the presence of formed Jesuits, who could provide direction, encouragement, and probably some discipline. The success of these houses—or "colleges," as they were referred to in sixteenth-century Europe—became so well known that parents wanted to send their (non-Jesuit) sons to them to enjoy the benefits of Jesuit supervision. The school established in Gandiá, Spain, in 1546 broke with this pattern since there were no institutions of higher learning nearby. In Gandiá the Jesuits provided both supervision and teachers for the young Jesuits in formation, and soon parents desired that this education be made available to their sons. A year later the leaders of the city of Messina requested Jesuits to serve as teachers at a school that they would fund for the benefit of the city's youth. Such schools quickly multiplied.

Ignatius and other Jesuits soon realized that the work of education was admirably suited to carry out the primary goal of the order: "The progress of souls in Christian life and doctrine." According to the Jesuit *Constitutions*, the best ministries were those that influenced individuals who, by their improvement, would cause the improvement of others.[5] These *Constitutions* also noted the importance of ministries that continued longer as opposed to those works that were less durable, that is, that "gave help on a few occasions and only for a short while."[6] Such a ministerial goal made sense in light of the ever increasing population of Western Europe.[7] While Jesuits initially devoted themselves to works of mercy that did not require the purchase of buildings or entail institutional structure, within a few years the order was focusing its efforts on ministries of a "more lasting value," particularly schools. It is false to presume that Ignatius did not favor this transition or saw it somehow as a deviation from the Society's fundamental mission. One of the last sections amplified in the

Constitutions was part 4, the material that dealt with universities and colleges run by the Society. Thus the educational philosophy provided in this section embodies a lifetime of experience and an abundance of supernatural gifts. For Ignatius, the ministry of education was not just one apostolate among many; rather, it quickly became the principal means by which the order achieved its fundamental apostolic goals. When Ignatius died in 1556, there were thirty-three schools in operation, with others ready to begin. By the death of Superior General Claudio Acquaviva in 1615, there were ten times that number.

From these roots grew a vast network that gained the Jesuits the appellation "the schoolmasters of Europe." Many of the great achievements in philosophy, theology, science, and the arts in the early modern era grew directly from the Jesuit school system. The growth in the 1600s gave way in the 1700s to a more defensive position against the new philosophies and sciences that challenged the strong religious foundations of the Jesuit system of education. These new philosophies, and especially the politics that they supported, opposed the general worldview of the Jesuits. Bourbon monarchs motivated by agnostic philosophers and adventurous ministers of state sought to eradicate the Society of Jesus. Although the church officially suppressed the Society in 1773, the papacy must be considered more pawn than protagonist in this episode of Jesuit history. The battered Pope Clement XIV, who signed the bull of suppression, was as much a victim of the political currents that swirled around him as was the suppressed Society of Jesus. After the French Revolution, the leaders of Europe attributed the excesses of the Reign of Terror to an abandonment of religion and considered restoration of the Society of Jesus as an important ingredient in the return to a stabilized Europe.

Restoration of the Society in 1814 inaugurated a new phase in its history, particularly in North America. Prior to the suppression, the Society's work in North America had emphasized the evangelization of indigenous peoples. After restoration in 1814, however, Jesuits, in addition to working with indigenous peoples, responded to the frequent requests of bishops to staff churches and schools to meet the needs of immigrants. Such was the case when the first bishop of Milwaukee requested Jesuits to help him in his new diocese.

In the early 1800s, Milwaukee was a small trading post at the confluence of the three rivers that emptied into Lake Michigan. Within a few decades the small trading village had become the principal city in the new Wisconsin Territory. Opening the territory to farmers triggered a population boom, consisting primarily of Yankees from New York and Boston. But by midcentury, when the fertile fields of Wisconsin became more widely known on the East Coast and in Europe as well, a new wave of immigrants began to overwhelm the earlier settlers. Before railroads, Milwaukee's strategic lakeside location made it a natural focus for shipping, and it quickly became the principal commercial center of the new territory.

Interesting parallels can be drawn between the Jesuit experience in Milwaukee and that in Rome. First, both cities had a dramatic increase in population as Jesuit schools were being founded. Rome numbered about 45,000 people at the death of Ignatius in 1556. Fifty years later, the population had more than doubled to over 110,000. Milwaukee's population at the time of the 1870 census was 71,616. Forty years later in 1910 the census reported the city's population had reached 373,857.[8] Another similarity is that in both cities ecclesiastical authorities saw a need for better religious instruction, and in both places the Jesuits responded to the call.[9] In Rome it was Ignatius himself who initiated the educational apostolate. The Jesuits in Milwaukee, on the other hand, opened schools only after tremendous coaxing from the bishop. In both cases, however, fiscal support from the laity provided an important ingredient for success.[10]

Milwaukee quickly became a city of immigrants, so much so that according to the 1890 census it had more foreign-born residents than any other of the twenty-eight largest cities in the United States.[11] Many immigrants came to this country because they were poor; therefore, many were poorly educated, even illiterate. Many of these immigrants were Catholics, and the church now faced the challenge of maintaining the faith of its now much larger and far more diverse flock with few existing parishes and even fewer schools, often in the face of nativist and anti-Catholic opposition. Bishop John Martin Henni, the first bishop of the diocese (founded in 1843) desperately wanted Jesuits to come to Milwaukee and set up a school. While on a begging trip in Europe during the winter of 1848–49, Henni discussed starting a Jesuit school with the provincial of the Upper German Province, Fr. Anthony Minoux. Providence, Henni thought, might have dealt him an opportunity. The revolutions that consumed most of Europe in 1848–49 made it impossible for many Jesuits to continue their previous work there. Henni saw this crisis in Europe as a benefit for his own diocese and discussed with the German provincial the possibility of finding a new home for these recent exiles. But money was an obstacle, and Fr. Minoux noted that the Jesuits could barely support themselves in their native country, much less undertake new foundations in the United States. On his way back to the States, Henni convinced a merchant from Antwerp, Guillaume Joseph de Boey, to give his new diocese $16,000 for an educational institution. Armed with the promise of money and still eager to have a Jesuit school, Henni returned to his diocese and petitioned the Society of Jesus in the United States to send him Jesuits to staff a school. Two were sent: Fr. Frederick Hubner and Fr. Anton Anderledy. The fathers arrived in Milwaukee in August of 1849. Within ten days of their arrival, however, Fr. Hubner sickened and died, thus giving to the Society of Jesus the dubious distinction of having one of its members be the first priest to die in the diocese. Since Fr. Anderledy spoke no English, he was sent to Green Bay to learn the language. He was soon called back to Europe and eventually to Rome, where he became Superior General of the order in 1883, perhaps as a consolation for not being able to live in Milwaukee.[12]

When de Boey died in 1850, Bishop Henni received the $16,000 and renewed his quest for Jesuit educators. He turned again to the provincial of the Missouri Province, Fr. John Elet, a man who governed the vast territory embracing almost the entire Missouri-Mississippi valley. The provincial's authority may have extended over an enormous domain, but he had only a few men to serve the needs of both indigenous peoples and new immigrants who were pouring into the lands between the Rockies and the Appalachians. Besides, Bishop Henni was not the only one asking the provincial to send Jesuits, and it is not surprising that such requests were not warmly received. As a sign of his commitment, in 1856 Bishop Henni purchased a plot of land on a ridge that overlooked what was then Milwaukee's city limits.[13] This plot was to be the site of Marquette College, a name the bishop suggested in honor of the great Jesuit missionary and cartographer Jacques Marquette. But in 1857, when the Missouri provincial sent two Jesuits, instead of establishing a college on Henni's site, they worked at a church and school closer to the village center. The local newspaper heralded the event, stating that these two Jesuits "will teach all branches of a commercial, classical, scientific, and philosophical education. They [members of the Jesuit order] are the most renowned educators in the World."[14] This effort inaugurated Jesuit-directed education, but it did not mark the beginning of Marquette College. Years of economic turmoil after 1857 meant that Henni's dream of a Jesuit college had to wait. Eventually, with renewed prosperity in the 1870s, Jesuits established Marquette College on the bishop's land and admitted its first students on 6 September 1881.[15]

A few important points should be noted in this abbreviated sketch of Marquette's early history. First, although the Jesuits proclaimed in their 1900–01 catalog that "Marquette College is under the sole and exclusive control of the members of the Society of Jesus," they failed to recognize in this statement the indispensable role of non-Jesuits in the founding of the school. Pride of place must go to the Milwaukee's ordinary, Bishop Henni, who petitioned for the Society's presence in Milwaukee, did the initial fund-raising, and bought the land for the college. De Boey deserves much credit for his initial gift, but his name is strangely absent from any monument or building on the current Marquette University campus. The parcel of land his bequest financed was crucial to the founding of the school. The $27,000 cost of the building and all future expenses became the responsibility of the Society of Jesus. Marquette College opened its doors thanks to the laity, the church hierarchy, and the Society of Jesus—all of whom worked together to promote Catholic education in the city of Milwaukee. It was a team effort from the beginning.[16]

By 1901, Marquette College was instructing 230 students under the direction of twenty Jesuits. In addition to the Jesuit faculty, the school hired five lay faculty who taught "accessory branches" such as bookkeeping, stenography, business, and athletics. Marquette College was for men only, as were all other Jesuit schools at the time. Soon, however, things changed. Within the first decade of the twentieth century, laywomen and nuns began attending classes.[17] There were more important characteristics of a Jesuit education than the male environment, however, characteristics that Jesuits themselves identified in their mission statement.

(2) The Content of Jesuit Education

Marquette College accepted boys between the ages of eleven and thirteen, the age a young man would enter high school today. A young man desiring the benefits of a Jesuit education one hundred years ago had two choices: he could choose either the classical course or the commercial course. The Jesuits had their preference:

> The classical course is designed to impart a thorough liberal education. In the accomplishment of this purpose the Ancient Classics hold the first place as the most efficient instrument of mental discipline. Besides Latin, Greek, and English, the course embraces Religious Instruction, Mental and Moral Philosophy, Astronomy and Mathematics, History, Literature, the Natural Sciences—in a word, all the usual branches of a complete education. It has been found by long experience that this is the only course that fully develops all the faculties, forms a correct taste, teaches the student how to use all his powers to the best advantage, and prepares him to excel in any pursuit, whether professional or commercial.[18]

The second track, referred to as the "commercial," was for those who did not "wish to avail themselves of a regular classical training," but instead to prepare for "commercial pursuits." Those who took this four-year program graduated with a certificate, not a degree. Space does not allow us to examine the commercial track here since our concern is the traditional Jesuit degree program. Such professional preparation did, however, play an important role in Jesuit education, especially after the 1950s.

The classical course had two phases: the *academic*, for those of the age of today's high school students; and the *collegiate*, for college age students. A student taking the classical course would enter into *third academic*, then *second*, and finally progress to *first academic*—the reverse of contemporary numeration. Another important difference from mainstream contemporary custom was class attendance on Saturdays, with Thursdays off. The fathers defended this European practice by claiming that Thursday afforded a more "natural break in the routine of study" and "enabled the students to come fresher to their tasks."[19] (Chart 1 provides the weekly schedule of classes.)

A quick glance at this chart reveals the absence of some subjects ordinarily included in the high school curriculum of the time. For the purposes of brevity, English was the catchall title for such disciplines as history, geography, elocution, and penmanship. The catalog provided summaries of the content offered in each of these classes. One example must suffice. The third academic English course presented the material in the following sequence: precepts, models, and practice. In precepts, the young man "learned the elements of composition: Words, Sentences, Punctuation, Figures, Epistolary Composition." After the instructor instilled the basics of grammar, the students examined models of good writing, such as Washington Irving's "Rip Van Winkle" and "The Legend of Sleepy Hollow"; Oliver Goldsmith's poem *The Deserted Village;* "easier selections" from Longfellow; and "choice selections from Catholic authors." Skills acquired in the study of precepts and models were put into practice in the next stage, where the students tried to imitate the styles of the authors they had read and then attempted their own original exercises. The content of other courses was specified just as precisely. In Latin, Cicero reigned, and students used the series composed by Thomas Kerchever Arnold as their guide.[20] In religion, Deharbe's *Catechism* was the book of choice.[21]

The course content embodied two important means toward the goals described in the 1900–01 catalog. The first means attempted to combine study of the classical authors of Greek and Latin antiquity and respected contemporary authors with development of skill in communicating—in elegant speech and clear composition—the ideas espoused by these authors. In striving to fulfill these goals, Jesuits of the early 1900s continued the pedagogical tradition of humanism, a tradition that stressed both awareness of the human condition as described by classical authors and a student's ability to communicate these thoughts effectively in speech and writing. This dual goal was a modern recapitulation of the ideas of Leonardo Bruni (1369–1444) whose *On Studies and Letters* argued for a balance between proficiency in literary form and firm acquisition of the facts.[22] The Jesuits considered the classics "branches of study absolutely necessary in any scheme of liberal education. Without a knowledge of these no man can be called educated."[23]

The second means toward the mission of Marquette College was training students for the needs of society. For some educators, training a young man to be an effective citizen was primary. Not so for the Jesuits. A cursory reading of the catechisms used by Marquette College in 1901 demonstrates the fidelity to the concept articulated by Ignatius in the First Principle and Foundation of his *Spiritual Exercises*.[24] In this Foundation, actions and things are identified as means toward attaining one's eternal salvation, never a terminus of human existence in themselves. This same idea was echoed in the Jesuit-authored catechisms used at Marquette College. According to these catechisms, one's profession should be skillfully performed; the profession itself was not the person's ultimate goal, but simply the means by which a person acted out his salvation.[25] In order to provide their students with the skills they would need to best perform their appointed tasks in life, Jesuits introduced into the curriculum content that reflected the needs of the times. Of course, they taught these skills in the light of instructing the students on the most important point of their existence, that is, achieving union with God.

At the turn of the twentieth century, Milwaukee witnessed a growth in commerce. A year later, in 1902, the college catalog gave a detailed description of its response to this growth. By providing its students with

> a working knowledge of the natural sciences, of physics and chemistry; a fair acquaintance with surveying and astronomy; a systematic training in mathematics . . . an acquaintance with sociology, political science and economic laws, it finds place for the rules of harmony, it unfolds the constitution of the United States and the principles underlying a popular form of government.[26]

Of course Jesuit schools were not the only educational institutions in the United States. Other schools, private and public, were frequently the laboratories for the new philosophies of education. Among these new philosophies, one that was finding greater acceptance in the better schools was the idea that students could choose electives and form their own curriculum. This popular theory was "proven" by Edward Thorndike in the early 1920s when he demonstrated that the development of intelligence was not contingent upon *what* was studied; rather, development depended on the baseline intelligence of the child. Briefly, Thorndike argued that "good thinkers" would develop at the same pace whether they took Greek or physical education.[27] John Dewey (1859–1952) was particularly insistent that courses should stress "lived experience" and not subject matter outside the more immediate experience of the child.[28] These theories made little headway at Marquette in 1901.[29] Since the Jesuits had the reputation of being the "most renowned educators in the world" (as the local newspaper had itself testified), they firmly believed that they knew what was best for their charges, not the other way around. Taking a stand against contemporary trends, particularly those that allowed students to choose their own courses, the Jesuits held that "young scholars are not proper judges of the studies essential for success in life" and "selection of studies should be permitted to none but those whose own minds have already been formed by the studies essential to character building and who have themselves practically determined upon their own life work."[30]

(3) The Order of Classes

Jesuit educators were as decisive about the proper order of classes as they were about the content of these classes. They could not, however, claim the merits of good order in education as their own theory. This idea first emerged in the West in classical Greece and was later transplanted to classical Rome, where it flourished—especially with the codification of Quintilian (A.D. 35–c. 100). Although the High Middle Ages witnessed an interest in classical pedagogy, the reemergence of classical texts—especially the complete version of Quintilian's *Institutione Oratoria*—reinvigorated interest in education's classical roots.[31] With the rebirth of classical education during the fifteenth and sixteenth centuries, great pedagogues of the Renaissance such as Pietro Paolo Vergerio (1370–1444) and Vittorino de Feltre (1378–1446) added substantially to the educational theory first developed during the classical period. Ignatius of Loyola received his master of philosophy degree at the University of Paris, the locus of the "method of Paris" system of education influenced by humanistic studies and the emphasis on a well-ordered presentation of the liberal arts, philosophy, and theology.[32] Ignatius insisted on this well-ordered accession of knowledge for Jesuit studies.[33] Systemizing the curriculum for Jesuit schools was a long process begun as a conversation when the first schools were being formed and continued until the promulgation in 1599 of the definitive plan of studies known as the *Ratio Studiorum*.[34] Soon after 1599, adaptations began to be made, and the conversation concerning curriculum in Jesuit education still continues.

The well-ordered classical curriculum may require further elaboration for the modern reader. For example, a young man in fifteenth-century Florence (and here again we note that education for the most part was restricted to men) began his education with the *trivium*. The three studies consisted of grammar, logic, and rhetoric, respectively. The order here is important. Grammar initiated the program of studies with its emphasis on the correct formation of individual sentences, logic instructed the pupil on the correct ordering of these sentences so as to present a cohesive idea, and rhetoric taught a student how to assemble these ideas in a focused manner. Both the material being studied and the order in which it was studied were equally important. This idea of good order was instilled into the minds of the students from the very beginning. In the study of grammar a student first learned that sentences required proper syntax. Syntax comes from the Greek word *syntassein*, referring to the orderly arrangement of a military division. Words within sentences and soldiers within a division could not be situated randomly lest chaos ensue. This idea of *syntassein* permeated classical and renaissance pedagogy and was a vital principle of the *Ratio Studiorum* of 1599 as well.

Good syntax was a crucial part of the educational endeavor at Marquette College in the early 1900s. This proper ordering of the classes was equally present in the next phase of education, the collegiate level. At the turn of the century, the entire eight-year experience of syntax was known as the college program. Chart 2 identifies the courses taken at the collegiate level. This four-year series of courses continued the idea of syntax, or proper ordering of the classes, so cherished by classical educators and Ignatius. This phase continued the syntax established by the academic class (the first four years covering the *trivium*) by including studies particular to *quadrivium* and then a continuation of studies into philosophy and religion.

The *quadrivium* was the study of mathematics, geometry, music, and astronomy. Like its predecessor, this unit of disciplines followed a specific order. In the classical understanding of the *quadrivium*, mathematics was the first subject studied: the examination of numbers and basic rules of number theory. Next was geometry, the study of numbers in three dimensions and their relation to spatial objects. Note here the analogy between the disciplines in the *trivium* and those in the *quadrivium*: grammar is to logic as mathematics is to geometry. Both grammar and mathematics are "one-dimensional"—or linear, so to speak—while the logical syllogism, like geometry, has extension. The next subject studied was music, and while its connection to geometry may be a bit of a stretch for us today, it was not so for someone of Ignatius's time. For a student of that era, music, especially the music of the sixteenth century, represented order, the following of basic rules. Just as a building was considered harmonious when it followed architectural principles based on the geometric principles of Euclid and then applied by Vitriuvius, good music was considered the extension of geometry into the realm of sound. This concept of harmony may seem difficult for us to understand today, especially if we are accustomed to the music of Igor Stravinsky or Philip Glass, whose music has broken with traditional Western harmonies.

The next discipline in the *quadrivium* was astronomy. Again the transition from music to astronomy may not be self-evident to the modern scholar. At this point we must look at the world, not through the model of modern Einsteinian relativity, but rather as presented by the Greek cartographer and astronomer Ptolemy (d. A.D. 150). In this system the planets and earth moved around the earth in perfect order, an order analogous to the order of good music and good rhetoric. The planets moved in harmony, that is, a proper order, and it was the teacher's task to reveal this order to his students. Astronomy was the furthest extension of this order in the natural world, a study of the order that began with the examination of an individual sentence and ended with the cosmos. Modern science has dispensed with the notion of the music of the spheres, but this same science has not abandoned the idea of the orderly progression of disciplines. Contemporary evidence of this orderly curricular progression can be seen in medical school, where specific courses are taken in series and few if any electives are allowed.

A student who attended Marquette College at the turn of the last century took courses that were particular to the *trivium* and the *quadrivium* (with adaptations to modern science) in their proper sequence during the first four years of the academy and then in the first years of the collegiate phase. The program of studies continued in the collegiate phase with courses in higher mathematics and the hard sciences, such as geology, after which the student was introduced to philosophy. In philosophy the student went beyond the investigation of the physical world to what could be known by natural reason concerning the student's obligations to himself, to his society, and to God. The object of this last year was to "form the mind to habits of correct reasoning, and, as the crowning perfection of the Whole Course of Instruction, to import sound principles of mental and moral philosophy."[35] This philosophical outlook began the first day a student started declining Latin nouns. He was presented with a sense of order, an order that permeated his course of studies and had as its terminus the truths of revealed religion taught in courses on Christian doctrine. Christian doctrine was not a single course taken at the end of the student's career nor was it considered one of many courses. Christian doctrine permeated the entire curriculum, serving as both foundation and focus of the course of studies begun in the first year of studies and continuing through the eight-year program.[36]

(4) Direction in a Jesuit Education

The seven disciplines had an internal cohesion, or order, but religion provided the direction and definitive trajectory of these studies. Jesuits considered the educational endeavor "a drawing out rather than a putting in; it is the cultivation of the ability to gain knowledge and use facts, rather than the actual imparting of information."[37] The Jesuits took seriously the etymology of the word *educate*, a derivative of the Latin verb *educare*, used to indicate the action of pulling or drawing out something that was already there, not putting in something that was absent. Jesuits taught facts, but the ultimate truths of human existence had greater priority. These truths had as their basis the immortality of the soul, whose supernatural end was union with God. Natural reason, especially as systematized by Thomas Aquinas, revealed the inherent truths of the human condition, a condition supported by the study of good literature. Moving a student toward an awareness of his supernatural end was the primary purpose of education, and in this movement Jesuits "drew out," or educated, him toward this awareness of what they considered innate knowledge. For this reason, Jesuits considered the classical course superior to the commercial one. In the classical course Jesuits used the humanities, the auxiliary courses, and philosophy to "draw out" of their students an awareness of their supernatural purpose, a purpose fully revealed in the classes of religion. The commercial course, on the other hand, was more a "putting in" than a "drawing out." Although the commercial course lacked much of the humanistic content of the classical course, it did entail religious instruction every semester. The Jesuits held that "religion should not be divorced from education; that morality is impossible without religion, and that it is far more important than knowledge for the welfare of the individual and the safety of society. The commonwealth needs good men more than it needs clever men."[38]

The commercial course included the terminus of the classical course, Christian doctrine, but without its academic underpinnings. The method of presenting religion as a course versus as the culmination of an academic effort was better than nothing, but the Jesuits' opinion of such a course of studies was made clear when they granted a certificate, not a degree, to students of the commercial course. These high ideals for religious education were not offered as a theoretical balm to some hypothetical problem. In 1903, there were seventy grand-jury indictments against aldermen and supervisors in the city of Milwaukee.[39] Anyone reading the Marquette catalog, with its emphasis on the necessity of good morals, knew that Jesuits were commenting on the state of humanity in general and offering advice to the city of Milwaukee in particular. Bishop Henni's purchase of a hilltop property for Marquette College was intended to give his city a moral beacon, not just another institution of learning.

Jesuit concern for moral development transcended the shores of Lake Michigan. In 1901, the same year that the catalog was published, another work saw the light of day. This was the English translation of Ernst Haeckel's *The Riddle of the Universe*.

Haeckel's opinions about the relationship between God and his creation directly contradicted the Jesuit view articulated in the 1901 catalog:

> The anthropomorphic notion of a deliberate architect and ruler of the world has gone forever from this field [science]; the "eternal, iron laws of nature" have taken his place. . . . Throughout the whole of astronomy, geology, physics, and chemistry there is no question today of a "moral order," or a personal god, whose "hand hath disposed all things in wisdom and understanding."[40]

Haeckel was not merely expressing an opinion; he was declaring an intellectual war against the idea of a providential God. The vision of a God who "over the bent / world broods with warm breast and with ah! Bright wings," as poetically described by Gerard Manley Hopkins in his poem "God's Grandeur," was soundly ridiculed by Haeckel.[41] His popular text gave ample ammunition to those who wished to jettison from academia any reference to God or disciplines that would lead to that knowledge, particularly "that dead learning which has come down from the cloistral schools of the Middle Ages. In the front rank we have grammatical gymnastics and an immense waste of time over a 'thorough knowledge' of classics and of the history of foreign nations."[42]

The Jesuits considered these opinions a challenge and, as they had done in the past, rose to the occasion and fought back as best they could. They used the tried-and-true means for which the church had turned to them in the past and for which Bishop Henni had turned to them in mid-nineteenth-century Milwaukee—they established schools. In order to "secure the just development of mind and heart," the Jesuits included content in their classes that embraced the innovations of modern science but set these against the full range of human experience as told by the classics. The content of these courses was well-ordered, as were the courses themselves, each in relation to others and each building on material learned in the previous class. This pattern was based on the classical progression established by the *trivium* and the *quadrivium*, which culminated in a philosophical and theological inquiry into the purpose and goal of human existence: union with God. The inquiry into the human person's relationship occurred in the classroom but was supported by extracurricular activities as well. These occurred within the greater environment of Jesuit education at Marquette College at the turn of the century.

(5) The Environment of the Educational Endeavor

Within the experience of the Spiritual Exercises, Ignatius asks the retreatant to examine the setting in which the salvation of the human race takes place. Jesuits have always been conscious of integrating their fundamental mission within specific cultural contexts. Although the extent to which Jesuit missionaries have adapted to foreign cultures has been debated, most historians credit the Jesuits with a greater sensitivity to surrounding culture than European merchants and government officials. In 1901, the Jesuits conducted their educational effort in an environment that transcended the confines of their single-classroom building and included extracurricular activities of interest to both their students and the community. At this time, Marquette College did not accept boarders, but it did supply its students with an environment that complemented classroom learning. Although the term was not used a century ago, these activities became what is now known as student life. These activities included various associations as well as contests and pageants that supported the goals of the institution.

There were two types of associations for students: those of a more religious nature and those that reinforced academic life.[43] Religious activities included participation in the Sodality of the Blessed Virgin, the Apostleship of Prayer, and the St. John Berchmans Acolythical Society. Each of these provided its members with the means to promote their spiritual welfare. The more academic societies supported the humanities. Good reading was fostered by participation in the Marquette Literary Society and Students' Library Association. Debating societies helped hone the rhetorical skills of students and were made available to the two language groups of Milwaukee, a city that had been dubbed the

"German Athens." The performing arts had their clubs, specifically the Marquette Mandolin Club and the Glee Club. Athletics had its own club as well. The debating, dramatic, and rhetorical societies frequently sponsored events or programs—entertainment for students, faculty, and parents—that demonstrated skill and provided the urban population with wholesome diversion. Besides plays, students of rhetoric competed in oratorical contests, and prizes in the form of medals were awarded for best in the class and best in subject matter. These prizes hearken back to a venerable Jesuit tradition known as Prize Day. The 1599 *Ratio Studiorum* allowed for such events and encouraged them as a means of promoting "holy rivalry" among the students so that they would strive for even greater academic heights. Sometimes Marquette students competed in contests that extended to other schools in the Missouri Province, and no doubt school pride induced no little fervor.[44] The plays presented at Marquette College also could trace their roots to the dramas that were performed on the stages of the Jesuit schools in the seventeenth century. Though they continued a great Jesuit tradition, the dramas offered at Marquette or any other contemporary Jesuit school would have been a mere shadow—and a weak one—of those vast spectaculars that were the talk of Rome and Vienna in the seventeenth century.[45] Whether on the stage or at a contest of oratory, the fundamental direction identified by "sound religious convictions" was never ignored.

Conclusion

The educational mission of the Society of Jesus articulated in the 1901 catalog of Marquette College echoed the first mission statement established by Ignatius: "For the defense and propagation of the faith and for the progress of souls in Christian life and doctrine." In order to achieve this mission, the Jesuits depended upon both the laity and the church. Thanks to these groups the Jesuits were able to implement their curriculum at Marquette designed with a specific content, order, and direction as well as an environment in which extracurricular activity both advanced and supported the material learned in the classroom. At the same time that Jesuits at Marquette were promoting their own educational theories, which were firmly rooted in classical antiquity, other educators, such as Ernst Haeckel, were attempting to eradicate the classical past. Although some pedagogues disparaged the efficacy of classical languages and methods that developed from that tradition, the Jesuits presented Milwaukee and the world with an alternative. A year later, in another catalog, these same Jesuits even admitted to the apparent lack of utility of some of their offered courses: "All the studies pursued need not be directly useful [after graduation]; the scaffolding may be discarded when the edifice is completed."[46]

Today we may ask whether the methods employed one hundred years ago—methods that included a "thorough knowledge" of the classics or "dead learning from the Middle Ages"—have anything to offer to the modern academic venture. Recent authors seem to defend the position firmly held by the Jesuits a century ago, arguing that excising classical thought from the curriculum disables the whole academic endeavor.[47] Jesuits a century ago believed that the scaffolding of the classics was the best way to build the edifice of their fundamental mission. The Jesuits presumed (perhaps from experience) that years after graduating from Marquette College, a gentleman may have forgotten his Greek, but he would not have forgotten that just as there was an order to Greek syntax so too was there a moral order given by God. The scaffolding of this education did, in fact, come down. But thanks to the nature of the scaffolding, the building remained sound. For those Jesuits a century ago, progress toward union with God—what was then considered the ultimate goal of a Jesuit education—occurred by grasping the essential truths of the past, along with the innovations of the present, firmly grounded in the truths of the Catholic faith. It was by these means that the Jesuits worked toward a specific articulation of their fundamental mission: the just development of mind and heart.

Chart I
Academic Classes

TIME	DAY	1ST ACADEMIC	2ND ACADEMIC	3RD ACADEMIC
8:00–8:30	Mon. Tues. Wed. Fri. Sat.	Stenography (optional)	(no class)	(no class)
9:00–10:00	Mon. Tues. Wed. Fri. Sat.	Latin	Latin	Latin
10:15–11:50	Mon. Tues. Wed. Fri. Sat.	Bookkeeping	(no class)	(no class)
1:10–1:40	Mon. Tues. Wed. Fri. Sat.	Christian Doctrine (Mon., Tues., Wed.) French or German	Christian Doctrine (Mon., Tues., Wed.) French or German	Christian Doctrine (Mon., Tues., Wed.) French or German
1:40–2:30	Mon. Tues. Wed. Fri. Sat.	English	English	English
2:40–3:30	Mon. Tues. Wed. Fri. Sat.	Algebra	Arithmetic	Arithmetic
3:30–4:30	Tues. Fri.	English Debating Society or German Debating Society		

Chart II
Collegiate Classes

TIME	DAY	PHILOSOPHY	RHETORIC	POETRY	HUMANITIES
8:00–8:30	Mon. Tues. Wed. Fri. Sat.	Stenography (optional)	Stenography (optional)	Stenography (optional)	Stenography (optional)
9:00–10:00	Mon. Tues. Wed. Fri. Sat.	Calculus (1st Term) Astronomy (2nd Term)	Latin	Latin	Latin
10:15–11:00	Mon. Tues. Wed. Fri. Sat.	Rational Philosophy (10:15–11:15)	Greek	Greek	Greek
11:00–11:50	Mon. Tues. Wed. Fri. Sat.		Physics Chemistry	Physics Chemistry	Bookkeeping
1:00–1:40	Mon. Tues. Wed. Fri. Sat.	Christian Doctrine (Tues., Sat.) French or German (Mon., Wed., Fri.)	Christian Doctrine (Tues., Sat.) French or German (Mon., Wed., Fri.)	Christian Doctrine (Tues., Sat.) French or German (Mon., Wed., Fri.)	Christian Doctrine (Tues., Sat.) French or German (Mon., Wed., Fri.)
1:40–2:30	Mon. Tues. Wed. Fri. Sat.	Rational Philosophy	English	English	English
2:40–3:30	Mon. Tues. Wed. Fri. Sat.	Geology (1st Term) Mechanics (2nd Term) Elocution (Saturday)	Higher Algebra (1st Term) Analytical Geometry (2nd term) Elocution (Saturday)	Trigonometry (1st Term) Surveying (2nd Term) Elocution (Saturday)	Geometry Elocution (Saturday)
3:30–4:30	Tues. Fri.	German Debating Society or English Debating Society			

Endnotes

1. The *Formula of the Institute* may be found in St. Ignatius of Loyola, *The Constitutions of the Society of Jesus,* trans. George E. Ganss, S.J. (St. Louis, Mo.: The Institute of Jesuit Sources, 1984), 66–72. Hereafter the *Formula of the Institute* will be cited as *Formula* and citations taken from the *Constitutions* as *ConsSJ*. Standard text enumeration will be given [in square brackets], and the page where the citation is found will be given in each note. For a synoptic reading and commentary of the 1539 *Formula* and the final version approved in 1550 (the version provided in the Ganss translation), see Antonio Aldama, *The Formula of the Institute: Notes for a Commentary* (St. Louis, Mo.: The Institute of Jesuit Sources, 1990).

2. *Formula,* 66, [1].

3. Marquette University Archives (hereafter abbreviated as MUA), Box A-6.2: 1900–1901 Marquette College Catalogue, 8 (hereafter abbreviated as 1900 Catalog).

4. George Ganss, *Saint Ignatius' Idea of a Jesuit University* (Milwaukee, Wis.: 1954), 20. Hereafter abbreviated as Ganss, *Jesuit University.*

5. *ConsSJ,* 275, [622, e].

6. *ConsSJ,* 276, [623, g].

7. For a general survey of European demography in the early modern period, see Jan de Vries, "Population," in *The Handbook of European History,* vol. 1, edited by Thomas Brady, Heiko Oberman, and James Tracy (Grand Rapids, Mich.: 1994), 1–50. For material specific to Italy and Rome, see A. Bellettini, "La popolazione italiana dall'inizio dell'era volgare ai giorni nostri. Valutazioni e tendenze," in *Storia d'Italia,* 5: I *I Documenti* (Turin: 1973), 509–21; C. M. Cipolla, "Four Centuries of Italian Demographic Development," in *Population in History,* eds. David Glass and D. E. C. Eversley (London: 1965), 570–87 and Jan de Vries, *European Urbanization* (Cambridge: 1984).

8. Bayrd Still, *Milwaukee: The History of a City* (Madison, Wis.: 1965), 570–71.

9. In preparation for calling a general council of the church Pope Paul III (1534–49) created a select committee of cardinals and other leaders to identify those areas that needed greatest reform. The document that issued from this committee, "The Proposal of a Select Committee of Cardinals and Other Prelates concerning the Reform of the Church, Written and Presented by Order of His Holiness Pope Paul III (1537)," specifically identified the need for greater care in providing good teachers

and especially good instruction for those studying for the priesthood. For a translation and commentary of this and other important documents, see *Reform Thought in Sixteenth Century Italy*, ed. Elisabeth G. Gleason (Ann Arbor, Mich.: 1981), 81–100.

10. This essay mentions the contributions given to help create Marquette College. For the important part played by donors—particularly women— to the Roman College, see Carolyne Valone, "Piety and Patronage: Women and the Early Jesuits," in *Creative Women in Medieval and Early Modern Italy: A Religious and Artistic Renaissance*, ed. E. Ann Matter and John Coakley (Philadelphia: 1994), 157–184.

11. Still, *Milwaukee*, 257.

12. Raphael Hamilton, *The Story of Marquette* (Milwaukee, Wis.: 1953), 5.

13. For a good study of the relationship between city life and the placement of Jesuit institutions in both Europe and America, see Thomas M. Lucas, *Landmarking: City, Church and Jesuit Urban Strategy* (Chicago: 1997).

14. *Milwaukee Sentinel*, 26 August 1857. Quoted in Hamilton, *Marquette*, 9.

15. Hamilton, *Marquette*, 9.

16. Ibid., 17

17. Ibid., 125.

18. 1900 Catalog, 8.

19. Ibid., 11.

20. The following texts were used for the study of Latin by Thomas Kerchever Arnold, *A Practical Introduction to Latin Prose Composition* (London: 1894) and *Select Orations of Cicero* (London: 1866). Arnold edited other texts and sources that were popular for the study of the classical languages.

21. *Large Catechism* (New York: 1882).

22. For a translation of Bruni's work consult William Harrison Woodward, *Vittorino da Feltre and Other Humanist Educators* (Cambridge: 1921), 119–33.

23. MUA, Box A-6.2: 1901–1902 Catalog, 9 (hereafter 1901 Catalog).

24. The 1900 Catalog mentions two specific catechisms: Deharbe's *Large Catechism* and Wilhelm Wilmer's *Handbook of the Christian Religion* (New York: 1891). The first line of Wilmer's catechism states that "Religion implies man's union with God." This echoes Ignatius's First Principle and Foundation given in his *Spiritual Exercises:* "Human beings are created to praise, reverence, and to serve God our Lord and by this means to save their

souls" (Ignatius Loyola, *Spiritual Exercises and Selected Works*, ed. and trans. George Ganss [Saint Louis, Mo.: The Institute of Jesuit Sources, 1991], 130). The *Constitutions* reiterates this same idea concerning the human person's supernatural end: The Society of Jesus "is directly ordered to dispose souls to gain their ultimate end from the hand of God our Creator and Lord" *(ConsSJ,* 129, [156]).

25. Wilmer, "Christian duties towards ourselves and our neighbors," *Handbook,* 464–80.

26. 1902 Catalog, 12.

27. Edward Thorndike, "Mental Discipline in High School Studies," *Journal of Educational Psychology* 15 (January 1924): 1–22.

28. John Dewey, *The Child and the Curriculum* (Chicago: 1902), particularly 11–12, 19–27, 30–32.

29. Concerning the state of public education at the turn of the century consult Daniel Tanner and Laurel Tanner, *Curriculum Development: Theory into Practice,* 3rd ed. (Englewood Cliffs, N.J.: 1995), particularly chaps. 1–3.

30. 1901 Catalog, 9.

31. *The Institutione Oratoria of Quintilian,* trans. H. E. Butler (New York: 1921).

32. Gabriel Codina Mir, *Aux sources de la pédagogie des Jésuites: le "modus parisiensis"* (Rome: 1968).

33. *ConsSJ,* 191, [366].

34. For a translation of the *Ratio,* see Edward A. Fitzpatrick, *St. Ignatius and the Ratio Studiorum* (New York: 1933).

35. 1900 Catalog, 17.

36. The relationship of Christian doctrine to the entire curriculum became a hotly debated point in late-nineteenth-century Minnesota. In an attempt to finance Catholic education, certain cities in the diocese of St. Paul under the direction of Archbishop John Ireland attempted to combine Catholic and public education so as to partially relieve the financial burden on the parish and diocese. Known as the Faribault Plan, it required that parochial schools be under the control of the city board of education "so long as its [their] religious integrity was preserved." Implications of such an arrangement were that no religious instruction would occur during mandated school hours; also, that there were to be "no prayers in school hours" and that all religious pictures were to be removed (Marvin O'Connell, *John Ireland and the American Catholic Church,* [St. Paul, Minn.: 1988], 326). The Jesuits disagreed with this position, arguing that Christian doctrine permeated the

disciplines and could not be abstracted from them. After the collapse of the Faribault Plan, thanks to Jesuit criticism of it in Rome, particularly in the newspaper *La Civiltà Cattolica,* relations between the Society of Jesus and Archbishop Ireland became strained.

37. 1901 Catalog, 8–9.

38. 1901 Catalog, 9.

39. Still, *Milwaukee,* 310.

40. Ernst Haeckel, *The Riddle of the Universe at the Close of the Nineteenth Century,* trans. Joseph McCabe (New York: 1900), 261–70.

41. A complete text of "God's Grandeur" can be found in most Hopkins anthologies. One such anthology is *A Hopkins Reader,* ed. John Pick (London: 1953), 13.

42. Haeckel, *Riddle,* 9

43. The organizations, and in some cases their members, are listed in 1900 Catalog, 39–45.

44. 1900 Catalog, 58. Intercollegiate contests were organized between the schools of the Missouri Province. In 1901, these schools were St. Louis University, St Louis, Missouri; St. Xavier College, Cincinnati, Ohio; St. Mary's College, St. Mary's, Kansas; St. Ignatius College, Chicago, Illinois; Detroit College, Detroit, Michigan; Marquette College, Milwaukee, Wisconsin; and Creighton University, Omaha, Nebraska. The subject for the English composition for that year was "The American Catholic Graduate and Patriotism: A Lesson from the Life and Writings of Orestes A. Brownson." The Latin contest essay had as its subject "Callista's Vision."

45. There is a substantial bibliography on Jesuit drama. Works that demonstrate the spectacular efforts of these productions include *I Gesuiti e i primordi del teatro barocco in Europa: Convegno di studi,* eds. M. Chiabò and F. Doglio (Rome: 1995); William McCabe, *An Introduction to Jesuit Theater,* ed. Louis Oldani (St. Louis, Mo.: The Institute of Jesuit Sources, 1983); and Edna Purdie, "Jesuit Theater," in *Oxford Companion to the Theater* (Oxford: 1983).

46. 1902 Catalog, 10.

47. The bibliography concerning the role of the classics in the curriculum increases almost daily. For a recent contribution to this genre see Victor Davis Hanson and John Heath, *Who Killed Homer: The Demise of Classical Education and the Recovery of Greek Wisdom* (San Francisco: 2001).

Contributors

Michael J. Buckley, S.J., is professor of theology at Boston College, Chestnut Hill, Massachusetts.

William A. Barry, S.J., is codirector of the New England Province tertianship program and spiritual director at Campion Center, Weston, Massachusetts.

Martin D. O'Keefe, S.J., is associate editor at the Institute of Jesuit Sources and professor of classical languages at St. Louis University, St. Louis, Missouri.

David L. Fleming, S.J., edits *Review for Religious,* St Louis, Missouri.

Joseph A. Tetlow, S.J., directs the Secretariat for Ignatian Spirituality at the Jesuit General Curia in Rome, Italy.

Howard J. Gray, S.J., is rector of the Jesuit Community at John Carroll University, Cleveland, Ohio.

Gauvin A. Bailey is professor of history at Clark University, Worcester, Massachusetts. He prepared his essay while a fellow at Villa I Tatti, Florence, Italy.

Evonne Levy is professor of art history at the University of Toronto, Toronto, Canada.

John W. O'Malley, S.J., is professor of church history at Weston Jesuit School of Theology, Cambridge, Massachusetts.

Peter J. Togni, S.J., is associate dean of arts and sciences and professor of theology at the University of San Francisco, San Francisco, California.

Paul V. Murphy is professor of history and director of the St. Ignatius Institute at the University of San Francisco, San Francisco, California.

Thomas M. Lucas, S.J., chairs the visual and performing arts department at the University of San Francisco, San Francisco, California.

Paul Begheyn, S.J., directs the Nederlands Instituut voor Jesuïeten Studies, Amsterdam, Netherlands.

Thomas M. McCoog, S.J., serves as British Province archivist and as a member of the Jesuit Historical Institute, Rome, Italy.

Gerald L. McKevitt, S.J., is professor of history at Santa Clara University, Santa Clara, California.

Michael W. Maher, S.J., is professor of history at St. Louis University, St. Louis, Missouri.

Index

2 Corinthians, 10–11

A

Abbey of Chiaravalle, 151
Abraham, 56
Academia del Disegno, 147, 152, 153
Acquaviva, Claudio, 137–38, 289, 407
    angelic intercessions, importance of, to, 161
    on secular clothing, 330
Acts of Supremacy and of Uniformity, 328
Adam, 8
Adams, David Wallace, 388
Administering Alms, Rules for, 91
Adorno, Francesco, 228, 229, 230
Agazzari, Alfonso, 335
Aldobrandini, Cardinal Pietro, 272
Alegambe, Philippe, 303
alienation, 9
Allori, Alessandro, 143–44
American Indian education. *See* Native American education
Ammannati, Bartolomeo, 137, 138, 139, 145, 146, 147
Amsterdam guild of booksellers, 308
Anderledy, Anton, Fr., 409
Andreas, Valerius, 303
angels
    cult of Guardian, 161
    evil. *See* evil: angel
    intercessions, importance of, to Ignatius, 161
    of light, 40

Annunciation, Gospel, mystery of, 82
anti-Catholicism, 107. *See also* anti-Jesuitism
    persecution in England, 329–30, 338–45
anti-Jesuitism. *See also* anti-Catholicism
    antirevolutionary, 189
    in England, 329–30, 338–45
    in France, 189
    in Germany, 189
    internationalism as critical component of, 183
    nineteenth-century, 189
    Ultramontast, 189
Anti-Pelagians, 211
Apollinare, S., 163
apostolic integrity, 123
Aquinas, Thomas, 418
architecture, Jesuit
    as anti-national style, 182–83, 185–86, 187
    Architecture Jesuitique, 191
    excess, criticism of supposed, 190
    infleunce in European cities, 181
    international dimension, 182, 192–93
    Jesuit style, as negative term, 182, 184–85, 193, 194, 195
Architecture Jesuitique, 191
Arnaldi, Marchese Domenico, 157
Arrupe, Pedro, 3
art, of Jesuits, 144–45. *See also* S. Giovannino

433

architecture, 149. *See also* architecture, Jesuit
artists, 145–50
fratelli coadiutori, 145
patronage, 156
Ascension, by Valeriano, 149
Aschenbrenner, George, Fr., 73
Augustine, 6, 8

B
Babylon, 83
Badia di Passignano, 142
Baglione, Giovanni, 148
Balde, Jakob, 310
Baldinucci, Filippo, 154, 156
Bannister, E. D., 391
baptism, as reconciliation, 14
Barbieri, Camillo, 236
Barone, Giovanni, 256
Bassano, Francesco Da Ponte, 144, 155
Battiferri, Laura, 137
Bellamy, Catherine, 341
Bellarmine, Robert, 161, 308, 309
Belting, Hans, 195
Benedetti, Giovanni di, 145
Benedict, St., 61, 62
Beringucci, Mario, 230–31, 235
Beringucci, Octavio, 247
Bernard, St., 60, 61, 63
Berrigan, Dan, 104
Berzera, Antonio, 248
Biaggi, Scipione, 235
Bitio, Ludovico, Br., 236, 239
Bizzelli, Giovanni, 144, 154, 156
Blaeu, Joan, 310
Blaeu, Willem Jansz, 308, 309

Bobadilla, Nicolo, 231
Bold, Richard, 342
Bolland, Jean, 303
Bonardi, Dorotheo, 249
Bonaventure, St., 79
Bondinaro, Pietro, 251
Book of Common Prayer, 328
book production, Netherlands
Amsterdam publications, 307–10
analysis of publications, 311–13
commission of books, 312
Leiden publications, 311
overview of history, 304
publications by four Jesuit colleges, 304–6
range of publications, 312
Rotterdam publications, 311
Borgia, Francis, 19
Borgmann, Albert, 95
Borja, Francisco de, 228, 289
Borromeo, Charles, St., 206, 222
Boscoli, Andrea, 153
Boston College, 119, 124
Branch Davidians, 109
Breda, college at, 306
Brocca, Melchior, Fr., 236, 239
Bronconi, Francesco, 158
Bronzino, Agnolo, 142, 143, 153
Brooksby, Eleanor, 342
Brown, Peter, 272
Brown University, drift to secularism, 93, 94
Browne, Francis, 342
Buckley, Michael, 119
Burckhardt, Jacob, 185, 186
Bureau of Catholic Indian Missions, 373, 378, 392, 394

burial of Jesus Christ, 85
Busselim, Pietro, 251
Buti, Lodovico, 156

C

"Call of the King," 80–85
Call of the Temporal King, 8, 9
Calvin, John, 100
Calzaetto, Antonio, 248
Cambiagi, Gaetano, 153
Camillo, Count, 244
Campiglia, Giovanni Domenico, 157
Campion, Edmund, 328, 331–38
　disguises self, 331
　imprisonment, 337–38
　travel, secretive, 332, 333, 334, 335, 336, 337
Canisius, Peter, 284, 285, 289, 290
　catechism, 305
　negotiation of sites for colleges, 291–92, 296
　retirement, 297
　sermon, final, 283
　sites, choosing, for colleges, 296
　urban centers, commitment to, 297–98
　Vienna imperial college, 295
Cappella Canigiani, 143
Cardi, Ludovico, 153
Carducci, Bartolommeo, 154
Carlisle Indian School, 377
Casa Buonarroti, 143
Castagneri, Giovanni, 236
Cateni, Cammillo, 153
Cateni, Giuseppe, 154
Catesby, William, Sir, 333
Catherine of Siena, Saint, 217

Catholic colleges. *See also* Jesuit colleges
　concerns about secularism, 93
　political challenges, 94
　theoretical challenges, 94
Catholicism. *See also* Catholic colleges
　church, union with as a Catholic, 128
　conveyance of term to others, 126
　God, union with as a Catholic, 128
　persecution in England, 343, 350–53
　radical, assoicated with Jesuits, 192
　reactionary, associated with Jesuits, 192
Cel-Born, Thomas, 311
Centurione, Francesco, 259
Certosa del Galluzzo, 143
Cesura, Pompeo, 149
Chapel of the Madonna della Strada, 149
Charity, 22
Charles V, Emperor, 96, 144, 207, 208
Chesterton, G. K., 104
Chierici, Bartolomeo di, Br., 236
Chiostro Grande, 143
Chizzuola, Ludovico, 257
choir monk, 18
Christ, Jesus
　burial. *See* burial of Jesus Christ
　Ignatian view of, 81
　mysteries of, 75, 81
　as object of devotion, 128
　objectification. *See* objectification of Christ
　risen, 81

436 INDEX

values of, 83
Christology, nature of, 34
Chrysostom, 56
church, the, definition of, 14–15
Church of the Gesù. *See* Gesù, Church of the
Church of the Madonna della Quercia, 142
Church of the Ognissanti, 142
Ciampelli, Agostino, 135
Cibò, Steffano, 235, 236
Cigoli, Jacopo, 153
Circignani, Niccolò, 135
Clement VII, Pope, 207
Clemente, Rutilio, 145, 146, 148, 151
Cocco, Nicolo, 250
Cohen, Thomas, 253
College at Innsbruck, 291
College de France, anti-Jesuit lectures at, 189
College de Sainte-Barbe, 21
Collegio Romano, 147, 184
Committed Worship, 104
Commodi, Andrea, 135
compassion, growth in, through power of imagination, 85
Confalonieri, Celso, 240
Confession of Augsburg, 95–96
Confessions, 8
confusion, grace of, 78
consolation, Ignatian view, 101
Constitutions, 23, 105, 117, 118
    on education, 125
    on reverence, 127
Contarini, Filippo, 240, 252
contemplation
    Ignatian view of, 82, 88

on the Love of God. *See* Contemplation on the Love of God
Contemplation on the Love of God, 82
conversion
    affective, 99, 105
    definition and usage of term, 103–104
    five elements of, 97
    intellectual, 99, 100–3, 104, 105, 108–9, 110, 111, 112
    moral, 98, 104, 105
    religious, 98–99, 104, 105
    sociopolitical, 99, 105
    transmutations of, 109
Cosimo III, Grand Duke, 157, 158
cosmopolitanism, 182–83
Costa, Giovanni Battista, 239
Council of Florence, 218
Counter-Reformation, 149, 206
Credia, Giacomo, Br., 236
Cresti, Domenico, 142. *See also* Passignano, il
Creswell, Joseph, 330, 343
Cross, imagining self on, 78
Cult of the Guardian Angel. *See* Guardian Angel, cult of
Cuninggim, Merrimon, 94
Curradi, Francesco, 143, 153
Curry, John, 344–45, 346

D

da Sangallo, Antonio, 273
da Sangallo, Giuliano, 273
da Siena, Matteo, 136
Dandini, Pier, 159
Day, Dorothy, 17, 97
de Aldama, Antonio M., 329

De Boey, Guillaume Joseph, 409
decree six, 14
del Conte, Christoforo, 249
Del Migliore, Ferdinando, 153
demons, cast out by Jesus, 40–41
de Rouge, Stephen, 382
de Smet, Pierre Jean, 366
DeSmet Mission, 384, 385, 387, 388
desolation, Ignatian view, 101
d'Este, Cardinal, 243
de'Vecchi, Giovanni, 135
discernment, 88–90
    apostolic, 286
    Ignatian art of, 89, 286
    preparation for, 89
    Rules for. *See* Discernment, Rules for
Discernment, Rules for, 88–90
Doctrine spirituelle, 6
Domènech, Jerónimo, 231
Dominic, St., 34, 75
Donahue, John, 96, 106
Donnelly, Francis P., 105
Doria, Cesare, 235, 236
Dova, Girolamo Paolo, 239
Drexel, Francis, 373
Drexel, Jeremias, 308, 310, 312
Drexel, Katharine, 373
Dudley, Robert, 338
Duke of Parma, 306
Duomo, in Pisa, 161
du Pree, Caspar, 306
Dutch Revolt, 308

E

Eating, Rules for, 90–91
education, Jesuit. *See* Jesuit education
Election, Ignatian, 84–85, 88, 127
Eleonora of Toledo, 137
Elet, John, 409
Elizabeth, Queen
    excommunication, 328–29
    Supreme Governor, declaration as, 328
Elmi, Cesare, 231
Elzevier, Lowijs, 310
Elzevier family, 311
Emerson, Ralph, 328, 331, 340
Enlightenment, 182
    collapse of, 183
    internatiolism of, 183
episcopacy, 209
Epistle of James, on meekness, 62
Eucharist
    celebration of, 128
    daily, 22–23
    role of, 15
Eve, 8, 56
Everard, Thomas, 344
evil, 10
    angel, 40
    mystery of, 78
    war against, 81
examen
    daily, Ignatian concept of, 73–74
    prayer period, after, 74, 78–79
excommunication, 328–29
Ex Corde Ecclesiae, 126

F

Faber, Peter, 20
faith, 41
    obedience, similarities between, 57
Farnese, Alexander, 306

Favre, Pierre, 37
Fei, Alessandro, 153
Ferdinand, Emperor, 295
Fiameri, Lisabetta, 146–47
Fiammeri, Giovanni Battista, 145, 146, 147, 148, 151
Fiammeri, Lorenzo, 147, 148
Fioravante, Giulio Cesare, 145
First Week prayer, 77–80
    exercises, 78
    gratitude in response to, 78
    overview, 78–80
    Principle and Foundation, 77–78, 80
Fitzherbert, Thomas, 337, 348
Flathead Reservation, 369
Flogni, Francesco, 243
Florentine reform movement, 143
Florentine Reformers, 135–163
Fondo Gesuitico, 236
Fontebuoni, Anastasio, 153
forgiveness, 10
Forlì, Melozzo da, 273
Formula of the Institute, 4, 5, 20, 21, 287, 288
Fortoul, Hippolyte, 190
Foucault, Michel, 216
Fourth Week prayer, 86–88
France
    anti-Jesuitism in, 189
    Catholic anti-Jesuitism in, 191
Franchi, Antonio, 159
Francis I, King, 207
Francis of Assisi, St., 34, 75
fratelli coadiutori, 145
Freedburg, Sydney, 140
French Revolution, 407

Freux, André des, 290
fundamentalism, 107

G

Galleria degli Uffizi, 144
Ganss, George, 96, 105, 106, 118
Garnet, Henry, 330, 342, 344, 345, 346, 354
Gelpi, Donald, 104
General Congregation, Third, 327–28
General Congregation, Thirty-fourth, 4, 14
General Congregation, Thirty-second, 3, 4
    formulations of the promotion of faith and service of justice, 22
    papal address to, 3
General Congregation, Thirty-third, 4
Georgetown, 107
Gerard, John, 342, 344, 346
Germany
    anti-Jesuitism in, 189, 191
    architecture in, 192–93, 194
    Catholic population in, 191
Gesù, Church of the, 161, 162, 184, 185
Gethsemani Abbey, 7
Giard, Luce, 119
Gifford Lectures, 41–42
Gilbert, George, 333, 346, 347
Giovane, Alfonso Parigi il, 139
Gisbert, Gisberto, 145, 146
Gisbert, Matteo, 145, 146
God, union with. *See* union, with God
Gonçalves da Câmara, Luis, 23, 34
Gonzaga, Camillo, 246, 247

INDEX 439

Gonzaga, Ercole, 270
Gonzaga, Aloysius, St., 155–56
Gorla, Bartolomeo, 251
Gospel, preeminence of, 15, 16
Gottuccio, Battista, 240
Gouda, Johannes van, 305
Graffoglietti, Gio. Battista, 235, 239
Gramatica, Antiveduto della, 135
Grant, President, 371, 372
Grassi, Biagio de, 248
gratitude, in response to First Week prayer, 78
Gregory, St., 60
Gregory XIII, Pope, 327
Griffin, Nigel, 252
Gualteri, Bernardus, 308
Guardian Angel, cult of the, 161
Guigno, Antonio, 240
Gunpowder Plot, 349
Gurlitt, Cornelius, 192, 193
Guzzone, Hipolito, 248

H

Habington, Dorothy, 344
Haeckel, Ernst, 419–20
Haigh, Christopher, Dr., 350, 351, 352, 354, 355
Hartoghvelt family, 307
Harvard University motto, original, 106
healing, 10
Hebrews, reconciliation theme in, 11–12
Heine, Heinrich, 194
hell
  choosing, 80
  imagining self in, 79, 80

Henni, John Martin, Bishop, 409
Hertogenbosch, college at, 305
Heywood, Jasper, 339–40, 353
hiereus, 14, 15, 17
Hitler, Adolf
  Catholicism, opinion of, 194, 195
  Jesuit architecture, opinion of, 194, 195
Holt, William, 330, 339, 353
Holtby, Richard, 344–45, 346
Houthaak, Tymon, 310
Howard, Philip, 340
Howlet, John (pseudonym of Robert Parsons), 335
Hubner, Frederick, 409
Hübsch, Heinrich, 187, 195
Hugo, Herman, 308
humanism, 109
humility
  Ignatian exercises on, 84
  Ignatian paradigm for growth in, 102
hunger, religious, 6

I

ICIM. *See* Bureau of Catholic Indian Missions
Ignatius, St., 19
  advice to early Jesuits, 288–89
  angelic intercession, importance of, to, 161
  art depicting, 158
  contemplation, 75–76
  daydreams, 34–35
  discernment, 35
  examen, 73–74
  excommunication, threat of, 39

ideas, traditional, fresh approach to, 101
imagination, 74–76, 78
Mass, devotion to, 22–23
meditations. *See* meditations, Ignatian
memoirs, 38–39
missionaries, advice to, 351
pilgrimages, 275–78
priesthood, on, 21
recovery at Loyola, 34
reflection/remembering, 72–74
scruples, 35–36
Spiritual Diary, 23
spirituality, 71–72, 117
suicidal feelings, 36
travels, 284, 285
vision of Jesuit preisthood, 25
Ilg, Alfred, 195
imagination, role in discernment, 74–76, 90
Imoda, Camillo, 368
Indian Citizenship Day, 388
Indian education. *See* Native American education
internationalism, ties to nationalism, 182
Isaac, 56
Ishay, Micheline, 182, 183

J

Janssonius, Johannes, 310
Jedin, Hubert, 205, 206
Jerome, St., 60, 63
Jerusalem, Ignatian view of, 83
Jesuit colleges. *See also* specific institutions; Catholic colleges
administration's role in culture of, 110
foundational criterion, 292–94
humanism, role of, 109
identity, importance of, 93–94
lay students, founding of first school for, 290
in Netherlands, 304, 305, 306
nonbelievers' role in culture of, 110, 121
pietas, importance of, 106–7
sites chosen, 290, 292, 296–97
staff's role in culture of, 110
urban settings, 294, 296, 297
Jesuit education. *See also* Jesuit colleges
academic societies, 421, 422
classes, order of, 415–18
classical curriculum, 415–16
cohesion, 418–21
experience of, 96–97
foundation, 403–4, 406
humanistic tradition, 290–91
importance of, to Jesuits, 106
Jesuits, role of, 105–6
in Milwaukee, 408, 410, 419
ministry of education, 405–11
of Native Americans. *See* Native American education
non-Jesuit students' admittance to schools, 289
religious activities, 421
reputation, 414–415
as a work of charity, 291
Jesuit style, as architectural term. *See* architecture, Jesuit
Jesuit Volunteer Corps, 124

Jesuits. *See also* anti-Jesuitism; Jesuit education
  architecture. *See* architecture, Jesuit
  art partronage. *See* art, of Jesuits
  artistic ties with Florence, 135
  behavioral principles, 105
  book production, Netherlands. *See* book production, Netherlands
  character of, 21, 22
  community of, 120
  cultic nature of, 22
  education, power of, belief in, 106
  General Superior, united to, 120
  God, link to, 120
  Mass, celebration of, frequency, 23–24
  mission, priestly, 26
  missionary work. *See* missionary work
  novices. *See* novices
  religious life. *See* religious life, Jesuits
  seminaries, early, 289
  social justice. *See* social justice
  Spritual Exercises, relationship between, 105, 106
  teaching commitment, early, 289
  traditions of, 120–21
Jesus and the Victory of God, 34
Jesus Christ. *See* Christ, Jesus
John, Abbot, 58
John of the Cross, 8–9
Jones, Jim, 109
Jones, Robert, 348
Joset, Joseph, 366, 367, 368
Judith, book of, 213

Julius II, Pope, 273
Jurado, Manuel Ruiz, 233
Jurado, Ruiz, 260–61
justification
  through good works, 211
  through grace, 211
  at Trent, discussions of, 212

K

Kalcoven brothers, 308
Kedd, Jodok, 306, 310, 312
Kegan, Robert, 108
Keine, Michael, 146
Keller, Robert H., Jr., 392
King's College
  drift to secularism, 93
  motto, original, 106
Kinschot, Caspar, 311
Kircher, Athanasius, 309
Kolvenbach, Peter-Hans, 107, 122–23
Kostka, Stanislas, 156

L

Laínezí, Diego, 136
Lallemant, Louis, 6
Lapwai Agency, 368
Last Supper, 85
lay brother, 18
Leo X, Pope, 143, 273
Levi, 90
Lewine, Milton, 146
Ligozzi, Jacopo, 142, 153, 156, 160
Living Flame, The, 8
Lonergan, Bernard, 103–4
Loreto. *See* Santa Casa di Loreto
Loyola, Ignatius's recovery at, 34
Lucifer, 56, 83

Lukács, László, 234–35
Luke, as gospel within the gospel, 8
Lumen Gentium, 15
Lusco, Ciro, 235
Lusk, Charles, 378
Luther, Martin, 95, 194
    challenge to the church, 207, 208
    grievances, 208
    "Scripture alone," as basis for teaching, 213, 220
Lutheran crisis, 208

M

Maastricht, college at, 305
Macchietti, Girolamo, 157
Macmurray, John, 41–43
Maffei, Francesco, 248, 249
Magnano, Agostino, 154
Maniera, 136, 141–44, 149, 157–59
Mannerist painting, 141
Manners, Lady, 348
Manners, Roger, 348
Manresa, 34, 35, 38, 123
Mantuanus, Battista, 270
Marazzi, Ascanio, 241
Marcel, Gabriel, 17
Marcellini, Carlo Andrea, 161
Mariani, Antonio, 152
Marquette College, 405, 410. *See also* Jesuit colleges; Jesuit education
    activities offered, 421
    catechisms used at, 413
    classics, 416
    mission statement, 422–23
    tracks, 411, 412, 413
marriage, Christian, 17
Martinskirche in Bamberg, 186

Marty, Martin, 129
Martyrdom of St. Catherine, 155
Mary, Virgin
    devotion to, 272
    obedience of, 56
Masi, Georgio, 248
Masius, Gisbert, 305
Matthew, St., 38, 90
McGrath, Patrick, 346, 350, 352, 353
McNickle, D'Arcy, 390
Medici, Cosimo I de, 135
meditations, Ignatian
    "Call of the King," 80
    First Week, 77–80
    Fourth Week prayer, 86–88
    Gospel Annunciation mystery, contemplations of, 82
    on mercy, 81
    Second Week, 80–85
    Third Week prayer points, 85–86
    "Two Standards," 84
Meier, John, 41
Melcetti, Bernardo, 145
memory, role in discernment, 90
Mercurian, Everard, 327, 328, 329
mercy, 80
Merton, Thomas, 7
Method in Theology, 104
Michelangelo, 144, 147, 149
Michelet, Jules, 189
Micheli, Antonio, 229
Mildmay, Walter, 338
Ministerial priesthood, 4, 5, 6–26
    in the church, 13–17
    church, relationship with and to, 16
    purpose of, 17

as representaiton of people of
  God, 16
 union with God, longing for, 7–8, 9
Minoux, Anthony, 409
missionary work
  mobility, vow of, 284
  radicalness when first suggested,
   284–85
Morais, Sebastião, 232
More, Henry, 334, 349
Morelli, Girolamo, 156
Morelli family, 156
Morgan, Edward, 348
Morgan, Thomas J., 392
Morone, Giovanni, 214
mortification, 230
Mount Olivet, 275, 276
Mullan, John, 375, 381
Munich, Catholic population of, 181
Murtio, Francesco, 235
Murtio the Cypriot, 247

N

Nadal, Jerome, 45–63, 123, 146, 290
Nasini, Giuseppe, 155
nationalism, 182
Native American education
  academic achievement,
   encouraging, 388
  apex and decline of boarding
   schools, 391–95
  assimilation, 390
  boarding vs. day school, 376–77
  Carlisle model, 377
  Catholic teachings, 386–88
  communities, placing schools near
   native, 378
  contract-school system, 374
  craft training, 383–86
  desertion, 390
  English vs. native tongue, 384–85,
   386
  faculty, 381–82
  federal tribal policy, 372–76
  funding, 368
  industrial schools, 381
  location, 366
  as missionary activity, 366, 367
  overview of, 365–66
  Peace Policy, 372–76
  preaching of example, 367–68
  recreation, 389
  requests for schools, tribal, 371–72
  resistance to, 379–80
  segregation of sexes, 380
  skills, teaching of, 368
  unhappiness of students, 389–90
  white encroachment, rapid, 370
Nativity, mystery of the, 82
Negroni, Giulio, 235
Newman, Cardinal, 24
Nez Percé, 368
Nichesoli, Lelio, 251
Nigetti, Giovanni, 153
Nihusius, Bartholdus, 308
Northwest Ordinance of 1787,
 106–7
Novella, S. Maria, 142, 143
Novellara, 231, 233. *See also* novices
  chronicles of life there, 237–38
  classes (social) of novices, 252
  deaths of novices, 247, 250, 251
  doctrine instruction, 242
  economics, 262, 263

education, 253
educational background of, 240
experiments, 246–47, 252
French novices, 246
home cities of novices, 241
illnesses, 250
novices entered at, 234, 235–36, 239, 240, 241, 244
numbers of novices accepted, 262
novices. *See also* Novellara
    accomplishments of, 255–56
    break with previous life, 256–57
    conversation, 233
    customs, 232–33
    daily life at Novellara, 260–61
    discipline, 232
    educational background of, 240
    home cities of, 241
    housing for, 227–28, 229
    mortification, 230
    probation, 228, 230–31, 256
    reasons for joining, 253
    rules, 232
    Spiritual Exercises, 258, 262
    studies, courses of, 245–46
    work of, 228, 229
nuns
    Third Orders, 217
    Trentian decrees on, 217

O

obedience
    blindness, 49, 55–57
    burden, in the face of, 58
    canons, 50–55
    character of, 47
    faith, similarity to, 57
    hindrance and weakness of, 59–63
    impossible commands, 48
    intellect, surrender of, 57
    judgment, simplicity of, 58–59
    nature of, 46
    perfection of, 49
    practice of, 47
    simplicity of, 48
    threefold nature of, 47
    will, surrender of, 57, 58
objectification of Christ, 14
O'Connor, Flannery, 109
Oldcorne, Edward, 344, 346
O'Malley, John, 106, 123
Oratorio della Confraternità della SS. Annunziata, 143
ordination of Jesuits, 3
orphans, dignity of, 123
Orton, Henry, 333

P

Pacifism, 104
Padberg, John, Fr.
    higher education, Jesuit, 129
    Ignatian spirituality, study of, in higher education, 117
    Jesuit life, chronicle of changes in, 355
    Society of Jesus, importance to, 4–5
Paets family, 307
Pagano, Mark Antonio, 239
Painted Red, 371
Palazzo Capponi, 143
Palazzo Ducale, 144
Palazzo Vecchio, 142, 144
Palladino, Lorenzo, 367, 383

Pallavicino, Gasparo, 235, 257
papacy reform at Trent, 214
Parigi, Giulio, 146, 151, 152
Paris, Catholic population of, 181
Parsons, Robert, 328, 331, 332, 333, 334, 335, 336
Passeto, Gio. Battista, 240
Passignano, il, 142, 153. *See also* Cresti, Domenico
Paul III, Pope, 96, 207, 208, 294
Paul VI, Pope, 3
Paul, St., 38
    on Abraham, 56
    change from persecutor to apostle, 90
    reconciliation, concept in 2 Corinthians, 10–11
Peace of Westphalia, 191
Pelagians, 211
perfection
    of obedience. *See* obedience
    striving toward, 46
Phillip II, King, 222
Piazza della Signoria, 147
Pierrepoint, Gervase, 333, 336
Pietas
    importance, 106
    promotion of, by Jesuit colleges, 107
pilgrimages, 259–260, 269
Piombo, Sebastiano del, 149
Pius II, Pope, 272
Pius IV, Pope, 221
Pius V, Pope, 18, 328
Plantjin, Chrisoffel, 303
Poccetti, Bernardino Barbatelli, 143, 159
Poiana, Andrea, 153
Polanco, Juan de, 227, 228
Pole, Reginald, 211
poor, dignity of, 123. *See also* poverty
Portrait of the First Century of the Society of Jesus, 303
Pounde, Thomas, 333
poverty, 330, 355. *See also* religious life, Jesuits
Power, Edward J., 365
Pozzo, Andrea, 148, 184
Prague, Catholic population of, 181
Prando, Pietro Paulo, 370, 377, 379
Pratt, Richard Henry, 377
Praying, Ways of, 90
presbyteroi, 14, 15
Presbyterorum ordinis, 15
Presupposition, Ignatian, 95
priesthood
    of Christ, 12
    of the church, 12–13, 17
    ministerial. *See* ministerial priesthood
    theology of, 4
Princeton University, drift to secularism, 94
Principle and Foundation, 72, 77–78, 80–82, 84
Prucha, Francis Paul, 392
Puccio, Cosmo, 243, 244
Pulse Program, Boston College, 124

Q

Quinet, Edgar, 189, 190

R

Rafaello, Giovanni di, 160
Rahner, Karl, 7, 16, 17

Raphael, 136, 142
Ratio studiorum, 96, 106–7
rationality, in discernment, 89
reconciliation, 9–12
  between human and divine, 26
  Jesuit ministry, role in, 25
Reformers, Florentine. *See* Florentine Reformers
Regimini militantis ecclesiae, 19
religious life, Jesuits
  attire, 355
  Catholic households, staying in, 349, 352, 353, 354, 355
  in hiding, 345, 346, 347, 348, 349, 352
  persecution in England, 329–30, 338, 339, 341, 345
  poverty, 330, 355
  routine, 328
  secular dress, 330
  standards, 328
  Third General Congregation rules, 327–28
retreats, role of, 33
Revelation, book of, 17
Ricca, Giovanni di, 239
Riccadi, Marchese Gabbriello, 158
Richa, Giuseppe, 153
Rimini, Gio. Battista da, 236, 239
Riva, Giovanni, 236
Roermond, college at, 306
Roger, Exupirus, 246
Ronan, Peter, 383
Rosenberg, Alfred, 194
Rosweyde, Heribert, 305, 309, 311, 312
Rotondo, S. Stefano, 163

Rouse, Anthony, 344
Rowe, Joy, 346, 350
Roy, Joannes, de, 305
Royce, Josiah, 112
Ruggieri, Annibal, 248

S

S. Andrea al Quirinale, 145–46, 147, 228
S. Giovannino, 138, 141, 145–46, 148
  Angels Chapel, 160, 161, 163
  apostle martyrdom paintings, 152–53
  artists, 142, 143, 149
  Chapel of St. Francis Xavier, 157, 158, 161, 163
  Chapel of St. Ignatius, 158, 161, 163
  fresco panels, 150, 153
  frescoes, 156
  Gesù, similarities to, 161, 163
  history of, 137, 140
  Immaculate Conception, 159
  Jesuit patronage, as monument of, 136
  martyrdom cycles, 150–51
  Martyrdom of St. Catherine, 155
  Martyrs Chapel, 163
  Nativity Chapel, 159, 163
  paintings, 150
  Passion Chapel, 163
  payments, to artists, 152
  refectory paintings, 152
  renovations, 150
  Saint Helen Adoring the Cross, 156
  Scolopian fathers, 150
  Seven Archangels, 161

side chapels, 142, 144, 150, 155–58
St. Aloysius Gonzaga, painting of, 155–56
St. Matthew, 153
stuccoes, 150, 151, 152
Transfiguration, 153, 154
S. Luigi dei Francesi, 144
S. Stefano Rotondo, 150
S. Tommaso di Cantorbery, 150, 163
S. Vitale, 163
sacraments
role, 15. *See also* specific sacraments
Saint Helen Adoring the Cross, 156
Salimbeni, Ventura, 135, 161
salvation, nature of, 81
Sansovino, Andrea, 273
Santa Casa di Loreto. *See also* Torsellini, Orazio
cult of, 270
historical overview, 269
Jesuit devotion to, early, 270–71
notoriety among Protestants, 270
papal patronage of, 272, 273, 274
as pilgrimage departure/arrival site, 277–78
pilgrims to, numbers of, 271
Pius II cured at, 272
shrines, 278
Santa Maria della Strada, 294
Sarto, Andrea del, 142
Saul, 90
Savonarola, 135
Scaduto, Mario, 230
Scherer, Georg, 310
Schmalkaldic League, 96

Schurz, Carl, 385, 386
Schwickenrath, Robert, 105
Sciorina, Lorenzo della, 144
Scolopian fathers, 150
Scribani, Charles, 307
Second Week prayer, 80–85
"Call of the King," 80–85
Gospel Annunciation mystery, contemplations of, 82
self, Ignatian view of, 101–2
Seripando, Girolamo, 210–11
Seven Archangels, 161
shame, grace of, 78
Signorelli, Luca, 273
Simpson, Richard, 333
sin, 9
analogy to drug use, 10
God's influence, absence of, 10
mortal, 46
mystery of, 78
Sisters of Charity of Providence, 370
Sixtus V, Pope, 221
Sledd, Charles, 333
social justice
Boston College's Pulse Program, 124
contemporary focus on, 123
universities' commitment, 124
Socialists, as threat to national interests of France and Germany, 181
Society of Jesus, 3
Constitutions, 45
Declaration, 21
Deliberations, 19–20
care of souls, 123
character of, 18, 19

final vows, 18
formation of, 45
history of, 18–19
ministerial priesthood within, 22–26
priesthood, role within, 4
spirituality, 5
tradition, 5
university/college connections, 94–95
Somerset, Henry, 348
sorrow, grace of, 78
Southwell, Robert, 330, 346, 354
Spalding, Jack, 153–54
Spinola, Nicolo, 235, 236, 238, 239, 241
Spinoza, Baruch, 307
spirits, discernment of, 33–43. *See also* Ignatius
by Jesus Christ, 41
rules of, according to Ignatius, 34–35, 37–40
Spiritual Exercises, the, 18, 22
conversions, five, 97
First Week prayer. *See* First Week prayer
novitiates' use of, 258–59, 262
Presupposition, 95–96
rules for discernment of spirits in, 34, 38
thirty-day experience, 76–77
Spiritual Exercises, The
composition of, 123
First Time, The, 38
spiritual virgins, 307
spirituality
apostolic, 91

Ignatian, 117
term, usage of, 103
St. Francis Regis Mission, 370
St. Gervasius church, 190
St. Ignatius Mission, 374–75, 378, 385, 386, 389, 391, 392
St. Labre Mission School, 380
St. Mary's Mission, 382
St. Paul's Mission, 381
St. Paul-St. Louis church, 190
St. Regis Mission, 382
Strada, Famiano, 310, 311
Sue, Eugène, 189
Switzerland, Jesuit presence in, 185
Synod of Southwark, 333

T

Tagliaferri, Guido Maria, 235
Tempesta, Antonio, 135
Teresa, Mother, 17
Teresa of Àvila, 117, 217
Third Week prayer points, 85–86
Thorndike, Edward, 414
Tillich, Paul, 103
Titian, 144
Tito, Santi di, 140, 142, 153
Torsellini, Orazio. *See also* Santa Casa di Loreto
facets of career, 275
Ignatius, sought to model himself after, 276–77
Latin, universality of, in his opinion, 274
papal involvement with Loreto, accounts of, 272, 273, 274
as pastor of souls, 275

shrine of Loreto, association with, 271
Spiritual Exercises, use of, 276–77
Virgin, devotion to, 272
Tosini, Michele, 142, 143, 157
Trennert, Robert A., 377
Trent, Council of, 141
   bishops, transformation of role, 214, 215
   catechism, 217
   confraternities, position on, 219
   disciplinary decrees, 215–16
   historical overview, 207–10
   implementation of decrees afterwards, 221–23
   Latin mass, statements on, 220–21
   nuns, decrees on, 217
   reform issues, 209–10, 214–17
   scholarly review of, 205–7
   seminaries, creation of, 215
Tresham, Thomas, 333, 342
Tridentine doctrine, 212, 214
Trinity Chapel at the Roman Gesù, 144
Tronchi, Bartolommeo, 145, 149, 151
Turnell, Philip, 388
Turnhout, Jan van, 305
Twelve-Year Truce, 305

U

Uffizi, Galleria degli, 144
union, with God, 6–9, 10
universalism, 182–83
University of Dillingen, 290
University of Ingolstadt, 290

V

Valentino, Antonio
   arrival at Novellara, 234
   on Cocco, 250
   on departing novices (assignments), 243, 244
   descriptions of life at Novellara, 233
   on educational backgrounds of novices, 253. *See also* Novellara
   on group of novices, 241–42
   on homesickness of novice, 248–49
   importance of remaining at Novellara without absence, 254
   as novice master/rector of Novellara, 245, 248–49, 250, 251–52
   pilgrimages, recordings of, 259–60
   Report on the Spiritual Practice at Novellara, 240
   on Spinola, 237–38, 239
   testimonies, 251–52
Valeriano, Giuseppe, 146, 149–50, 154
Valla, Lorenzo, 274
van den Enden, Franciscus, 307
van der Mye, Isaac, 311
van Egmond, Cornelis, 308
Van Gorp, Leopold, 376, 378, 391
van Sichem, Christoffel, II, 307
van Waesberge, Jan, 306
Vasari, Giorgio, 142, 146, 147
Vatican II, Jesuits role in the church following, 3–4
Vaudoyer, Léon, 190, 191

Vavasseur, François, 311
Vecchio, Alfonso Parigiil, 152
Veracini, Agostino, 139, 157
Verbier, Giovanni (Johannes), 244, 245
Vezzani, Gio. Antonio, 235
Vezzano, Giovanni Antonio, 249
Vienna, Catholic population of, 181
Villa Medici, 143, 147
Vitelleschi, Father General Muzio, 352
Vossius, Gerardus Johannes, 309

W

Waco, Texas, 109
Ways of Praying. *See* Praying, Ways of
Weston, William, 340, 341–42, 343
widows, dignity of, 123
William of Orange, assassination of, 341
Williams, Rowan, 117
Wischaven, Cornelius, 290
Wisdom, book of, 213
Wiseman, John, 344
Wiseman, Thomas, 344
Woiwode, Larry, 118–19, 120, 122
Word, ministry of the, 15
Wright, N. T., 34
Wulf, Friedrich, 7–8

X

Xavier, Francis, St., 157, 311
Xavier, Jerónimo, 311

Y

Yale University, drift to secularism, 93, 94

Z

Zuccaro, Frederico, 160
Zuccaro brothers, 142